Tourism and Recreation Handbook
of Planning and Design

Architectural Press Planning and Design Series
Edited by Fred Lawson

Published books in the series:

Shopping Centres: Retail Development, Design and Management
Second edition – Nadine Beddington
Published 1991

Hotels and Resorts: Planning, Design and Refurbishment
Fred Lawson
Published 1995

Restaurants, Clubs and Bars: Planning and Design Investment for Food Service Facilities
Revised paperback edition – Fred Lawson
Published 1995

Airport Terminals
Second edition – Christopher J. Blow
Published 1996

Buildings for the Performing Arts
Ian Appleton
Published 1996

Tourism and Recreation Handbook of Planning and Design
Manuel Baud-Bovy and Fred Lawson
Published 1998

Forthcoming in the series:

Conference, Convention and Exhibition Centres
Fred Lawson

Tourism and Recreation Handbook of Planning and Design

Manuel Baud-Bovy and Fred Lawson

Architectural Press

OXFORD   AUCKLAND   BOSTON   JOHANNESBURG   MELBOURNE   NEW DELHI

Architectural Press
An imprint of Butterworth-Heinemann
Linacre House, Jordan Hill, Oxford OX2 8DP
225 Wildwood Avenue, Woburn, MA 01801-2041
A division of Reed Educational and Professional Publishing Ltd

 A member of the Reed Elsevier plc group

First published as *Tourism and Recreation Development* 1977
Second edition 1998
Reprinted 2000

British Library Cataloguing in Publication Data
A catalogue record for this book is available from the British Library

Library of Congress Cataloguing in Publication Data
A catalogue record for this book is available from the Library of Congress

ISBN 0 7506 3086 8

FOR EVERY VOLUME THAT WE PUBLISH, BUTTERWORTH-HEINEMANN
WILL PAY FOR BTCV TO PLANT AND CARE FOR A TREE.

Composition by Scribe Design, Gillingham, Kent, UK
Printed and bound in Great Britain by The Bath Press, Bath

Contents

Foreword   ix

Preface   xi

1   **Background to planning**   1

1.1   Interface of recreation and tourism   1
1.1.1   Leisure and recreation (definitions)   1
1.1.2   Visitors and tourists (definitions)   1
1.1.3   Uncertain boundaries   2
1.1.4   Demand for tourism and recreation   2
1.1.5   Tourism and recreation: similarities and differences   3

1.2   Complexity of the tourism/recreation system   3
1.2.1   Interface within the overall socio-economic policies   4
1.2.2   Interface of international tourism, domestic tourism and recreation   4
1.2.3   Interface with competing destinations   4
1.2.4   Interface and roles within the tourism/recreation sector   4

1.3   Planning with tourism products   5
1.3.1   Tourism products   5
1.3.2   Planning with products   6

1.4   Development versus conservation   7
1.4.1   Environmental impacts from tourism   7
1.4.2   Environmental impacts from recreation   9
1.4.3   Sustainable development   9
1.4.4   Alternative forms of tourism   12
1.4.5   Carrying capacities   12
1.4.6   Limits of acceptable charges   13
1.4.7   Environmental impact assessment   13
1.4.8   Environmental auditing and quality control   14
1.4.9   Pressures on resources: alternative policies   14

1.5   Evaluation of development proposals   14
1.5.1   Feasibility analysis   15
1.5.2   Cost benefit analysis   15
1.5.3   Planning balance sheet   16
1.5.4   Goals achievement matrix   16

2   **Basic standards for accommodation, catering and shopping**   17

2.1   Influences on planning   17
2.1.1   Types of facilities   17
2.1.2   Main types of accommodation   18
2.1.3   Feasibility of hotel accommodation   19
2.1.4   Effects of investment on hotel planning   19
2.1.5   Balance of hotel and private accommodation   21
2.1.6   Impact of accommodation mix on resort development   21
2.1.7   New objectives in planning   21

2.2   Hotels   23
2.2.1   Types of hotels   23
2.2.2   Planning standards: built areas   23
2.2.3   Variations in rooms sizes   25
2.2.4   Circulation planning   25
2.2.5   Planning of public areas   25
2.2.6   Back-of-house areas   26

2.3   Other forms of accommodation   26
2.3.1   Apartments, bungalows, villas, condominiums   26
2.3.2   Site planning   27
2.3.3   Standards in winter resorts   28
2.3.4   Standards in seaside and countryside resorts   28
2.3.5   Standards for commercial holiday villages   28
2.3.6   Standards for social tourism villages   28
2.3.7   Youth hostels   31

2.4   Camping and caravanning   31
2.4.1   Camping sites, caravan sites   31
2.4.2   Categories of camps   33
2.4.3   Densities and sizes of camps   33
2.4.4   Facilities: minimum standards for 100 persons (25 units)   34

2.5   Food services and shopping   34
2.5.1   Food service provisions   34
2.5.2   Shops and related services   35
2.5.3   Standards for shopping and related services   35

3   **Support services and technical infrastructures**   37

3.1   Administration, technical and support services   37
3.1.1   Employees and resident non-tourist populations   37
3.1.2   Direct employment   37
3.1.3   Indirect and induced employment   37
3.1.4   Size of non-tourist populations in resorts   38
3.1.5   Housing of non-tourist population   38
3.1.6   Administrative, technical and other ancillary services   38

3.2   Infrastructure provision, roads and parking areas   39
3.2.1 Access for traffic   39
3.2.2 Planning data for roads   40
3.2.3 Parking areas   40
3.2.4 External lighting, street furniture and utilities   40

3.3   Sanitation and engineering services   41
3.3.1 Water supply   41
3.3.2 Sewerage, sewage treatment and standards   41
3.3.3 Outfall and irrigation systems: phased extension   43
3.3.4 Refuse disposal   43
3.3.5 Electricity supplies   43
3.3.6 Communication systems   44
3.3.7 Heating and air conditioning systems   44
3.3.8 Coordination of underground utilities   44

4   Basic standards for recreation, cultural and sport facilities   46

4.1   Indoor social and cultural activities   46
4.1.1 Facilities   46
4.1.2 Standard facilities in integrated resorts   46

4.2   Land-based sports facilities   48
4.2.1 Important factors   48
4.2.2 Sports grounds   48
4.2.3 Built sports halls   48
4.2.4 Horse riding   51
4.2.5 Golf courses   51
4.2.6 Standards for sports facilities in holiday resorts   53

4.3   Land-based recreation facilities   53
4.3.1 Picnicking   53
4.3.2 Parks, rest and playing fields   54
4.3.3 Walking and hiking trails   55
4.3.4 Other types of trails   55
4.3.5 Allotment gardens   57

4.4   Water-based facilities   57
4.4.1 Natural bathing places   57
4.4.2 Swimming pools   58
4.4.3 Sailing and boating   59
4.4.4 Other water-based activities   60

4.5   Densities, land requirements and costs   61
4.5.1 Densities   61
4.5.2 Land requirements   61
4.5.3 Cost requirements   62

5   Programmes for resorts and recreation complexes   63

5.1   Main categories of tourist resorts and recreation complexes   64
5.1.1 Main categories   64
5.1.2 Average specific densities   64
5.1.3 Average overall densities   66

5.2   Beach resorts and marinas   66
5.2.1 Beach development   71

5.2.2 Public beach facilities   72
5.2.3 Beach in an integrated resort   73
5.2.4 Facilities for yachting: types of havens   73
5.2.5 Basic facilities for harbours   74
5.2.6 Planning standards for medium-sized pleasure harbours   74
5.2.7 Yachting centres or 'dry harbours'   74

5.3   Mountain resorts   77
5.3.1 Categories of skiers   77
5.3.2 Ski trails characteristics   81
5.3.3 Cable transporters   83
5.3.4 Other mountain resort facilities   84
5.3.5 Principles in planning a ski resort   84

5.4   Resorts in the countryside   85
5.4.1 Second residences   85
5.4.2 Social holiday villages   88
5.4.3 Country resorts for rent   89
5.4.4 Holiday parks   89

5.5   Spas and health resorts   95
5.5.1 Markets and resources   95
5.5.2 Spas facilities   95
5.5.3 Non-specific facilities   95
5.5.4 Planning spa resorts   96
5.5.5 Thalassotherapy and health centres   96

5.6   Fun, safari and aquatic parks   96
5.6.1 Categories   96
5.6.2 Attraction and theme parks   96
5.6.3 Safari parks   98
5.6.4 Aquatic parks   101

5.7   Suburban relaxation parks   104
5.7.1 Favourable sites   104
5.7.2 Specific facilities   107
5.7.3 Average densities   107
5.7.4 Suburban relaxation and leisure parks   108
5.7.5 Suburban relaxation and sports parks   108
5.7.6 Suburban relaxation and nature parks   109

5.8   Nature parks   117
5.8.1 National parks   117
5.8.2 Regional parks   123
5.8.3 Forests and recreation   126
5.8.4 Protected natural areas   126

6   Planning tourist resorts and recreation complexes   129

6.1   Tourist resorts   129
6.1.1 Tourist resorts and tourist towns   129
6.1.2 Traditional resorts   131
6.1.3 Post-war developments: uncontrolled urbanization   131

6.2   New resort development   132
6.2.1 Integrated resorts   132
6.2.2 Developers   132

6.2.3   Failures and criticisms   132
6.2.4   Operation of resorts   133

6.3   Recreation and leisure complexes   133
6.3.1   Attraction, theme and aquatic parks   133
6.3.2   Recreation and nature parks   135

6.4   Principles of development (tourist resort or
         recreation complex)   135
6.4.1   Objectives, ways and means   135
6.4.2   Environmental integration   141
6.4.3   Contact with nature   141
6.4.4   Increasing value of the resources   141
6.4.5   Grouping of activities   142
6.4.6   Landscaping   143
6.4.7   Distribution of buildings and focuses of interest   143
6.4.8   Separation of traffic   143
6.4.9   Quality of construction   143

6.5   Phasing and extension   146
6.5.1   Phasing development   146
6.5.2   Phases of development   147
6.5.3   Changes in requirements   147
6.5.4   Rehabilitating existing resorts   148

6.6   Planning procedures   152
6.6.1   Framework   152
6.6.2   Broad concept   152
6.6.3   Draft project   154
6.6.4   Final project   156
6.6.5   Phase One and operational projects   157

7   Framework for tourism/recreation master
         plans   158

7.1   Interrelation of tourism and recreation   158
7.1.1   Aims in planning tourism/recreation
         development   158
7.1.2   Differences in planning for tourism and
         recreation   158

7.2   Fundamental planning consideration   160
7.2.1   Definitions   160
7.2.2   Governmental structures and policies   160
7.2.3   Processes   160
7.2.4   Scales and levels of planning   163
7.2.5   Environmental protection and tourism image   163
7.2.6   Conflicts of interests   165
7.2.7   Planning for tourism and recreation at local
         administration level   167

7.3   Approaches to tourism/recreation planning   168
7.3.1   Priorities   169
7.3.2   Extent of studies   169
7.3.3   Timescales for implementation   169
7.3.4   Demand analyses   170
7.3.5   Planning models and simulation techniques   170
7.3.6   Comprehensive planning: approaches by alternative
         plans   173

7.3.7   Comprehensive planning: the PASOLP approach   173
7.3.8   Monitoring system   173
7.3.9   Flexibility in planning   175

7.4   Preliminaries for a master plan   176
7.4.1   Terms of references   176
7.4.2   Planning objectives   176
7.4.3   Organizational framework   176

8   Tourism/recreation master plans: surveys and
         formulation   177

8.1   Resources surveys   177
8.1.1   Principles in surveying resources   177
8.1.2   Methodology and stages   177
8.1.3   Existing features and activities of potential tourist
         interest   178
8.1.4   Recreational attractions   184
8.1.5   Facilities and infrastructures   187

8.2   Market assessment   188
8.2.1   Outdoor recreation activities   188
8.2.2   Specific aspects of the outdoor recreation markets
         189
8.2.3   Specific aspects of the tourist markets   190

8.3   Assessment of structures and policies   191
8.3.1   Socio-economic surveys   192
8.3.2   Survey of implementation framework   192
8.3.3   Survey of existing development plans   192
8.3.4   Development goals and policies   193
8.3.5   Sources of data   193

8.4   Formulation of tourism development plans   193
8.4.1   Additional facilities needed   194
8.4.2   Means of access   198
8.4.3   Resources: hierarchy of development   199
8.4.4   Priority areas for tourism and recreation
         development   199
8.4.5   Main tourist resorts   199
8.4.6   Towns and urban centres   200
8.4.7   Road networks and circuits   202
8.4.8   Isolated facilities   203

8.5   Formulation of regional recreation plans   203
8.5.1   The struggle for sites   203
8.5.2   Extent, methodology and content of a master
         plan for recreation   207
8.5.3   Outdoor recreation areas in the city   208
8.5.4   The green belt   209
8.5.5   The rural area   209
8.5.6   The greenways   209

9   Tourism/recreation master plans:
         implementation, protection of resources
         and outdoor recreation in the cities   219

9.1   Strategy for implementation   219
9.1.1   Involvement of other economic sectors   219

9.1.2   The need for a coordinated strategy   220
9.1.3   Adapting financing techniques   221
9.1.4   Implementing and controlling facilities   222
9.1.5   Training tourism manpower   222
9.1.6   Transportation   223
9.1.7   Organizing and promoting tourism and recreation products   224
9.1.8   Land control for tourism and recreation development   225

9.2   Protection of resources   226
9.2.1   Nature parks   226
9.2.2   'Sensitive areas' of environmental control   226
9.2.3   Planning nature parks and sensitive areas   229
9.2.4   Protection of roads   230
9.2.5   Tourists and historic monuments   230
9.2.6   Isolated monuments   231
9.2.7   Monument ensembles   231
9.2.8   Towns and centres of culture   232

9.3   Planning outdoor recreation in the cities   232
9.3.1   Principles   234
9.3.2   Urban parks standards   242
9.3.3   Park planning principles   244
9.3.4   Creation of new urban parks   245
9.3.5   'Eco parks'   251
9.3.6   Lakesides or seasides and stream banks   251
9.3.7   Pedestrian squares, areas and networks   251
9.3.8   Neighbourhood recreation areas   257
9.3.9   Planning outdoor recreation areas   257

Appendices: Useful data for planning development   264

Appendix A1: Markets for tourism and recreation – influences on demand and trends   264
A1.1   Measurement of recreation demand   264
A1.2   Market segmentation   264
A1.3   Influences on demand for recreation and tourism   265

A1.4   Tourism measurement   266
A1.5   International tourism   266
A1.6   Global projections to 2010   267
A1.7   Domestic tourism   268

Appendix A2: Investment in tourism and recreation – methods and sources   268
A2.1   Characteristics of tourism investment   268
A2.2   Revenue earning potential   268
A2.3   Accommodation   268
A2.4   Other facilities   269
A2.5   Public sector participation   269
A2.6   Forms of financial aid   269
A2.7   Main sources of capital finance   270

Appendix A3: Impacts from tourism and recreation – socio-economic data   271
A3.1   Collection of economic data   271
A3.2   Evaluation of costs   271
A3.3   National or regional income and tourism   271
A3.4   Employment   272
A3.5   State revenues and regional benefits   272
A3.6   Negative and unquantifiable impacts   272

Appendix A4: Tourism transportation – recent developments and trends   273
A4.1   Developments in transportation   273
A4.2   Development in air transport   273
A4.3   Aircraft developments   274
A4.4   Airport development   274
A4.5   Road transport   275
A4.6   Rail transport   275
A4.7   Sea transport   275
A4.8   Cruising   275

Select bibliography   277

Index   281

Foreword

Over the last four decades, tourism has rapidly become a vital vector of social and economic development in the different regions and countries of the world.

Over the last twenty years, the conservation of natural resources and preservation of cultural resources have progressively become global concerns by generating commitments amongst growing numbers of individuals, organizations and nations.

Concepts of sustainability are now widely accepted as an essential approach for all types of development including tourism and recreation.

According to the World Tourism Organization's new Tourism Vision 2020, the travel and tourism sector will globally continue to grow strongly during the first two decades of the forthcoming century. WTO forecasts that there will be 700 million international arrivals by the year 2000, one billion in 2010 and 1.6 billion by 2020 – nearly three times the number of international arrivals in 1996.

In such circumstances, and twenty years after their widely acclaimed *Tourism and Recreation Development – A Handbook of Planning*, Manuel Baud-Bovy and Fred Lawson, two internationally renowned experts, have decided to publish a new edition of their previous book with coverage of the challenges facing tourism and recreation facilities for the twenty-first century.

The new edition provides very comprehensive guidance on basic standards, specific requirements and detailed procedures for programming, planning and implementing tourism and recreation development, ranging from national and regional plans to local community facilities' projects.

The authors have taken into account sustainability and environmental issues as well as new concepts and trends affecting leisure, outdoor recreation and tourism facilities. Special attention is given to revive the existing long-standing tourist resorts and to make the best use of natural resources by offering a spectrum of parks, green areas, sport facilities and leisure centres accessible to large urban populations.

Like the first edition, published in 1977, the new *Tourism and Recreation Handbook of Planning and Design* is richly illustrated with updated examples and case studies of a wide range of leisure, outdoor recreation and tourism development plans.

Undoubtedly, this new book will serve as a most useful source of reference, not only for architects, planners and developers, but also for all those involved in or interested in the management of tourism and recreation resorts.

On the eve of the new millennium, this publication will provide an invaluable contribution to the promotion of tourism's long-term sustainability development.

Francesco Frangialli
Secretary-General
World Tourism Organization

Preface

The first edition of this book, published in 1977, provided a unique source of reference for the comprehensive planning of tourism and recreation. With a foreword by the Secretary General of the World Tourism Organization, it set out procedures and standards and explained how the impacts and problems which can arise from anarchic and insensitive development should be addressed during the planning stage.

Most of these principles still apply and this new edition is arranged to provide a similar detailed and practical framework for reference. In addition to providing updated examples, the second edition covers current concerns over sustainability and other environmental issues. Although national and regional planning for tourism is still important, attention is also given to the need to revive the existing older resorts, to restore and improve the environment and to reduce the pressures on unique resources.

Over the last twenty years there has been a vast increase in demands for recreation, coupled with an increasing mobility and improved access to the countryside and coast. Tourists and weekend recreationists often use the same resources and facilities and the requirements of both must be taken into account in planning provisions.

More particularly, community needs for outdoor recreation have given rise to concentrated pressures in the countryside readily accessible to large urban populations. This necessitates positive action to provide a spectrum of parks, green areas, sports facilities and leisure centres, and calls for detailed studies to make the best use of natural resources within the limitation of the public funds available.

Tourism is the world's largest industry and planning is essential to safeguard unique natural attractions; recreation planning is a necessity for every urban community. It is hoped this new edition will serve both these needs and be a valuable source of reference not only for planners, architects and developers, but those involved in managing these important sectors.

In preparing this work the authors have drawn on their extensive international experience in tourism and recreation development. However, the coverage would not be complete without the numerous examples provided by others working in these fields. Although examples were generously supplied from all over the world, it has regretfully only been possible to include a small proportion and many excellent schemes could not be used because of difficulties in reproduction. Where possible, the names of the architects, planners and/or organizations are acknowledged for the projects illustrated, but the authors would like to thank collectively the many contributors who have assisted in this publication. In particular, our thanks are due to Francesco Frangialli, Secretary General of the World Tourism Organization, to Patrice Tedjini, Head of the Documentation Center, and to Enzo Paci, Chief Statistics and Market Research, both World Tourism Organization, and to Aristea Baud-Bovy who has participated in many of the studies outlined.

1 Background to planning

1.1 INTERFACE OF RECREATION AND TOURISM

Distinctions between leisure, recreation and many tourist activities are increasingly blurred by changing lifestyles and terms are often interchangeable. However, precise definitions are necessary for statistical comparisons, market analyses and product differentiation.

1.1.1 Leisure and recreation (definitions)

- **Leisure** is the free time available to the individual when the disciplines of work, sleep and other basic needs have been met. It is time which can be used in ways determined by the individual's own discretion. 'Basic needs' includes essential cooking, shopping, housework, child care and hygiene. 'Work' includes travel time to and from work.
- **Recreation** covers, broadly, any pursuit taken up during leisure time other than those to which people have a high commitment (overtime, second job, home study and various maintenance jobs about the house). In this book recreation and tourism are treated as separate but overlapping subjects.
- **Recreational activities** can be broadly grouped into six categories, taking into account their nature and the types of facilities used:

Category of activities	Examples
Taking place about the home	Watching television, reading, listening to music, gardening, do-it-yourself hobbies
Having a high social content	Entertaining, eating out, drinking in bars, party going, visiting friends and relatives
Cultural, educational and artistic interests	Visiting theatres, concerts, exhibitions, museums, attending non-vocational classes
Pursuit of sport, either as participants or spectators	Golf, football, swimming, tennis, bowls, darts, gymnastics
Informal outdoor recreation	Driving for pleasure, day excursions to seaside and countryside, walking, picnicking
Leisure tourism involving overnight stay	Longer distance travel, tours, weekend breaks, holidays and vacations

The first three categories, although a major constituent of leisure time, are outside the scope of this book. Social, cultural and indoor sports activities are more specialized subjects and have been included only where they form components of other recreation or tourism developments.

In view of the different needs for marketing, planning and funding, this book also draws a distinction between requirements which are primarily for *community recreation* and those which are mainly directed at *leisure tourism*.

1.1.2 Visitors and tourists (definitions)

A **visitor** is defined for statistical purpose by the World Tourism Organization (WTO) as a person who travels outside his/her usual environment and whose main purpose is other than the exercise of an activity remunerated from within the country or place visited. Visitors can be separated into:

- **international visitors** – travelling to another country (measured as arrivals in destination country);
- **domestic visitors** – residents travelling within their own country.

Further subdivision is determined by main purpose of visit (business, leisure, health, etc.) or length of stay:

- **tourists** are visitors staying at least one night;
- **same-day visitors** stay less than 24 hours without involving an overnight stay;
- **cruise passengers** may visit the country for several days but spend nights on board cruise ships.

For planning purposes, local users of recreation products are identified in this book as:

- **excursionists** – same-day visitors travelling some distance to visit one or more places for pleasure;
- **recreationists** – mostly townspeople, visiting suitable places and using facilities for informal outdoor recreation, sport and leisure pastimes for a day or shorter time.

Visits may involve (WTO 1991)
- **independent travel** – travel and accommodation etc. arranged individually for and by the visitor;
- **group travel** – visitors travelling or meeting together to attend events (conferences, exhibitions) and/or in inclusive tour arrangements (packaged vacations).

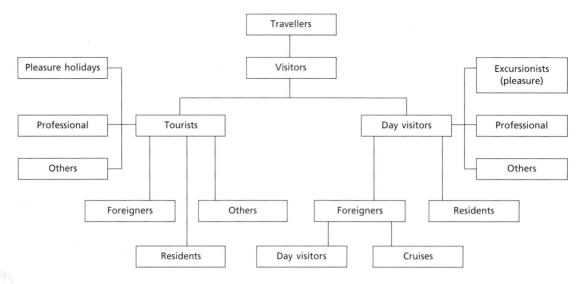

Figure 1.1

Tourism may thus be defined in terms of its components, namely the facilitation of travel of tourists, the activities they undertake at their destinations and the facilities and services provided to cater for their requirements.

1.1.3 Uncertain boundaries

Boundaries between recreation and tourism are indistinct, as both activities often share the same environments and facilities and compete for space and finance:

*   steps taken to improve the environment and to conserve and restore the national heritage benefit both recreation and tourism;
*   high quality provision for local recreation (ice rinks, yacht moorings, golf courses) will often enhance tourism interest

in the area and generate demands for accommodation and other services. Tourism products may also be created by improvements in cultural resources (museums, concert halls, theatres);
*   exotic leisure developments such as theme parks or ski resorts invariably need to attract tourists as well as day users. Hotels and resort facilities may partly rely on revenues generated by local users (functions, club membership, restaurant usage, etc.).

1.1.4 Demand for tourism and recreation

The demand for outdoor recreational activities mainly arises from cities and densely populated areas. It exerts a strong impact on resources and sites within convenient travelling

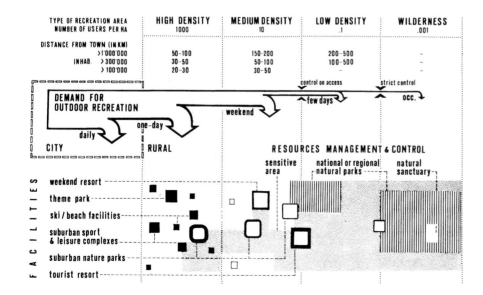

Figure 1.2

Location	Requirements for recreation	Typical densities (persons/ha)	Examples
Within urban areas	Local facilities for school, employees, club users, local community	2000–3000 (much more for spectator sports)	Sports grounds; urban parks; built leisure centres
Near city or town	Concentrated facilities for high density of users; with opportunities for more green and leisure activities	2000–3000 100–200	Theme parks; public beaches Suburban sports and leisure complexes
Within area (weekend use)	More dispersed facilities; control over location, densities and character	10–150	Weekend resorts; ski, seaside/ lakeside and country resorts
More distant regions	Protected areas; strict control and management of resources	below 0.1	Natural parks

distance. This demand takes different forms corresponding to the time available to reach these destinations (*time-distance*) and the type of activity involved (*participation time*).

Overall times	Locations for recreation	Distances
Few hours	In the city or its surroundings	1–10 km
One day	In the suburban area	20–100 km
Weekend	In the region	50–200 km
Short/long holidays	Usually more distant travel for sojourning/sightseeing	

The distance covered by recreationists usually increases with the size of their town of origin. The number of recreationists decreases as the distance from the urban centre generating demand increases. The pressure on resources also decreases with time-distance thus enabling greater opportunities in remote areas for protection and management of resources (national parks, nature reserves) (see Figure 1.2 and table at top of page).

1.1.5 Tourism and recreation: similarities and differences

Like tourism, recreation may take the form of inclusive tours, excursions or organized events. More commonly the recreation product is an individual arrangement in which time (time-distance to the destination and time available for recreational use) and opportunity cost are important considerations. Although recreation often shares the same interests and resources as tourism there are often significant differences (see table below).

Comparisons in marketing, operation and financing are summarized in 7.1.2.

1.2 COMPLEXITY OF THE TOURISM/RECREATION SYSTEM

Tourism and recreation are activities which involve

* other sectors of the economy (transportation, education, urban development, industry, forestry, telecommunications, information, etc.);
* national, regional and local socio-economic policies;
* socio-political traditions.

Although this book is primarily concerned with requirements for physical planning, decisions on land use and resources allocation must also take account of – and are often determined by – their economic and social environment and consequences.

Comparisons	Tourism	Open air recreation
Facilities	Developed by private sector; commercial feasibility critical	Usually with public sector funding
Choice	Wide choice of destination; strong international competition	Restricted by time-distance; alternatives usually limited
Quality of environment	Unique or distinctive character and image of destination are important factors	Important in suburban areas and in the countryside
Organization	Intermediaries (tour organizers, agents) play a major role	Clubs, societies, associations may be involved
Numbers of users	Limited by accommodation provided in the area	Determined by catchment population, access and facilities
Demands on resources	Continuous over season(s) of use; sensitive to excessive demand	Highly concentrated in weekends and public holidays; tolerant of crowding
Economic benefits	High with inflow of capital, employment and tourist expenditure	Low with limited (mainly part-time) employment and expenditure

'Recreation planning is a process that relates the leisure time of people to space. It is an art and a science that uses the concepts and methods of many disciplines to provide public and private leisure opportunities in cities. In practice, recreation planning blends the knowledge and techniques of environmental design and the social sciences to develop alternatives for using leisure time, space, energy and money to accommodate human needs. . . . Recreation planning is a hybrid of physical and social planning.'

(Gold 1980, p. 5)

Many plans have failed because of insufficient attention to the means of financing and implementing the proposals, to the existence of competing destinations or as a result of insufficient monitoring of progress.

1.2.1 Interface within the overall socio-economic policies

The development of tourism, an industry which relies almost entirely on other sectors, has to be planned in accordance with a number of principles:

- The measures to be implemented for the development of tourism/recreation (training, financing, infrastructures, land control, protection of resources, and so on) must be coherent with other relevant national policies (education, budget, public works, environment, etc.).
- All pressures on the land and the natural environment, from any origin (tourism, mining, industry, agriculture), must be controlled with the aim of avoiding any irreversible damage to the resources.
- The tourism master plan must be integrated within the country's economic development plans and programmes as well as with the physical (land-use) plans at national, regional and local levels.
- The tourism development plan must reflect the political, social and economic priorities so far as employment, revenues, regional development, image of the country, social tourism and community recreation, etc. are considered.

Financial and socio-economic procedures are detailed in Chapter 8 and in Appendices A2 and A3.

Similarly, public recreation has to be integrated with education, health, housing, transportation, environment, agriculture, forestry, welfare services and employment policies.

1.2.2 Interface of international tourism, domestic tourism and recreation

Whilst the economic benefits (high expenditure, foreign exchange) of international tourism often exert a dominant influence in tourism planning, the needs of domestic tourism and local recreation cannot be neglected:

- many facilities are shared by the three clienteles (especially in developed countries);

- there is often competition for appropriation of favourable sites (and finance);
- social policies include the development of recreation and domestic tourism.

In developing countries, where the charges for tourism facilities often exclude most of the local population, compensatory benefits may be provided through investment in community recreation (public beaches, sports grounds).

1.2.3 Interface with competing destinations

The development of tourism in any country depends, in part, on the steps being taken in neighbouring countries and, more generally, in similar competing destinations: the competitive introduction of new facilities and the tariffs and agreements concluded with large-scale operators or transporters may fundamentally modify the international markets. An evaluation of alternative destinations and competing tourism products is an essential part of any tourism development plan.

The same applies to recreation: the latent demand in any catchment area for particular sport and recreation facilities is sometimes finite and excessive provision can lead to market saturation (tennis courts, for example). Existing facilities can be affected by competition from new, more sophisticated, developments and require life cycle reinvestment in upgrading.

1.2.4 Interface and roles within the tourism/recreation sector

The implementation of any development calls for the participation of all parties concerned in tourism:

- **Developers** are the entrepreneurs or organizations who initiate a project and bring together the various resources and skills required to carry it out: site, finance, professional inputs. These may be an individual (hotelier, landowner), a commercial company or a public organization. The character of the development will, to a large extent, reflect the developer's motivation, interests and objectives. Commercial development proposals and strategies for their implementation are largely dictated by external conditions such as the market feasibility, costs of finance and land, political and economic conditions, and viability of the investment.
- **Intermediaries** are those bodies, agencies or operators who establish links between the actual facilities and the potential clientele. They include tour operators and travel agents; air, sea and ground transporters and the specialized press and promotional agencies. Intermediaries are in direct contact with their clienteles and may have a strong influence orientating their choice of activity and destination.

Intermediaries play a major role in
- packaging tourism products (assistance+travel+accommodation+after service);
- participating in development (through investment, finance, management);
- selling products and associated services;
- providing reservation services (independently and through franchises);
- organizing events and conferences.

- **National, regional or local public authorities** play a major role in tourism and recreation development:
  - in planning, decision making, monitoring and legislative programmes;
  - through investment in infrastructure and facilities, both directly and by means of incentives;
  - by setting up organizational structures involving public agency and/or private sector collaboration (tourism authorities, joint operating companies).

A tourism development plan has to conform with the various and often conflicting interests of all these parties, with their respective responsibilities, importance and influences, and with the decision-making organization.

Similar parties are concerned, alternatively or working together, in the development of recreation facilities and the implementation of a recreation development plan:

- **public bodies** (e.g. recreation commission, recreation and parks department, schools and other public agencies, etc.);
- **private non-profit sector** (e.g. youth organizations, sports associations and clubs, managements of firms creating facilities for their employees, etc.);
- **commercial sector** (e.g. for amusement parks, bowling greens, golf courses, etc.).

1.3 PLANNING WITH TOURISM PRODUCTS

The tourism (or the recreation) sector forms a complex system, with numerous decisive elements which affect and depend on the actions of others.

Compared with the difficulty of planning for tourism generally, taking into account the many and often conflicting relationships, as indicated in Figure 1.3, it is more practical to examine specific tourism products.

1.3.1 Tourism products

Tourism products are an amalgam of resources, facilities and services. Tourism products are evident in inclusive tours in which the tour operator brings together all the elements of a

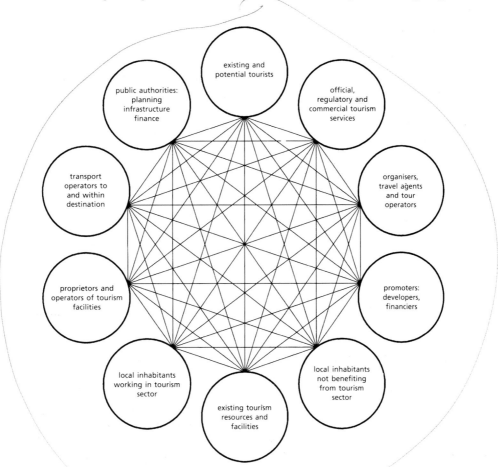

Figure 1.3

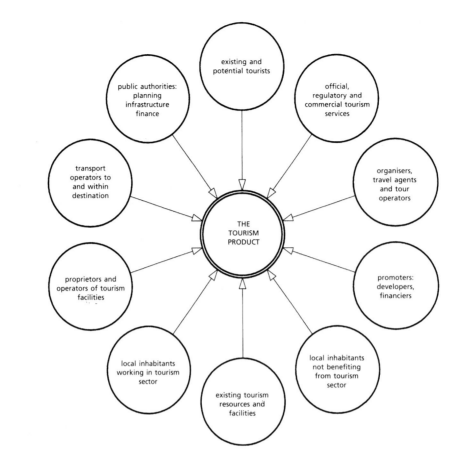

Figure 1.4

holiday and sells this package at an inclusive price. However, all tourists buy package, whether or not they use travel agents: individual tourists travelling on their own create their own products, when visiting resources or buying available facilities.

Tourism products may be centred on one place (e.g. a packaged resort holiday) or spread over a region (as in touring). They may be formulated for special interest groups (organized conference, golfing holiday) or framed around the use of a particular facility (cruising, hotel 'mini breaks').

Most tourism products are a blend of several interests: the primary attractions provide the main motivation but other attributes – such as the quality of accommodation, social activities, convenience of travel, and so on – have a strong influence on choice.

Product differentiation enables packages to be designed to attract particular segments of the tourism market and provides the basis for planning facilities and standards. *Product positioning* is pursued to establish prominence and reputation; it enables a destination to become identified with particular attributes (exotic, sophisticated, exclusive).

Note that from the supplier's viewpoint, products may have another meaning and represent the range of goods, facilities and services each supplier is able to offer.

1.3.2 Planning with products

Planning for tourism products – using a succession of optional tourism products aimed at increasing attractiveness, reducing costs or attracting new segments of the market – has many advantages:

Advantages	Details
Identifies the proposals which are fully implementable	Takes into consideration, from the planning stages, the motivations, customs, needs, spending power and other characteristics of the intended markets
Enables consultation with all parties liable to be affected by the tourism development	Combines their common interests and settles potential conflicts
Considers the competition from similar destinations	SWOT (strengths, weaknesses, opportunities and threats) can be specifically assessed
Allows detailed analysis of socio-economic and environmental impacts of each product created, achievement of strategic goals, etc.	Appraisal of feasibility, costs and benefits in local and foreign exchange, added value, employment

It is then easy to select the products whose impacts are adapted to the development policies. Comparisons may also be made with the potential benefits which could be derived from the same level of investment in other sectors of the economy (agriculture, handicrafts, etc.).

As can be seen from the two examples, product analyses do not apply to tourism only – recreation products may also be analysed and compared.

Examples of tourism and recreation product analyses

<u>Evaluation of tourism products in Niger</u>

As part of the Tourism Development Plan for Niger, a detailed evaluation was made of the main tourist flows and products in order to compare the benefits (see 7.3.7). As an example, the analysis of a camel riding circuit through the Aïr Range as a tourism package over 15–16 days took account of the local and external (leakages) revenues and costs incurred, the local and foreign investments required and jobs created.

The economic impact per annum was calculated in terms of

- *added value of the expenditure in Niger;*
- *integration ratio (added value:turnover);*
- *capital ratio (investment:added value);*
- *foreign exchange ratio;*
- *average cost per job created.*

Similar calculations of the potential alternative flows and products on the same basis:

Tourist flows	Integration	Ratios of capital	Foreign exchange
International business tourism	0.58	3.8	2.1
Nigerian business tourism	0.60	4.0	–
Regional business tourism	0.61	3.7	1.6
Nigerian traditional tourism	0.70	2.5	–
Relaxation and leisure centres	0.25	over 20	–
Individual international tourism	0.77	3.2	–
Circuits in the Aïr	0.72	2.6	1.7
Circuits in the Ténéré	0.70	2.0	1.5
Circuits to the Niger River	0.53	7.6	1.6

The advantage to the country of developing, for example, camel rides through the Aïr Range rather than circuits to the River and small adjacent animal reserve are shown by the better added value compared with turnover, much lower capital investment ratio and reduced leakages in foreign exchange.

Source: M. Baud-Bovy (1980), Tourism Development Plan, Niger, UNDP.

<u>Recreation product analyses</u>

In a study of sports and recreation activities in the canton of Geneva, the actual costs of amateur tennis and football were compared taking account of the size of the playing areas, number of hours of weekly use, duration of a play-period, number of simultaneous players, number of hours of weekly use per player, and the costs of providing and maintaining these facilities, including the cost of land and players' equipment:

The results showed that the costs to the community of providing facilities for football in a town were three to ten times those for tennis courts in the open. Similar comparisons were drawn between other sports as indicated in section 4.5.

Source: A. and M. Baud-Bovy (1988), Délassement, Sports et Loisirs de plein air à Genève, DTPE Genève

Average figures for one field/court	Area/player	No. of players	Investment cost	Costs per player operation only	operation and amortization	Typical allocation of costs Community	Player
Football in a village	165 m²	50	100 000	150	200	200	100–200
Football in a town	55 m²	150	1 000 000	700	1000	1 000	100–200
Tennis courts (summer only)	25 m²	60	150 000	50	300	100–300	50–250
Tennis Club (partly indoor)	25 m²	60	300 000	300	800	200–800	100–600

1.4 DEVELOPMENT VERSUS CONSERVATION

The first studies concerning the environmental impacts of tourism appeared after the mid-seventies (Tangy, 1977; Baud-Bovy and Lawson, 1977), followed by more research activity in the 1980s. (Briassoulis and Van der Straaten 1992)

Many tourism/recreational impacts are quantifiable; they will be dealt with in section 1.5. Others, in particular those related to the conservation of resources, are of a qualitative nature and more difficult to evaluate.

1.4.1 Environmental impacts from tourism

Unlike most other export-earning industries, tourism is invasive: the consumers purchase opportunities to visit and experience the attractions, amenities and other benefits offered by a destination. This involves close contact and, to some degree, competition with the local community for the resources of their environment. Tourism impacts (socio-cultural, economic and environmental) vary in both scale and intensity from one destination to the next and depend, to a large extent on their vulnerability (see 1.4.5) and accessibility to mass markets.

Both visitors and residents may have different perceptions of the detrimental effects of changes:

- **Visitors** seeking peace and solitude, an experience of history or socio-cultural exchange will have a low threshold of sensitivity. For others, gregariousness, social contact, range of services and activity choice may be key attractions.
- **Residents** also view impacts in different ways depending on whether they gain benefit (ownership of land, business interests, employment) or experience some loss. Losses may be measurable (higher costs of housing, depopulation of rural areas) or intangible (intrusion, changes in lifestyles and surroundings).

Agenda 21 for the travel and tourism industry:
Towards environmentally sustainable development

Agenda 21 was adopted in June 1992 by 182 governments at the United Nations Conference on Environment and Development (UNCED), the Earth Summit. The document prepared in 1996 by three major tourism organizations translates Agenda 21 into a programme of action for travel and tourism.

Nine priorities are defined for government departments, NTAs and representative trade organizations:

1 assessing the capacity of the existing regulatory, economic and voluntary framework to bring about sustainable toursim
2 assessing the economic, social, cultural, and environment implications of the organization's operations
3 training, education, and public awareness
4 planning for sustainable tourism development
5 facilitating exchange of information, skills, and technology relating to sustainable tourism between developed and developing countries
6 providing for the participation of all sectors of the society
7 design of new tourism products with sustainability at their core
8 measuring progress in achieving sustainable development
9 partnerships for sustainable development.

Ten priorities areas are defined for companies:

1 waste minimization, reuse and recycling
2 energy efficiency, conservation and management
3 management of fresh water resources
4 waste water management
5 limitation of hazardous substances
6 responsible use of transport
7 land-use planning and management
8 involving staff, customers, and communities in environmental issues
9 design for sustainability
10 partnerships for sustainable development.

Source: World Travel and Tourism Council, World Tourism Organization, The Earth Council (1996) Agenda 21 for the Travel and Tourism Industry – Towards Environmentally Sustainable Development, WTO, Madrid, 78 pp

Negative	Positive
Natural environment	
Modification of ecosystem	Actions for environmental conservation, such as creation of nature parks (in particular where natural beauties, rare animals, etc., are major tourist attractions)
Urbanization, degradation of countryside	
Sea pollution (not only from tourism)	
Coastal erosion (jetties, harbours)	Initiatives to provide treatment and purification systems for wastes
Deforestation	
Air pollution, litter	
Excessive water consumption	
Pollution of groundwater	
Socio-cultural environment	
Loss of identity and traditional culture	Rise in the available income
Rapid wealth-creation (in particular by selling properties)	Opportunities for work and business
Economic discrepancies between those active in tourism and the others	Contact with other cultures
Subordination to external decision-makers and investors ('colonization')	Improvement in cultural and educational standards
Inflation of purchase price or rent of properties	
Immigration of marginal strata with illegal, semi-legal or criminal activities	
Urban environment	
Over-intensive urbanization	Provision of public and private services
Uniformity/anonymity of areas of mass tourism	Improvement of communication and transport networks
Overburdening the resort's capacities	Concern for urban appearance
Illegal building	Making the most of local architecture, features, identities
Degradation of urban environment	Rehabilitation of decayed buildings and deteriorated urban areas
Negative aesthetic changes	
Noise and air pollution	

Source: ECONSTAT 1993, European Union, Brussels

Impacts may be tolerable for short intervals (holidays, peak seasons) and can be ameliorated by evident gains (improvements in infrastructure, amenities and environment). They are most evident when the character of an area changes dramatically by excessive and dominant building, but of equal concern are the insidious changes arising from the loss of place and natural harmony (coastal ribbon development, urban sprawl, insensitive design, ecological disturbance).

The approach towards impact analysis usually involves environmental assessment (see 1.4.7) and determination of carrying capacity (see 1.4.5). Negative impacts may be lessened by concentration in place (*enclave development*) or small-scale dispersion (*distributed development*).

1.4.2 Environmental impacts from recreation

Sustainability and the assessment of carrying capacities of vulnerable environments (national parks, areas of natural beauty) are essential considerations in recreation planning. Like tourism enclaves, recreational activities can be concentrated into areas or zones specifically equipped for the purpose (organized camping grounds, mooring jetties, playgrounds, leisure centres, visitor centres).

The development of certain categories of outdoor recreation facilities in the vicinity of a town calls for attractive sites. Conflicts may arise between:

- the environmentalists, giving priority to the absolute conservation of valuable natural sites, and
- the needs of the inhabitants of the town.

It has, however, been demonstrated (Sideway 1993) that the impact on sites from sport and outdoor recreation is not of major significance and that local damage to fragile habitat may be ameliorated by good conservation practice. Impacts from tourism development may be much more significant. The alternative policies which can be adopted in order to solve such conflicts are described in 1.4.9.

1.4.3 Sustainable development

Sustainable development is broadly defined as 'meeting the needs of the present without compromising the ability of future generations to meet their own needs' (The Brundtland Report 1987).

Forces promoting sustainable tourism

- Consumer pressure – destination choice influenced by environmental quality; increase in alternative forms of tourism (green tourism, ecotourism, special interest groups).

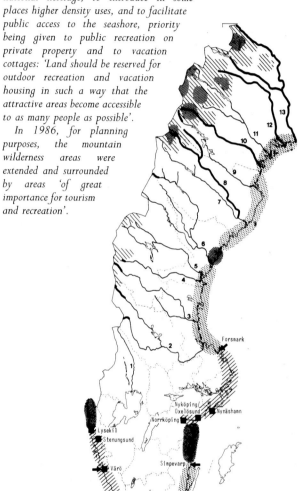

Sweden: An early ecological approach to the protection of natural resources

As early as 1971 a first outline national physical plan, entitled The conservation of land and water resources, was issued in Sweden, and approved by the parliament in 1972. It aimed in particular at controlling the extension of polluting industries and the development of vacation cottages.

More precise guidelines to control the development of vacation cottages were proposed in the late 1970s, in order to protect the national heritage, to introduce in some places higher density uses, and to facilitate public access to the seashore, priority being given to public recreation on private property and to vacation cottages: 'Land should be reserved for outdoor recreation and vacation housing in such a way that the attractive areas become accessible to as many people as possible'.

In 1986, for planning purposes, the mountain wilderness areas were extended and surrounded by areas 'of great importance for tourism and recreation'.

Key

⧄ Continuous coastlines: industry prohibited, recreational activities, protection of nature.

⧄ Heavily developed coastlines: strict control over industrial developments, public access to attractive shorelines, tourist and recreation facilities.

■ Main industrial sites.

➡ Expansion of nuclear power plants.

⧅ Wild areas to be kept free of roads, industrial developments and, to some extent, forestry.

▩ Centres of mountain wilderness areas: protection against heavy development, limited tourism only.

⤳ Rivers unaffected by hydroelectric plants to be protected.

- Public authority – not simply regulating development but encouraging good environmental practice (e.g. 'polluter pays' policies)
- Conservation concerns and local opposition – requiring environmental impact assessment and environmental auditing for major developments (e.g. Channel Tunnel, EuroDisney).

Counter forces

- Economic imperative – developers' interests in obtaining best return on investment and commercial profit in the short term.
- Developing countries – needs of foreign exchange and employment often outweigh environmental considerations.

Conservation and preservation of natural resources and cultural heritage are global as well as local concerns. For tourism to be sustainable, the type and extent of tourism activity must be balanced against the carrying capacity of the natural and man-made resources available.

Requirements

Sustainable tourism calls for:

- a long-term view of tourism with a regard for future inheritance as well as present needs;

- measures to ensure that consumption of tourism does not exceed the ability to provide;
- optimization to ensure equity in development between tourism requirements and community concerns, and investment returns and environmental safeguards;
- carefully planned economic growth: with worthwhile jobs, without dominating the local economy;
- effective management and maintenance of quality in both development and conservation of sites and traditional values to ensure continuation of benefits.

Environmental guidelines

In a dynamic world change is inevitable but it should not be at the expense of the basic principles of sustainability. In general these involve

- positive management of the relationship between tourism and the environment;
- limitation of damage to the resources or actions prejudicial to their future use; recycling;
- tourism activities and developments that respect the coherence of the landscape, the scale, nature and character of the places in which they are sited;
- in any location, a harmony or balance between the needs of visitors, the site and the host community;

Selected indicators for the tourism sector

The World Tourism Organization (WTO) recently proposed the use of selected indicators for sustainable tourism. In order to be useful to tourism sector managers and administrators, the selected indicators are demand-driven; they respond to decision-makers' need to know; they are practical for most nations or regions to provide. The selected core indicators are:

Indicator	Specific measures
1 Site protection	*Category of site protection according to IUCN (International Union for Conservation of Nature and Natural Resources) index*
2 Stress	*Tourism numbers visiting site (per annum / peak month)*
3 Use intensity	*Intensity of use in peak period (persons / hectare)*
4 Social impact	*Ratio of tourists to locals (peak period and overtime)*
5 Development control	*Existence of environmental review procedures or formal controls over development of site and use densities*
6 Waste management	*Percentage of sewage from site receiving treatment*
7 Planning process	*Existence of organized regional plan for tourist destination region (including tourism component)*
8 Critical ecosystems	*Number of rare / endangered species*
9 Consumer satisfaction	*Level of satisfaction by visitors (questionnaire-based)*
10 Local satisfaction	*Level of satisfaction by locals (questionnaire-based)*
11 Tourism contribution to local economy	*Proportion of total economic activity generated by tourism only*

Composite indices

A	*Carrying capacity*	*Composite early warning of key factors affecting the ability of the site to support different levels of tourism*
B	*Site stress*	*Composite measure of levels of impact on the site (its natural and cultural attributes due to tourism and other sector cumulative stresses)*
C.	*Attractiveness*	*Qualitative measure of those site attributes that make it attractive to tourism and can change over time.*

The WTO's study details the specific measures for these and other indicators; defines the role of indicators in managing sustainable tourism; and describes how to conduct indicator studies.

Source: Consulting and Audit Canada (1995)

- consideration being given to the region around the site and the effects of changes on the whole regional system;
- low energy consumption and promotion of a renewable energy base;
- respect for these principles by the tourism industry, local authorities and environmental agencies who need to work together to achieve their practical realization (English Tourist Board, 1991);
- participation of the local population in the decision process.

1.4.4 Alternative forms of tourism

The definitions of sustainable tourism are many, varied and often ambiguous. Terms like 'alternative', 'appropriate', 'responsible', 'green', 'eco-' and 'soft' generally refer to alternative forms of tourism. These are usually small scale, locally controlled, value conscious activities which take place in rural rather than urban areas, minimize the overall impact on the environment, benefit the host community and are sustainable. Within this overall coverage are a number of more specific definitions:

- **Green tourism** is an attitude or philosophy of a kind of tourism which is sustainable and which has regard for and respects the landscape, the wildlife, the existing infrastructure and cultural heritage of tourism destinations.
- **Alternative tourism** has been described as approaches which promote a just form of travel between members of different communities. It seeks to achieve a mutual understanding, solidarity and equality among participants.
- **Ecotourism** generally refers to travel to relatively undisturbed or uncontaminated natural areas with the specific objective of studying, admiring and enjoying the scenery and its wild plants and animals as well as any cultural manifestations found in these areas. The Australian definition is 'nature-based tourism that involves education and interpretation of the natural environment and is managed to be ecologically sustainable'. (Smith Evans 1994)

Although strict controls on numbers, activities and changes are often necessary to protect vulnerable resources, alternative forms of tourism are not a panacea. By interacting with local populations over extensive areas, trekking parties and 'backpacking' tourists may alter their ways of life much more than tourists concentrated in enclaves.

Conflicts between tourism and local traditions often occur in areas where the tourist activity is dictated by foreign interests (foreign developers, operators, tour organizers) but can be ameliorated where local people have a hand in developing tourism themselves. Planners should try, as far as possible, to conceive forms and products of tourism, and facilities which can be implemented and operated by the local population or at least by nationals of the country.

Tourism Concern and WWF-UK propose the following 'Ten Principles for Sustainable Tourism' in their paper *Beyond the Green Horizon*:

1 Using resources sustainably
2 Reducing over-consumption and waste
3 Maintaining diversity
4 Integrating tourism into planning
5 Supporting local economies
6 Involving local communities
7 Consulting stake-holders and the public
8 Training staff
9 Marketing tourism responsibly
10 Undertaking research

Source: Enviro, 17 June 1994

1.4.5 Carrying capacities

Carrying capacity is a measure of the maximum extent to which a particular location or resource can be used without detriment to its image and sustainability (Inskeep 1991). The early definition provided by J. Tivy

> Number of user-unit use-periods that a recreation site can provide (each year) without permanent biological and physical deterioration of the site ability to support recreation and without appreciably impairing the quality of the recreation experience
>
> (Tivy 1972)

is still relevant. The ways in which recreational activities interact with natural ecosystems has to be considered (Cocossis and Parpairis 1992, p. 26).

The World Tourism Organization defines the carrying capacity as:

- the levels which can be maintained without damage to the surrounding physical environment and without generating socio-cultural and economic problems to a community;
- the maintenance of balance between conservation and development;
- the numbers of visitors that are compatible with the image of the tourist product and the types of environmental and cultural experiences that visitors are seeking.

Carrying capacities vary from place to place depending on factors such as

- the fragility of the environment and local socio-cultural lifestyles and customs;
- the quality of experience sought by tourists in choosing that destination;
- the benefits sought from tourism and the extent to which the local community is involved;
- the facilities and services available and the extent to which the infrastructure can meet demand.

In practice carrying capacity may be measured in a number of ways:

Criteria	Examples of measurements
Physical	Density of development (beds/ha), intensity of use (visitors/ha), ratios (tourists/residents), floor coverage, plot ratios
Psychological	Perception of crowding and spatial quality (area/user), disturbance, conflicts with other user activities (behavioural studies, travel behaviour models)
Biological	Changes in land use, damage to vegetation, disturbance of wildlife, pollution (environmental impact analysis and audits)
Social	Extent of interaction and tourism dominance acceptable to host community (social surveys)
Economic	Benefits achieved (economic models), employment gains (direct and indirect), opportunity costs and negative impacts, congestion models
Infrastructure	Costs of infrastructure provision (cost/head), capacities available (roads, water, power, waste treatment), benefits to community

Carrying capacities provide the basis for planning resource utilization and scale of facilities to be provided. In most locations, carrying capacities can be increased without detriment by resource management (zoning, limiting numbers/activities, substitution) and provision of support facilities (visitor centres, public transport, museums).

Carrying capacity is broadly determined by three considerations:

- **Recreation** – types of activities, levels of use, spatial and temporal variations, user behaviour and social interactions, perceptions of resource quality.
- **Ecology** – natural processes of, and human impacts on, vegetation, soil, water, fauna etc.
- **Socio-economic impacts** – extent of change imposed on and the benefits gained by the host communities.

Determination of carrying capacity requires an analysis of each site and each planned activity to assess the level of use which would be tolerable to the visitor, the resources and the host community.

Difficulties in quantifying standards of carrying capacities for various types of recreational activity (see 4.3) are increased for those in which 'wilderness' or 'solitude' are important components. Sites requiring strict control to protect unique resources are usually reserved for scientific interest (for a discussion of carrying capacity and its implications in this respect see the publications of the Ecotourism Society).

> 'The concept of carrying capacity has already been employed in several outdoor recreation projects and can serve as a useful conceptual tool in the studies, especially when it is seen as a means to encourage tourist planners and others to give greater consideration to environmental matters, to qualitative aspects such as the experiences of both hosts and guests and as a supportive tool for the specification of goals and objectives. At present, the possibility of establishing quantitative limits through carrying capacity

expressions as absolute figures seems rather remote. In any case, the concept of tourist carrying capacity is not the panacea it may seem to be.'

(Coccossis and Parpairis 1992, p. 31)

1.4.6 Limits of acceptable charges

The concept of limits of acceptable charges (LAC) provides an interesting alternative to the concept of carrying capacity. Developed by the US Forest Service (Stankey *et al.* 1985) the LAC system is a framework for defining acceptable resource use, emphasis being given to the conditions desired in the area rather than to how much the area can tolerate. It requires a political decision about what is acceptable and may be based on a collective agreement (by managers, users and experts) on the limits of use which should not be exceeded. Agreed conservation/use standards corresponding to these objectives are then defined and permanently monitored.

This monitoring applies to both resources and visitors (patterns of use and satisfaction). This approach calls for a good match between the site and its resources on the one hand, and corresponding segments of the tourism market on the other.

1.4.7 Environmental impact assessment

Environmental impact assessment (EIA) is an approach used to identify the key attributes of the natural environment and the natural systems of a site or region. The objective is to identify, in advance, factors which may affect the ability to build a desired development, or be affected by the proposed activity.

The results can then influence the decision whether or not to proceed, the choice of design and phasing, and identify the need to mitigate unwanted effects.

EIA stems from the United States National Environmental Assessment Act 1972. The US Department of Commerce requires a comprehensive approach which includes (Manning and Dogherty 1994):

- inventory of social, political, physical and economic environments;
- forecast or projection of trends;
- setting of goals and objectives (usually or project level);
- examination of alternatives to reach these goals;
- selection of preferred alternatives;
- development of implementation strategy;
- implementation;
- evaluation.

Other authorities may accept simpler review procedures. For example, *site focused EIAs* examine the engineering concerns (drainage, soil depth, stability) and selected on-site phenomena (vegetation, fauna) which would be directly disturbed. Whilst site-specific reviews have value in identifying key physical and biological factors there is no examination of alternative sites or options, nor of the off-site effects (damage downstream or cumulative impact of pollution). The trend in EIA is towards evaluating ecological damage or disturbance against the wider benefits which the ecosystems provide (ecosystem evaluation, 'ecosphere' approaches).

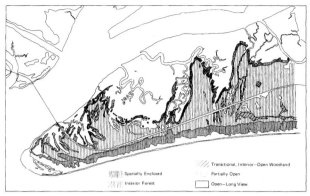

Spatially Enclosed
Interior Forest
Transitional, Interior—Open Woodland
Partially Open
Open—Long View

Landscape perception

Amelia Island, Florida, USA

Now recognized as one of the first ecological approaches to tourism planning, this ecological and land-use study of a coastal island of great natural beauty was undertaken to determine the optimum fit between the requirements for development of a resort community and the existing ecological and physical conditions. Amongst the subjects studied were climatic variations, exposures, probable tidal inundations, geology, physiography (dune stability, slope, areas of scenic or scientific value), hydrology (water quality and ground water levels, estuarine water), soils, marshes, vegetation cover and wildlife.

Architects: Wallace McMarg Roberts & Todd

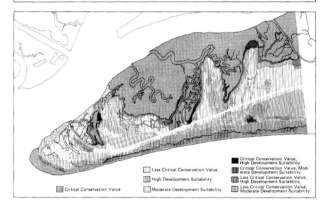

Ocean Front
Ocean Related, Marsh Front Southern Exposure
Marsh Front, Northern and Western Exposure
Marsh Front Lower Elevation, Woodland Interior Higher Elevation
Woodland Interior Lower Elevation

Synthesis of development opportunities

Less Critical Conservation Value
High Development Suitability
Critical Conservation Value
Moderate Development Suitability
Critical Conservation Value, High Development Suitability
Critical Conservation Value, Moderate Development Suitability
Less Critical Conservation Value, High Development Suitability
Less Critical Conservation Value, Moderate Development Suitability

Synthesis of all land-use suitabilities

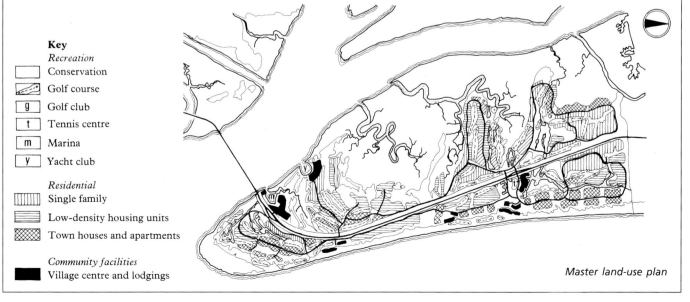

Key

Recreation
Conservation
Golf course
g Golf club
t Tennis centre
m Marina
y Yacht club

Residential
Single family
Low-density housing units
Town houses and apartments

Community facilities
Village centre and lodgings

Master land-use plan

1.4.8 Environmental auditing and quality control

The purpose of environmental auditing (EA) is to evaluate the performance of existing activities and procedures. In many countries this forms part of the *environmental management system (EMS)* of a destination or site. EA is widely practised by planning authorities to provide a systematic and objective evaluation of their performance in protecting the environment, and their compliance with environmental policies, standards and regulatory requirements.

As part of this procedure a *state of the environment (SOE)* report may be provided which identifies particular impacts and concerns which need to be addressed together with proposals for remedial action.

Environmental management control can be further achieved through the introduction of *environmental quality standards (EQS)* for destinations and *environmental performance standards (EPS)* for private companies.

1.4.9 Pressures on resources: alternative policies

There is a fundamental and continuing conflict between those for whom the preservation of the natural inheritance (natural or man-made) is an absolute priority and those who seek to utilize resources for beneficial use. The planning problem is to weigh conservation values against development suitability and against the recreational needs of the neighbouring population. In cases where it is necessary to **meet the demand**, a number of principles must be applied:

- irreversible degradation of unique resources must be avoided, a certain level of local damage accepted;
- as far as possible the policies adopted and the facilities provided must be sufficiently flexible to allow reintroduction of controls where necessary;
- facilities and activities which are not essentially linked to sensitive environmental areas should be located some distance away (without losing their attractiveness).

In many situations when the problem is acute and on a large scale, decisions between conservation and utilization will often be based on political rather than technical considerations.

When a resource with a finite capacity for visitors is or may become overcrowded or exposed to incompatible uses, various procedures may be considered to **alleviate the pressure** by restricting, regulating or reducing its use:

- **Restricting access**: limiting car park provision; prohibiting access by car; regulating the number of entrance tickets (advanced booking); charging high and/or differential admission prices, etc.

- **Limiting the facilities**: prohibiting the building of additional roads, accommodation and other facilities, not renewing licences or granting leases.
- **Zoning the various activities**: separating quiet activities (walking, fishing, etc.) in contact with the most valuable and sensitive part of the resource, from those which are fast-moving and noisy (motor boating, snowmobiles, water-skiing etc.).
- **Scheduling**: excluding one or more activities at different times of the day, week, month or year; for example, allocating water skiing 0900–1200 hrs, swimming 1200–1800 hrs, fishing 1800–2100 hrs.
- **Developing alternative destinations** of similar character, for example, relieving demand on an area of forest by building a road to another part, or putting private wooded areas to public recreational use, or reforesting demand areas: e.g. country parks (state parks in the USA) are developed to take part of the pressure away from national parks.

Even where priority is given to the recreational needs of the local population or the economic benefits expected from tourism, steps must be taken to **minimize degradation** of the resources:

- **increasing carrying capacities**: for example, by drainage, stabilization or other land improvements, landscaping, installing hard-wearing surfaces;
- **multiplying the facilities**: roads, parking places, vantage sites, different trails for walkers, horse riders and cyclists to separate conflicting uses and reduce inconvenience;
- **replacing crowded low-density activities** (free bathing, picnicking and camping in the wild) by planned equipped areas (organized public beaches, built facilities and standings for picnicking and camping);
- **concentrating facilities** in high-density 'absorption' sites ('honey pots') conveniently near the access points, thus alleviating the pressure on more vulnerable areas;
- **creating facilities for mass activities** (sports grounds, youth centres, recreational centres, club facilities) on the periphery of the resource area;
- **improving standards** of management, supervision, preservation, maintenance and interpretation.
- **excluding activities** which are not compatible with the resource or cannot provide a satisfactory recreational experiences.

1.5 EVALUATION OF DEVELOPMENT PROPOSALS

Evaluation of proposals for development of tourism and recreation may be at different levels of involvement and judged against different criteria:

- **At unit level** investment decisions are generally made by private entrepreneurs, companies, single-purpose authorities or local authorities and take into account only those inputs and outputs of a project which affect market pricing, their relative internal costs and values and the degree of risk or uncertainty involved.

- **At national and regional levels** the decisions will be more complex, requiring consideration of the environmental implications and the broader and long-term effects on the socio-economic development of the country. The latter will include the regional income-generating effects of tourism/recreation and comparisons with alternative developments in other economic sectors.

This section presents the main methods of evaluation. Data and sources useful in evaluating development projects (sources of economic data, investment costs, employment ratios, state revenues) are provided in Appendix A2: Investment in tourism and recreation – Methods and sources, and in Appendix A3: Impacts from tourism and recreation – Socio-economic data.

1.5.1 Feasibility analysis

Feasibility analysis is used for the commercial appraisal of alternative investments and involves comparisons of investment profitability using the normal commercial criteria of revenues and costs (internal benefits and costs) and return on capital. For each investment project a cash flow forecast is prepared giving a breakdown of receipts and expenditures – including subsidies and taxes – over the periods of time they are expected to occur, taking into account the timing of life cycles and loan repayments.

Examples of purely commercial investments:

- hotels and property investments (condominiums etc.);
- high revenue generating leisure attractions (gambling, entertainment, spectator sports);
- private membership facilities (health and fitness, golf);
- associated commercial services (restaurants, bars, shops).

Commercial development is highly sensitive to changes in interest rates and the opportunity costs of alternative investments. Incentives affect feasibility by reducing capital costs (grants) or by improving investment returns (tax credits, low interest loans etc.).

Similar methods of analysis can be applied globally to a mixed development such as a tourist resort or recreational complex. However, large-scale developments involve broader issues such as

- the balance between revenue earning and non-revenue earning expenditures;
- the apportionment of external and joint costs to individual projects;
- the phasing of development and investment streams (programming, resource levelling etc.).

Individual feasibility studies must be applied to determine

- requirements (financial, locational, spatial) which the developers will have to satisfy in order to resell or lease plots for

various facilities such as hotels, commercial properties and housing;
- overall costs which will be incurred in implementing other development needs (infrastructure, parks, promenades, recreational amenities).

In order to obtain approval for development and financial contribution from public sector sources, it is usually necessary to consider wider issues than investment criteria. These will include such aspects as:

- environmental impacts and measures to be taken for conservation (including cost and location implications – see 1.2.8)
- employment and other benefits (purchases of goods and services, by tourists, improvement of local amenities and services), taking into account costs of training and other services.

Example: Evaluation of tourism products in Mauritius

Taking into account the expenditures of each flow of tourists (origins, characteristics) and the products involved (holiday, honeymoon, business/incentive travel, visiting friends and relations, and others), a forecasting model was prepared to evaluate the economic and environmental impacts of future strategies. The continuously revised outputs include multiplier values, employment generation, government revenues, balance of payments and environmental impacts (land allocations, accommodation requirements, etc.).

Source: Professor J. Fletcher, for the Mauritius Government, May 1996

1.5.2 Cost benefit analysis

Cost benefit analysis provides a framework for long-term evaluation and for a wider view of development issues. It enables values to be attached to various external costs and benefits which stem from a development. In comparing alternatives, particular consideration can be given to the community's interests which is usually assumed to be best served by maximizing the socio-economic benefits.

Cost benefit analysis gives a more comprehensive picture of the true impact of tourism, defining ratios such as

- gains in foreign exchange by unit of investment;
- capital cost per job created;
- state revenue gain by unit of investment.

These ratios measured against those for competing economic sectors assist in determining preferential sectors for development and support.

Local planning regulation of tourism development may positively contribute towards this end by transferring to the developer many of the external costs which would otherwise have to be borne by the community. The potential financial gain resulting from planning consent may also be used as a means of directly funding other community needs (amenities, environmental improvements).

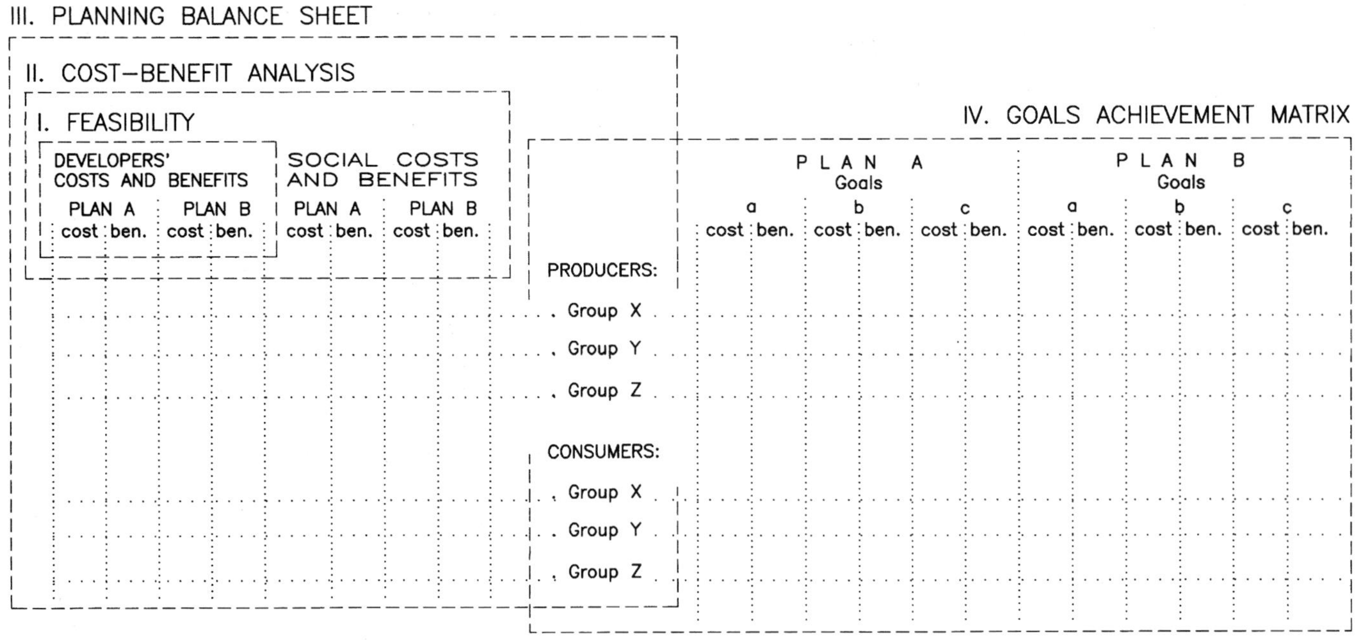

III. PLANNING BALANCE SHEET

Figure 1.5

1.5.3 Planning balance sheet

A community is not homogeneous and various groups may have different, and sometimes opposite, points of view. Costs and benefits are not necessarily the same, for example, those taking part in tourism and recreation development have different requirements from those pursuing traditional activities or otherwise affected by them.

The planning balance sheet allows these various interests to be considered in detail. The balance sheet enumerates for each project or groups of projects the parties who will be concerned in producing and/or operating the facilities, or consuming the services provided – whether they buy them in the market or (collectively) through taxes. For each party, the costs and benefits which will accrue can be more specifically forecast.

Compared with separate evaluations of costs and benefits, the balance sheet provides a more comprehensive analysis of alternative plans: it enables social and/or environmental costs to be offset by other benefits and both costs and benefits to be more equitably distributed by adjustments in the plan.

From the viewpoint of the developer, a planning balance sheet may be used to demonstrate the benefits which will accrue to the community if permission for a proposed development is given. In resort development the use of a fully quantified econometric model applying fuzzy programme techniques is usually not practicable. A simpler approach may be adopted based on

- a quantified analysis of tangible criteria (economic benefits and costs);
- a descriptive expression of the foreseeable social and environmental effects on each of the main groups involved;
- a comparison of the inherent risks of each alternative.

1.5.4 Goals achievement matrix

This is an alternative approach which takes into account the *goal orientation* of planning. For analysis a number of goals or desired objectives for the plan are established and weighted in terms of their relative importance and values. Benefits represent progress towards the desired objectives whilst costs represent retrogression from these objectives. This approach takes explicitly into consideration unquantifiable environmental impacts with a view to defining the sustainability of the proposed development.

Costs and benefits are recorded for each objective according to the parties that are affected. Alternative plans can be compared in terms of the goals which can be achieved and this procedure may also be used to enable strategies to be progressively shaped and evaluated in relation to specified long-term objectives.

The goals achievement matrix is significant in planning for tourism and recreation but may also be adapted to monitor the effects of developments in relation to planning strategies and long-term objectives.

2 Basic standards for accommodation, catering and shopping

This chapter provides standards for the essential facilities required in tourist or recreation resorts of various sizes and characteristics.

2.1 INFLUENCES ON PLANNING

2.1.1 Types of facilities

Tourist facilities fall into two main categories, namely those which are

- **basic** or common to all types of resorts or recreation complexes, wherever they are located, providing for general tourist needs such as accommodation, catering, entertainment,

leisure and relaxation and providing the necessary technical infrastructure for resort operation.
- **specific** – identified with particular localities, utilizing the resources of the site and surroundings for more specific pursuits which characterize the nature of the resort or of the recreation area. Seaside, mountain, spa and themed resorts and holiday centres or suburban parks are examples of specific developments.

The basic facilities described in this chapter are not limited to resorts. Hotels, restaurants and other services are located along tourist and traffic routes, in cities and towns and in strategic places where there is a market demand for transient or staying visitors. In general, the same planning standards and technical details apply, although with variations depending mainly on the markets (pricing, grade, level of sophistication)

The Pousadas of Portugal

The Pousadas de Portugal form a network of 41 units spread throughout the most beautiful regions of the country. Each one is unique: regional pousadas take their inspiration from local architecture, whilst the historical pousadas are created from restored castles, convents and palaces. Few have more than 30 rooms and emphasis is given to traditional hospitality and service. In 1996 this project won the international ASTA–Smithsonian Foundation Award.

Pousada de D. Maria   Pousada do Castelo Alvito

Baan Taling Ngam Resort, Thailand

Located on Ko Samui Island on a ridge with spectacular views of the sea and offshore islands, this luxury resort, built in 1994, has only 44 rooms in a boutique hotel, plus 42 traditional Thai village huts and a beach combo area with six units, a beach club and swimming pool. A service area provides support services for the whole of this self-contained site.

Architects: RMJM (Hong Kong)

and location (indoor/outdoor facilities, degree of concentration).

The figures quoted are based on the average provision for new integrated resorts (see 6.2.1 for a definition of integrated resorts), in which at least 50 per cent of the beds are available for rent and in which there are few competing facilities in the hotels. Adjustments will need to be made for local circumstances, such as the availability of similar facilities in the vicinity of the resort.

Further details are given in *Hotels and Resorts: Planning, Design and Refurbishment* (Lawson 1995).

2.1.2 Main types of accommodation

In terms of investment, accommodation represents the most expensive facility in holiday resorts: a 10 per cent saving in the cost of hotel accommodation may, for example, be equal to the total investment needed for other recreation, sports and cultural facilities. Accommodation, whether in hotels or rented units, also represents the major source of service for a resort and is the main contributor to net income. In other cases the capitalization and sale of accommodation units, such as in condominium or real estate properties, is the key motivation for investment. A detailed survey of accommodation requirements and trends is, therefore, essential in the initial stages of resort planning as well as in determining design features of individual premises.

In most countries the requirements for various grades or classifications of hotels and other tourist accommodation are laid down in compulsory regulations or voluntary schemes. Registration or licensing and other conditions for financial aid towards the costs of providing tourist hotels, etc., also indicate the standards and services to be provided.

Resort accommodation may be grouped into a number of categories:

- **Hotels** provide accommodation, meals and refreshments, for irregular periods of time and not necessarily by pre-arrangement. In practice, resort hotels may be under contract to accommodate specific groups (for example, for tour operations), may restrict meals to residents only and may remain open only during the holiday season.
- **Guesthouses and pensions** are generally smaller private units offering exclusive accommodation and meals for residents, for longer, regular periods of time.
- **Motels and lodges** are specifically sited and planned to provide convenient accommodation for the motorist. Meals are often available separately on an independent basis. While motels have evolved to serve transient needs, many of the lodges and motor hotels sited in resort areas provide extensive facilities, including self-catering, for the holidaymaker.
- **Hotels garnis** and similar establishments provide bed and breakfast or accommodation without meals. Bed and breakfast or self-catering accommodation may also be provided by owners of domestic properties.

- **Hostel accommodation** is generally provided for specific groups of users (young people, associations, pilgrims etc.) and facilities are invariably shared. The accommodation may be basic (for economy) or provide dining, social and recreational services.
- **Condominiums** are groupings of properties which are individually owned but share common facilities (elevators, building, engineering services etc.) and communal areas (grounds, entrances, recreation facilities). Responsibilities for maintenance and security are also collective and these and other services – including leasing to vacationers -may be carried out by management associations or agencies.
- **Holiday villages** are essentially multiple units of accommodation individually grouped around central catering and recreational facilities. The accommodation units may provide self-catering as an alternative to inclusive meals, and are designed mainly for family or individual use. The villages are conceived as self sufficient entities offering, under one management, all the facilities of a planned resort. Some holiday villages are built for social tourism, others (such as Club Méditerranée or Valtour) as commercial developments. They are usually distinct from the main holiday resorts but sometimes integrated for social tourism. Commercial holiday villages usually provide around 500 to 2000 beds (800 to 1000 being considered an optimum for centralized activities) and may be developed by phasing (see section 6.2). Villages of a social character are generally much smaller (see 2.3.6).
- **Individual housing** units in resort areas include apartments, villas, chalets, maisonettes and houses. The accommodation may be used as the main or second (holiday) home of the owner, leased on a short- or long-term basis to tourist agencies or managed as a condominium.
- **Camping sites, caravan sites** are equipped with sanitary services, drainage and site works and may include restaurants or cafeteria, vehicle service stations, shops, indoor and outdoor recreation facilities and other features. Most resort sites are restricted to holiday season use, although permanent parking of caravans may be allowed under more stringent licensing conditions.

2.1.3 Feasibility of hotel accommodation

The economic aspects of investment in tourist accommodation are outlined in 1.5, 9.1.3 and Appendix A2. The high proportion of capital tied up in fixed assets for long periods (20–25 years in the case of the building shell) means there is little scope for flexibility to meet changes in market or operating conditions.

The break-even point is often finely balanced in the case of resorts, relying on very high occupancy figures during a relatively short period of use and, in some cases, on governmental or regional financial aid.

Feasibility analyses of hotels and similar types of accommodation need to take account of projected elements for sales, costs and profit margins for different rates of occupancy and periods of use.

Methods of increasing the feasibility of investment

Approach	Examples
Increased occupancy	Extension of season with promotional activities, enclosed facilities, market development in conferences, incentive travel, special interest groups
Reduced building costs	Economical forms of building; standardization, prefabrication, rationalization, separation of public and residential areas
State aid for tourism	Reduction of capital costs (grants, loans, subventions) or fiscal incentives, training and promotion services
Capital sales and concessions	Sale of supplementary accommodation, leasing of shops, food services, sports and leisure services, serviced units
Shared investment	Joint venture projects, sale and leaseback of land and properties, mixed development with shops and commercial property

2.1.4 Effects of investment on hotel planning

In developed market economies, faced with high building and labour costs, the steps suggested for increasing the feasibility of investment have generally proved to be insufficient to attract adequate investment in lower and medium priced resort hotels. Hotel development has tended to polarize into

- *high standard hotels* orientated to business and higher spending tourists, in city centres and prime locations which ensure high annual occupancies;
- *budget hotels* with minimal public facilities, serving mainly transient and short-stay users, along highways and in low cost out-of-centre sites including urban redevelopment areas;
- *resort complexes,* new concepts and changes in existing resorts to provide self-catering/inclusive options, part enclosed recreation and entertainment (all weather, extended seasons), sophisticated sports and themed attractions in landscaped settings.

In developing countries inward investment is usually in higher standard hotels, which can attract international tourists and provide confidence in the standards of amenities and security, whilst local investment is mainly in small budget hotels (usually operated on a family basis). Lower land and operating costs generally allow lower density development and more spacious rooms.

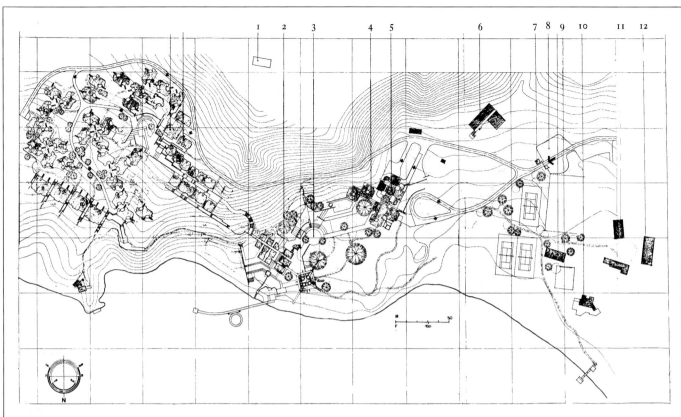

a *Site plan: Phase 1 showing the entrance (west aside), public areas (central) and residences (east)*

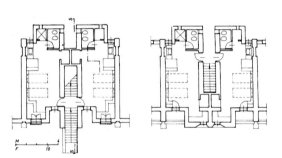

Key
1 Traditional baths and infirmary
2 Bazaar
3 Theatre
4 Restaurant
5 Kitchen
6 Staff quarters
7 Entrance control
8 Parking
9 Sports area
10 Beach bar
11 Sewage works
12 Maintenance

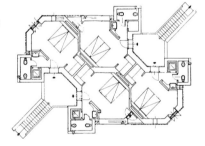

b *Houses with upper and lower units in rows*

d *Houses in clusters, surrounding courts*

Tourist Village, Kemer, Antalya, Turkey

One of the first developments in this designated tourist region, the village is situated on a rocky promontory amongst pine forests. The starkly simple forms of architecture echo the character of the region and its archaeology. Under Turkish law all trees are the property of the Government and are protected, dictating the layout of the site and buildings. A low area is concentrated with open buildings around a garden plaza; the upper area contains the residences with paths to rows and clusters of two-storey units.

The planned capacity is 1200 beds, with the first phase (completed in 1973) providing some 700 beds. The resort village includes a restaurant with open-air terrace, bar pavilion, coffee terrace, Turkish baths, a night club, open-air theatre, bazaar, tennis courts, sub-aqua and sailing schools and a landing stage. A high proportion of the staff are housed on site and the village provides its own power station and laundry. The village is now run by Club Med.

Architects: Luciano Giovanni, Giorgio Giovanni,
Tuncay Cavder, with Christine Leserre

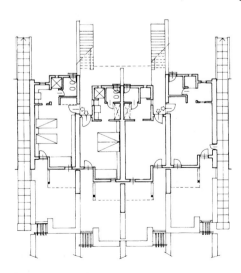

c *Houses in terraces*

2.1.5 Balance of hotel and private accommodation

Much of the past large-scale tourism development in the 1970s and early 1980s stemmed from individual private investments in holiday accommodation. The attractions of owning a villa or apartment in a tourist resort for holidays (and eventual retirement), with the prospect of appreciation in property values as a form of security for personal savings, was often combined with the financial advantages of low interest on long-term mortgages and tax concessions for ownership of property.

Real estate developers have introduced various formulae aimed at making the acquisition of private properties even more affordable and attractive, for example:

- multi-ownership: with two, four or more owners sharing the costs, with agreed programmes for occupation;
- creating an organization for letting the apartment/residence when the owner (often a shareholder in a condominium) is away, sometimes with a guaranteed rate of revenue;
- selling at reduced prices, the developer (or agent) reserving rights to income from letting the units for a fixed number of years;
- time sharing: selling transferable shares giving a right to one (or more) weeks of occupation in a specific unit each year at the same date;
- selling shares in the ownership of the whole resort (as in Les Arcs, France) giving the right to a corresponding stay free of charge at stated periods;
- selling shares in a company investing in a number of resorts, allowing choice of location for the entitled period of stay.

As a result, the ratio of hotel beds, even in traditional resorts, has significantly declined. In new mountain or seaside resorts in developed market economies, hotel beds often make up less than 10 per cent of the total accommodation. The situation is different in centrally-planned economies and in developing countries where the main demand is from packaged tours requiring inclusive hotel or resort accommodation or where reassurance of standards is an important marketing consideration.

2.1.6 Impact of accommodation mix on resort development

The long-term consequences of this orientation towards private accommodation have become increasingly apparent and can be summarized as follows:

- heavy state assistance and financing tends to result in accelerating and often massive provision of private units, uninhabited for much of the year and bringing in little revenue to the country and limited employment opportunities;

- precious (often prime) tourist sites, which are or would be required for more profitable types of tourism, become occupied by private users – often by foreigners;
- the development of private units creates sprawling urban resorts, often with traffic and parking problems, few viable amenities and little vitality outside the short periods of seasonal (or weekend) use.

Similar changes tend to occur in the character of existing resorts, but with increasing ratios of retired residents together with shifts in tourism towards short-stay and excursion visitors.

2.1.7 New objectives in planning

At least 50 per cent, and more if possible, of the accommodation of a resort should be made available for rent. The policies which may be suggested or imposed by the authorities include:

- providing incentives (for example, through fiscal adjustments) for the private owners of existing units to make them available for renting;
- stipulating, as planning conditions for new resorts, the number of private units which must be made available, for tourist rental, in the absence of their owners;
- developing para-hotel condominiums: selling studio and small apartments for personal occupancy for some weeks each year with, at other times, rental as hotel rooms;
- providing social accommodation such as hostels, holiday villages, camping and caravan sites as part of integrated tourism development;
- combining traditional hotels with apartments or villas (aparthotels), with food service, cleaning, laundry and other services being undertaken by the hotel;
- mobilizing private investment for the financing of hotels by:
  - selling hotel units (including a percentage of public areas) to co-owners, in the absence of whom the unit is rented (Eurotel);
  - selling shares corresponding to one (or more) hotel room and giving the right to stay free of charge for a given period in the year, with reductions in tariffs and priority in other establishments of the same chain (Club Hotel).

With these new formulae the traditional distinction between hotel and non-hotel beds loses significance: it is replaced by the distinction between those beds which are available for overnight and short-term let and those which are not. It is generally accepted, in particular in winter resorts, that about half of the beds should be available for rent in order to maintain life and activity in the resort.

The availability of alternative forms of accommodation is advantageous in extending marketing opportunities, including out-of-season inducements (organized events, group travel, special activities or interests).

Belek Hotel, Antalya, Turkey

Under construction in 1996, the high-grade Belek Hotel has 253 guest rooms arranged in terraces around spacious public areas on one side of the site overlooking the pool and beach beyond. Fifty aparthotels form a village grouping on the other side, with extensive landscaped recreational areas between. The site extends to 68 731 m² with a built area of 27 146 m². The design echoes traditional Turkish architecture and, although buildings are concentrated, their outline is broken with separate blocks of rooms, varied heights and external landscaped spaces flowing between and into the areas. Technical services are housed in under-corridor galleries extending from the basement plant.

Architect: Professor Cengiz Eren

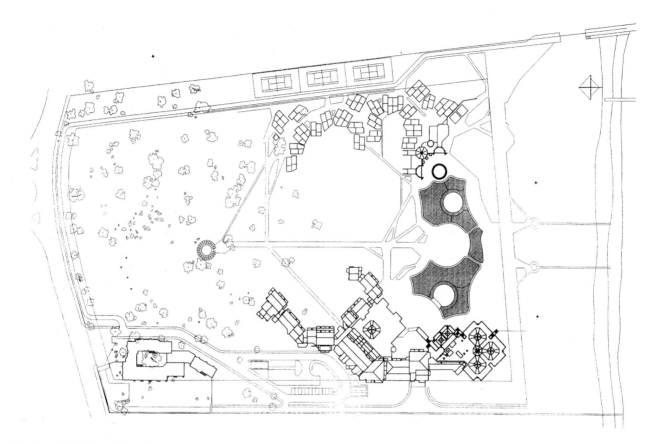

Site plan, Belek Hotel, Antalya

View from sea towards restaurant

2.2 HOTELS

2.2.1 Types of hotels

Hotels range over many types, catering for different market requirements (luxury or economy, meals, specific to particular groups or catering for the general public, with or without additional facilities and services) and operating under different conditions of scale, ownership and management. Hence definitions of hotels are often imprecise and subject to continuous change.

Optimum sizes for hotels increase in steps, the threshold of size being determined by operating requirements:

- family-operated hotels, guesthouses, pensions   10–20 rooms
- supported by professional management   50–70 rooms
- choice of restaurants offered   100–150 rooms
- resort hotels for packaged tours (economies of scale)   150–300 rooms

In pavilion hotels and village resorts (such as holiday parks, see 5.4.4), the residential accommodation is separate from public areas and generally arranged in small-scale clusters or groups of rooms. This permits greater flexibility in layout and better integration with the landscape, although greater land areas are usually required. The resorts are generally traffic free and, as a rule, room service is limited to basic cleaning.

Investment in very large hotels of more than 500 beds in resorts is constrained by the difficulties and uncertainties of marketing and finance in a world of rapidly changing economic and social patterns. Development of resort accommodation is now more likely to be carried out in smaller self-financing stages of buildings and extensions, with three main exceptions:

- *casino hotels* which often require 500–1000 or more rooms to support the high investment in elaborate public facilities;
- *convention hotels* which market large convention and banqueting areas;
- *mixed developments* of hotels with aparthotels, condominiums and other accommodation options within the same site.

2.2.2 Planning standards: built areas

Room sizes and the extent of public and support facilities provided in hotels are largely dictated by

- *grade* – classification of the hotel standards;
- *location* – relative costs of land, surroundings;
- *market emphasis* – packaged tours, conventions;
- *design* – arrangements of rooms, circulation space;
- *size* – economies of scale, range of amenities;

Apart from hostel type accommodation, practically all new hotels and resorts provide guestrooms en-suite with bathrooms or shower rooms. A typical bathroom takes up between 16 and 20 per cent of the total unit area of a guestroom and emphasis is usually given to compact ergonomic design with layouts

Gross areas for typical hotel two-bed units (by category or grade of hotel) are normally:

		Economy *	Some comfort **	Average comfort ***	High comfort ****	Deluxe *****
Twin-bed room (net) including bathroom	m²	17.5ᵃ	21.7	25.2	30.0 (+5%)	36.0 (+5%)
	sq ft	188	234	271	323	387
Room circulation and servicesᵇ	m²	4.5	5.3	7.8	14.0	17.0
	sq ft	48	57	84	151	183
Residential areas (total)	m²	22.0	27.0	33.0	44.0	53.0
	sq ft	236	291	355	474	570
Public and support areas (total)ᶜ	m²	5.5	8.0	12.0	18.0	22.0
	sq ft	60	86	129	194	237
Residential areas	% of total	80	77	72	71	71
Total per unit	m²	27.5	35.0	45.0	62.0	75.0
	sq ft	296	377	484	668	807
Total per bed	m²	13.8	17.5	22.5	31.0	37.5
	sq ft	148	183	242	334	404

Notes:
(a) Shower rooms or shared bathrooms (1:2) reduce areas by 7–10%.
(b) Corridors, stairs, elevators, floor service rooms, etc. Rooms with external entrances reduce these areas by 60%.
(c) Includes support services (kitchen, housekeeping, etc.) but not technical services in basement (plant) or staff accommodation.

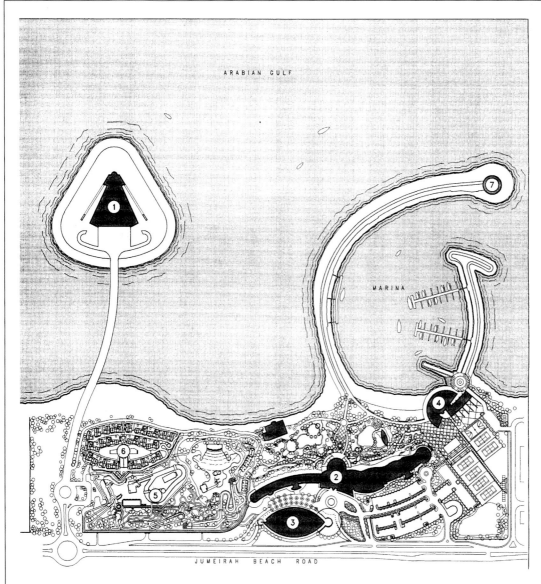

Site plan, Chicago Beach, Dubai

1 Tower Hotel
2 Resort Hotel
3 Conference Centre
4 Sports Centre
5 Aquapark
6 Chalet
7 Marina restaurant

Chicago Beach, Dubai

Situated 15 km from the city of Dubai on the shores of the Arabian Gulf, the new Chicago Beach development occupies a site of 12.5 ha. The resort area includes a marina, two hotels, 21 beach chalets, a conference centre and ballroom, aqua park, sports club, golf and tennis academies, restaurants, pools, a children's area, staff village and central service compound.

The Resort Hotel, completed in September 1997, is a 5-star tourist hotel, having a curved profile, which accommodates 551 rooms and 49 suites, all enjoying sea views, and ten speciality restaurants. Built on

a man-made island with a link bridge to the shore, the Tower Hotel is due to be completed in 1998. A super luxury 202-suite hotel, this is 321 m high, shaped like a fluted sail around an atrium, forming a dramatic feature and image for the area. The hotel facilities include four world-class restaurants, luxury health floor, and pool deck on the island.

Architects, engineers and project managers:
W. S. Atkins, UK
Project Director/Chief Architect: T. Wills-Wright

grouped around service ducts. Some economy may be gained by the use of showers in lieu of baths, particularly for single rooms. Important considerations include:

- the number and format of beds (permanent and convertible);
- luggage transfer, unpacking and stowage;
- extent of hanging and drawer/shelf space;
- room facilities (television, telephone, service);
- drying facilities (for wet clothes, towels etc.);

- family needs (additional/convertible rooms);
- self catering (location of equipment, ventilation);
- design (lighting, decor, mirrors, furnishings).

In multi-storey hotels, room widths are most critical, affecting frontages and travel distances. Standard rooms are normally based on 3.65 m (12 ft) models, with a minimum of 3.5 m (11 ft 6 in). Greater flexibility is allowed in *pavilion* style hotels.

2.2.3 Variations in rooms sizes

Rooms planned for family use, with twin double beds or convertible settees, increase the room areas by 5 to 10 per cent. The room sizes of international hotels in developing countries and of chain hotels in America are also generally 5 to 10 per cent larger than the standards provided in 2.2.2.

In mountain ski resorts, the rooms are often reduced by 5 to 10 per cent with emphasis on cosiness (bunk beds, compact designs). Apartments provided in a hotel (aparthotels) require a space of 32 to 50 m² (340 to 540 sq ft) for two rooms and 65 to 80 m² for three rooms.

Resort hotels generally have twin-bedded rooms, with the facility of joining the beds together as large doubles. In cities and places serving mainly business travellers, a proportion of the rooms may have one double bed allowing more space for work areas. Single rooms may also be used in economy grade rooms such as hostels, two single rooms requiring about 20 per cent more space than one twin-bedded room. The ratio of twin- to double-bed rooms and family room options is determined by market analysis, which must take account of variations in use (weekday, weekend, seasonal holiday) and foreseeable changes in requirements (e.g. self-catering needs).

Rooms planned for the disabled need specific consideration. Statutory requirements usually stipulate 1 or 2 per cent of rooms must be equipped for ambulant disabled use, allowing

- easy access (signed, level, ramped and/or elevator circulations);
- space within the room and bathroom (for wheelchair manoeuvres);
- suitable fittings within convenient reach.

2.2.4 Circulation planning

In the early stages of planning, decisions must be taken on:

Requirement	Consideration
Access for guests and visitors	Mode of transport; parking; protection; impression
Access for goods, services and staff	Routes; location of services; areas; separation; screening
Guest circulation within the hotels	Locations of public areas, rooms, facilities, services
Service circulation and locations	Food and beverage, housekeeping maintenance; administration
Leisure areas and vantages	Maximum benefit to rooms and public areas

2.2.5 Planning of public areas

The range of public facilities is closely related to

- availability of *alternative facilities* in the resort or vicinity (as in integrated resorts);

- *market requirements*: standards of service and facilities expected for the grade of hotel;
- potential *external markets* for restaurants, conference and function rooms and leisure facilities;
- *size*: sufficient numbers of uses for viable operation.

Resort hotels generally offer inclusive accommodation with meals (full- or half-board) but in other locations the extent of meal service may be rationalized. Higher grade hotels, particularly large units, offer a choice of restaurants. In a resort having a large residential population and in other urban areas, the restaurants and entertainment lounges may be designed to attract local custom, with external access, conspicuous frontages and a measure of separation from the hotel residential areas. This also applies to conference, function and banquet areas. On the other hand, the extent of public space may be reduced in budget hotels where alternative restaurants, etc., are available elsewhere.

Lobbies: serve as a reception and information centre, a place to meet and often the hub of circulation for the guestrooms and public areas (including shops). In a seaside resort the design of the lobby should allow views of the leisure activities and beach, and may extend into balconies and terraces to create interest and linkages. Typical areas:

	m²/room	sq ft/room	Notes
Seaside resort hotels	1.0	10.0	(a)
Village style resorts	0.6	6.0	(b)
Mountain resorts	0.6	6.0	(c)

Notes:
(a) Extending to other areas, landscaped.
(b) More functional (reception, luggage, information). More space allocated to entertainment.
(c) Relatively small but attractive (fire, features) leading to lounge(s), bars, restaurants etc.

Shops: the number and type depends on the market (grade and number of hotel rooms, outside customers). In a high-grade hotel these may be arranged in a mall or terrace – with visible frontage. In an integrated resort providing a great variety of shops and commercial malls, individual hotels do not need shops (except a bazaar in high-grade hotels): see 2.5.2.

Restaurants and coffee shops (1.5 to 2 seats per room): 2/room at least in small hotels and hotels serving packaged markets. For hotels of 100 plus rooms, these are usually separated into:

- coffee shop/brasserie – two-thirds of total seats provided (also used for breakfast)
- speciality restaurant – one-third of total seats (mainly evening/party use).

To facilitate rationalization, in peak season may use terraces (with umbrella shading), or use function rooms for groups of tourists. Pool bar and barbecue – additional.

Bars and lounges (0.8 seat per room): often adjacent to lobby or restaurant to allow spillovers for entertainment evenings. A nightclub and/or discotheque may also be provided with screening for noise (basement or separated area).

Meeting and function rooms (1 to 2 seats per room): in a small or budget hotel meeting rooms are often omitted or used also for general purposes (games rooms, children's play). High-grade hotels may provide for large conferences – with some delegates accommodated in other hotels, condominiums etc. May be replaced by a convention centre in integrated resorts.

Children's/games rooms (net area of 30 to 50 m² for 100 rooms): wet weather games room and library common in mountain resorts. Larger children's play centres may include a nursery, crèche and adjacent outdoor play area. Games rooms are used by adults and children.

Pool and deck (net area of 80 to 120 m² for 100 rooms): outdoor swimming pools (or access to adjacent beach) are essential to seaside and rural resorts and often form a featured focus for the development. Smaller indoor pools (combined with health–fitness centres) are provided in mountain resorts and elsewhere where the weather is unreliable or the season extended. Profitably replaced by a complex of large pools in an integrated resort.

Fitness room/gymnasium (net area of 30 to 80 m² for 100 rooms) or replaced by communal facilities in an integrated resort

Ski room, lockers etc. (net area of 50 to 80 m² for 100 rooms): in winter resorts, ski rooms at the place of entry for skiers provide changing and storage (lockers) and are often located next to a bar and lounge (open fire) for relaxation. Similar provisions may be made for other club facilities (golf, sailing, diving).

First aid centre (net area of 20 to 30 m² for 100 rooms: ranges from a small restroom to an equipped medical centre in large integrated resorts. In a spa hotel this area is developed to include treatment/massage rooms, hydrotherapy areas, specialist facilities.

Changing rooms (net area of 30 to 50 m² for 100 rooms).

2.2.6 Back-of-house areas

The areas required for storage, plant, laundry, housekeeping, food preparation, employee and other support needs depends on the sophistication of the hotel (its grade). Furthermore, individual hotel service facilities may be replaced by services supplied from external sources. In integrated resorts central organization of services can reduce the back-of-house areas in individual hotels by 30 to 50 per cent.

A number of support services (in particular laundry, maintenance and part of food preparation) may be omitted from hotels and restaurants and centralized as a collective service elsewhere in an integrated resort. In the case of food and beverage services, as an example, the use of relatively small premises, often under leasehold and for short seasons of activity, does not, as a rule, warrant large investment in individual food preparation facilities, and there are often both economic and practical advantages in buying prepared food (whether fresh, chilled or frozen). Economic appraisal of central production must take into account the relative costs of food, labour, space, equipment, energy and transportation, which will depend very much on the size of the population area served and the state of development of the region. Similar considerations apply to laundries and to many maintenance services in which the economies and advantages of scale apply.

The central food production areas include storage of bulk food and beverage purchases, pre-preparation and refrigeration. In an integrated resort, where catering is mainly centralized, the production kitchens employ about 0.02 employees per tourist bed. Planning standards for commercial food service facilities and equipment selection are covered in the book *Restaurants, Clubs and Bars: Planning, Design and Investment* (Lawson 1994).

	Number of tourist beds (in thousands)					
	1	2	4	7	12	20
Number of hotel beds (50% assumed, see 2.1.5)	0.5	1	2	3.5	6	10
Central laundry (for hotels etc.) m²	50	100	200	300	400	800
Central food production (for hotels/restaurants) m²	150	300	700	1200	1800	2400
Maintenance depots and stores (hotels and other premises) m²	100	200	300	400	600	800
Total area m²	300	600	1200	1900	2800	4000
Area per hotel bed m²	0.6	0.6	0.6	0.55	0.45	0.4
Area per tourist bed m²	0.3	0.3	0.3	0.3	0.2	0.2

2.3 OTHER FORMS OF ACCOMMODATION

2.3.1 Apartments, bungalows, villas, condominiums

Estate development of private residences and condominiums often comprises the major sector of resort development and has a significant impact on tourism resources. The private residences may form

- **Part of a hotel or resort complex** – to provide alternative accommodation (for families, long stay guests, etc.) using services provided by the hotel. Aparthotels and similar properties may be hotel owned or individually owned but managed by the hotel. Independent condominiums may also be leased to a hotel to add to its accommodation at peak times (high season, conventions);
- **Estates** – with properties individually owned or operated on a condominium basis. The long-term value of property investment depends on:
  - the benefits of the location and surroundings;
  - the degree of quality control over planning, harmonious design, construction, maintenance and management;
  - the extent of landscaping (hard and soft) and amenities.

Accommodation in the form of rented chalets or bungalows is usual in the case of

- **country resorts for rent** (see 5.4.3 and 5.4.4), with space standards similar to those of private bungalows in the countryside (see 2.3.4);
- **social tourism villages**, where the space standards are lower (see 2.3.6 below);
- **commercial holiday villages**, where accommodation is usually provided in twin bed rooms located in bungalows.

2.3.2 Site planning

Property development broadly falls into three main groups:

- individual self-contained residences which may be detached, linked or terraced together;

- concentrated row or cluster groupings giving a high local density of small- to medium-sized units;
- apartments and collective housing within common structures often several storeys high to gain advantages from view and central location..

The type of accommodation provided and its standard will depend on

- market requirements (attitudes, accessibility, attraction, fashion);
- site characteristics (surroundings, area, planning regulations, cost of land);
- tourism policies (aims for development, products, desired images).

Individual properties require extensive (and expensive) roads and infrastructures. Large estates of buildings create suburban conditions with limited opportunity to separate traffic or green areas, or to create focuses of tourism interest. Advantages to the developer arise from the opportunity to sell plots of land with phased expansion and reduced outlays. Individual plots can also be located around golf courses (fairway homes) and other landscaped attractions.

Cluster groupings allow better use of sites and more interesting, compact developments amongst large landscaped areas for recreation and amenity. A sense of community and social interest can be generated and collective services can be more easily managed, including the letting of units in the owners' absence. This form of development requires control over layout, design and construction of the properties.

Groupings for recreational residences

Small duplex bungalows are grouped together in farm-like buildings using traditional materials where possible to retain the character of the area

Cluster group sharing a common access allowing individual rear gardens

Planners: A. & M. Baud-Bovy, Geneva

Apartments enable maximum use to be made of prime sites (centres of urban resorts, marinas): units can be more easily served and more land can be set aside for open space and recreation. Well-designed taller buildings concentrated in the centre of a nondescript resort can create a dynamic focus and sense of vitality. Comprehensively planned apartments and hotels often form attractive, unified street frontages to promenades, squares and shopping areas.

2.3.3 Standards in winter resorts

Closely grouped apartment buildings are particularly advantageous in winter resorts, facilitating access, snow clearing, central heating and maintenance as well as a centre for social activity. Facilities such as swimming pools, saunas, ski rooms, children's playrooms can be incorporated. Apartments in winter resorts are usually compact, offering studios or separate living rooms which can be converted into bedrooms. Beds may be superimposed (as in bunk beds or in alcoves) and duplex arrangements in the form of a chalet and balcony are often provided.

Similar figures apply to chalets, the saving in circulation space required being used for additional facilities such as a ski room, cupboard spaces, etc. The distribution of space shown in the table at the top of p. 29 is typical but will vary with different layouts. Minimum standards are based on high season bed occupancies (including convertible beds).

Summary standard (per bed)	Minimum	Comfortable
Low occupancy	12 m² (130 sq ft)	17 m² (185 sq ft)
High occupancy	7 m² (75 sq ft)	13 m² (140 sq ft)

2.3.4 Standards in seaside and countryside resorts

To allow for the longer sojourn and more relaxed use the rooms in seaside and countryside resorts are more spacious and usually separate from bedrooms (or in a separate part of a studio). A loggia or terrace is usually essential. Occupancies also tend to be lower, giving an appreciably larger area available per bed.

Most developments in prime locations (seaside, lakeside, marina) are in the form of apartments or terraced units for which the following standards generally apply. Individual properties (villas, bungalows) are located outside the central area of a large resort in Western developed countries. In countries where the building costs are low, their area may be much higher than the figures in the table at the bottom of p. 29.

Summary standard (per bed)	Minimum	Comfortable
Normal low occupancy	14 m² (150 sq ft)	18–21 m² (190–230 sq ft)
Higher occupancy	11 m² (120 sq ft)	15 m² (160 sq ft)

2.3.5 Standards for commercial holiday villages

Commercial holiday villages (such as Club Méditerranée or Valtour) present examples of various types of accommodation: from thatched sheds to bungalows arranged in rows or clusters, sometimes even hotels. They are characterized by

* full board accommodation;
* diversified activities and facilities, with lively organized programmes;
* reserved for use of residents only.

Space standards for average commercial villages

2 bed unit	Sea	Mountain
Bungalow or room	20 to 24 m²	24 to 30 m²
Public areas	6 to 10 m²	8 to 12 m²
Total per unit	26 to 34 m²	32 to 42 m²
Total per bed	13 to 17 m²	16 to 21 m²

Seaside villages may have smaller residential units, but provide much more external landscaped areas, sports and recreation activities. The rooms often provide an original design aimed at accentuating the character of a holiday.

A good zoning of activities is essential in order to avoid the problem of nuisance:

* access: parking, reception, luggage, security;
* central: information, catering, shops, snacks, bars;
* outdoor: sports, swimming pool, outdoor games, amphitheatre;
* children: supervised play areas, near but distinct from other activities;
* recreation: disco, night club, bars (usually linked to the centre);
* accommodation: quiet area, calm, intimacy;
* services: stores, kitchen, plant area, staff quarters, etc.

2.3.6 Standards for social tourism villages

The basic unit of social accommodation consists of

* a living room (with two beds for the parents);
* a children's room (with two bunk beds or beds on the floor plus one bunk bed);

Planning standards for apartments and chalets in winter resorts

		Studio		1 Bedroom		2 Bedrooms		3 Bedrooms	
		Min.	Comf.	Min.	Comf.	Min.	Comf.	Min.	Comf.
Number of beds		2–4	2–3	3–5	3–4	5–8	5–7	7–10	7–9
Net area (m²)									
Living		12	18	12	18	16	20	18	25
Kitchen		1.5	2	2	3	2.5	4	4	5
Sanitary		2.5	4.5	3.5	6	4.5	7	5	8
Bedroom 1				8	10	10	12	10	12
Bedroom 2						8	10	8	10
Bedroom 3								8	10
Circulation etc.[a]		2	2.5	5	7	8	10	12	15
Total net area	(m²)	18	27	30.5	44	49	63	65	85
	(sq ft)	195	290	330	470	530	680	700	920
Gross area[b]	(m²)	23.5	35	39.5	57	64	82	84.5	110
	(sq ft)	255	375	425	610	690	880	910	1180
Occupancy	low	12	17.5	13	17	13	16.5	12	16
(m²/bed)	high	6	6	8	14	8	12	8.5	12

Notes:
(a) Cupboards, storage, internal circulation.
(b) Net area plus 30% for access, services and structure.

Planning standards for seaside or countryside apartments and bungalows used for holidays or short-term letting

		Studio		1 Bedroom		2 Bedrooms		3 Bedrooms	
		Min.	Comf.	Min.	Comf.	Min.	Comf.	Min.	Comf.
Number of beds		2–3		3–4		5–6		7–8	
Net area (m²)									
Living		14	20	14	20	16	24	18	30
Kitchen		2	2	2	3	4	5	5	6
Sanitary		3	4	3	5	4	8	6	10
Bedroom 1				8	9	8	10	8	10
Bedroom 1						8	9	8	9
Bedroom 3								8	9
Circulation etc.[a]		2	3	5	8	8	11	12	15
Total net area	(m²)	21	30	32	45	48	67	65	89
	(sq ft)	215	310	345	485	520	720	700	955
Gross area[b]	(m²)	27	39	41	58	62	87	85	116
Terrace	(m²)	(4)	(6)	(6)	(10)	(10)	(12)	(12)	(16)
Occupancy	low	14.5	21	14.5	21	13.5	17.5	12	16.5
(m²/bed)	high	10	14.5	11	15.5	11	14.5	10.5	14.5

Notes:
(a) Cupboards, storage, internal circulation.
(b) Net area plus 30% for access, services and structure.

- a bathroom with shower, washbasin and WC (separate WC in higher-grade units); for self-catering units a small kitchen is provided off the living room.

The number of bedrooms may be increased to two for large families or combined with the living area for studio units. In budget accommodation, the showers may be communal, together with sanitary and laundry facilities.

Gross areas for basic two-room units

| | | Integrated catering | | Self-catering | |
		Mini-mum	Some comfort	Mini-mum	Some comfort
Living room	m²	11	15	12	15
Children's room	m²	7	8	7	8
Bathroom	m²	2	3	2	3
Kitchen	m²			3	4
Residential	m²	21	26	24	30
Public areas	m²	12	18	6	10
Total area	m²	32	44	30	40
	sq ft	345	475	325	430
Number of beds		(4) (6)	(4) (6)	(4) (6)	(4) (6)
area per bed	m²	8 5.5	11 7.5	7.5 5	10 5
	sq ft	85 60	120 80	80 65	110 70

The same considerations apply to the zoning of activities as for commercial holiday villages.

Social Holiday Village, Port Barcares, France

The accommodation in this village includes 1800 beds in family apartments, most having a second small room for children (total gross area for 4 beds: 23 m²) and 600 beds in family apartments with a small kitchen and a patio or terrace.

All apartments are in two-storey buildings, the units on the upper floor being linked by foot-bridges, and grouped in clusters around service cores. Total gross built areas, including public areas, services and staff quarters amount to only 10 m² per bed. The very dense layout (illustrated) is aimed towards economic operation.

Architect: G. Candilis

1 Administration
2 Reception
3 Restaurant bar and information
4 Services
5 Staff village
6 Cultural centre
A Family units with kitchen
B Units without kitchens

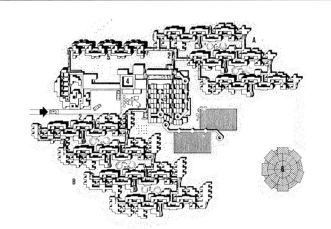

Layout plan

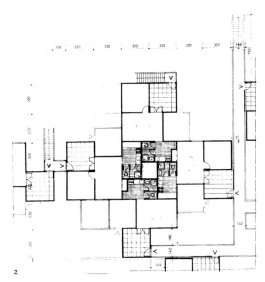

Apartments with kitchen (upper level)

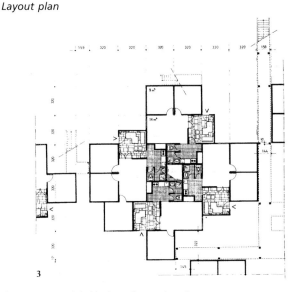

Apartments with kitchen (lower level)

2.3.7 Youth hostels

Hostel standards vary widely and the following recommendations are based on typical basic requirements, excluding recreational areas but including circulation space and communal facilities (sanitary and minimum dining areas).

Gross area for basic units		Single bedroom	Double bedroom
Per room	m²	16.5–18.5	23–25
	sq ft	180–200	250–270
Per bed	m²	as above	11.5–12.5
	sq ft		1256–135

Minimum standards are lower. Hostels with dormitory accommodation have a gross area of about 5 to 6 m² per place (55 to 65 sq ft per place).

2.4 CAMPING AND CARAVANNING

2.4.1 Camping sites, caravan sites

Camping and caravanning provide the cheapest form of tourist accommodation and in Western Europe more bed spaces are provided in tents and caravans than in hotels. Sites for this purpose must have easy access, good drainage, limited slope, good orientation to the sun and, where possible, interspacing with trees and hedges (against wind and for privacy).

Pilgrims' resthouses in Sri Lanka

In 1991, domestic tourism in Sri Lanka was mainly pilgrimages (40 per cent), with family holidays amounting to 22 per cent, group holidays 21 per cent, studies and sightseeing 14 per cent and other reasons for travel 3 per cent.

Twenty-nine per cent of the tourists stayed with friends and relatives, 24 per cent stayed in pilgrim halls/religious places, 23 per cent in resthouses, only 12 per cent in hotels and guesthouses and 16 per cent in youth hostels and other places.

As part of the Tourism Master Plan, proposals for development of domestic tourism identified a number of potential sites for domestic tourist accommodation and included model layouts for resthouses.

UNDP/WTO Master Plan for Tourism 1991–2001,
Project Director: M. Gerty.
Resort Architects: M. Pugsley/A. De Vos.

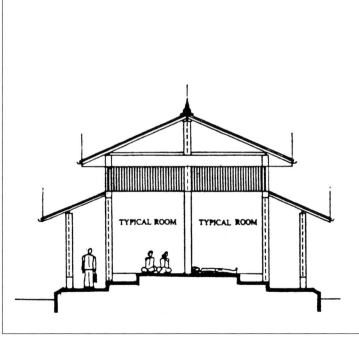

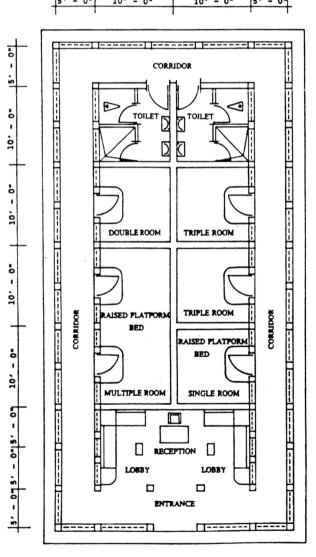

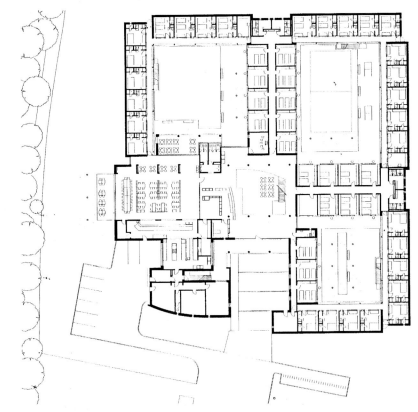

Plan of ground floor

'Jeunotel' in Lausanne, Switzerland

This high quality two-storey 'Youth Hostel' opened in 1993 for young tourists (individuals or groups) and/or resident students. It provides

- *five dormitories (16 beds each);*
- *40 rooms without shower (two/three or four beds);*
- *58 rooms with shower and mini-kitchenette (two beds);*
- *six rooms for accompanying adults (one bed);*
- *sanitary and laundry facilities;*
- *160-seat self service restaurant, etc.*

The building used some prefabrication: concrete blocks for shower cubicles/kitchenettes and concrete or studded walls between rooms.

Area per bed: 14.5 to 17.7 m^2 according to occupancy. This is more than usual hostel standards but justified by the large dining room and quality accommodation.

Architects: Atelier Cube: G. & M. Collomb, P. Vogel, architects, Lausanne

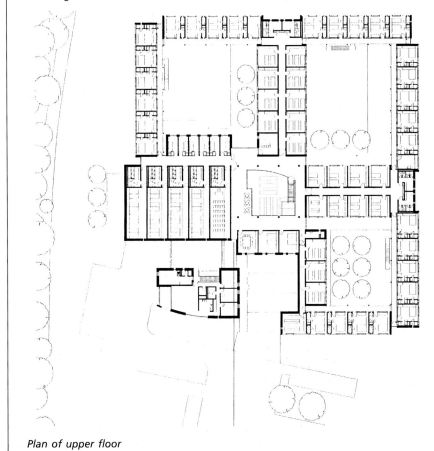

Plan of upper floor

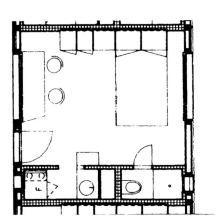

Plan of room unit with shower and kitchenette (20 m^2 for one or two beds)

Most countries lay down standards for camping and caravan sites with several categories, depending on the ratio of facilities, space and amenities.

Types of structures:

- tent: canvas folding structure;
- camping tent: canvas folding structure erected on site for temporary use;
- motorized home or camper van: portable dwelling as an integral part of a self-propelled vehicle;
- travel trailer or caravan: vehicular towed structure built on a chassis for temporary dwelling;
- mobile home: movable or portable dwelling unit built on a chassis for year-round dwelling.

Caravan plots have to be separated from the areas used for tent camping where both are accepted in the same site. The two clienteles have different interests which may be in conflict and caravans need heavier infrastructures (solid access and parking places and, generally, connections to water, electricity and sewerage services).

Mobile homes (camper vans or trailers) which are more common in the USA than in Europe may be used for vacationing. Their maximum size for road transport is 3.60×18.30 m (12×60 ft). Generally mobile homes have a short life span (about 10 years) and tend to present a disorganized and poor appearance which must be tempered by landscaping, insetting in plantations etc.

2.4.2 Categories of camps

Apart from individual camping in the 'wild' (which threatens the environment with visual pollution, risk of fire etc., and is often *verboten*) camping sites fall into seven main categories:

Category	Description
Transit camps	With minimum facilities, the stay being generally no more than 48 hours
Day camps	In certain recreation parks camping sites are limited to the day, or sometimes one night only (see 5.7.2)
Weekend camps	In rural surroundings allowing opportunities for outdoor recreation and facilities for sport. Playgrounds for children and other amenities are usually provided. Often rented on a year-round basis (80 per cent of French trailer owners use their trailers as weekend bungalows)
Residential camps	More permanent than weekend camps. Used for trailers, mobile homes or light construction bungalows. Plots (minimum 200 m² for bungalows) rented on a year-round basis or sold in full or leasehold property ownership.
Holiday camps	Near valuable resources (sea, lake, forest) with communal facilities. Caravan sites may also be developed in ski resorts (on whole winter basis) with parking in ribbons for easier snow removing, drying rooms, play rooms for children and other indoor services
Forest camps	In the USA this is a typical campsite for families, associated with forest recreation: medium/low density, up to 25 units, at least 35 m between two units, full range of facilities
Tourism camps	Higher standard holiday camps, in or near tourist resorts.

In developing countries, tents are generally provided by the camp's operating company. Elsewhere, self-ownership or independent rental of tents and equipment is usual, the site operator providing space, services and communal facilities.

2.4.3 Densities and sizes of camps

The minimum area per unit (tent or caravan plus car) varies from 90 m² in France to 120 to 150 m², according to circumstances, in Germany. Lower densities are recommended by the Netherlands Forest Administration: 150 m² per unit (but surrounded by larger areas of undeveloped land). The USA recommended densities in parks, in order to achieve some contact with nature, vary widely from (a) central camps with all facilities (300 m²/unit), (b) forest camps for 400 to 1000 persons with road access and facilities (800–1000 m²/unit, but surrounded by large areas of forest land), and to (c) back country (hunter) camps for 50 to 100 persons without any facilities (1500 m²/unit, surrounded by wilderness) (See Fig. 2.1).

Area per unit	Coverage	Density* Persons/ha	Persons/acre
100 m² per unit	on three-quarters of total area	300	120
150 m² per unit	on three-quarters of total area	200	80
150 m² per unit	on three-eighths of total area	100	40
800 m² per unit	on one-tenth of total area	5	2
800 m² per unit	on one-twentieth of total area	2.5	1

*Assuming each unit is occupied by an average of four people

For a dense camp, accommodating 200 to 300 persons per ha (80 to 120 persons per acre), a suitable camp size is 3 to 5 ha (8 to 12 acres), which allows viability with a capacity limited to 600 to 1500 persons.

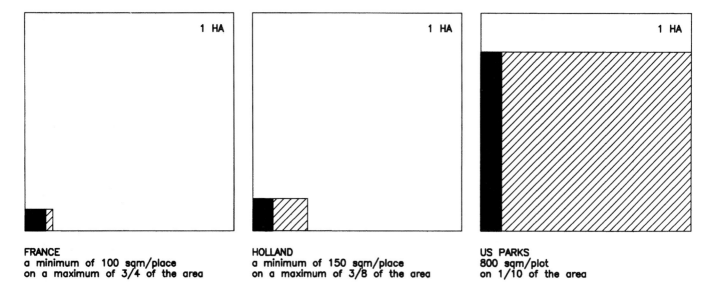

FRANCE
a minimum of 100 sqm/place
on a maximum of 3/4 of the area

HOLLAND
a minimum of 150 sqm/place
on a maximum of 3/8 of the area

US PARKS
800 sqm/plot
on 1/10 of the area

Figure 2.1 *Dimensions/densities of camping/caravanning plots*

2.4.4 Facilities: minimum standards for 100 persons (25 units)

- Sanitary facilities (four WCs, four to five washbasins, two showers, two double sinks, three refuse bins), ideally no more distant than 100 m (maximum 150 m) from any unit.
- Rubbish receptacles (one receptacle per two to three units).
- Additionally in holiday camps, laundry, clothes drying and ironing facilities.
- Provision for administration and site maintenance; depending on the size and category of camp, a food shop and lounge facilities may be provided.
- Spaces for recreation (volleyball, children's playgrounds, tennis, miniature golf, etc.).
- One-way road (3 to 3.5 m width) with car parking near the entrance to avoid traffic in the camp during the night; lighted pedestrian alleys (1 to 1.5 m width).
- Water supply (40 to 60 litres per person per day); drainage and sewage treatment, including a pumping station and/or means to dispose of waste from sewage holding tanks.

Large tourist camps may offer much more than these minimum facilities, operating restaurant and garage services and providing more sophisticated forms of recreation and entertainment. Day camps often provide only minimal facilities, such as water points and refuse bins. The facilities provided in nearby resorts and, conversely, those which may be supported by other developments must be taken into account in considering the opportunity for, and feasibility of, such investments.

2.5 FOOD SERVICES AND SHOPPING

2.5.1 Food service provisions

The changing habits and preferences of tourists have a considerable influence on the design of food service facilities in an integrated resort. As a rule the trend is away from formal set meals taken in the same hotel dining room. Opportunities could be provided for greater variety and individual choice by

- designing a large hotel restaurant as a number of smaller dining areas, each having a distinctive character and identity;
- making arrangements for hotel guests to use other comparable restaurants elsewhere in the resort for all or some meals;
- providing a range of restaurants, coffee shops, grill and fast food bars, cafes, etc. to attract both residents and non-residents. These may be grouped around (or supplied from) a central food production unit or be arranged in food courts;
- including a number of speciality restaurants and bars serving meals (fish or fondue restaurants, barbecues, taverns with food specialities of the country etc.) which may be operated in association with hotels or independently.

Most existing resorts provide one extra restaurant seat and one extra coffee-shop or bar seat (additional to hotel provision) for each group of five to twenty tourist beds in the resort, depending on the proportion of beds in traditional hotels as compared with hotels garnis, apartments and other forms of accommodation. The same numbers of seats are also provided in cafes, bars and similar informal eating places. Design information on restaurants is given in *Restaurant, Clubs and Bars: Planning, Design and Investment* (Lawson 1994).

Planning data: space per seat provided including all services

Types of meals		Dining area (net)	Total incl. services[a]
Haute cuisine restaurant	m²	1.8–2.0	3.6–4.0
	sq ft	20–22	40–44
Standard restaurant	m²	1.7–1.9	3.0–3.5
	sq ft	18–20	33–38
Coffee shop	m²	1.5–1.7	2.7–3.0
	sq ft	16–18	25–32
Speciality grill	m²	1.7–2.0	2.7–3.2
	sq ft	18–22	29–32
Snack bars	m²	1.3–1.5	1.9–2.1
	sq ft	14–16	20–23

Note:

(a) Overall gross areas with preparation and circulation. Range: minimum – self-contained.

To reduce the difficulties of operating many different restaurants in one resort, each requiring its own expensive kitchen, storage and service facilities, the tendency is to centralize much of the food preparation into a few larger food production units. Prepared food may be supplied to restaurants and hotels fresh, chilled or deep frozen depending on the distance and scale of operation.

2.5.2 Shops and related services

The commercial facilities of a holiday resort are quite different from those of towns or villages of the same size, not only in the types of shops, but also in their numbers.

In most residential situations the inhabitants of small villages or suburbs will shop in nearby towns for anything other than essential items. Tourists, however, expect to find a large range of shops in resorts, particularly if they do not have private cars at their disposal or if, as in mountain resorts, access is difficult. Thus small resorts (up to 3000 beds) may need more shops and services than could be commercially feasible. The developer may be obliged to provide and operate some of these facilities during the launching stage.

Shopping in a holiday resort should be a pleasure. It should provide an extension to recreation, an atmosphere of bustling activity, opportunities to meet and make friends in informal interesting surroundings. The ideal is illustrated by the examples of the busy streets of Zermatt or Rhodes and the squares of traditional Mediterranean towns, the harbours of Hydra or the promenades of Morcote or St Tropez.

In many ski resorts, protection from the weather is provided by a commercial gallery or enclosed shopping precinct which enables customers to go under cover from one shop to the next. It is questionable whether this urban approach is appropriate for a resort area in which the experience of walking out in the snow is part of the recreational enjoyment.

In holiday parks, shops are often combined with the catering facilities in the form of a 'plaza', protected from the rain by a large glass structure and decorated with fountains, tropical vegetation, etc.

2.5.3 Standards for shopping and related services

The size of a commercial unit, such as a shop, varies from 50 to 200 m² (550 to 22000 sq ft) with an average of 90 to 100 m² (950 to 1100 sq ft). Some of the shops may be grouped together under one central management, but it is important to retain the character of a boutique rather than an impersonal store. Shops of different types should be intermixed in order to create interest and variety: those for essential grocery and other provisions should be side-by-side with shops selling luxury goods.

Shopping and related services	Number of tourist beds (in thousands)					
	1	2	4	7	12	20
Daily food and groceries: general grocery, bakery, dairy, butcher, fruit/vegetable store	1	2	3	7	10	20
Other day-to-day purchases: drugstore/pharmacy, newsagent/bookshop, tobacconist, florist, handicrafts/gifts/souvenirs	2	3	5	8	12	20
Equipment: clothes and fashion shops, sports goods, photographic equipment, domestic appliances, furniture etc.	2	5	10	20	35	50
Services: hairdresser/beauty parlour, laundry/dry cleaning, petrol station/garage, repairs etc.	1	2	4	7	12	30
Travel agency/car hire		P*	1	1–2	2	2–3
Bank agency			1	1	2	2
Real estate agency			1	2	2–3	3
Total number	6	12	26	47	75	123

*P = Possibly

These figures are those of a completely autonomous holiday resort, without easy access to the shopping facilities of a neighbouring town or village. They correspond to a net provision of 0.6 to 0.7 m² per tourist bed (6 to 8 sq ft.). Average: three to five employees per shop or commercial agency.

Manchester Velodrome, UK

Completed in 1994 in a derelict part of the city, at a cost of £9 million, this indoor velodrome is run by Britain's Sports Council and the National Cycling Federation.

The 250 m long 7 m wide cycling track required an overall 10 000 m² plan providing peripheral support to a 122 m clear span arch as the skeletal backbone. The oval shape has been modified by quadrants housing local plant (air-conditioning, heating, electrical) with zoned supplies to the spectator terraces and central arena for a variable occupancy up to 4000. Lighting levels range from 400 lux (training) to 1200 lux (TV coverage) with permanent camera positions.

Spectator surfaces have been moulded to the complex raking shape of the track to opitmize sightlines, and the central arena can be used for other forms of sport (badminton, tennis hockey, etc.). The main upper concourse includes toilets, bars, hospitality boxes and first aid facilities, whilst below are changing areas, offices, cycle workshops, weight training rooms and the national sports medical clinic.

Architects: FaulknerBrowns with
AMEC Design and Build Ltd

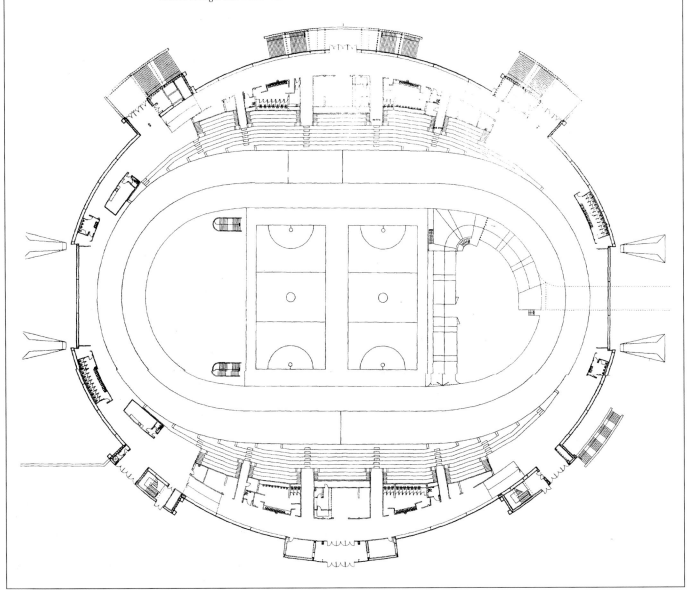

3 Support services and technical infrastructures

3.1 ADMINISTRATION, TECHNICAL AND SUPPORT SERVICES

The extent to which these services are implemented within the resort itself will depend on its location, the size of the non-tourist population, the proximity of other market towns and extent of regional administration of public services. The table below indicates the requirements for an isolated, integrated resort and should be reduced where services and facilities are provided in part elsewhere.

3.1.1 Employees and resident non-tourist populations

The non-tourist population can be divided into a number of different categories:

- permanent employees of the facilities used by tourists;
- their families;
- seasonal workers (usually without their families);
- other permanent residents working indirectly for the tourism industry (in handicrafts, gardening, maintenance etc.);
- people living in the resort but without any association with tourism;
- unemployed persons often attracted – particularly in developing countries – by employment prospects in the resort.

The size of the non-tourist population of a resort is often difficult to identify as a general standard:

- ratios of employee per tourist bed vary with different categories of accommodation and countries (see below);
- percentages of permanent to seasonal workers and of female to male employees vary according to economic and social circumstances;
- percentages of working population to total population depend on the location of the resort and the extent of other development;
- percentages of seasonal and permanent workers to be accommodated on site depend on many factors, particularly on the isolation of the resort.

3.1.2 Direct employment

Most of the direct employment in a resort is generated by the hotels, the ratio of employees per tourist bed increasing with the standard or grade of hotel. Other accommodation and other activities in the resort have lower employment ratios. The planning standards outlined are representative for resorts in developed areas. These figures may be increased (by an average of 20 per cent or much more) in developing countries where productivity is often lower and one of the primary objectives in promoting tourism is the creation of job opportunities and training.

Planning standards: ratio of direct employees

Accommodation	Employees per tourist bed
Hotel de luxe *****	1.0
****	0.6–0.9
***	0.4–0.6
**	0.3–0.4
*	0.2–0.3
Boarding house	0.1
Hotel garni	0.1
Holiday villages	0.1–0.2
Camping/caravanning/hostels	0.05
Secondary homes	0.05
Cruise boats	0.2
Other activities	
Additional food services	less than 0.02
Recreation, sports and culture	less than 0.05
Shopping and services	less than 0.01
Administration and technical	less than 0.02
Total other activities	0.05–0.1

Some 10 per cent of employees are in a managerial or professional capacity; 20 to 30 per cent skilled and/or technically qualified; and 60 to 70 per cent partially skilled with on-the-job training.

3.1.3 Indirect and induced employment

Based on the figures for direct tourism employment, it is possible to estimate, successively, the proportions of permanent and seasonal employment, the off-site, indirect or induced employment, the proportion of male permanent employment, the family status of the employees and the total population depending on the employment, including the families.

Indirect and induced employment can be determined from employment multiplier factors calculated for each situation. A ratio of one indirect for one direct employment is met in many countries. It may be much higher (up to three indirect for one direct) in poor developing countries with an extended informal sector.

3.1.4 Size of non-tourist populations in resorts

Actual figures show a wide variation as demonstrated by a few examples (1997 figures):

Port Camargue, France 5300 residents for 105 000 tourist beds: 5 per cent.
This low figure (typical of many new resorts) is explained by the high number of privately owned second homes (76 per cent of the total) and high proportion of seasonal workers commuting from other areas. Excluding second homes, the resident population:tourist beds ratio is 18.2 per cent.

Verbier, Switzerland 2100 residents for 25 000 tourist beds: 8.5 per cent.
1500 beds in hotels, 9500 in other rooms to rent and about 14 000 in second homes. Excluding second homes the ratio is 19 per cent.

Zermatt, Switzerland 5500 residents for about 16 000 tourist beds: 34 per cent.
6500 beds in hotels, 4500 in other rooms to rent and about 5000 in second homes. Excluding second homes the ratio is 52 per cent.

In developing countries much higher figures are usually involved. The Diani Resort (Kenya) was one of the first resorts where the needs of the dependent population were considered from the planning stages (KCP 1975). Plans for 5900 direct and 5800 other employees were made for 6500 tourist beds, giving a total population (including dependants) of 42 300, with 28 100 accommodated in the resort area and the remainder in neighbouring villages or commuting from other areas. 28 100 residents for 6500 tourist beds: 430 per cent.

3.1.5 Housing of non-tourist population

The problem of accommodation for employees and their dependants has often been ignored by the developers of new resorts leaving the provision of lodgings to the private initiative of employers. Among the methods used are

- employees commuting from neighbouring areas where they are resident or have lodgings;
- accommodating some of the staff in the hotels themselves;
- providing room in flats or hostels for seasonal workers (sometimes the same accommodation is used out of season by building operatives employed in developing the resort).

This problem is particularly acute in *developing countries* where the resort is developed some distance away from existing built-up areas. Shanty towns sometimes appear around the resort built by the employees and their families; dormitories provided for singles are often of a low standard, with minimum space and facilities. In these cases, it is necessary to plan the resorts as a whole, not only for tourists, but for the total resort population and with consideration both of permanent and seasonal needs. However, provided real economic benefits return to the local community (in the form of improved sanitation, schools, housing, medical and social care etc.), there are many long-term advantages to be gained for both tourism and for community life by retaining some form of separate development in the initial phases.

For *developed countries* this is primarily a question of determining appropriate levels of expenditure, locations and design standards for the non-tourist accommodation.

In developing areas other problems may emerge: domestic standards of housing may be too low to allow juxtaposition with tourist accommodation; and wide gaps in the standards of living may even necessitate steps to limit the general population from using the same areas and facilities as tourists (for the sake of security) and the provision of separate, less expensive shopping facilities.

Planning standards for housing, sanitation and other service needs for the non-tourist population are those which apply generally in the country in which the resort is situated. As a guide, single accommodation in hostel-type establishments will take up about 4 to 5 m² (45 to 55 sq ft) per bed.

3.1.6 Administrative, technical and other ancillary services

A resort has to provide all the services of a small- or medium-sized town, plus others required specifically for tourism. The organization of the necessary facilities and services will be dependent on the administrative statutes of the new resort and the involvement of neighbouring towns and regional administration which may assume responsibility for some of the services.

Cultural and educational facilities will vary according to the size and characteristics of the population to be served. At least one primary school is usually required, if not already provided in the neighbourhood.

Planning standards: administrative and other services

	Number of tourist beds (in thousands)					
	1	2	4	7	12	20
Administration and maintenance						
Resort's administration by developer or operator	X	X	P			
Community administration (town hall or delegation)			P	X	X	X
Tourist board		P	X	X	X	X
Post Office (telephone exchange)	P	X	X	X	X	X
Fire brigade		P	X	X	X	X
Police station (seasonal)			P	P	X	X
Maintenance (roads, gardens, refuse, snow removal)	X	X	X	X	X	X
Average number of employees	10	24	40	70	100	160
Health and social services						
Medical care: first aid (100 m²) Area (m²)	P	100				
Medical centre (200 m²)			200			
with dispensary (400 m²)				400		
Clinic (from 500 to 5000 m²)					1000	2000
Baby minding service		P	X	X	X	X
Crèche, nursery area (m²)		100	150	250	400	500
Average number of employees						
Physicians			1	1–2	2–6	2–10
Chemists		P	1	1	1–2	2–3
Dentist			P	P	1	1
Masseur/physiotherapist			P	1	1	1
Others	1	1	2	3	5	5

P = provision possibly required; X = provision required

The gross building area required in most seaside and rural resorts is about 0.1 m² per bed (1 sq ft) for each category, or some 0.2 m² per bed (2 sq ft) for all administrative, health and social services. In mountain resorts, where numerous vehicles and plant are required for road clearance, snow removal and trail maintenance, an additional space of 0.1 to 0.2 m² per bed (1 to 2 sq ft) should be allowed for workshops and associated buildings.

3.2 INFRASTRUCTURE PROVISION, ROADS AND PARKING AREAS

In considering infrastructure requirements for resort development it is necessary to distinguish:

- *Connecting infrastructure:* main supplies, highway and communication networks and other services which originate outside the resort's boundaries and are planned and operated on a regional or national scale.
- *Distribution infrastructure:* within the area of the resort, for the development.

It is often the provision of connecting infrastructure – such as the construction of a new highway or new airport – which provides the stimulus for secondary investment in tourism. Conversely, inadequate connections or supplies will add significantly to local costs (for example, in the provision of power generating plant, water distillation or treatment works) and may affect the feasibility of development.

Distribution infrastructure, including means of collection and disposal of sewage and waste, must be planned at the outset for the whole of the intended resort development. While the installation work may be carried out in stages as construction proceeds, it is essential that the capacities of mains, space provisions for plant and connections for future equipment are adequate to meet the eventual load requirements.

3.2.1 Access for traffic

The proportion of areas covered by roads, footpaths and parking spaces in a resort depends on the concentration of the development and its accessibility to the main modes of transport for tourists (air, coach, motor car etc.).

Percentage of total area used for traffic:

- for resorts with limited access and roads: 5–10 per cent
- for urbanized high-density resorts: 20–25 per cent

The general policy in new resort development and in most recreation areas is to regulate the entry of cars and thereby reduce the noise pollution, traffic, congestion, hazard and environmentally destructive parking of cars – urban conditions which the majority of tourists are seeking to escape – as well as the high costs of extended asphalt or concrete roads.

Integrated resort development allows an opportunity to introduce new solutions, such as:

- Provision of a large car park or garage (which can extend in stages as the resort increases in size) at the point of entry to the resort. Secondary transport into the resort proper for people and their luggage by cable lift, rail, electric trucks etc.
- Access to accommodation for private cars strictly limited to unloading and loading of luggage – the car being kept in a central car park or garage during the period of stay.
- Where the size of the resort makes walking distances excessive (more than 8000 beds), private cars may be allowed to use peripheral roads. Alternatively, novel systems of local

transport to and within the resort may be introduced, particularly where tourist arrival is mainly by public or group chartered transport. Examples include the use of electric trucks and trailer combinations, installation of rail track (narrow gauge, mono) or suspended cable systems, provision of free horse cabs, electric taxis or buses, bicycles etc.

It is particularly important to control access of those cars used by weekend recreationists, which tend to create high peaks of traffic congestion. Alternative arrangements include the use of buses to transport commuters from nearby towns or the obligation to park private cars away from the resort with access by teleferic or skis (Flaine resort, France), etc.

3.2.2 Planning data for roads

Standards for road construction are usually dictated by legislation, particularly where the road is to become part of the public highway system. The following data (with rounded conversions) are typical:

Carriageway widths:
- District distributor roads: single or dual two-lane carriageways leading to small resorts: minimum 7.30 m (24 ft) wide, increasing to 13.5 m (44 ft) minimum for single four-lane roads used by through traffic
- Local distributor roads: single two lane carriageways in commercial districts of resort: 6.75 m (22 ft) wide reducing to a minimum of 6 m (20 ft) width in residential districts
- Access roads and driveways: single two-lane carriageways in entrance driveways and back or service roads for freight deliveries to hotels, shops, restaurants: usual width 5.50 m (18 ft).
- One-way system restricted to cars, usual width of one-lane carriageway: 3.50 m (11 ft 6 in)

Waiting bays:
- for service vehicles: 3.0 m (10 ft) wide
- for cars: 2.50 m (8 ft 6 in) wide
- for buses: 3.25 m (10 ft 6 in) wide

Sightseeing roads in parks and reserves: (interior roads in nature parks are generally subject to speed restrictions, usually under 40 km per hour):

- one-lane carriageway: 5 m (16 ft) wide, surfaced, plus shoulder 0.6 m (2 ft) each side
- minor two-lane carriageway: 7.5 m (25 ft) wide, surfaced plus shoulder 0.8 m (2 ft 6 in) each side.
- major two-lane carriageway: 9.0 m (30 ft) wide, surfaced, plus shoulder 1.2 m (4 ft) each side.

Maximum longitudinal gradients:
- for trunk roads: 1:25 (4 per cent)
- for other roads: 1:10 (10 per cent)
- in mountains (snow conditions):1:15 (6.5 per cent)
- if undercover or underground: 1:8 (12 per cent)

Vertical clearance for bridges over roads: 5.1 m (17 ft) minimum

Over-width for mountain roads: 2 m (6 ft 6 in) (for snow removal)

3.2.3 Parking areas

Car parking provision is typically on the basis of one car parking space per:

- 0.8   rooms in a motel (including staff)
- 3–5   places in a public restaurant
- 2–4   rooms in a resort hotel (substantial reductions for hotels catering only for group travel)
- 10   places in a hotel restaurant
- 1   apartment or villa (with extra space for boat, caravan or second car where appropriate)

The area required depends on the number of cars and the spacing allowed, the layout and provisions for access and circulation. Areas of 25 to 30 m² (270 to 325 sq ft) for open-air parking and 30 to 35 m² (325 to 372 sq ft) for parking in a garage are typical.

In mountain resorts, open-air car parks should never be more than 20 m (65 ft) wide (for snow clearing) and covered garages should be provided for residents. Access roads leading to the car park should be one lane (one- or two-way) and edged with insurmountable obstacles to avoid random parking. Parking areas should be landscaped to reduce the impact of the large space and planted to provide shelter, the planted areas being concentrated into dividing banks and hedges for both safety and maintenance and allowing variations in levels. As a rule, parking should be within 200–300 m (maximum 500 m) of the tourist facilities or transfer station. Total capacity should not normally exceed 400 car places (one attendant) in any one area. In hot climates, concrete or gravel surfaces are preferable to dark bitumen.

For further planning data (space standards, manoeuvring spaces, constructional features etc.), reference should be made to specific literature.

3.2.4 External lighting, street furniture and utilities

Lighting is an important factor in creating interest and social atmosphere, extending the use of resort facilities into the evening. It is also necessary as an aid to security, public safety, traffic control and for the illumination of signs and directions. To obtain the best effects, without glare and confusion, all forms of external lighting should be considered as part of a coherent scheme. The daytime appearance of columns and light fittings is equally important.

Traffic controls and the equipment of statutory undertakings are usually subject to regulatory standards but, accepting the need for functional requirements, a coordinated scheme of landscape design must be adopted which appropriately reflects the character of the resort. Street furniture must be part of that total design. An unsightly clutter of unrelated signs and hoardings, mediocre and badly sited buildings and other unimaginatively visualized public utilities, no matter how practical, will often ruin the care which has been put into planning attractive estates and buildings.

3.3 SANITATION AND ENGINEERING SERVICES

3.3.1 Water supply

An adequate and reliable supply of pure and wholesome drinking water must be provided for resort development to meet all the requirements for domestic and related purposes. The mains supply may also serve in emergency for fire-fighting as well as filling and supplementing the water recycled in swimming pools and other circulatory systems.

The minimum water consumption per person varies with location and standards:

Camp sites and day employees	50 litres/person/day (13 US gals)
Non-tourist residential population	100–150 litres/person/day (26–40 US gals)
Hotel and resort tourists	150–170* litres/person/day (40–45 US gals)

(*High grade hotels and beach resorts in hot climates)

For resort development, the overall water supply requirements (including tourists, employees and support services) are usually based on:

Minimum supply	300–400 litres/tourist bed/day (80–106 US gals)
Beach resorts in hot climates	500–700 litres/tourist bed/day (132–185 US gals)

This does not include the extensive use of water for irrigation of gardens and grounds which, in hot weather, can be 5 litres/m^2 per day. Irrigation may be supplemented by alternative sources or by the recirculation of treated sewage effluent (see 3.3.2).

When the mains water supply is very limited, a dual supply may be implemented: the waste water of baths, showers and washbasins may be reused for flushing the toilets.

Where mains supplies are inadequate, supplementary sources may be used such as desalination of sea water, underground boreholes and stored rainwater. It is essential that the mains supplies are kept separate from other circulations and, in some cases, a separate system of pipes for drinking water may be installed.

Treatment. Supplies of drinking water must comply with the physical, chemical and biological standards of quality recommended by the World Health Organization. The European Union lays down broadly similar requirements. Local purification plant is required for water which is supplied from private sources, for improving the quality of mains supplies which are unreliable and, separately, for water recycled in swimming pools. Typically this involves chemical dosage, pressure filtration and controlled sterilization (using chlorine, ozone or, less commonly, ultra-violet light).

Distribution. Local storage must be provided, usually based on 48-hours' supply: 1000 litres/tourist bed (379 US gal), but increased where supplies are unreliable. Distribution of water through a resort is usually via a system of mains and sub-mains divided into zones of controlled pressure – determined by the heights of the tallest buildings and requirements for fire-fighting. Pressure may be maintained by local storage in service reservoirs or water towers or by pumping systems (mechanical/pneumatic). Water towers can be used to create a dynamic feature for the resort.

Specific provision must be made for fire-fighting supplies, such as the use of alternative sources of water (possibly from swimming pools and garden lakes) with suitable pumping systems to hydrant points to meet fire authority standards.

3.3.2 Sewerage, sewage treatment and standards

Requirements for sewage treatment depend on the availability of mains sewerage in the area. A dual system of surface (storm) water and foul water drains is invariably used, the drains being of a size and depth to allow extension in future phases of the resort development.

Design. The size of surface water drains is determined by the highest intensity of rainfall (including 'flash floods') determined from records for the area and the relative impermeability of the planned zones of development. The outfall may be to the sea, rivers, lakes or 'soakaways' with sufficient capacity.

The quantities of foul water and size of the drains are related to the pattern of water consumption. Peak hours are generally 8.00–10.00 and 16.30–18.30 with a flow rate/hour of 10 per cent of the daily demand. The maximum rate of flow from a resort – depending on location and climate – will vary from 0.01 to 0.025 litres/tourist bed/sec and the biochemical oxygen demand is usually based on 70 grammes/person. Sewers in the resort are normally laid at a gradient to ensure a self-cleansing velocity of 0.75 m/sec (2.5 ft/sec) with pumping systems installed where it is necessary to discharge to a higher level.

Sewage treatment is often in the vicinity of the resort but may be conveyed through a regional scheme to a central plant.

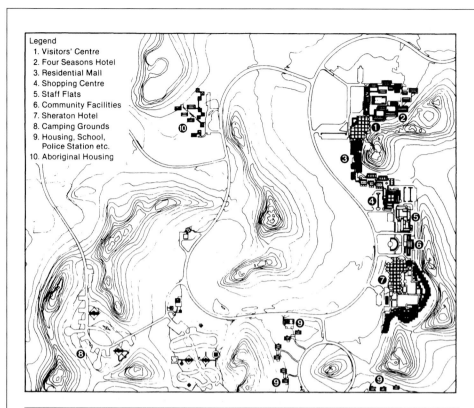

Yulara tourist resort: site plan

Legend
1. Visitors' Centre
2. Four Seasons Hotel
3. Residential Mall
4. Shopping Centre
5. Staff Flats
6. Community Facilities
7. Sheraton Hotel
8. Camping Grounds
9. Housing, School, Police Station etc.
10. Aboriginal Housing

Yulara's sails (tension fabric membrane structures) provide shade from the harsh desert sun

Yulara Tourist Resort, Australia

Ayers Rock in central Australia is a major national tourist attraction and is surrounded by the Uluru Federal Park (1325 km²) which has been given to the Aboriginal people to control and manage. To relieve rising visitor pressures and damage to the local environment a new airstrip and resort was constructed 16 km away outside the park boundary.

The Yulara resort, on a site about 2 km × 2 km, has been designed for a mixed population of 5000 tourists and 500 permanent residents, including park staff. It is arranged around an S-shaped spine built on a raised podium contoured over the sand dunes and provides a visitor centre, two hotels, retail area and communal and staff facilities in clusters around squares and spaces. A separate service area contains water and sewage treatment and maintenance plant. Peripheral components include a

school, aboriginal housing and four camping grounds (for 3600 in total) each with a swimming pool.

The buildings are simple domestic scale with blockwork and light metal frames. Shading is provided by tension fabric membrane structures — the dominant architectural feature of the resort.

The climate is arid and water supplies are obtained from an aquifer having a dissolved salt content of 2500 mg/l, reduced to 500 g/l by automatic electrodialysis. Storage is provided for 200 000 litres, about two days' peak demand. Four types of supplies are reticulated: treated — for drinking and bathing, untreated — cisterns and fire hydrants, blended — trickle irrigation, and recycled — sports stadium, plantations.

Architects: Philip Cox & Partners
Consulting Engineers: Ove Arup & Partners`

Where the development is carried out in phases, the site for the treatment plant must be planned to allow for the eventual total capacity.

Physio-biological processes of treatment include:

• *Septic tank* (anaerobic decomposition) with ground or percolating filtration. Requires periodic emptying by tanker vehicle (access, pumping)	For small developments in isolated sites, caravan and camp sites. Minimum area: 100 m² increased to 1000 m² for land irrigation
• *Activated sludge process* – screening, oxygenation and settlement tanks	Power supplies essential – minimum area per 1000 person: 800 m² (*)
• *Sedimentation and aeration* processes	For larger developments – minimum area per 1000 persons: 1200 m² (*)

(*) With minimum areas for treatment of sludge – assuming this is removed from the site. For permanent populations in excess of 5000 it is usually feasible to install a sludge digestion plant.

3.3.3 Outfall and irrigation systems: phased extension

The siting of proposed sewage plant is often difficult to decide, taking into account recreational and environmental requirements and future extensions of the resort. Usually the natural slope of ground is towards the greatest asset of the resort (beach, lakeside) and pumping will be required to transfer the sewage to a more convenient site inland. In some cases it may be practical to provide initial treatment, prior to pumping, in tanks constructed under paved promenades and jetties and this is often done when existing resort outfalls are redesigned to reduce pollution.

Outfall must be carefully surveyed in relation to possible pollution of nearby beaches and aquatic life or groundwater. Where a sea outfall is necessary, it must be extended well beyond the lowest tide level in a position which allows adequate dispersion of the treated effluent. In sensitive areas tertiary treatment, such as chorine dosage in effluent tanks, is required prior to disposal and this is essential when effluent is recycled for irrigation of grounds.

Recent research aims at treating and processing outfall by natural means (after primary traditional processing), utilizing soil filtering or the activity of wetland plants and micro-organisms. This solution provides ponds and wetland habitats in places where fresh water is expensive.

In Europe and elsewhere, beaches are assessed for their suitability for recreational use taking into account pollution and other conditions.

3.3.4 Refuse disposal

Three areas of planning are involved in devising arrangements for refuse disposal:

- *collection*: characteristics of the collection area; methods of collection (returnable containers, disposable sacks) and vehicle design; separation of recyclable items;
- *storage*: requirements for individual properties (location, types of containers, compression equipment); requirements for recycling; problems of nuisance, flies, rodents, etc;
- *disposal*: location of disposal point; alternative methods for disposal; potential damage to the environment (unsightliness, pollution, fire, scavenging); seasonal variations (in quantities and conditions).

In most cases, the collection of refuse is undertaken by the local authority for the area but sometimes private contractual arrangements may be necessary. Environmental considerations must be taken into account in comparing alternatives as well as economic feasibility. Where resort development is carried out in stages, the long-term requirements may justify greater initial investment.

3.3.5 Electricity supplies

Loadings. Electricity demands are calculated from the individual loadings of the connected equipment together with a diversity factor determined by the probability of coincidence in use. For any resort, the total load will depend on many factors:

- *numbers accommodated*: peak numbers of tourists, employees, residents;
- *climate*: air conditioning and space heating needs; design features of buildings;
- *sophistication*: standards; range of recreational and food service facilities;
- *alternative sources of energy*: gas, oil, combined heat and power, district heating systems.

For a typical seaside resort in a hot climate, having 1000 rooms (2000 beds) and 600 resident employees, using electricity for cooking and air-conditioning, the total loading is estimated at 3000 kW. Allowing a diversity factor of 0.7, the electricity loading is about 2000 kW.

The main areas of consumption (allowing simultaneous demand coefficients) are:

air-conditioning (700 kW), guestrooms (450 kW), restaurants and bars (300 kW), kitchens and cold rooms (500 kW), laundry (200 kW), hot water (40 kW), plant (150 kW), staff rooms and facilities (200 kW), swimming pool, sauna, etc. (130 kW), external lighting (130 kW), disco/theatre (50 kW), and miscellaneous uses (150 kW).

In winter resorts the electrical load may be significantly reduced if space heating and cooking requirements are met by alternative forms of energy (gas or oil combustion). Combined power and heating systems are also widely used, with surplus power being sold to the utility supply company and heat recovered for domestic hot water and space heating needs. This also applies to district schemes in which electricity is generated for a wider area and the recovered heat circulated in mains to individual properties (metered).

Transmission voltages for the mains supply of electricity depend on regional or national practice and the distances and loadings involved. Transformation to primary supply voltages (large hotels and primary users) and to lower secondary voltages (residential premises) is necessary for distribution with the resort area. The voltage is set by the utility supply company and varies widely. 120/208 V, 240/415 V and 277/480 V, single/three-phase supplies are fairly common and almost all electricity is distributed as alternating current with a frequency of 50 Hz.

Emergency generation of electricity supplies must be provided within the resort. As a rule this covers emergency lighting, refrigeration, pumps and essential equipment (up to 30 per cent of normal load) but is higher where supplies are unreliable. Three synchronized generators are usually recommended for a 1000 room resort, with automatic battery start and delay switch back to normal current.

Distribution within the resort may be in the form of *ring main systems* with substation transformers and switchgear at intervals and *radial main systems* direct to substations and heavy users such as large hotels. Both distribution mains and services to properties may be constructed above or below ground, the latter being preferred to avoid the unsightly appearance of poles and cables in and around the resort, although costs are increased by a factor of 2 to 10 depending on the terrain and distances.

Outside the resort, the planning of overhead lines (electricity, telephone) must take account of the visual amenity value of the landscape, which will ultimately be of greater importance for the success of the resort than the additional cost incurred for its protection. Lines must be integrated into the folds of the contours so that they cannot be seen against the skyline; they should be constructed underground or diverted away from areas of high scenic attraction and from recreational zones (such as ski pistes) where they could create hazards.

3.3.6 Communication systems

Infrastructure services include public telephone networks and television and radio broadcasting systems. In both cases, wired or cable connections or aerial transmission via ground stations or satellites may be involved.

Telephone services in resorts normally use private automatic branch exchanges (PABX) connected to the utility supply company network, supplemented with local systems within the resort (intercom, direct dialling and PAX systems).

Television systems generally require a master antenna system to boost the signal, and careful siting of satellite dishes is important for good reception and appearance. With increasing sophistication services may provide in-room films and guest information.

Public address systems are essential in most resorts, with controlled relays to the recreational and social areas and acoustic screening for quieter areas.

Emergency safety, security and control systems are essential and cover a wide range of requirements, including protection (monitoring), alarm (fire, security, system failure, etc.) and specific action (switch to fire mode, emergency supplies, etc.). Most systems are computer-controlled and this may be linked to other installations such as computerized locking systems. Safety provisions also include lightning conductors and electrical grounding and overload protection.

Computerized management systems cover administration requirements like reservations, accounting, billing, employee records and maintenance. Billing may be operated by the locking system card allowing use for individual purchases throughout the resort.

3.3.7 Heating and air-conditioning systems

Internal environmental services may be planned as central or unitary systems:

*   *Central systems* allow more convenient location of plant, more sophisticated control and higher efficiencies and are more suitable for public areas, space heating generally and air-conditioning in high grade hotels.
*   *Unitary systems* provide individual choice and, often, more instant local response. Unitary air-conditioning (mainly split systems) is widely used in resort guestrooms and self-owned apartments or condominiums. The noisy compression/ condenser equipment should be sited way from the rooms and screened from view (on the roofs or elsewhere).

The location of central plant must take into account the need for vehicle access, methods of distribution of air and hot water and possible nuisance from noise and air pollution (chimneys, exhaust outlets). Most air-conditioning and heating systems, including domestic hot water supplies, are arranged to supply zones within the properties for easier control, less transmission loss and energy savings.

Heat distribution is usually by means of hot water circulation, but in large winter resorts steam heating may be employed for both internal and external (under pavement) requirements. Heat may be generated in boilers or heat exchangers (combined with power generation) and transferred to other supplies (domestic hot water, recreational uses) in calorifiers.

3.3.8 Coordination of underground utilities

Site works involve extensive changes to the area (construction, change and intensification of use, landscaping). An *environmental survey* may be required prior to planning consideration (see 1.4.7). Coordination of site and infrastructural works is essential to avoid subsequent disturbance or difficulties. The programme of work will usually include:

Surveys

Land use — surroundings, existing local plans and strategies for the area

Access — roads, junctions, traffic patterns, proposed changes, noise levels

Physical — topographical map, climate, extreme conditions and risks

Environment — characteristics, assets, natural vegetation, habitats, surroundings

Geotechnical — geological and seismic data, adverse conditions, risks, water levels

Specific — archaeological areas, conditions for specific resorts

Site plans

Conceptual — preliminary layouts, sketches and visual images, features

Development — zones, optimum locations for facilities, parking, services

Landscape — ground moulding, water-filled areas, retained vegetation, planting schemes

Engineering

Grading — finished grade elevations, excavation and fill volumes, stabilizing works

Structural — foundations, basements, retaining structures, structural design

Technical — plant locations, underground structures, drainage and services circulations

Roads — access, vehicular/pedestrian circulations, parking, paved areas

4 Basic standards for recreation, cultural and sports facilities

4.1 INDOOR SOCIAL AND CULTURAL ACTIVITIES

Indoor facilities are particularly important in ski areas and in resorts and recreational complexes where variable climatic conditions or demands for use in the evening make this feasible. In other situations, such as beach resorts, they are less critical.

4.1.1 Facilities

The types of facilities required depend on the clientele structure and the image to be projected, but the following should be considered:

- *Cinema* — In a small resort designed to allow alternative uses (conventions, plays)
- *Multi-purpose hall* — For variety, music, folk entertainment, social meetings and conventions. From 200 m² (2000 sq ft) in small resorts to 1000 m² (11 000 sq ft) in a large tourist centre. Combined with other facilities if conventions are an important market target.
- *Open air theatre* — May replace both cinema and hall in small resorts with mild climate.
- *Youth centre* — Meeting place for young people in large resorts and recreation centres. From 200–800 m² (2000–9000 sq ft) with a lobby, main hall, games rooms and workshops.
- *Night clubs and dance halls* — Required for two main age groups: 16–25: discotheque and dance halls 25 and older: ballrooms and night-clubs
- *Library and reading room* — Mainly in larger resorts. Often combined with facilities for lectures, music recitals, local information.
- *TV room* — Where television is not provided in the rooms. May also serve as a lounge for beverages.
- *Casino* — Gambling facilities are usually restricted by national policy and planning conditions. Special requirements apply.
- *Visitor centre* — For regional and national parks. May be located near a resort.

The facilities may be grouped together or arranged to extend interest and animation throughout the resort. Other facilities may be considered:

- to add to the attractions of the resort and, particularly, its season of use, and
- to compensate for limitations in weather or natural resources on the site.

4.1.2 Standard facilities in integrated resorts

The standards indicated below are averages for new *integrated* resorts in which at least 50 per cent of the beds are available for rent and where there are few competing facilities available in hotels. The data is taken from surveys of Italian seaside resorts (SOMEA 1968), French ski resorts (CSFSH 1974, PROMOTOUR), earlier studies by M. Baud-Bovy (ACAU 1967), surveys of resorts in developing countries and special studies in this subject (BACOPA 1972).

		Numbers of tourist beds in thousands					
		1	2	4	7	12	20
Cinema 300–600 seats	S			1	1	1	2
(300–600 m²)	M		L	1	1–2	2–3	2–5
Multi-purpose hall	S					1	1
(200–1000 m²)	M				1	1	1
Open air theatre	S	L	1	1	1	1	1
(500 m²)							
Library (150–500 m²)	M/S			P	P	1	1
Youth Centre	M/S		L	P	1	1	1
Dancing, night club	S	L	1		1–2	2–3	3–4
(150–200 m²)	M		L	1–2	1–3	2–5	3–8	6–12

M = mountain
S = sea
P = possibly
L = when launching a larger resort

Approximate gross built area:
- 0.1 m² per bed (2 sq ft) in seaside resorts
- 0.2 to 0.3 m² per bed (4 to 6 sq ft) in mountain resorts

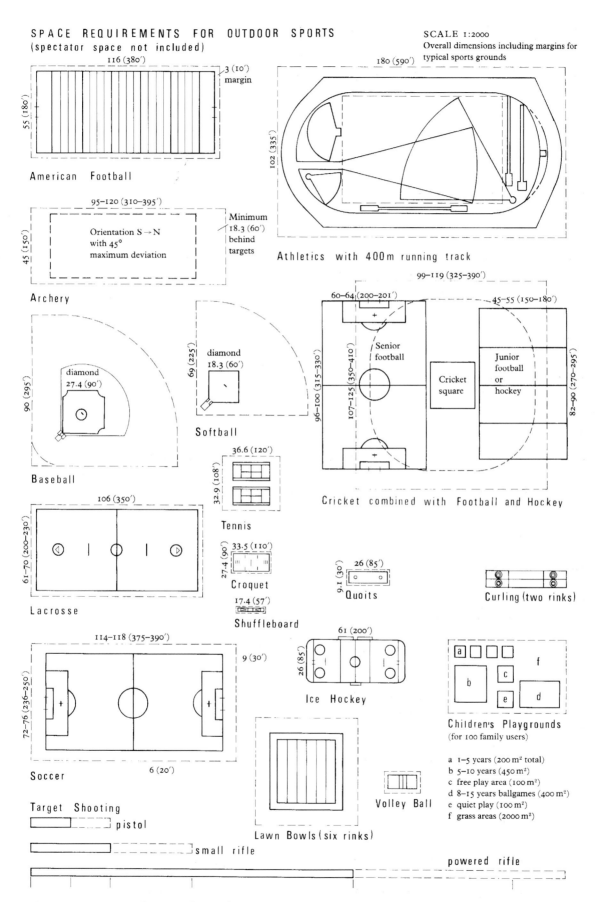

Figure 4.1 *Space requirements for outdoor sports*

4.2 LAND-BASED SPORTS FACILITIES

This section covers general facilities provided for outdoor sports. The details consider local recreational needs as well as typical standards for tourist resorts (see 4.2.6). Specialized requirements for winter resorts are examined separately (see 5.3).

4.2.1 Important factors

Most sports facilities provided for local communities are in or near urban areas where land is scarce and expensive. To ensure that the best use is made of resources it is necessary to evaluate carefully, for each type of sport:

- the numbers of potential users and the areas of land required;
- investment costs (usually borne by the community);
- the apportionment of operating costs between the community and users.

4.2.2 Sports grounds

Figure 4.1 indicates the space requirements for most outdoor sports. The following notes should also be considered:

- **Tennis courts**: Most courts are constructed with semi-porous synthetic surfaces and, often, have floodlighting to allow extended use. They are provided by most local authorities for public (hourly hire charges) as well as private use (membership fees). Large tennis centres often include some lawn and indoor tennis courts as well as squash courts and other clubhouse facilities. Tennis is a relatively inexpensive facility:
  - in land area: one court (1500 m^2) is sufficient for 75 regular amateur players: 20 m^2 per player
  - in investment cost
  - in cost per player in small clubs (but increasing with club sophistication(.
- **Team sports on grass pitches**: Football, soccer, rugby, hockey, baseball, etc. are considered as 'popular' sports and range from local clubs to national teams. Pitches are often shared by local schools and clubs. The intensity of use usually varies with the scarcity of land available:
  - 50 regular players in a village (about 200 m^2 per regular player),
  - 150 regular players in a town (about 65 m^2 per regular player),
  - 250 regular players on synthetic grass (about 40 m^2 per regular player).

  The higher intensity of use in urban areas reflects the scarcity of land and high upkeep costs (multiplied by a factor of 10 in towns). Although cheap for the players, team sports on grass are expensive for urban local authorities.
- Playing fields and playgrounds (for adults and children) for badminton, free volleyball, handball and so on should be located near the beach (in a seaside resort) or at the start of the ski pistes (in a ski resort, for the summer season) and carefully landscaped with trees, etc. A few hard semi-porous surfaces may be used in areas of intensive use (table tennis or basketball). Urban playgrounds are dealt with in 9.3.3.

4.2.3 Built sports halls

Indoor sports facilities are necessary in many areas to allow intensive use over long periods of the day, independent of weather. Sports halls can be grouped into four types:

- **Village hall and community recreation centre** serving a catchment population of 5000 to 10 000. Typically this has an undifferentiated hall which can accommodate many activities (gymnastics, dance, badminton) or other social uses, with or without some provision for separation of space The hall size is based on 1–2 badminton courts: minimum 16.4 × 8.4 m with clear height 7.6 m. The hall is usually equipped with a stage, cloakrooms, storage areas, a cafe/bar and, usually, one or two small meeting rooms.
- **Small sports centres** for populations up to 25 000. This has a large hall which is usually sized for four badminton courts (16.4 × 15.4 m) with a number of smaller multi-use rooms for various leisure and social activities. Whilst 'dry' sports use is more common, sports centres may include or be linked to indoor swimming pools, with saunas, jet pools, steam baths and other facilities.
- **Medium and large sports centres** serving larger regional needs. These provide extensive facilities for both leisure and competitive sports, including spectator areas. The buildings are differentiated into 'wet' and 'dry' areas with purpose-designed activity halls. Larger centres provide leisure pools as well as standard competition pools (often with a separate training pool and diving pool – see 4.4.2) and may include an ice rink. External sports grounds and playing fields are normally provided as part of the complex, as well as extensive parking areas and public transport services.
- **Leisure centres**: The trend in regional developments is towards a greater range of leisure interests which cater for the whole family. Most large centres have landscaped leisure pools, ice rinks, ten-pin bowling alleys, indoor bowling greens, fitness centres and extensive cafe/refreshment areas as well as competitive sports facilities. Some provide rooms for art and handicrafts, yoga, dance, and other activities as well as services like a crèche, beauty-care and massage.

Ponds Forge Sports Centre, Sheffield, UK

Designed to FINA standards (Fédération International de Natation Amateur), this sports centre has been built on the site of a former steel works as part of the regeneration strategy for Sheffield and used for the World Student Games. The facilities include a ten-lane 50 m × 25 m × 2–3 m deep competition pool, incorporating a floating floor and movable bulkheads, and a diving pool in which an underwater system creates surface agitation (for distance judging) and a safety cushion of bubbles for practice. There is a separate leisure pool (with flumes and waves), a sports hall and ancillary facilities.

Architects: Faulkner-Brown
Engineers: Ove Arup & Partners.

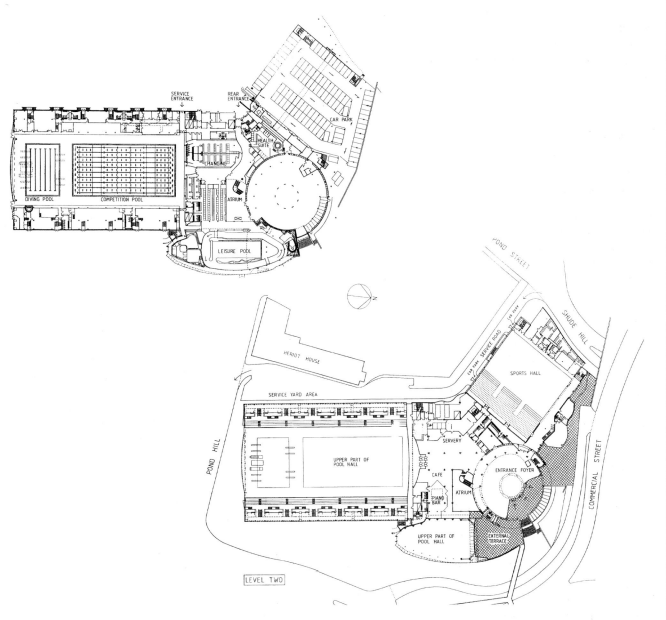

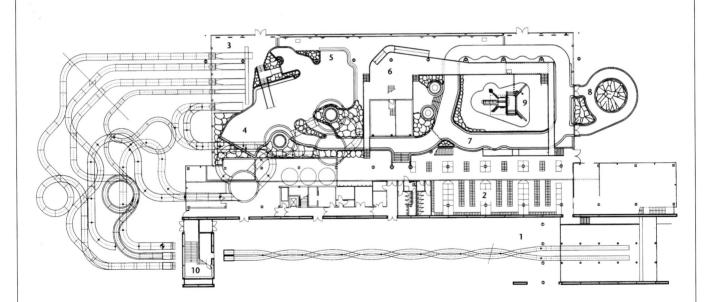

Wet 'n Wild Water Park, Newcastle, UK

Providing a leisure focus for the redevelopment of Newcastle, this centre contains 14 different water activities mainly within a simple elegant steel and glass enclosure under a curved roof. The rides include a 110 m 'lazy river' winding in and out of the building with the current carrying bathers in rubber tyres, three waterfalls, water jets, a wave canyon, and white-knuckle twisted flume. Pools are sited on the south side with a cafe, bar, changing areas and offices, etc. on the north.

Architects: Faulkner Browns

The first two types of sports centres may be provided in tourist resorts, sometimes linked to squash courts, swimming pool, fitness rooms, etc. A large bar and sports shop may provide animation and an atmosphere of social relaxation.

4.2.4 Horse riding

Horse riding and pony trekking are popular for both local recreation and tourism. A riding centre needs space for exercising the horses (at least 1 ha for 12 to 15 horses). Riding stables range in scale from 10 to 100 horses or more.

On average a horse is used by 15–20 persons/week at novice level (40–50 m² /rider), by four persons per week at more advanced level (150–200 m² /rider), or by one owner (600–700 m² of land/rider).

Recreational horse riding is an expensive hobby, particularly for more advanced riders. In urban areas it is often necessary to travel some distance to riding centres with access to trails (bridleways) in attractive rural or forested surroundings away from traffic. Riding centres are usually private enterprises, or belong to associations, with 30 to 100 horses, some privately owned (livery) and some for hire. Local authorities are usually responsible for designating and maintaining public bridleways; occasionally they provide the land, or even a loan. Conflicts often arise from motorists, farming and forestry interests, walkers and ecologists, and this needs to be taken into account in preparing regional development plans.

In tourist areas, horse riding is a major attraction, particularly in offering opportunities for instruction, gallops (along remote beaches and heaths) and extensive trails (see 4.3.4). The latter may be combined with overnight accommodation and services about every 30 km (20 miles). In a mild climate, using tough ponies (requiring no stabling, etc.) trekking and riding can provide a relatively cheap attraction.

Horse riding trials of a few days to two weeks are developing as a product. The accommodation is usually spartan (farms, dormitories), but there is a new trend toward more comfort, such as in 'horstels'.

An example of horse riding trials: 'La Drôme à cheval' France

2500 km of trails – 80 alternative day-itineraries – 45 simple accommodation locations (farms with twelve stalls or boxes and paddock). The association maintains trails, prepares maps and itineraries, promotes and controls standards.

4.2.5 Golf courses

Land requirements. Golf requires large areas of land with high landscape construction and maintenance costs. Typically, an 18-hole (6000 m round) course takes up about 45 to 60 hectares (100–150 acres) for up to 250 golfers daily (i.e. about 500 to 600 active members per golf course). This represents 1000 m² of land per active golfer playing an average of two rounds a week.

The construction of an 18-hole golf course, including clubhouse facilities and mechanical services, involves a *high capital investment* ($2–4 millions, up to $8 million on difficult sites), although this is often seen as a way of enhancing low-value farmland whilst also adding to amenities and inducing new leisure and tourism markets. The *operating costs* are also very high ($500 000 to $1 million/year), the courses requiring upkeep, watering (250 000 m³/year on the Mediterranean coast) and fertilizers. These figures are much lower, for example in France (AFIT 1996), for elementary 9-hole courses in favourable locations ($400 00–$800 000 investment; $100 000 maintenance).

Arguments against new developments are usually based on the additional traffic generated, damage to the natural landscape and ecology and the risk of pollution from fertilization. Relatively few jobs are created, perhaps five to ten per development.

Provision. Golf courses fall into four main categories:

- *Private clubs:* privately owned or owned collectively by members who pay a joining fee and annual subscription. Other attractions (swimming pool, fitness centre, tennis courts, horse riding, etc.) may be added to extend the membership.
- *Residential developments:* with building plots, houses and chalets arranged around the fairways to benefit from the landscape and contribute to the development costs, sometimes substantially or even totally. With additional attractions, this may become a weekend resort (see 5.4.1).
- *Public golf courses:* provided by the local authority for community use and to enhance the tourist attractions of an area. A fee is charged for each round of use – often with the cost subsidized as part of the recreational amenities budget. The costs involved in providing public golf courses are high and the subsidy per regular player may be almost the equivalent of private club fees.
- *Golf hotels and resorts:* using golf and the landscaped surroundings as a key attraction. Courses are often designed – and operated – by well-known professionals and usually include some residential developments (for sale or rent) and club membership. Some tourist regions (such as the Costa

Typical provision	Small unit	Standard unit	Large centre
Horses (employees)	10 (2)	25 (4–5)	100 (15–20)
Stables and services	Numbers of horses + isolation bay + staff and visitor facilities		
Track m (ft)	20×12 (66×40)	20×30 (66×100)	20×60 (66×200)
Outdoor manége m² (sq ft)	1000 (11 000)	2000 (22 000)	5000 (55 000)
Grass paddock ha (acre)	0.2–0.5 (0.5–1.3)	1.0 (2.5) min.	6–8 (15–20)

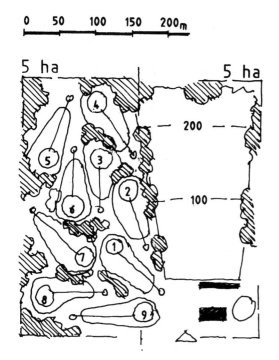

Figure 4.2a *Pitch and putt with driving range*

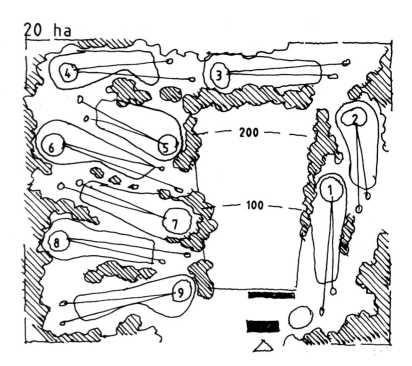

Figure 4.2b *9-hole (par 3) with driving range*

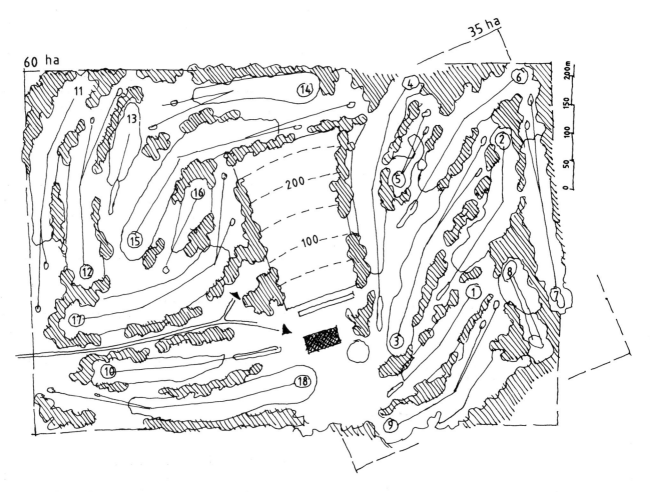

Figure 4.2c *Standard 9-hole with driving range, extended to 18-hole with driving range*

del Sol in Spain, with 48 golf courses on a coastal stretch of 120 km) have become privileged golfing destinations with the opportunity to play on several courses within 30 minutes of each other. The courses are mainly private, owned by the hotels or foreign investors, and occasional green fees are high and access is not always available.
The basic elements of a golf course are:

- 9- or/and 18-hole fairways with bunkers and greens;
- driving range: 250–300 m × 100–125 m in area, designed for intensive use by golfers practising long drives (usually with 25 persons on each side, sometimes floodlit);
- large putting green and training green with pitches and bunkers (two or three holes);
- beginners' training area (often with artificial grass);
- clubhouse and services (including video monitoring);
- parking, maintenance and equipment stores.

Feasibility. Without cross-subsidies (from property and hotel interests) the feasibility of a new golf course is generally low. In most cases the revenues only cover operating costs, some cover a return on the investment and, exceptionally, land acquisition. Local authorities are often under pressure to provide golf facilities and need expertise to determine the extent to which they should be involved: by providing land only, controlling development or even undertaking the investment and operation.

A number of alternatives may be considered (for land economy, wider use):

- driving range and practice putting greens only (for beginners and training);
- 'pitch and putt' course (in USA 'chip and putt') for holiday-makers requiring 5-6 ha of land (9-hole) to 12 ha (18-hole), in some cases with artificial lighting for extended use;
- 9-hole, par 3, course next to a driving range, on about 20 ha;
- 'executive' golf course (especially in USA) 18 holes but about ten par 3 and only one par 5, for a shorter length, on 25 to 30 ha.
- regulation course, possibly through a phased extension: from an initial 9-hole course (30–35 ha) to full 18-hole competition standard (50–60 ha).

4.2.6 Standards for sports facilities in holiday resorts

Most of the basic sports facilities for community recreation (summarized above) are also provided in resorts for the use of tourists. The arrangements may include:

- *exclusive use:* hotels, commercial resorts, private estates/condominiums;
- *extended commercial use:* by guests/tourists, club members and fee-paying users;
- *separate provision:* for local residents (in newly-developing areas);
- *public and private use:* local authorities enhancing the recreational attractions.

Other forms of land-based recreation may also be developed – where the resources and climate are suitable – to create more specific products and a distinct image for marketing the resort, such as scenic parks and gardens, enhanced cultural activities, hill walking, mountaineering, river rafting, fishing, wildlife viewing, nature studies and special interests. (see 4.3 and 4.4). More specialized resorts are described in 5.2 to 5.5.

		Number of tourist beds in thousands					
		1	2	4	7	12	20
Playgrounds (about 2000 m²)	M/S	1	2	4	6	10	15
Basket/volleyball (800 m²)	M/S			1	1	2	4
Tennis (650 m²)	M/S	P	1–4	2–8	4–10	6–12	8–20
Tennis indoor	S						1
(25 m×40 m)	M			P	1	1–2	2
Sports halls (250–1000 m²)	M/S	P	P	1	1	1	
Outdoor swimming pool (500–2500 m² pools)	S	P	1	1	1	1	
Indoor swimming pool	S				P	P	1
(200–1500 m² pools)	M	P	1	1	1–2	2	
Riding centre (No. of horses)	M/S			P	(10)	(15)	(20)

M = mountain, S = sea, P = provision possibly required

Average space provisions for basic sports facilities in resorts are:

	Area per bed	
	m²	sq ft
Open space, including playgrounds	5–8	55–85
Built area in mountain resorts	0.4–0.5	4–5
Built area in seaside resorts (with warm climates)	< 0.2	2

In mountain resorts, part of the open recreation area may be utilized during the ski season 'la Grenouillère', the area where skiers congregate at the base of the pistes (see 5.3.5).

4.3 LAND-BASED RECREATION FACILITIES

4.3.1 Picnicking

Facilities for picnicking are provided in:

- picnic sites beside a road or a highway;
- designated large picnic areas with internal road and gravelled parking sites, sometimes provided for an admission fee;
- picnic areas as one of the elements in suburban parks (see 5.7).

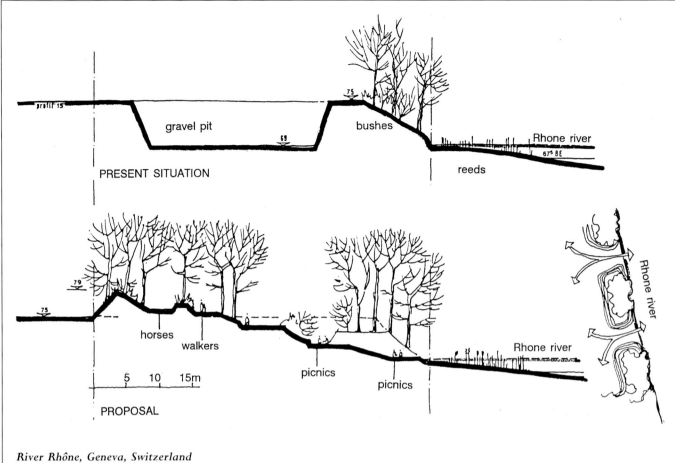

River Rhône, Geneva, Switzerland

Landscaping a river bank for outdoor activities: by developing the contact with the river, creating recreation 'spaces' (trails, meadows, trees) and banning recreation 'facilities' (tables, benches, etc.).

Source: A&M Baud-Bovy (1984), Aménagement des rives du Rhône, DTPE, Canton de Genève (work report)

Planning standards usually encompass a wide range of densities depending on the location and the extent to which the site is equipped with car hard-standing, turfed areas and tree or shrub screening.

- Recommended standards for specific picnic sites: 15–40 units per ha (6–16 per acre), of 40 m² each, with one or more benches, a table, firegrate for barbecues and rubbish receptacle. Each unit serves four to eight persons and includes both picnic facilities and car parking. Where possible, cars should be screened from view and kept about 100 m from the site. Under normal use 40 units (or 150 persons) per ha permit the normal growth of durable grass.
- Maximum concentrated usage may reach 300 and even 500 persons per ha at peak times but this is excessive and causes a serious deterioration in the visual environment and enjoyment of the experience.
- Specific picnic sites should not be more than 100 m from car park areas.
- In suburban parks, however, cars may be parked up to 300 m from the picnic areas.

The picnickers often bring their own camping tables, chairs and barbecue. Drinking water and flush toilets should be provided.

4.3.2 Parks, rest and playing fields

Parks provide opportunities for people living in towns and cities to enjoy contact with nature and relax in pleasant surroundings free from traffic (see 8.5.3). Grassed areas allow informal games with children and gardens provide visual interest and enjoyment for older users. People living or working in the area have the opportunity to lunch in the open air or to take exercise. Areas may also be set aside for children and for dog owners to exercise their pets, but the feeling of being in a natural environment is jeopardized by the incorporation of sports fields, tennis courts, or playgrounds which are too conspicuous.

- **Urban parks**: Parks in the centres of towns and cities are attracting increasing attention, in many cases after a long period of decline and neglect. An urban park with large lawns can accommodate about 150 persons per ha at any one time. With higher intensities of use it is necessary to provide more paved or gravelled areas, ultimately replacing lawns with trees, shrubs and flower beds.

The planning of a new park or rehabilitation of existing areas calls for consultation with local users to resolve conflicts of interest and identify the true role of a park. Most concerns relate to safety, vandalism and maintenance (see 8.5.3 and 9.3.3 to 9.3.8).

- **Suburban parks**: Parks located on the edges of towns usually offer large spaces and opportunities for a wider range of activities (see 5.7.2). Undulating grassed areas, with lines or groves of trees for shelter, are provided for quiet relaxation and informal family games, the latter being associated with picnic facilities. Because the pressure on the grass areas is much lighter than in urban parks, lawns are not necessary: meadows mowed three or four times each year are sufficient. Space must be allowed for large machinery for mowing and removal of rubbish.

	Persons/ ha at any one time	Daily turnover rate	Persons/ ha per day	Persons/ acre per day
Dense picnic site	200–300	1.5–2	300–600	120–240
Lightly used picnic site	40–100	1.5–2	60–200	25–80
Playing fields	50–100	2–3	100–300	40–120
Urban parks	150–200	3–4	450–800	180–320

4.3.3 Walking and hiking trails

Recreational trails and paths fall into three categories:

- **Trails for short walks**, generally allow alternative choice of time-distance ranging from half an hour to two hours (1–8 km) depending on the topography. Usually the paths are arranged as loops around a car park, restaurant or picnic area and extend to features of interest and viewing points. The density of trails in a popular area depends on the geomorphology and vegetation. With good screening by clusters of trees a density of five persons per day per km of trail (eight per mile) allows a feeling of wilderness and closeness with nature, whilst 50 persons per day per km (80 per mile) gives a sense of crowding.
- **Trails for getting about** from one place to another may be in the country (for example, from a holiday resort to a neighbouring village or lake). In towns, signposted trails are often used to:
  - provide pedestrian access between destinations (schools, parks, sports grounds, etc.),

  - link associated recreational areas (*linear parks*) and tourist sights (*paths of discovery*).

These trails must be protected – preferably separated – from traffic and have 'green' or interesting surroundings. They may follow canal towpaths, river banks, disused railway lines or pedestrianized streets and are important in urban planning (see 8.5.6 and 9.3.6). Trails are easy to implement on community land; institutions and public agencies may accept a trail throughout their open spaces; on private land it may be necessary to consider rights-of-way, utility easements, lease of a track of land, conditional approval of a new property development or compulsory acquisition.

- **Trails for long distance hiking** may extend for hundreds of kilometres along ancient paths followed by pilgrims, travellers or migrants (such as the route of St-Jacques-de-Compostelle) or extend through attractive, and often remote, natural areas. Long distance paths extend all over Europe from Germany through the Alps to the Mediterranean, and in Britain there are many, such as the Pennine Way.

Depending on their density of use, location and possible access for the disabled, trails may be of asphalt, gravel on stone base or natural (with drainage and reinstatement where required). Trails should avoid the disturbance of travel patterns and habitats of wildlife, provide for erosion control and diversion of water, avoid fragile soils and preferably use low-impact solutions (e.g. boardwalk) to paving. A carefully built trail reduces maintenance and reconstruction costs. Other provisions include:

- signposting or marking;
- diversion of pathway from hazardous features;
- instructional/educational facilities along nature trails.

4.3.4 Other types of trails

Cycle touring, cyclocross, mountain bikes: Bicycle trails fall into four main categories:

- *Urban trails* and dedicated cycle tracks linking urban centres to suburban parks and recreational areas in the countryside.
- *Cycle touring* along road systems selected to avoid the main flows of traffic or along special cycle tracks (as through the pine forests of Aquitaine, France).
- *Cyclocross* or cross-country cycling around a rough track circuit, typically 1.6 to 3.2 km (1 to 2 miles).
- *Mountain bike* routes in mountain areas, around mountain resorts, through pastures or on rough pedestrian trails. Specifically designed trails have been implemented in the USA, for various categories of difficulty, with the following standards:
  - length of daily trips: 15 to 80 km
  - maximum pitch: 10 to 30 per cent
  - maximum sustained pitch: 5 to 15 per cent

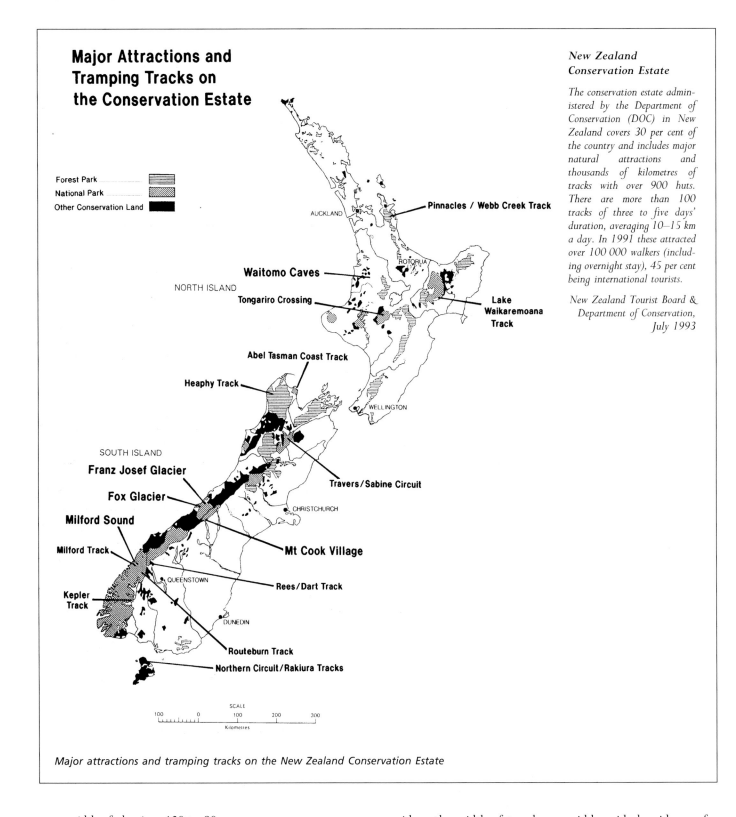

Major Attractions and Tramping Tracks on the Conservation Estate

Forest Park
National Park
Other Conservation Land

NORTH ISLAND

AUCKLAND

ROTORUA

Pinnacles / Webb Creek Track

Waitomo Caves

Tongariro Crossing

Lake Waikaremoana Track

Abel Tasman Coast Track

Heaphy Track

WELLINGTON

SOUTH ISLAND

Franz Josef Glacier

Fox Glacier

Milford Sound

Milford Track

Travers/Sabine Circuit

CHRISTCHURCH

Mt Cook Village

QUEENSTOWN

Rees/Dart Track

Kepler Track

DUNEDIN

Routeburn Track

Northern Circuit/Rakiura Tracks

SCALE
100   0   100   200   300
Kilometres

New Zealand Conservation Estate

The conservation estate administered by the Department of Conservation (DOC) in New Zealand covers 30 per cent of the country and includes major natural attractions and thousands of kilometres of tracks with over 900 huts. There are more than 100 tracks of three to five days' duration, averaging 10–15 km a day. In 1991 these attracted over 100 000 walkers (including overnight stay), 45 per cent being international tourists.

New Zealand Tourist Board & Department of Conservation, July 1993

Major attractions and tramping tracks on the New Zealand Conservation Estate

– width of clearing: 120 to 90 cm
– width of tread: 60 to 30 cm
– surface: relatively smooth to rough with some portage required.

Horse riding, pony trekking. This generally involves groups of three to five persons on trails 2.5–3 m (8–10 ft) wide – the width of two horses ridden side by side or of a maintenance vehicle. Stopping places are required at intervals for resting the horses, usually with space for up to ten horses. Earth or gravel on a stone foundation is preferred, with sandy sections for gallops. The required clearance for a horse with rider is typically 2.4 m (7 ft 9 in) high, 1.2 m (4 ft) wide.

Space standards for trails

On-trail activities	Persons per km at the same time	Daily turnover rate	Persons per km per day	Persons/ha per day for trails separated by:		
				400 m	200 m	100 m
Walking (urban park)	500	4	2000			400
Walking (sub-urban park)	5	4	200		20	
Walking (natural surroundings)	10	4	40		4	
Short hiking (2 hours)	10	2	20	1.0		
Long hiking (5–8 hours)	10	0.5	5	0.2		
Bicycling (10–20 km)	10–20	3–5	20–50		2–5	
Horse riding (5–10 km)	6–20	4	25–80	1.2–4	2.5–8	

Motor cycle scrambling and similar forms of cross-country racing require careful zoning to minimize the nuisance from noise, servicing of vehicles and concentrations of spectators. Training is often provided in disused pits and on waste heaps.
Snowmobile trails are common in Canada and the USA: 15–50 miles long, 2–5 m wide, with turning radiuses over 7.5 m
Trails of discovery trace back and link various places associated with historic, archaeological, agricultural (e.g. vineyards) or social development subjects. They may be urban or rural, followed by car, on bicycle or on foot.
Navigable waterways and canals available for cruising, sailing, or canoeing, with land-based facilities and services, with towpaths for walking or bicycling.
Nordic ski trails (see 5.3.2).

As a rule motorized bicycles and motor bikes are prohibited on footpaths, bridleways and cycle routes. Separate trails for walkers, horse and cycle riders are recommended where the usage is high and conflicts or danger liable to arise. Otherwise they might share lightly used trails, which provides a less expensive solution with lesser impact on the environment than several parallel trails.

4.3.5 Allotment gardens

Dating from the nineteenth century, allotments are small garden plots, about 250 m² in area, created by ad hoc associations, by corporations for their employees or by municipalities, usually on public land available for short time leases, sometimes pending future redevelopment. The individual occupiers can erect garden huts and glasshouses and this disorganized appearance often gives rise to local opposition.

The areas of individual plots are related to their use and distance from the home of the users. For medium and large towns this is typically:

- 1.5 to 2 km for *vegetable gardens* (125–200 m²) with water supply only;

- 7 to 8 km for *mixed gardens* (200–300 m²) with vegetables, flowers and/or lawns;
- 15 to 20 km for *weekend gardens* (300–400 m²).

Today, a great number of these Sunday gardeners grow more flowers than vegetables: in some countries allotment gardens are becoming a kind of small weekend residence, an attractive alternative to a caravan in a residential camp.

Sites for allotments may be:

- designated in urban master plans (France);
- considered as public 'mini-parks' or 'community gardens', with alleys between plots open to the public (Bremen, Germany);
- integrated into urban parks together with playgrounds and sports fields (former East Germany);
- created on vacant lots in abandoned inner city areas (USA);
- provided near residential areas, in the form of mini-plots (6 to 48 m²) with water supply but prohibiting sheds, trees or lawns, creating links between apartment dwellers and their immediate environment as well as diversifying the town's vegetation (Lausanne, Switzerland) (Anonymous 1997);
- developed into higher standard 'leisure gardens', with weekend summer houses, some additional landscaping, tree planting, etc. (CIAG 1969).

The average land consumption equates to 125 m² (two users per plot) and the costs of provision and use (land, fencing, water, parking etc.) are relatively high for quality developments.

4.4 WATER-BASED FACILITIES

This section considers water-based facilities for community recreation and countryside resorts. The requirements for large beach resorts and marinas are detailed in 5.2.

4.4.1 Natural bathing places.

Bathing in 'natural' surroundings may be provided in streams, ponds and lakes and may be exclusive or associated with other compatible activities like boating. Increasingly, reservoirs, disused quarries and abandoned clay workings are being adapted for recreation.

Key issues are:

- control of bacteriological quality, diving places and submerged hazards;
- regulation of use (including zoning) and densities;
- restriction on building and unsightly development around the area;
- strict control over pollution from boats and shore-based activities or from vegetation, algae, mosquitoes, etc.

Planning. For intensive use, the banks must be modified and reinforced to withstand wave action and scouring (whether natural or created) and to allow direct access for bathers, boat launching, or landings. Landscaping and tree planting is invariably required to provide shelter, stabilization, surface drainage and screening for various activities, in addition to heightening the sense of contact with nature. The densities for bathing spots are similar to those for seaside beaches. Extreme densities of 6000 simultaneous users/ha (1.7 m²/user) have been reached on some crowded Dutch beaches but these are excessive for planning purposes. The number of swimmers in the water at the same time never exceeds one quarter of the people present on the beach, and generally much less. Turnover rates per day vary from 1.5 to 3.

Facilities usually include:

- a sandy/gravel beach with adjacent lawns for picnics and games;
- floating platforms, safety float lines or boundary buoys;
- showers and changing rooms, lifeguard service;
- provision for various concessionary services.

Lockers are not obligatory since most bathers undress in the open: even with purpose-built outdoor swimming pools there is a tendency not to use changing rooms.

Recommended standards

Facilities	Average beach area per user		No. of simultaneous users per ha	No. of daily users per ha
	m²	sq ft		
Outdoor swimming pools (1 m² of water/user)	5–10	55–110	1000–2000	2000–5000
Beach on lake (water area not included)	5–15	55–160	650–2000	1300–5000
Beach around pond (2–4 m² of water/ user)	10–20	160–270	500–1000	1000–2500

These areas do not include car parking space. As a general rule:

- for small ponds up to 20 ha (50 acres) the aggregate area required for recreational lawns, picnicking and viewing areas; the various facilities, paths and parking will be the same as the water area;

- for a beach around a lake or river, each swimmer occupies 5 to 15 m² of the guarded water area (inside safety lines), the total number of users of the site being four to five times the number of simultaneous swimmers.

4.4.2 Swimming pools

Built swimming pools are important facilities for recreation and often form a focus for other activities. During the summer, open air pools are the preferred destinations for many urban recreationists and an indispensable element of most tourist resorts, whilst indoor pools have a high intensity of use all year round. All built pools require pumped water circulation and treatment to maintain the clarity and hygiene of the water. In most cases heating (or cooling, in very hot climates) is also involved. Pools can be grouped into three main types: open air, indoor sports pools and indoor sports and leisure pools.

Open air pools. In temperate countries, the use of open air pools is seasonal and the water is invariably warmed. Pools and basins are generally landscaped and surrounded by paved areas and lawns sheltered by shrubs and trees. They are often adjacent to a lake or river to provide an associated setting and alternative choice. Access to public transport services is important and the facilities should be planned for a wide range of users. Typical characteristics:

- 2000 m² of basins (swimmers, non-swimmers, divers, small children);
- 16 000 m² of lawns for rest and play;
- 2000 m² of built area (lockers, snack bar/cafe, toilets/changing facilities, etc.);
- a total area of 20 000 m², not including parking areas.

Such a pool complex may accommodate a maximum of 4000 simultaneous users at peak times (based on 0.5 m² of water per user) and about 140 000–200 000 users yearly. The land 'consumed' by a regular user may be evaluated at 5 m² (assuming that a regular user uses the pool 35 times during the season).

$$\frac{2000 \text{ m}^2 \times 35 \text{ annual entries}}{140\,000 \text{ annual entries}} = 5 \text{ m}^2$$

Demand-related standards for outdoor swimming pools vary from 0.5 m² to 2.0 m² swimming pool area per inhabitant: hence the 'typical' pool described above would be appropriate for a neighbourhood population of 10 000–40 000 but would probably cater for more.

Outdoor pools are usually provided by local authorities as public recreation amenities. Revenues rarely meet operating costs and the costs of investment may be partly funded by grants and donations.

Indoor sports pool. Indoor pools are used for year-round exercise, training and competitions as well as local school classes. Pools are usually rectangular and the length of the main pool may range from 16.6 m (50 ft) to 50 m (Olympic size). In large swimming centres there are normally two or three pools (for swimming, learning and diving), including a main competition pool with tiered spectator seating. Depth variation may also be provided using a movable bottom. Indoor pools require extensive plant, technical services and changing rooms. Both the investment cost and costs of operation are very high, whilst the number of users is limited. The high cost per user is normally extensively subsidized as a community charge. High operation deficits, a limited number of users, and the need for expensive repairs after some years has often resulted in the closure of public pools.

Indoor sports and leisure pools. As an alternative to closing sports pools, other communities have successfully extended the market use by transforming them into sport and leisure pools (with landscaping, some vegetation, a snack bar, sauna, fitness installations, table tennis, billiards, children's pool, jacuzzis), usually by adding new space. These sports and leisure pools may be considered as miniature aquatic parks (see 5.6.4).

Example: Tranformation of a swimming pool

After transformation from an indoor swimming pool the sports and leisure pool of Petit-Couronne, France, received 240 000 visitors a year instead of 55 000 as before, for a smaller operating deficit (Mallet 1988).

More exceptionally, leisure pools may be provided as part of a commercial investment, combined with other financially viable leisure activities (bowling alley, fitness centre, cinemas, discotheque, bars and foot outlets) or as an attraction to large shopping areas.

4.4.3 Sailing and boating

User standards for a pond or lake vary with the water area and the types of boats involved. The table below relates to a relatively small lake of 50 ha (125 acres) and lower figures should be used for more extensive waters, reducing down to about 50 per cent for very large lakes and estuaries.

Activity	Area (m²) per boat at any one time	No. of boats per ha* at any one time	No. of users per ha* at any one time	No. of users per ha* daily
Boats for angling	2500–5000	2	2–4	5–8
Small boats**	1800–5000	2–6	4–12	10–30
Medium sailing boats	5000–10 000	1–2	3–6	10–15
Windsurfers	2000–5000	2–5	2–5	8–20
Speed power boats	15 000–30 000	0.3–0.6	1–2	5–10
Water skiing	20 000–40 000	0.25–0.5	0.7–1.5	5–15

* divide by 2.5 to give capacity per acre
** small dinghies, rowing and pedal boats, low powered motor boats, very light sailing craft

Sailing. The minimum area for competitive and recreational sailing with light craft is 6 ha (15 acres) but an area in excess of 10 to 20 ha (25 to 50 acres) is preferable for multiple sailing activities. The banks should be straight or have gradual curves, with a clear width of 45 m (150 ft) between banks and any islands or shallows. The minimum depth for the sailing areas is 1.6 m (5 ft) and, preferably, 1.8 m (6 ft). Larger, keeled yachts require more specific provisions (see 5.2.6).

Power boats. The minimum area on open water is 6 ha (15 acres) and more than 10 ha (25 acres) is preferable. The water must be free from weeds and debris and zoned to restrict other use. Launching and mooring requirements are similar to those for sailing boats. For racing, a speed stadium course, with minimum dimensions 2000 m × 200 m, should be provided. Power boating and water skiing are usually prohibited on areas of less than 25 ha (60 acres) in reservoirs, rivers and canals because of risks of accident, wash damage to banks and wave action.

Windsurfing. Windsurfing is a relatively cheap and popular alternative to sailing. A breezy site of at least 20 ha (preferably more) is required with a depth of 0.5 m or more. Surfboards may be removed from the site or stored there on suitable racks.

Water skiing. A zone for water skiing must be separate from other activities and requires a minimum area of 10 ha (25 acres) with a clear channel of 20 m or preferably 50 m (165 ft) width, zoned for the purpose. A permanent slalom course with jumps may be established.

Small rowing and pedal boats. Channels for small boats must be shallow and sheltered from turbulence. They are usually an irregular shape, about 700 m long, extending along the shore, around islands or in a serpentine route to create interest.

Berth capacity. On a lake the berth capacity may extend up to three times the water area capacity for boating since it is rare for more than one third of the boats to be in active use at the same time. An exception applies where many of the boats are available for hire. The demand for berths is often difficult to accommodate. In many lakes only about 10 to 20 per cent of the moored boats are in use, even at the weekend, the majority only being used four or five times a year and some not at all. Possible solutions include increasing the charges and increasing dry land storage (see 5.2.7). Separate moorings may be required for larger keeled boats and these should be designed, where necessary, to allow for fluctuations in water level (by floating pontoons, lock-closed basins, etc.).

Launch capacity. A 4-m wide slipway or ramp is suitable for up to 40 medium sized boats per day. This should have road access and be set back in the bank sloping down below low water level.

Shore facilities. In a developed centre these will include sanitary facilities, changing rooms, first aid and safety provisions, open and covered storage for landed boats, clubhouse, car parking and spectator vantage area.

The following comparative annual costs have been estimated (Baud-Bovy 1987) for water-based activities on the basis of 10 for the user of a windsurf board:

		Apportionment of cost	
		User	Local authority
Windsurfing		10	1
Light boat, land-parked	per boat	15	2
(1.5 users per boat)	per user	10	1.3
Medium boat, land-parked	per boat	90	12–20
(2.5 users per boat)	per user	35	5–8
Moored boat	per boat	90	30–50
(2.5 users par boat)	per user	35	15–25

4.4.4 Other water-based activities

Angling is one of the most popular sports in many countries and extends to rivers and streams as well as purposely stocked ponds. Ponds of 0.5 to 2 ha are preferable for easier control and fish stocking. Zoning for this use is important to avoid disturbance, and angling may be limited to banks on one side to allow a greater free area for fish. Usually controlled by licensing, restricted to specific seasons and subject to conditions operated by river authorities, land ownership, club membership, etc. If linked to picnic sites, facilities must be provided for fish cleaning (preparation table, water supply, covered waste bin).

Rowing. Olympic courses are 2000 m long (2200 m overall), 1500 m being sufficient for amateur competitions. Rowing lanes are 12.5 m wide with four lanes being the minimum and six lanes (75 m) required for international competitions, in each case with 5 m clearance on each side. The minimum depth is 2 m (6 ft) increasing to 3.3 m (10 ft) for international competition courses. Launching of boats is usually sideways and a landing stage 18 m (60 ft) long with a ramp or steps is required for 'eights' rowing boats.

Canoe racing. Sprint competitions require a straight course 1000 m long, 45 m wide (six lanes of 7.5 m) and a minimum depth of 2 m.

Canoe slalom. This requires turbulent water along a fast-flowing river or below a weir, the flow being regulated to maintain conditions. The course, through a series of gates, is generally about 500 m to 700 m long and may be concentrated into a relatively small area below a weir. White water rafting, aquaplaning and similar sports use highly turbulent river waters along a natural course (which may involve regulation of flow by a dam).

Inland cruising. Inland waterways (river systems and canal networks) are widely used for boat cruising, mainly in hired craft. The minimum water area per cruiser is about 75 m × 9 m. Waterways are usually regulated by the river authorities and include locks (for changes in level and flood control) and

mooring basins at intervals with some shore facilities for provisions, meals and recreation. Cruising is developed as a tourism product in many areas (Norfolk Broads, River Shannon, Canal du Midi). Special requirements apply to the large river and seagoing cruise ships accommodating tourists (see Appendix A4).

Underwater diving. In suitable locations, permanent shore facilities for divers may provide mooring jetties for boats, with equipment stores and clubhouse including changing and sanitary accommodation together with instruction, communication and safety/first aid facilities. Specialized centres may require decompression chambers and other emergency services.

Model boats. Ponds of 30 m width and up to 200 m length, which may also be round or naturally shaped, with edged and paved sides for easy access, are often provided in parks and other recreational areas.

Nature reserves. Areas reserved for nature studies, bird watching, etc. should have minimum access and disturbance. They provide an attractive backcloth for quiet water-based recreation and views from the opposite shore. Facilities may include 'hides' for observation studies.

Compatibility. The extent of compatibility of the various activities is shown in the Fig. 4.9. Where activities are liable to be disruptive or dangerous, zoning by areas or scheduling by timetables may have to be considered.

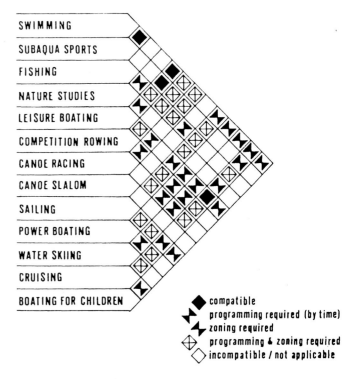

Figure 4.3 *Table of compatibility*

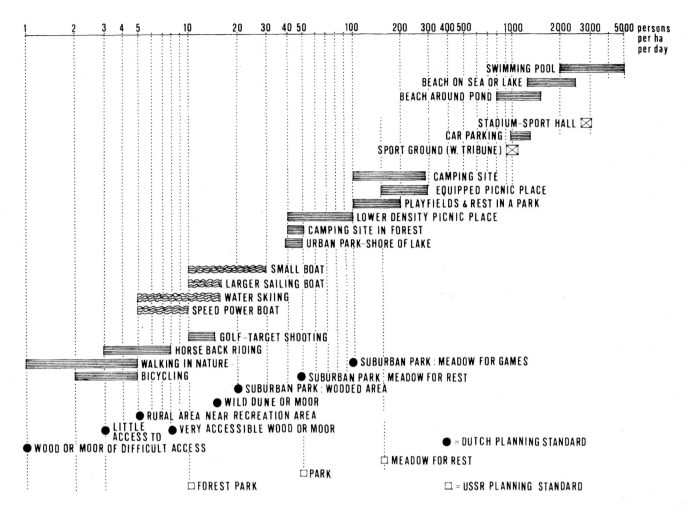

Figure 4.4 *Average densities for recreation facilities*

4.5 DENSITIES, LAND REQUIREMENTS AND COSTS

4.5.1 Densities

Fig. 4.4 indicates the typical numbers of daily users per ha for various recreational activities. The scale is logarithmic.

The graph demonstrates how nature-based recreation activities tend to fall into the four categories detailed in 4.2 to 4.4.

Density	No. of users per ha	Character
Very low	less than 5	Contact with nature
Low	5 to 50	Large spaces
Medium	40 to 300	Uncrowded to crowded
High	1000 to 5000	Very crowded

4.5.2 Land requirements

The land required for regular practice by a golfer is 40 times that required for regular use by a tennis player or 500 times

the area taken up by a regular user of an indoor swimming pool (see Fig. 4.5).

This significantly influences planning considerations when land is scarce and expensive near a town: the local community may divert the latent demand (see 8.2.2) towards less demanding activities.

Land usage	Area per regular user (m²)	(sq yd)	Types of activities
Very high	more than 600	more than 700	Golf, riding private horses, weekend residence
High	100–200	120–240	Riding hired horses, rural football, allotment gardens
Moderate	40–65	45–65	Urban football, picnics, recreation parks, camping
Small	5–25	6–30	Tennis, light sailing boats, public parks
Very small	under 5	under 6	Open or indoor pools, skating rinks, windsurfing

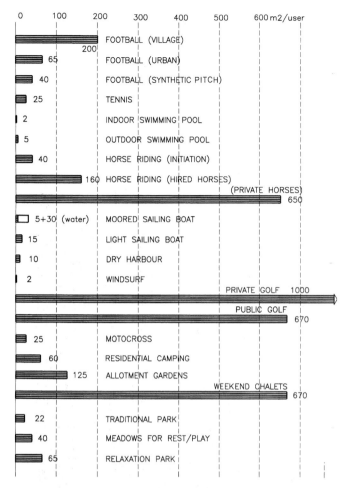

Figure 4.5 *Source: A. & M. Baud-Bovy 1987*

4.5.3 Cost requirements

The financial costs incurred in the regular practice of different sports and recreational activities can also be compared. Figure 4.6 shows the relative costs to the individuals and those normally supported by the local authorities.

Although this comparison is based on a sample, broadly similar ratios apply in many other urban areas.

Costs to participants	Examples of activities
Very expensive	Golf, horse riding, sailing, owning a weekend residence
Relatively expensive	Football in towns, indoor swimming and ice skating, residential camping
Less expensive	Tennis, football in villages, light sailing*, windsurfing*, allotments
Least expensive	Outdoor swimming, picnicking, walking, hiking

Costs supported by local authorities

Very high costs	Indoor sport and swimming, football in towns, boat moorings
High costs	Football in villages, allotments, open air swimming, dry harbours
Low costs	Tennis, light sailing and windsurfing*, horse riding**, urban and suburban public parks, walking and hiking (e.g. in forests)
*	depending on location
**	if not subsidized, (as usual)

Walking, hiking, picnicking, informal rest and recreation in natural surroundings, which are almost free for the user, are also amongst the cheapest activities for the local authority.

This type of analysis involves a detailed examination of the costs incurred by the local authority (amortization, maintenance, employees, energy and utilities, land values) compared with revenues (numbers of users, income streams). It is important, for planning purposes, to consider both the likely number of users and the relative costs before deciding investments in recreation and sports. Community policies based on analyses of this type, and taking into account the elasticity of the demand and the possible substitution of activities (see 8.2.2), will provide the population with convenient recreation and sports activities at a minimum cost.

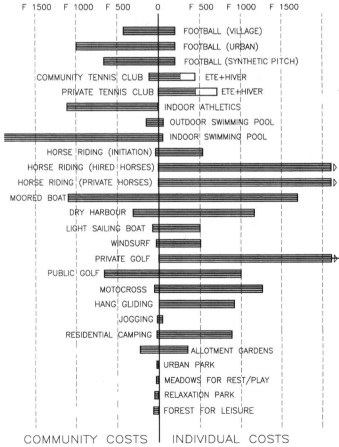

Figure 4.6 *Source: A. & M. Baud-Bovy 1987, p. 115*

5 Programmes for resorts and recreation complexes

Palace of the Lost City

Palace of the Lost City, Sun City, South Africa

The Sun City theme resort created in the dry bush of South Africa extends over 200 ha (500 acres) of planted jungle and water parks and is planned for an eventual 3000 hotel rooms and golf courses totalling 36 holes. In addition to artificial rivers, water flumes and a centre for children, a large lake with sand beach has been created in which surges form waves 2.5 m high for surfing.

A major feature of the resort, the five-star Palace of the Lost City, was conceived and built in 28 months at a cost of $300 million. Completed in 1992, the hotel has 328 rooms and 21 suites, plus extensive public and convention facilities in 35 300 m² (380 000 sq ft). Based on a fictional legend of 'archaeological discovery' it is built on a grand scale, featuring larger than life stone carvings interpreting African themes, vast halls and exotic interiors in a site of 20 ha (50 acres) of created jungle and water features. The Palace and neighbouring theme park have created nearly 1500 jobs.

Architects: Wimberly Allison Tong & Goo, for Sun International Ltd.
Associate architects: MV3 Architects

5.1 MAIN CATEGORIES OF TOURIST RESORTS AND RECREATION COMPLEXES

This section provides the standards required for planning specific types of resorts and recreational complexes. Chapter 6 deals with the planning methodology and procedures.

5.1.1 Main categories

The graph in section 1.1.4 illustrates how recreation facilities are affected – and largely determined – by the demand stemming from a metropolis, town or other densely populated area. As a rule, the nearest recreational sites are subject to the highest density of use but there are exceptions, for example where an attraction or theme park draws visitors from a wide catchment population.

Tourist resorts, recreation complexes and parks may be broadly classified as shown in Fig. 5.2.

Planning provisions for urban facilities are presented in Chapter 6. Requirements for a range of resorts and other recreational areas are detailed in this chapter.

5.1.2 Average specific densities

The figures summarized in the following tables are based on average requirements of land and built space and are intended as a guide in preliminary evaluation.

- **Accommodation**: the gross built areas per bed mentioned in Chapter 2 may be summarized as follows:

Traditional resort hotels	15–30 m^2
Hotels integrated in a resort	11–25 m^2
Hotels garnis and boarding houses	8–10 m^2
Motels	23–28 m^2
Hostels	11–13 m^2
Social holiday villages	5–11 m^2
Commercial holiday villages	13–21 m^2
Apartments and chalets in mountain areas	7–17 m^2
Apartments and bungalows at seaside areas	11–21 m^2
Employees in apartments	10 m^2
Employees in dormitories	5 m^2

- **Facilities other than accommodation**: as a summary of the details in Chapters 3 and 4, gross built areas for these facilities are as follows:

Total built area per bed

Facility	Seaside and countryside Built area in m^2	Mountain resorts Built area in m^2
Recreational and cultural	0.1	0.2–0.3
Basic sports (indoor)	0.2	0.4–0.5
Centralized services	0.3	0.3
Administration, technical	0.2	0.3
Total built area per bed	1.5	2.0

- **Roads, parking areas, pedestrian ways and squares**: the surfaced areas necessary for circulation within the resort vary with its density, average floor space index and overall

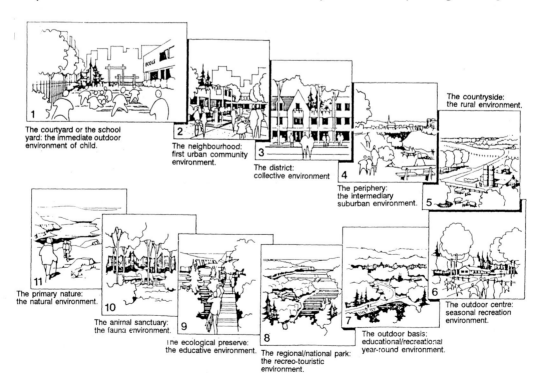

Figure 5.1 *A hierarchy of outdoor recreation spaces. Source: J-C. Jay-Rayon & J. Coquereau, Quebec*

Figure 5.2

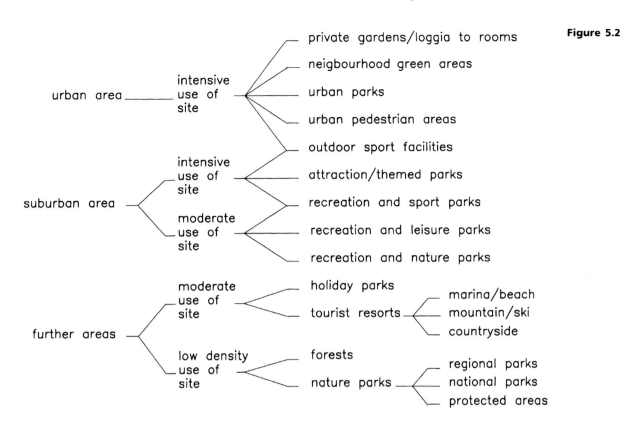

size (higher in larger resorts). Variations in requirements may be very wide. An evaluation of the area used for traffic has been provided in section 3.2.2:

Percentages of total resort area for roads and parking: with limited access and roads: 5–10 per cent; urbanized high density resorts 20–25 per cent

Examples of density for several categories of resorts

Calculation per bed and per ha	Seaside resort			Mountain resort		
	Individual properties (1)	Closely grouped (2)	Dense buildings (3)	Individual properties (1)	Closely grouped (2)	Dense buildings (3)
Built area per bed (in m²)	18+2=20	16+2=18	15+2=17	16+2=18	12+2=14	12+2=14
Floor space index	0.2	0.4	1.2 & .4	0.2	0.4	1.2
Site area for buildings (m²)	100	45	12+5=17	90	35	12
Area for beaches or ski pistes (m²)	20	20	15	15	10	10
Area for other outdoor sports (m²)	10	10	10	5	5	5
Squares, parks, green areas	20	20	20	15	10	10
(A) Area per bed (in m²)	150	95	62	130	70	47
Roads and parking: as percentage of total area (%)	10	10	20	15	20	25
Corresponding area in m²/ha	1000	1000	2000	1500	2000	2500
(B) Area apart from roads and parking (m²/ha)	9000	9000	8000	8500	8000	7500
Density in beds/ha – (B):(A)	~60	~85	~130	~65	~115	~160

(1) low rise, spread-out villas, chalets, houses
(2) low rise in rows or clusters
(3) concentrated 4–storey buildings

Based on such examples and on evaluations of density in existing resorts, average densities are presented in the graph in Fig. 5.3.

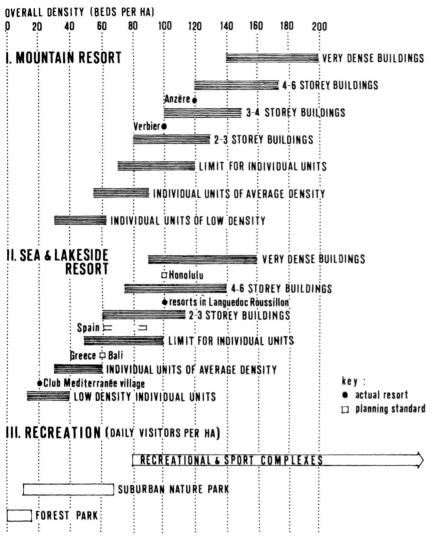

Figure 5.3 *Average overall densities in resorts related to the various types of structure used for accommodating guests**

*The corresponding net densities in the accommodation areas are much higher than the overall densities indicated in this table.

• **Public open green spaces**: in addition to the 'open areas' integral to the resort or recreation complex (beach area, ski trails, golf courses, etc.), additional public areas for tree planting and open recreational space depend on the standard of the resort:

winter resort: 5–15 m² per bed (to be increased if important summer season)
seaside and countryside resort   20–40 m² per bed

Note: these figures may be reduced if extensive open areas around the resort are irreversibly protected and classified as non-aedificandi areas open to the residents of the resort (as may be provided by a local zone plan).

5.1.3 Average overall densities

Overall densities in resorts may be evaluated on the basis of the previous figures. They range from 20 to 200 beds/ha, depending in particular on the type of accommodation used and the standard of the resort (see table on p. 65).

5.2 BEACH RESORTS AND MARINAS

The requirements for beach resorts and marinas outlined in this chapter apply to all types of resorts where the interest is centred on water, such as seaside resorts, lakeside resorts and resorts along major rivers and estuaries. Other water-based facilities used for community recreation (natural bathing places, fishing, angling, rowing, etc.) are dealt with in 4.4.

Hyundai Hotel   Concorde Hotel   Chosun Hotel   Amenity Centre and multipurpose hall

Hobanjang Restaurant   Hilton Hotel

Pomun Lake Resort, Korea

Pomun Resort is located near the city of Kyongju, ancient capital of the Shilla Kingdom, in a region with a rich cultural heritage (tombs, temples, religious grottoes, museums, etc.). Pomun Resort was planned from scratch in 1972, with the participation of the World Bank. Unlike most recent European resorts, developed with a low percentage of hotel rooms, Pomun Resort's accommodation is exclusively provided in hotels and condominiums.

The resort occupies about 1000 ha and provides (according to 1996 figures) 3000 hotel rooms (for both international and domestic tourists) in units of 50 to 450 rooms; the large hotels offer convention halls for up to 1000–2000 people. Other facilities: an amenity core in traditional architecture (handicraft and shops, restaurant, aquarium, theatre, 900-seat multi-purpose hall, etc.), golf courses (giving a total of 72 holes!), sports fields, fun park, etc. Being planned in 1996: a Shilla Folklore Village showing, on 165 ha, life during the Shilla Era, and a large amusement building with casino, games rooms and theatre restaurant.

Port Grimaud, St Tropez, France

As three-fifths of the total area is water, each of the 900 flats and houses has a berth. Cars are forbidden on the quays. The architect, Francis Spoerry, has created an instant eighteenth-century environment on reclaimed marshland.

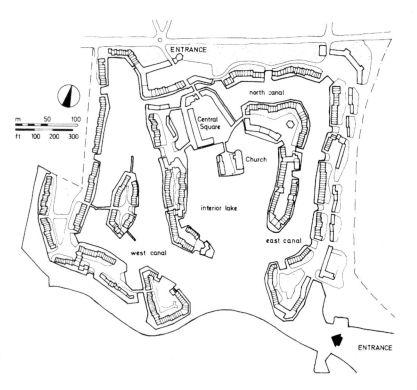

Port Grimaud, St Tropez, France: Plan of Stage 1

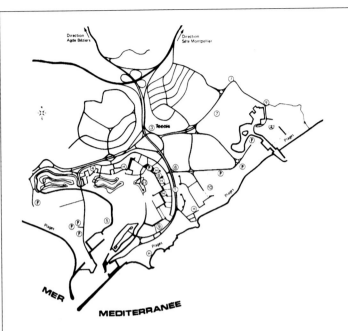

Key

1 Administration
2 Nautical village
3 Tennis club (21 courts)
4 Riding centre
5 Marine zoo
6 Cinema
7 Holiday village
8 Harbour master
9 Harbour services
10 Camping
H Buildings and hotel
P Parking

Cap D'Agde, France

About 30 000 beds were planned in this resort, partly housed in collective apartments which have been constructed in the character of a small traditional town, partly in holiday villages, campsites and individual houses. A major naturist village has its own beach and port. In total there are nine separate ports around a natural inlet from the sea extending over 80 ha (200 acres) with a capacity of 2000 moored boats and 1500 sailing dinghies.

To create a characteristic local architecture, regulations require:

- *a tiled roof (25 per cent gradient) or, alternatively, a flat roof covered with terracotta tiles;*
- *selected colours for the exterior walls;*
- *selected materials (including local basalt) for pedestrian streets and squares.*

The main pedestrian street, parallel to the quays, 1 km in length, links the main services, cultural and recreational facilities and commercial centres. The roads used by cars are distinct from the pedestrian ways but allow vehicles to reach every place in the resort (beach, port commercial areas, etc). provision is made for 1.5 parking places per apartment.

In addition to sailing, the accent is placed on tennis, with over 40 courts — several of which are covered.

Architect / Town Planner: Jean le Couteur

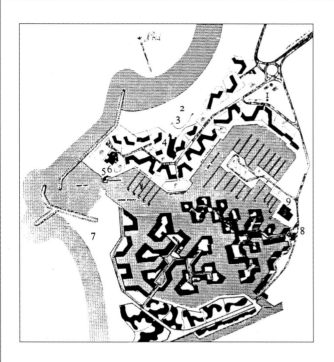

Key
1 Tennis playing fields, club
2 Children's club
3 Beach facilities
4 Commercial centre
5 Harbour Master
6 Mediterranean Yachting Centre
7 Hotel zone
8 Commercial centre
9 Harbour service

Port Camargue, France

Situated on the edge of the Camargue marsh delta this resort was part of the regional development of the Languedoc–Roussillon coast. Construction began in 1970, on an initial programme of 12 000 beds occupying a land area of 120 ha (300 acres). The plan allowed for a high proportion of low-rise marina apartments with private moorings and three-storey condominiums. The first phase 1970–7 provided some 6000 beds, 21 per cent being in apartments and villas, 21 per cent in holiday villages, 14 per cent in hotels and 44 per cent in camping/caravan sites. Subsequent development has produced a shift in the balance of accommodation and, in 1997, the resort provided:

Type	Apartments/rooms	Beds	Percentage
Second homes	19 000	76 000	72.4
Hotels	424	1046	1.0
Tourist residences	1015	4199	4.0
Social holiday villages		750	0.7
Joint enterprises		1591	1.5
Camping/caravan sites	6691	21 432	20.4

Harbour facilities were planned for 2500 boats (1000 quay-side berths in first phase) with extensive services, including the Mediterranean Yachting Centre which offers training courses.

Chief architect: Jean M. Balladur

Key

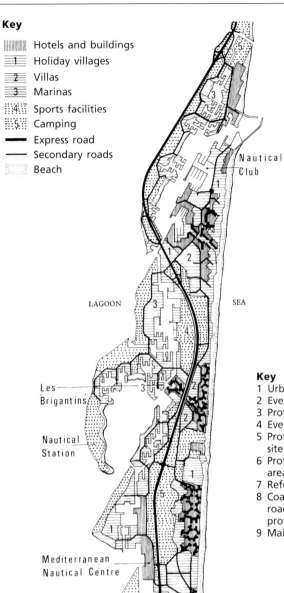

▦	Hotels and buildings
1	Holiday villages
2	Villas
3	Marinas
4	Sports facilities
5	Camping
▬	Express road
—	Secondary roads
⠿	Beach

Nautical Club

LAGOON   SEA

Les Brigantins

Nautical Station

Mediterranean Nautical Centre

Key
1 Urban Masterplan
2 Eventual extension
3 Protected village
4 Eventual evolution
5 Protected natural site
6 Protected tourist area
7 Reforestation area
8 Coastal express road (with protection)
9 Main highway

Port Leucate-Barcarès, France

The largest of the resorts planned in Languedoc-Roussillon, Port Leucate-Barcarès occupies a flat stretch of land between the sea and a large lagoon of 4000 ha (10 000 acres) The resort extends along about 10 km (6.2 miles) of beach and is planned to provide about 90 000 beds in a built area of 75 ha (185 acres).

Port Leucate and Port Barcarès form two distinct centres surrounded by protected areas.

Accommodation is widely diversified and includes:

* *marinas with individual moorings in front of each house;*
* *small condominium buildings of three or four storeys,*
* *units of eight apartments (each with a patio or terrace) on two levels;*
* *several social holiday villages;*
* *camp sites and other units.*

The image projected by the resort is not distinctive but reflects the use of modest, economic, unpretentious architecture adapted to the prevailing climate. Among the main attractions are:

* *Port Leucate for large yachts;*
* *Port Barcarès for smaller pleasure boats and fishing boats;*
* *the Mediterranean Nautical Centre;*
* *the ship Lydia, berthed on the beach, which includes a nightclub, swimming pool and casino.*

Town Planner: G. Candilis

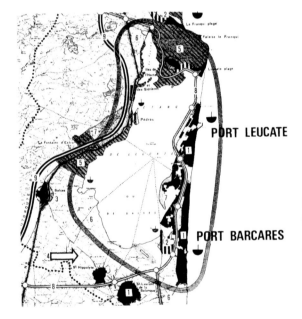

PORT LEUCATE

PORT BARCARES

5.2.1 Beach development

Beach surveys. Surveys are not limited to the beach but must extend over the adjacent sea and coastal areas and the countryside around the planned resort area. The data must include an analysis of previous readings and trends over the short-term and long-term in order to assess seasonal changes, wind and tidal effects, and extreme conditions liable to be experienced. Particular aspects which should be considered in relation to the recreational development of the area include:

- *Sea*

  Climatic conditions affecting recreational use (air temperatures, winds, sunshine)
  Water temperatures (including variations)
  Tides (reaches, effects, deposits)
  Currents (local or littoral)
  Waves (direction, strength, periodicity, seasonality)
  Ecology (seaweed, fish and shellfish varieties, etc.)
  Clarity of water (nature of seabed)
  Pollution (native vegetation, river silt, hydrocarbon, sewage, etc.)
  Possible attractions (islands, coral, fauna for underwater diving)
  Suitability for recreational use (fishing, sailing, surfing, water skiing)

- *Strand*

  Material and stability
  Gradient and regularity of slope
  Distance to which bathers may walk in the water
  Risks of danger from tidal movements

- *Beach*

  Material (texture, colour, purity, absence of silt, etc.)
  Stability (erosion through wind, sea, currents, disturbance)
  Depth and length (extent, rights of use, public access)
  Risks of sand/gravel extraction as building material

- *Back beach*

  Area available (width, depth, set-back and conditions for use)
  Views to sea and inland (risk of future obstructions)
  Geomorphology (cliffs, dunes, flat land, marsh, etc.)
  Vegetation and microclimate (winds, temperature, humidity, etc.)
  Protection against degradation (conservation, planting, screening)
  Access (location of roads, control, conditions, difficulties)
  Scope for improvement (drainage, excavation and filling)
  Phased development (optimum zoning and locations)

- *Coastal stretch*

  Beach environment (up to a depth of between 1 and 5 km)

- *Countryside*

  Natural attractions and features (countryside around and scope for excursions and extended interests)
  Existing development or proposals (detrimental or complementary)
  Infrastructures (availability, reliability, conditions, future plans)

Beach protection. Many beaches are in a state of fragile balance under the combined actions of winds and currents. An apparently insignificant change (a small breakwater or a building near the shore) may have serious consequences hundreds of metres away. The same applies to the coastal dunes: with the destruction of their cover of vegetation sand may be blown inland, over roads and properties, and be quite difficult to control. Hence, extreme care is required, leaving beach and back beach as untouched as possible, and making in-depth studies and tests before intervening.

Beach capacities. Maximum theoretical standards for the density of use of beaches have been defined in a number of countries and optimum standards have been used to determine the desirable number of tourists for sustainability (Albania). Such standards may be related to the beach area (persons per acre or hectare, m² per person) or to its extent along the seafront (per mile, kilometre or metre). In addition to the tourists, consideration must be given to the numbers of residents in the resort (40 to 70 per cent of whom may be on the beach simultaneously), as well as non-residents coming from neighbouring areas, whose numbers will tend to increase as the facilities improve. The following table gives typical densities or capacities and is based on averages. Actual distributions often show wide variations, with beach users tending to cluster around entry points and key attractions.

The depth considered for the beach may be more than the actual area of sand and include up to 50 m of lawns, green areas and terraces available to beach users. The widening of a narrow beach – or the transformation of a pebble beach or strand into a sandy one – may be considered: often by constructing breakwaters (parallel or at right angles to the shore to encourage natural sand deposit), with the dumping of gravel and sand. This involves precise studies (texture, currents, winds, tests on models, etc.) and may have unexpected results. It is usually much easier, cheaper and permanent to landscape the back beach with lawns and gardens, use sand deposits on firm ground, and create seawater basins on the rocks or in extended lagoons.

Typical standards for beach capacity analysis (facilities not included)

	No. of m² per person	Persons per metre of coast			Metres of coast per person			No. of sq ft. per person
		Depth of beach			Depth of beach			
		20 m	33 m	50 m	20 m	33 m	50 m	
Over-density (Rimini)	3	6.5	11.0	16.5	0.15	0.10	0.05	35
Public beach near town	5	4.0	6.5	10.0	0.25	0.15	0.10	55
Public beach (average)	8	2.5	4.0	6.0	0.40	0.25	0.15	85
Resort (low standard)	10	2.0	3.5	5.0	0.50	0.30	0.20	110
Resort (medium standard)	15	1.5	2.0	3.5	0.65	0.50	0.30	160
Public beach (high standard)	20	1.0	1.5	2.5	1.0	0.65	0.40	215
Resort (comfort)	20	1.0	1.5	2.5	1.0	0.65	0.40	215
Resort (de luxe)	30	0.7	1.0	1.5	1.5	1.0	0.65	320

Notes: Median beach depths taken. Usage constantly changes and the figures have been rounded.

Resorts with an image of 'solitude' located in remote areas should adopt the density of a de luxe development.

Quality standards for European beaches and marinas

The Blue Flag Campaign, operated by the Foundation for Environmental Education in Europe (FEEE), lays down standards for:
Beaches: *water quality; control of industrial, oil and human waste pollution and litter; regular cleaning; environmental plans for the coastal area; public toilets, drinking water, telephones; safe access, lifeguards, safety equipment; access for disabled; maintenance; management, control and information.*
Marinas: *clean water and surroundings; control of pollution and litter; facilities for disposal of waste, oil, tank sewage and bilge water; sanitary and washing facilities, drinking water; public lighting and power; life saving, fire fighting and other safety provisions; management and information.*
Water quality criteria are also stipulated under Bathing Water Directive 76/160/EEC

FEEE, Copenhagen

5.2.2 Public beach facilities

As a rule, no building on the beach should be allowed, only portable items such as parasols, sunshades and screens. All sanitary accommodation, changing rooms, cafes and other facilities should be located at the back of the beach within a defined zone and, preferably, built under lease or licence and designed to harmonize with the character and desired image for the area. The redevelopment of many resort areas is often frustrated by the difficulties of removing added, and often garish, eyesores from the seafront or lakeside.

The extent of development required for beaches open to the public varies widely: those adjacent to or near urban areas are often well equipped for concentrated use; others may have minimal facilities with strict control to retain their natural surroundings (see 4.4.1: Natural bathing places).

Developed public beaches should have lifeguard facilities, floating platforms and chains – where required for safety – one or more security/lifeguard posts and a first aid centre. Sports and play areas (for volleyball, table tennis, badminton and informal play) could be provided and a supervised protected area for children with a children's pool and playgrounds. Depending on conditions, there may be provision for sheltered moorings and hiring facilities for boats, windsurf boards, pedalos, surfboards and other equipment, removable kiosks for refreshments, often a snack bar and sometimes a restaurant.

Sanitary facilities are based on the ratios of five WCs and washbasins, plus four showers per 500 people together with one changing cubicle or cabin per 10 to 20 bathers – the first figure for highly concentrated use. Clothes storage is usually in baskets kept in individual lockers or attendant-operated cloakrooms. There is, however, a trend for people to come to the beach (or the open air swimming pool) with their swimsuits on and fewer cabins to be used. The numbers of employees and entrepreneurs may be estimated at one-tenth of the total numbers of beach users, 75 per cent working on a seasonal basis.

Parking places for vehicles should not be more than 150 to 200 m from the water's edge (except in the case of large para-urban public beaches) and must be sited and landscaped to minimize visual intrusion. In rural areas, picnic sites may be provided nearby. Special provision needs to be made for the disabled and elderly, together with suitable access and footpaths to viewing points overlooking the beach – which may also be linked to coastal walks.

More developed beaches are usually bounded by promenades – sometimes incorporating sea defences – with shelters and other facilities. Often the land adjacent to the beach is landscaped with gardens, green areas and trees to provide an attractive frontage and interconnected recreational area. In urban surroundings, a built swimming pool may be provided near the beach to provide an alternative to sea or lake bathing with a vista of the surroundings.

5.2.3 Beach in an integrated resort

In an integrated resort, many of the sports and some of the recreational facilities listed in sections 4.2 and 4.3 may be advantageously grouped near the beach. The main open air swimming pool (free form, landscaped) is often centrally located in the back beach area as a focus of interest and animation, with a children's pool and play area separated but within sight. Terraced restaurants and open-air buffets may be arranged to benefit from the pool view and, in a limited site, the pool may be extended or located inland with tourism accommodation grouped around the landscaped surrounds.

On the sea front, active sports, such as yachting, water skiing and skin diving, can be deliberately used to provide spectator interest but buildings (equipment, storage, facilities) should be located to one side of the prime beach frontage.

Whilst grouping together compatible activities, the master plan for a beach resort must also provide for the separation of others having different interests and needs. This is best achieved by locating (zoning) and designing areas in a way which will instil appropriate 'atmosphere'.

For quiet relaxation, guest-room accommodation should be sited away from the public activities in landscaped gardens, with shaded seated areas, small-scale buildings, in contact with the natural environment or isolated stretches of beach. For lively participation an opposite approach would be adopted. Aspects of zoning are covered in 6.4.5 and 6.4.7.

5.2.4 Facilities for yachting: types of havens

This subject is a specialized study and reference may be made to other publications (Adie 1984) for further details. The following outline summarizes the main details which must be taken into account in planning resort facilities.

Three main categories of sailing resources can usually be distinguished:

- inland areas of water (lakes, reservoirs, river and canal waterways);
- 'yachting stations' for light sailing (naturally protected from deep waves but with suitable exposure to winds);
- 'cruising basins': denticulated coasts of about 60 to 100 km (40 to 60 miles) offering havens at regular intervals (ranging from emergency shelters with no facilities to fully equipped ports).

Taking into account the heavy investment costs, a harbour will only be considered after a detailed feasibility study and the preparation of a regional plan for tourism and recreation development. The latter must include details of the various categories of boats to be accommodated and an assessment of the physical opportunities for harbour provision at reasonable cost. Various types of havens may be involved.

Type	Provision
Emergency haven	Storm protection, navigation aids, minimum moorage facilities.
Convenience harbour	Stopover place with limited moorage facilities; usually at or near a town or village for supplies.
Moorage harbour	For non-residents to moor their boats: may be feasible if the natural configuration (well protected and easily accessible basin) allows low investment costs.
Pleasure harbour (or marina)	The focal point of a resort or recreational residential complex.
Harbour resorts	Where each individual property opens onto a private quay (as in Port Grimaud).
Yachting centres (or 'dry harbours')	For sailing and motor boats which can be stored ashore (see 5.2.7).

According to local situations (type of harbour and coast, strand gradient, costs of land, breakwaters, retaining walls or dredging, legislation, etc.) ports may be located on the water, inland or in intermediate positions (see Figure 5.4).

Figure 5.4

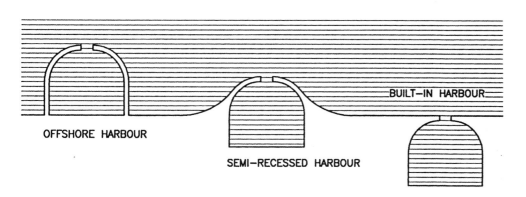

5.2.5 Basic facilities for harbours

Main elements of a moorage harbour:

- *protection:* natural or by breakwaters, groynes, levees, etc. to reduce wave and wind effects;
- *locked basin:* where the water level is trapped whatever the level of the tide – essential where the rise and fall exceeds 3 m (10 ft) at average tide or where the number of berths is greater than 500;
- *basin flushing:* by protected channel for tide or flow flushing. In enclosed basins mechanical aeration may be required to maintain balance;
- *navigation aids:* buoys, markers, lights, etc.;
- *moorage:* on fixed or floating (sometimes covered) piers;
- *hardstanding area:* between quays, boat store, trailer park, boat handling equipment and boat collection bay;
- *on-land boat parking:* for light drop-keel sailing or motor boats, on trailers, legs, or cradles;
- *launching ramp:* not steeper than 12 per cent grade, located near harbour entry for light sailing boats (avoiding navigation without motor in the harbour) or nearer in for outboard powered boats (up to 10 m length) on trailers;
- *derrick or crane lift;*
- *marine service station* and fuel storage;
- *stores and repairs,* boat washing areas and covered dry boat storage;
- *administration:* including harbour master and customs (typically 200 to 400 m²);
- *car park and trailer park;*
- *clubhouse:* with bar-lounge, dining room, toilets and showers, place for viewing races and regattas;
- *marine store, shops, sales office:* depending on scale and feasibility, food provisions, chandlery, sports and fishing gear, etc. Usually located near entrance.

The last two are generally introduced at a later stage in a development. As a first estimate the necessary land area (for car/trailers parking, technical and commercial services) is at least equal to the area of water.

5.2.6 Planning standards for medium-sized pleasure harbours

For profitability reasons, the minimum size of a pleasure harbour should, generally, cater for between 150 to 250 boats. It may extend to a thousand or more. The following standards may be applied, as first estimates:

- *Density:* the harbour should hold 75 to 100 boats per ha of water (30 to 40 boats/acre), plus an equivalent space for car and light boat parking.

- The *distance between piers* from axis to axis, should be 4 to 4.5 times the length of boats.
- The *place per boat* along the pier should be from 2.5 to 5 m, the average being 3.5 m (12 ft). A greater length is required if finger piers are provided, boats of Class I (the most numerous) requiring up to 5.0 m and those of Class II from 5 to 8 m.
- The *orientation of the piers* should be at right angles to the prevailing winds (the boats lying parallel with the winds).
- The *depth of the main basin channel* should be a minimum of 4.6 m (15 ft) and for berths from 2.3 to 3.7 m (8 to 12 ft).
- *Moorings* should be connected to water supply, electricity and even drainage services if possible and this is essential for larger boats.
- There should be *separate areas* for sailing boats, (with wider moorings for catamarans and other broad-beamed multi-hulls), power boats and – if required – fishing boats. Moorings for visiting boats should be located near the entry to the harbour.
- *Car parking* places should normally be provided at the ratio of 0.5 places per boat berth but increased where local usage is high (up to two places in US recreational marinas).
- A *trailer park* should be provided near the slipway plus some larger spaces for cars with trailers.

In pleasure harbours – and much more so in harbour resorts – the planning of the port has to take into consideration its function as a centre of activity and visual attraction. Prime locations around the water are allocated to public quays, coffee shops, restaurants and tourist accommodation. The technical services are limited in number and located in less conspicuous areas.

Harbour construction, particularly in tidal waters, involves heavy investment and maintenance and is not always feasible despite – in many areas – state assistance and good management. Feasibility is more likely in places where there is an assured market demand for mooring facilities and if complementary products – such as boat and equipment selling, maintenance and repairs – are added to the boat parking function. In other situations, pleasure harbours may be created out of disused commercial docks providing a recreational attraction and enhancing the value of the surroundings.

5.2.7 Yachting centres or 'dry harbours'

The yachting centre offers an alternative solution where the main need is for sport and recreational activities. It caters only for those sailing or motor boats which may be stored ashore, in particular outboard powered or drop-keel sailing boats, transported on trailers. Boats of this category often represent 80 per cent of the total number. Hoists may be provided to assist in taking larger, even keeled boats up to 10 m out of the water and placing them on trailers or storage cradles.

St Peter's Riverside before marina development

Tyne and Wear redevelopment, UK

Following changes in shipping requirements and decline of the traditional heavy industries in the area, extensive regeneration projects have been undertaken by the Tyne and Wear Development Corporation (TWDC) including:

St Peter's Riverside, *at the mouth of the River Wear, covers 90 ha and includes a new 300-berth marina, slipway and riverside promenades with a total investment of £150 million.*

Royal Quays, *North Shields is a mixed-use regeneration project extending over 80 ha of land on the north bank of the Tyne, at a cost of £245 million. The area forms an amphitheatre around a historic dock forming a lively harbour (9 ha) for fishing boats and a 200-berth marina. A new 5 ha linear park and greenways for pedestrians and cyclists extend through the centre with a subway link to an existing park which has been redeveloped.*

Tyne and Wear Development Corporation, 1996

St Peter's Riverside after marina development

La Grande-Motte, France

The most controversial of the resorts built along the Languedoc-Roussillon coast, with buildings of dominant architectural form, adapted to sun and wind, rising out of a flat landscape. A total of 43 000 beds was planned in the resort area of 1000 ha (2500 acres) of which 200 ha are lakes and 100 ha pine forests. Sixty-five per cent of the accommodation was intended to be in condominium apartments, 9 per cent in hotels and rooms for rent and 17 per cent in camp sites

and social villages. Construction commenced in 1967 and more than half of the proposed buildings had been completed by 1977.

The harbour provides about 1000 fully equipped berths and there are extensive boat servicing and repair yards. La Grande-Motte has a well-developed shopping area, night clubs, restaurants, sports grounds and land-based recreation areas.

Chief architect: Jean Balladur

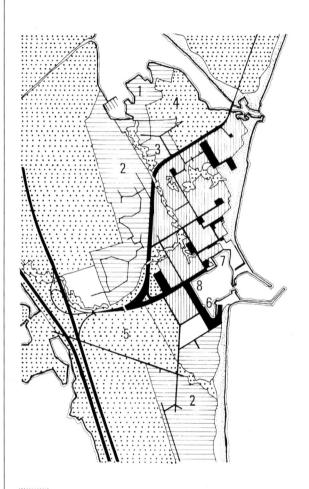

	Apartments
1	Holiday villages
2	Villas
3	Riding centre
4	Sports facilities
5	Camping
	Sea/Lagoon
	Beach
━━	Main road
—	Secondary roads

6 Light industry

7 Port services

8 Harbour facilities
For visitors and
residents

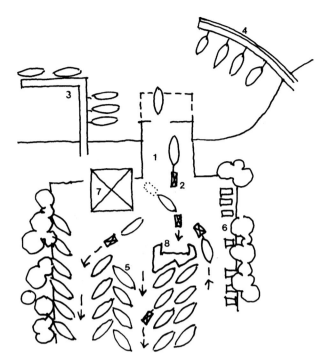

Key
1 Slipway
2 Tractor (boat on trailer)
3 Courtesy dock
4 Small breakwater (if necessary)
5 Boat parking
6 Car parking
7 Office
8 Back up area (not necessary if forklift instead of tractor)

Figure 5.5 *Main elements of a dry harbour*

The main requirements are:

- *Boat parking area* for boats staying on their trailers or on cradles. This should be concreted or paved and landscaped to separate it from the car parking area. An average space of at least 6 × 3 m (20 × 10 ft) per boat should be allowed, increasing to 9 × 3.6 m for boats other than sailing dinghies and 15 × 3.6 m for a boat plus car.
- *Launching ramp* of concrete, 4 m (one lane) to 32 m wide, calculated on the basis of one launching lane per 40 to 60 boats. Ramps should have a gradient of 8 to 10 per cent for hand launching and 12 to 15 per cent for launching with a car. A courtesy dock is also required.
- *Calm water* in the launching areas is necessary and may require the construction of a breakwater – which can also offer moorings for a limited number of heavier boats (including those required for control and safety in the centre). Otherwise the moored boats may be secured to chains, piles or submerged blocks.
- *Indoor storage of boats* is an optional provision and requires a large shed with stacking trucks. An internal space of 6 to 7 m^2 per small boat, when stacked on three levels, should be allowed.

A yachting centre should not be larger than 500 boats occupying some 2 to 5 ha (5 to 12 acres) of ground. An area of 150 to 200 m^2 should be allowed for services, equipment racks and sanitary facilities. In resorts where many holidaymakers have their own boats (usually nationals) or hire craft, a standard of one boat per ten beds is usual, i.e. 100 boats for a 1000-bed resort.

In other cases, provision may be made for a *yachting school* in which instruction can be offered as an attraction to tourists and local residents. A school typically consists of 250 to 600 m^2 of buildings accommodating classrooms, stores, and services together with a calm-water training area and other facilities. This would be appropriate for a larger resort of 7000 beds or more. In smaller resorts (2000 to 4000 beds) opportunities for sailing and instruction may be provided as part of the beach facilities, with one or two instructors, a few light sailing boats which can be pulled out onto the beach and one or more motor boats for water-skiing.

5.3 MOUNTAIN RESORTS

Most of the recently developed mountain resorts are in fact ski resorts, the high-altitude summer resorts in hot countries being more comparable to countryside resorts (see 5.4). The term mountain resort is preferred to ski or winter resort because it does not minimize the importance of the summer season.

5.3.1 Categories of skiers

Skiers may be classified into three categories, each having specific skills and capacities and requiring appropriate facilities; a good resort provides trails for all categories (including trails for nordic skiing).

Average standards for skiers by categories

		Begin-ners	Inter-mediate	Advanced
Vertical drop	m	100–300	500–800	over 800
skied per hour*	(ft)	350–1000	1600–2600	over 2600
Vertical drop	m	500–1000	2500–3500	5000–8000
skied per day	ft	1600–3200	8000–11500	16500–26000
Average trail	%	10	25	35
gradient	degree	6°	15°	20°

*Including time to go up again

Due to rapid improvements in equipment and materials, skiers rapidly progress from one category to the next. In some places specific ski-surfing areas – which is an increasingly popular sport, but liable to cause hazard to other skiers – have been introduced. Acrobatic skiing requires short steep pistes.

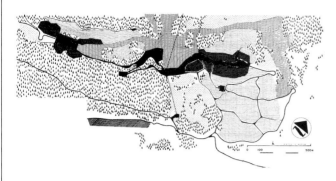

Zoning: decreasing density of shading represents reducing density of development. Other zones are reserved for sports and ski trails, forest, parking, and areas non-aedificandi

Anzere ski resort, Switzerland

This resort was planned for a total of 7500 beds, 3500 being built in the first phase to 1977. In 1997, 50 per cent of the beds were in private apartments, 40 per cent in apartments available for rent, and less than 10 per cent of the beds in hotels. The resident population was only 450 (equivalent to 12 per cent of bed spaces – excluding those in private use).

The main resort is characterized by large chalet-type condominiums built around a square, with shops and recreational facilities located in the basements linked by pedestrian arcades.

Public facilities include:

* indoor swimming pool with sauna; outdoor heated swimming pool
* ice skating and curling rinks
* tennis courts
* trails for skiing and ski bobs
* hotels, restaurants/cafes, bars and shops
* underground garages.

Town Planners: J. Hentsch and ACAU
Architects: J. Hentsch, J. F. Empeyta, C. Tobler

Site plan: main resort

Plan of circulation and car parking

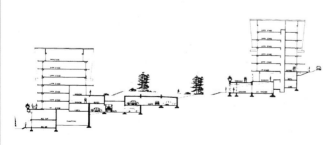

Section through the main square

Avoriaz ski resort, France

Development of Avoriaz has extended in phases from 780 beds (1967), to 6040 (1975) and to the planned capacity of 16 000 beds (1997). Concentrated on the southern slopes of a plateau with the buildings surmounting steep rocky cliffs, the unique designs reflect the rugged character of the surroundings. Visitors may arrive by teleferic from the valley below or by a rear road with car parking at the entrance. Trails through the resort, together with chair lifts, allow the skiers to go everywhere in the resort on their skis. A system of roads is used by horse drawn sledges in winter and carriages in the summer. Indoor streets, linked by lifts, are used by pedestrians.

Following the initial development of the village 'Les Dromonts', later phases have extended up the slopes to form other villages and across to the village 'La Falaise' with a few changes to the original master plan. In the initial phases most of the accommodation was provided in large apartments in co-ownership, with a high proportion of duplex units. Later phases have seen a reduction in the size of units, with an increasing number of studio units and the development of multi-ownership apartments for renting.

Architects: J. Labro, J. J. Orsini, A. Wujek and others

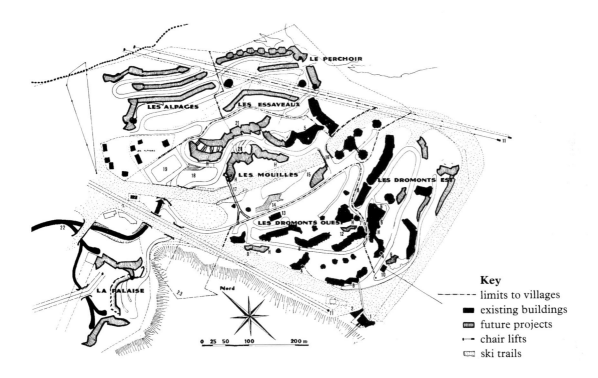

Key
- – – – limits to villages
- ■ existing buildings
- ▥ future projects
- ⊢• chair lifts
- ▨ ski trails

(photo, O. T. Avoriaz)

(photo, O. T. Avoriaz)

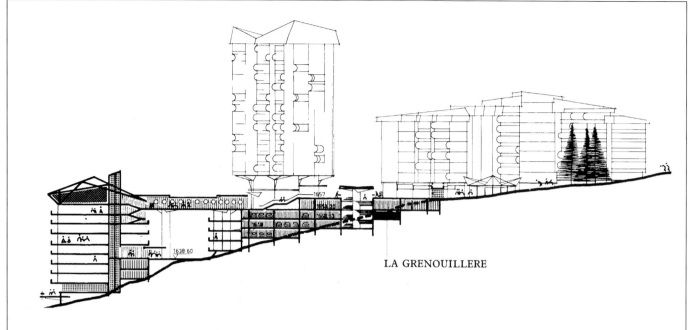

LA GRENOUILLERE

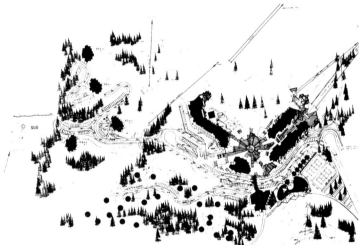

Les Orres, France

The master plan for this planned ski resort shows the skiing area and a Grenouillère (at base of pistes) surrounded by apartments and commercial buildings, with access roads and parking. Extensive provision has been made for parking: in addition to the spaces shown, garages are constructed in the basements of the buildings and a nearby outdoor parking area is provided for weekend visitors.

Developed in 1973–6, the resort had reached a total of 9520 beds by 1996.

Architect-planner: J. M. Legrand

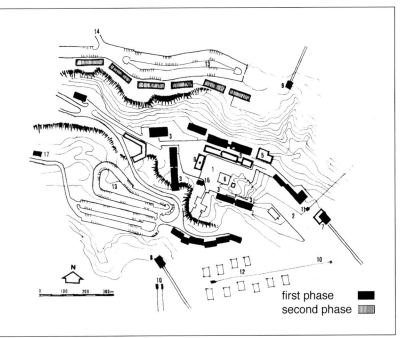

Flaine, France

Sited amongst the trees at an altitude of 1600 m (5200 ft), this ski resort was planned for development in two stages, initially for 4300 beds around a 'forum' with a later development further north along a cliff increasing the total to 9500 beds (1997), about half being in hotels or apartments to rent. The buildings in prefabricated concrete, assembled on site, are designed to take advantage of the contrasts of sun and shadows.

The facilities provide a balance of activities for both winter and summer seasons, with integrated arts and cultural interests, a convention hall and meeting rooms. Technical services are housed underground and traffic is segregated: weekend visitors leave their cars in parking areas above and away from the resort, reach the teleferics on skis and use a chair lift to return to the car park. The ski facilities are of a high standard and include provision for making artificial snow. Amongst the summer facilities are 26 tennis courts, a riding school, swimming pool and cinema.

Architect: M. Breuer

first phase
second phase

5.3.2 Ski trail characteristics

The following characteristics are typical for the European Alps, but standards vary from one country to the next:

- *Snow cover* allowing a minimum four months' season, corresponding to 1000–1200 m of altitude in Austria and 1500–1800 m (according to the orientation of slope) on the other side of the Alps. A shorter ski season may be considered for weekend use only, with light facilities (ski-lifts).
- *Average gradient* of 20 to 35 per cent, with steeper intermittent stretches up to 60 per cent for advanced skiers.
- *Orientation* of the slope preferably to the north or east (better snow, staying longer), except for beginners who prefer more sun and warmer places.
- *Convergence of trails* at a place where the lower station for the transporters can be built is important.
- *Vertical drop* sufficient for the skiers concerned; Alpine standards are:
  – 1000–1500 m for resorts of international interest
  – 500–800 m for resorts of regional interest
  – 200–500 m for resorts of local interest
  – but 80–100 m, often lit, for USA resorts of local interest (Great Lakes states).

The altitudes of resorts vary widely, as Fig. 5.6 shows.

- Traditional resorts were mainly developed from original mountain villages (1200–1550 m high)
- Recent resorts developed in the 1960s and 1970s have been planned higher on the mountain pasture grounds (1800–2000 m) with easier land control and a longer season of use but, being above the tree line, they are generally not attractive during the summer.

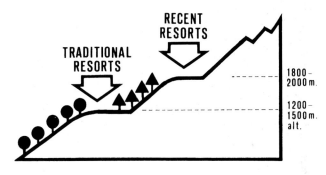

Figure 5.6

- There has been a renewed trend to develop resorts at lower altitudes, skiing at lower levels being facilitated by the use of artificial snow projected with snow guns.

Ski trails need careful planning (see 6.6.3), construction and maintenance:

- *construction* includes: opening the trails in otherwise impassable zones (forests, rocks), eliminating bottlenecks (minimum width: 30–50 m, less with slopes lower than 6 per cent, but more when the gradient increases to 50 per cent), levelling the ground;
- *maintenance* includes: compacting the snow when it is falling (with snow cats and ratracks); reducing the formation of snow bumps; producing artificial snow with 'snow guns' (generally to maintain a piste back to the resort at lower altitude, requires high consumption of water); and organizing permanent monitoring (to close trails becoming dangerous, to artificially start potential avalanches, etc.).

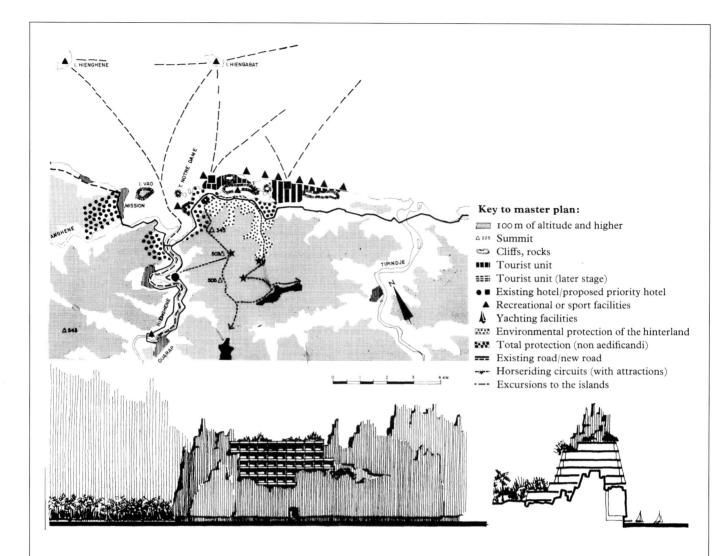

Key to master plan:

▨ 100 m of altitude and higher
△ 225 Summit
〰 Cliffs, rocks
▦ Tourist unit
▦ Tourist unit (later stage)
● ■ Existing hotel/proposed priority hotel
▲ Recreational or sport facilities
⚑ Yachting facilities
▨ Environmental protection of the hinterland
▨ Total protection (non aedificandi)
▬ Existing road/new road
⇢ Horseriding circuits (with attractions)
┄ Excursions to the islands

Regional tourism planning around a proposed resort at Hienghene, New Caledonia

The master plan (1970) illustrates some of the regional aspects of concern in planning a new resort:

* *protecting the attractions surrounding the resort;*
* *organizing circuits, excursions from the resort;*
* *extending to a larger area the benefits stemming from the activity of the resort.*

A hotel, with swimming pools, gardens, terraces on the roofs and lift access to the sea, was originally planned on some of the cliffs which characterize the site — which are now protected as a natural monument.

SCETO, ACAU and SCET-COOPERATION;
Architect-planner: M. Baud-Bovy.

The construction of ski trails can cause heavy damage to the environment, especially at high altitude (where plant regeneration is difficult) and throughout forests. For many years the trail areas may be unsightly during the summer.

The capacity of a trail corresponds to the number of skiers using it simultaneously. The capacity limit (on peak days) approaches twice the ideal capacity and corresponds to the lowest planning standards. Amongst many other methods used to determine the capacity limit, the Cumin method gives reasonably good approximations (Cumin 1966):

The average capacity of a trail is equal to its vertical drop measured in metres.

Sun Valley-Ketchum Resort, Idaho, USA

Sun Valley was the first grand destination ski resort in the USA, developed in the 1930s and served by the Union Pacific railway. It now has 78 runs on 2054 skiable acres (820 ha) over two mountains, with summits of 9150 ft (3002 m), and 17 lifts – including high-speed detachable quads – with a total capacity of over 28 000 skiers per hour (Fig. 5.22). The ski season extends over four months and the resort operates the world's largest automatic snow making system over 600 acres (240 ha) and 3400 ft (1660 m) vertical.

In addition to three new day lodges (Fig. 5.23) serving the ski runs, the immediate resort area has 740 rooms in full-service hotels, over 410 rooms in smaller hotels and lodges and extensive condominium developments. Summer programmes include trekking, paragliding, biking, horse riding, rafting, fishing, hunting, golf (two 18-hole courses), swimming and other sports as well as organized events.

Sun Valley Chamber of Commerce.

5.3.3 Cable transporters

Main types of cable transporters are listed by increasing cost of investment:

- *rope tows:* thick rope which skiers catch in their hands, for very short slopes only;
- *teleskis:* cable with disengageable hooks, T-Bars, etc., drawing skiers on snow;
- *chair-lifts:* aerial cable carrying open chairs on which skiers sit with skis on their feet (fitted with movable protection against cold and wind);
- *cabin-lifts:* aerial cable carrying a series of small cabins, the skis being fastened outside;
- *teleferics:* large cabins, one going up while the other goes down;
- *underground funiculars:* large counterbalanced cabins, guided by rails within a constructed shaft or tunnel.

In principle, teleskis and chair-lifts (usually disengageable for comfort and capacity) are preferred for small to medium vertical drops. Cabin-lifts and teleferics are installed for medium and important drops. Their use is continued for summer tourists.

Characteristics of cable transporters

Type of transporter (number of users)	Obstacles accepted	At risk from	Up Down	Speed m/sec	Capacity per/hour	Cost
Rope tows (1)	none	–	U only	1	200–300	–
Teleskis (1–2)	none	–	U only	4–5	600–800	1*
Chair lifts (2–4)	small	C/W	U (D)	2–3	600–1000	2–3
Disengageable chair-lifts (4–6)	small	W	U (D)	6–8	2000–3000	3–5
Cabin lifts (2–8)	ravines	W	U + D	6–8	1000–2000	5–10
Teleferics (50–200)	valleys	W	U + D	10–12	1000–2000	10–15
Underground funiculars	small	–	U + D	10–12	1000–2500	15–20

W = sensitivity to wind
C = sensitivity to cold
*base cost

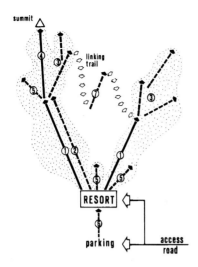

Figure 5.7

Cable transporter system

Typical arrangements are (see Fig. 5.7):

1 Basic transporter linking the resort with the main ski areas: usually cabin-lifts to carry skiers to the slopes and back.
2 Additional transporter to meet peak hourly demand (50–80 per cent of total number of skiers.
3 Light transporters in the main ski areas (for example, cheap teleskis).
4 Heavier cable transporters (ranging from chair-lifts to teleferics) to places not accessible by teleski.
5 Small teleski for beginners near the resort or accessible by cabin-lifts.
6 Large cabin-lift (or buses) linking the resort with car parking areas lower in the valley.
7 Additional light link allowing skiers to cross from one ski area to the next.

5.3.4 Other mountain resort facilities

In addition to the basic sports facilities (see 4.2):

- *Outdoor skating rink:* minimum size, 20 m × 40 m (two tennis courts), using natural ice in small resorts and ice-forming equipment in larger ones. For hockey contests a rink area up to 30 m × 60 m with spectator facilities is required and, in many resorts, this is provided as a permanent indoor attraction for year-round use.
- *Curling rinks,* according to character/clientele of resort: minimum two rinks (6 m × 45 m each).
- *Trails for nordic skiing:* 3 to 15 km (even up to 30) over slightly undulating ground; usual gradients for intermediate skiers: up to 8–10 per cent in some sections; clear width: 2.5 m (increasing to 4 m where gradient over is 10 per cent).
- *Slalom trail:* vertical drop 150–200 m, gradient is 45–50 per cent, lit.

- *Bobsleigh or toboggan runs* are exceptional features.
- *Snowmobile trails:* loop trails 25–50 km (up to 80) length; 2–3 m in width with a variety of landscapes (noisy and often damaging to the environment).

Planning standards: average sport facilities

Facilities	No. of tourist beds in thousands				
	2	4	7	12	20
Skating rink	P	20 × 40	20 × 40	30 × 60	30 × 60
Curling rinks			P	2–4	4–6
Slalom trail	P	P	R	R	R
Nordic trails	P	R	R	R	R

P = possibly required, depending on character of resort
R = required

The recreational and cultural activities are important for the long hours of *après-ski* and these facilities, together with shops and bars, are developed to a greater extent in mountain resorts than elsewhere (see 4.1.1).

The summer season is essential for the feasibility of a mountain resort and care for the surrounding landscape is of utmost importance. Large swimming pools, tennis courts and facilities for riding are important features (see 4.2). Special mountain activities usually include: organized excursions (hiking and climbing), golfing, flora and fauna studies, river rafting, paragliding, orienteering, mountain biking (see 4.3.3) and summer skiing on the glaciers.

5.3.5 Principles in planning a ski resort

Any study of a ski resort will be preceded by an analysis of the surrounding region. The methodology for regional planning is outlined in Chapter 6, while particular details which relate to skiing are summarized below. When surveying resources, special attention should be given to:

- *The skiable area,* taking account of the snow cover and geomorphology, and eliminating unsuitable areas such as:
  - areas where the snow period is inadequate due to altitude, orientation or winds,
  - areas too rocky, too steep (more than 60 or 70 per cent gradient) or too flat,
  - forests, except when specifically considering trails through a forest.
- *The main potential ski trails:* separate trails for beginners, intermediate and advanced skiers, with uniform standards for each class and possible combinations of the resort's skiable areas and neighbouring areas. This part of the study will be from maps, aerial photographs and ground surveys on foot and ski.
- *The potential sites for accommodation:* on moderate slopes and plateaux, in an attractive environment, protected from

wind, with maximum exposure to sun, clear from avalanches and conveniently located in relation to the convergence of the main ski trails.

A regional development scheme, would define:

- the access roads and car parking system (for both residents and day visitors),
- the main trails and the most economical cable transportation system,
- provisions for environmental conservation, agriculture, cattle grazing and forestry;
- the stages of progressive development.

In the vicinity of densely populated areas (as around Vancouver, Canada, or Innsbruck, Austria) it is feasible to implement 'snow stadiums' for use by day, with developed skiing facilities (in particular cheap teleskis) but very limited accommodation.

Master plan for a ski resort. In addition to the general principles presented in section 6.4, the following more specific requirements apply:

- Limiting the presence of cars, by providing peripheral or underground car parking and local transportation system (small buses, electric taxis, etc.).
- Reserving, in the resort, trails of a sufficient width (at least 10–15 m for a gradient of 10–15 per cent) to allow skiers to ski directly from their residences to the departure stations of all the cable transporters, and back to the residences when returning from the ski slopes.
- Creating a large, flat area (2 to 5 m^2 per skier in the resort) at the departure points of lifts (and convergence of trails). This area – known as *La Grenouillère* – is the arrival and meeting place for skiers and classes of the ski school. With its mingling of skiers and non-skiers and concentrated activities (information, tea-rooms, restaurants, snack bars, shops) this area is the real heart of most recent ski resorts.
- Considering, in the building design, the possible hazards from snow and ice: avoiding steep gradients on roads and paths, safeguarding pathways, terraces and balconies from dislodged snow, etc.

5.4 RESORTS IN THE COUNTRYSIDE

Mountains, seasides or lakesides are generally more appealing than open gently undulating country areas and the development of tourism or recreation in the countryside is essentially related to the proximity of large towns or densely populated areas.

Historically, the impact of tourism or recreation demand on the countryside has followed three stages:

- first, development of weekend residences;
- second, creation of social holiday villages in places nearer and less expensive than the seaside or the mountain resort;
- third, a relatively recent development and related to the growth of second or third annual holidays, the creation of country resorts and holiday parks, particularly for short stays.

5.4.1 Second residences

The demand for second – essentially weekend – residences, particularly in richer developed countries, is related to the deterioration in urban life conditions: the larger the town, the higher the percentage of owners of second residences.

Typical distances from town to second residence:

- less than 100 km (65 miles) for inhabitants of small towns;
- 150–200 km (95–125 miles) for those living in cities with a population of over one million.

Characteristic sequence in the development of individual second residences:

1 Renovation of abandoned rural buildings of character (mills, cottages, etc.).
2 Land acquisition and construction of villas, smaller bungalows and chalets, with positive economic local impacts (for landowners selling sites, local workers in the building sector) in the most attractive sites available.
3 Negatives impacts become evident: high infrastructure costs to be borne by local authorities, damage to the environment and the landscape, minimal benefit for the local communities as properties are left unused for much of the time.
4 Escalating land costs destroy the structure of the rural economy and result in more and more clearance for urbanization.

Many countries have introduced some form of planning control to regulate the development of second residences in environmentally sensitive areas:

- further building of second residences prohibited in areas where their density is approaching critical proportions, e.g. 5 residences/km^2 (13 per sq mile);
- designation of area as agricultural land, green belt zone (see 8.5.4.), area for recreation or local area of outstanding natural beauty.

In some cases, regulations may require the grouping of second residences together into fewer, more concentrated sites. These groups, often arranged in strips or clusters, may benefit from:

- individual outlooks and a large degree of privacy;
- integrated recreational and sports activities attracting, in particular, the owner's children.

These resorts of second residences (often planned as residential golfs resorts) are created by a developer who acquires and equips the site, sell plots or built residences, with the maintenance costs of common facilities being paid by yearly subscriptions from the owners.

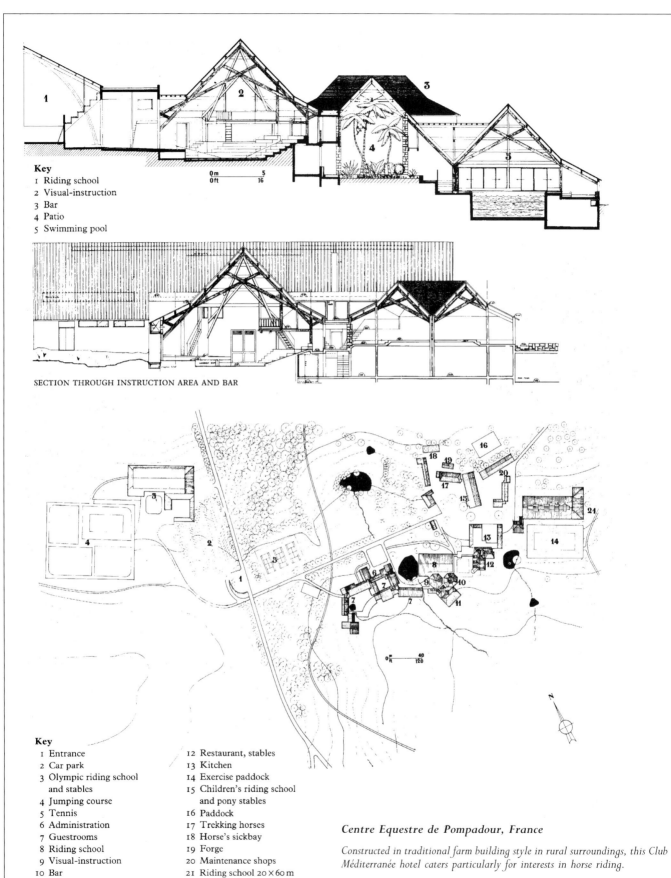

Key
1 Riding school
2 Visual-instruction
3 Bar
4 Patio
5 Swimming pool

0 m   5
0 ft   16

SECTION THROUGH INSTRUCTION AREA AND BAR

Key

1 Entrance
2 Car park
3 Olympic riding school
   and stables
4 Jumping course
5 Tennis
6 Administration
7 Guestrooms
8 Riding school
9 Visual-instruction
10 Bar
11 Swimming pool

12 Restaurant, stables
13 Kitchen
14 Exercise paddock
15 Children's riding school
   and pony stables
16 Paddock
17 Trekking horses
18 Horse's sickbay
19 Forge
20 Maintenance shops
21 Riding school 20 × 60 m

0 m   40
ft   120

N

Centre Equestre de Pompadour, France

*Constructed in traditional farm building style in rural surroundings, this Club
Méditerranée hotel caters particularly for interests in horse riding.*

Architects: Noëlle Janet and Christian Demonchy

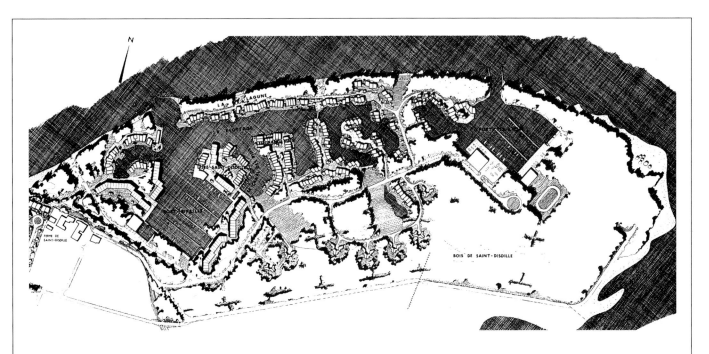

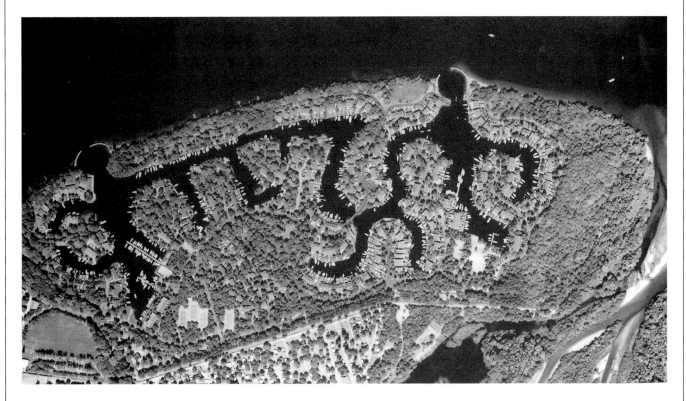

Port-Ripaille, Lake Geneva, France

Initiated in 1975 on the Dranse river delta on the French shore of Lake Geneva, much of the area of Port-Ripaille village (600 units) has been raised by dredged material from the canals and harbours which also give most of the houses direct boat access to the lake. The master plan (Fig. 5.26a) was dictated by the need to retain existing trees on the site, with additional plantations of similar species to ensure screening from the lake.

The village developed in phases, from west to east, up to 1990. The aerial photograph (Fig. 5.26b) shows the evolution of the initial concept with additional canalside rows of bungalows. Communal facilities are limited to two small harbours, a clubhouse and tennis courts. Food and beverage shops are provided at a nearby campsite.

Architects: ACAU/ATHUA;
Architect-planner in charge: M. Baud-Bovy

Activities to be provided: all the basic sport and recreational activities, making the best of local natural resources (lake or large pond, forest, etc.), with horse riding, golf, water-based sports, developed to create a more attractive, more specific image. These activities are often grouped together, creating a 'country club' sometimes constructed out of an old building (farm, manor house, monastery).

Size of second residences: standards provided in section 2.3.4 may be considered as average requirements, to be increased when second residences are intended for retirement, reduced when limited simply to weekend use.

Shopping facilities: not compulsory as residents, coming by car, generally bring their own provisions or go shopping in the neighbouring villages.

5.4.2 Social holiday villages

The development of social accommodation was particularly popular in Europe during the 1960s and 1970s. The initial aim was to provide the working classes with inexpensive accommodation for their paid holidays, social holiday villages being built in or near seaside resorts or near minor ski resorts. Later, some self-contained villages were created in the countryside nearer industrial towns to serve for both long holidays and weekend leisure breaks combined with weekday use for meetings, educational classes and disadvantaged groups (elderly, disabled, etc.).

Social tourism uses many categories of accommodation, from hotels to camping sites or chalets. Some of the social organizations involved in the provision of holiday accommodation specify standards for their facilities. Regulations governing the classification of holiday villages etc., have been laid down in a number of countries (for example, Spain and France). Operators may include specific associations, such as the Villages Vacances Familles (VVF) in France, or trade union groups and cooperative societies. Holiday accommodation as a social service to their employees has also been provided by some commercial companies, particularly in Japan.

The trend has been towards versatility of facilities, their location and characteristics allowing alternative and successive use, at different periods of time, by low-income families, various groups, adult education, aged people, parties of children (such as skiing parties), weekend visitors etc. Most forms of social accommodation provide fully integrated facilities (including special arrangements for ski lifts etc.) comparable to those in packaged holidays.

Main categories:

- **Hostels** are often converted from old buildings, sometimes in obsolete hotels, suitably transformed to accommodate groups, families or individuals. Youth hostels vary widely in their provision, from individual rooms to dormitories and from full meal service to self-catering in communal kitchens.
- **Holiday villages** of a social character fall into two categories: (a) those with inclusive food services (full board), requiring extensive dining rooms and communal lounges, and (b) those self-catering: each unit having a small kitchen and dining area. Collective facilities are less developed and usually limited to social and recreational uses. The distribution of cooked meals to individual units may be considered as a supplementary service. The self-catering category of a holiday village is more common, having advantages of economy in construction and in staffing (guest employee ratios 1:0.1 or 1:0.25), easier operation and greater individuality in accommodation and use.
- **Tent villages** differ from camping sites in that their clients are accommodated on an all-inclusive basis (generally with full board): the tents and camping equipment are provided and collective facilities are as extensive as in holiday villages.
- **Converted cottages, farm buildings and other properties** represent a more recent attempt to develop social tourism in old and obsolescent rural buildings (at a lower cost and for the direct benefit of the local owners). Grants are often available for the conversion of such buildings, including installation of sanitary facilities and a cooperative organization operates the letting of available apartments or rooms over an extensive tourist area. The rehabilitation of traditional buildings ensures that the character of the area is retained for the benefit of tourism.

The size of a village has to take account of the minimum threshold for feasibility and of the maximum beyond which operating problems (food services and recreation in particular) become arduous. An optimal size is usually found between 300 and 800 beds. Larger villages should be divided into neighbourhood areas of 300–400 beds.

In many European countries, the occupancy of social holiday villages (mostly created 20 to 30 years ago) has progressively declined with the rising disposable incomes of their traditional markets, competition from other destinations nearby (such as

---

An example of the social holiday market

The Danish Arbejdsmarketdets Feriefond (Labour Market Holiday Fund) is an independent, non-profit-making, fund founded in 1974 under the Danish Holiday Act. Financed by employers, the Fund spends about £15–20 million (1996 figures) on holiday activities and accommodation facilities for 800 000 workers who do not have holidays with pay. From 1974 to 1993 support was provided for 21 resorts all over Denmark. Since 1993 investment has been mainly in holiday activity centres, theme parks, entertainment parks and activity projects. Total investment amounts to about £75 million, of which 50 per cent was raised by the resorts themselves.

holiday parks) or abroad, and the acquisition of caravans and camper vehicles. The situation is better – but over a shorter season – for social holiday villages located in or near popular seaside and ski resorts.

5.4.3 Country resorts for rent

Most of the resorts created by tourism organizations (such as Club Méditerranée) and other developers are seaside resorts generally rented for a week or more, with access restricted to guests. But other resorts have been created in the countryside, accessible to densely populated areas for short holidays on a weekly basis or for weekends: in particular in Germany, Holland and Belgium. One of the first was Pompadour Village (Club Méditerranée), which uses horse riding as the main activity.

Like resorts for second residences (section 5.4.1), country resorts for rent are located in attractive surroundings (hills, forests, rivers or lakes) with many on-site activities and outside excursions to provide 'active' and 'total' holidays: sport, recreation, culture, nature, relaxation. Their capacity is generally limited to one or two thousand beds.

The accommodation is generally provided in individual bungalows, lodges or chalets, sometimes in an aparthotel, often converted from an existing hotel. The bungalows (see room standards, section 2.3.5) are arranged in rows or clusters, each having a small kitchen as an alternative to using a restaurant. There is no room service: cleaning and changing towels is carried out between lettings.

The climatic conditions are a major consideration and, since the 1960s, the large resorts in northern Europe have been planned for all-weather use with a wide range of indoor facilities and activity programmes.

Typical indoor facilities include:

- covered patios and sheltered walkways;
- a choice of restaurants, lounges, bars;
- billiards (pool) room, indoor games area;
- dance hall/entertainment area;
- indoor/outdoor bowls, tennis, squash, volleyball and badminton courts;
- landscaped indoor swimming pool (with outdoor extensions);
- whirlpool, sauna, steam bath, massage;
- fitness and beauty centre.

These facilities must be carefully designed and integrated into landscaped surroundings to retain contact with nature. Some separated areas should be provided for adults and for children.

Outdoor activities include: mountain bikes, excursions, promenades on horseback, mini-golf and outdoor sports facilities. Many facilities are provided for children, families with children being the main market: playgrounds, kindergarten, entertainment activities, excursions and competitions for the different ages.

5.4.4 Holiday parks

Holiday parks differ from country resorts by their large size and the extent of recreational attractions and indoor facilities. The concept of these large 'centres for active leisure and holidays' was first implemented in Holland and Belgium in the 1970s. By 1997, holiday parks had been developed on several sites throughout Europe, mainly in attractive parts of the countryside within easy travelling distance of large towns, although some have been sited in seaside areas to revive existing resorts. Holiday parks involve an investment of US $100–150 million, on 100 to 200 ha, and need a large population catchment area (10 million people and over) within a 2–3 hour drive time.

The **concept** of holiday parks was introduced by the Dutch firm Center Parks:

- an integrated resort of 2,000 to 4,500 beds (400 to 800 bungalows) with corresponding services and infrastructures;
- developed and operated by one company;
- mainly comfortable self-service bungalows, one to four rooms with kitchen (as in country resorts) of 'home from home' quality; occasionally an aparthotel;
- provision of the largest possible range of activities – extending those listed in 5.4.3;
- in particular, a huge free-form indoor pool – 'Aquatic subtropical Paradise' – with beaches, waves, flumes and slides, rapids, jacuzzis, salt water, waterfalls, waterside snack bars, etc., in 'themed landscape' with exotic vegetation, under artificially assisted sunlight;
- an indoor landscaped 'Central Plaza' combining 'gastronomic' catering in themed restaurants, shopping, social and cultural activities, with subtropical trees and flowers;
- a wide range of sports halls and courts, with vegetation;
- designed and marketed to provide all year round active short holidays, competing with Mediterranean destinations, in particular for:
  - families with small children needing babysitting and child supervision,
  - families with teenage children needing an activity programme,
  - all adult parties, at non-peak times, with sport, health, cultural or countryside interests,
  - people aged 55 and over looking for a taste of new activities.

About half the revenues earned are produced by catering, shops and sports. Most staff live outside the villages and are recruited from local residents. High standards of customer care and village servicing and maintenance are provided.

Center Park in Sologne, France

Built in 1993 on 110 ha (270 acres) of forested flat land, the park provides about 3500 beds in two, three and four–room comfortable bungalows: an average density of approximately 30 beds/ha. The park includes 17 ha of lake, ponds and canals, created for their landscape value and used for boating and fishing. The present water areas were used during the construction of the park for temporary access roads and materials storage, in order to protect the trees.

Cars are only allowed on site for baggage delivery, then parked at the entrance. Bicycles are available for rent. The roads and trails are carefully laid out, and the ranges of bungalows designed in order to create a feeling of independence. The main elements of the park are:

- A large glassed dome (about 100 metres in diameter) divided into two parts: (a) the Water Paradise with pools, waves, jacuzzis, rivers (extending outside), etc. and (b) the Park Plaza with six bars/restaurants, six shops (including fresh food for guests preferring to eat in their bungalows), children's facilities and launderette. Both areas are very carefully landscaped with small ponds or cascades and a great variety of well tended exotic trees, plants and flowers, even birds.
- The indoor sports club (4500 m²) includes an information desk and bar, three tennis courts, three squash courts, two short tennis courts, a bowling alley, three badminton courts, a fitness room, multi-purpose room, billiards and table tennis areas. These facilities are also being partly landscaped.

The park has about 450 employees, but the majority are part-time or limited to a few hours (cleaning of bungalows twice a week)

Key
1 Access/control
2 Entrance to dome
3 Dome (Water Paradise and Park Plaza)
4 Convention rooms
5 Services
6 Health and Beauty Centre
7 Sports Club
8 Outdoor tennis courts
9 Archery
10 Bicycles for hire
11 Boats for hire
PK Car parking

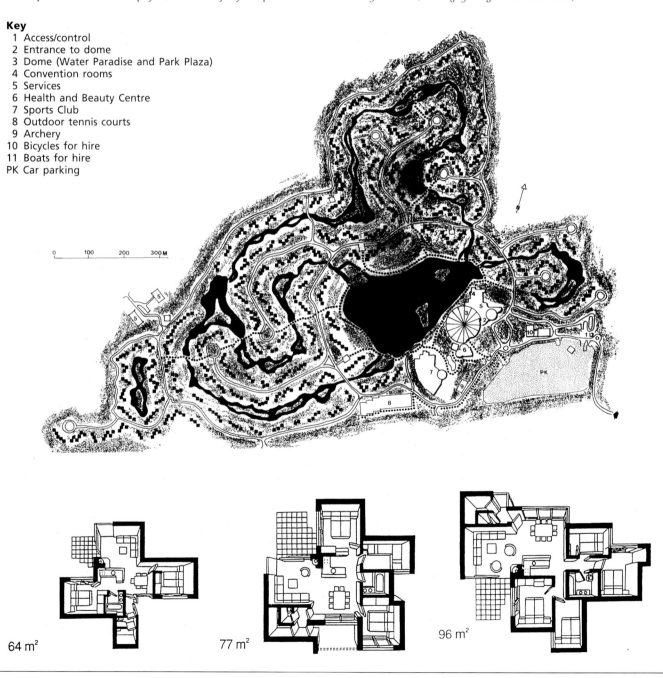

64 m²   77 m²   96 m²

a

b

c

Oasis Lakeland Forest Holiday Village, UK

The Oasis Village, opened in 1997, is the latest concept in the development of year-round 'holiday park' resorts. Located in the English Lake District, the village combines an enclosed exotic leisure complex with outdoor recreation in 160 ha of pine forest. A choice of high quality one, two, three or four bedrooms with living/dining areas and well-equipped kitchens and bathrooms is provided in forest or lakeside lodges and apartments.

Leisure facilities are centred on a vast 'World of Water' with landscaped pools, rapids, flumes and wave machines together with an area for quiet swimming and relaxation. There are also restaurants, shops and health and beauty spa facilities within the complex, which is covered by an inverted hyperbolic paraboloid roof having an overall span of 70 m with a double-glazed area of 4500 m².

Open air recreation includes nature trails, cycleways, sailing and water sports on the created lake. A policy of environmental management and ecological protection has been introduced. The Oasis Village is planned to attract a wide spectrum of tourists of all ages for both primary and secondary holidays. In 1997 plans were approved for a second village.

Architect: HMA Architects

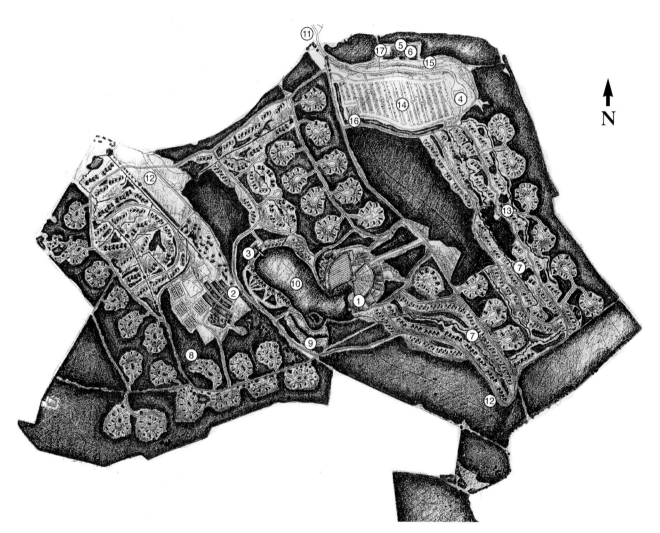

N

Site plan

Main Buildings
1. Village Centre
2. Sports Club
3. Waterside Inn
4. Reception
5. Maintenance
6. Staff Accommodation

Accommodation
7. Waterside Villas
8. Forest Lodges
9. Studio Apartments

External Works
10. 7.5 Acre Lake
11. Access Road
12. Service Road
13. Lanes
14. Car Parking
15. Staff Parking
16. Cycle Park
17. Service Yard

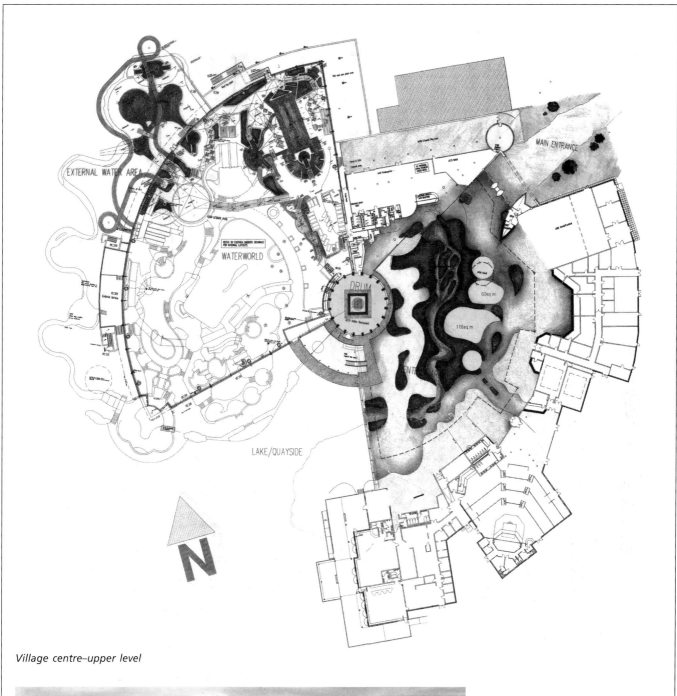

Village centre–upper level

Computer-generated model

Marketing. Packages, including accommodation and free use of the subtropical pool and of some (but not all) of the sports/recreational activities are usually offered for:

- long weekends of three nights (Friday to Monday)
- mid-week breaks of four nights (Monday to Friday)
- weeks during school holidays, etc.

Variations. Some parks are planned to be self-sufficient (like Club Méditerranée resorts), others are less exclusive:

- *Self-sufficient, exclusive parks:* most Center Parks are built on 60 to 130 ha or more (with facilities limited to 70 per cent of the total area), on an attractive site, either natural or man-made created with artificial ponds or lakes; forests of evergreen trees are preferred, despite their poor ecological value, for permanent screening (50 000 trees and shrubs have been planted for the Sherwood Forest Center Park). Such parks provide most activities – even nature-related such as horse riding – on their own grounds and restrict the access of non-residents (making the advance booking of day cards necessary); attractions are often extended and renewed to generate further market interest and repeat visits. Each park may have a 'special' attraction: surf school, deep diving or ski slope, etc. Average overall density: 30–60 beds/ha.

- *Open, non-exclusive parks*, such as Gran Dorado Parks or Sun Parks, are developed on 25 to 50 ha on possibly less attractive sites; guests are encouraged to go out for excursions and organized activities in the country and the parks are open to day visitors, with a fee for access to the 'Aquatic Paradise'. The individuality of each park is stressed according to the characteristics of the local environment. Average overall density: 60–100 beds/ha.

Since 1980, a vast enclosed pool – the 'Aquatic Tropical Paradise' of the marketing brochures – has been the basic element of both types of parks. Its main characteristics are described in section 5.6.4.

Over the last twenty years, there has been intense controversy over the siting and development of these very large resorts, with heated arguments for (by developers, investors, local communities) and against (by ecologists defending nature and landscape, existing resorts fearing competition) proposed projects (Büro für Strukturentwicklung 1994):

For	Topic	Against
Smaller than for more scattered developments	Land consumption	Large areas unable to be used for anything else
Average with guaranteed supply	Resources use (water and electricity)	Higher, shortages at peak periods
Comparable to traditional resorts	Wastes	Additional dumps
Normal, sufficient sewage plants	Sewage	Higher, additional plants necessary
Local vegetation reused	Vegetation (inside)	Loss of previous vegetation
Restoration through new planting	Vegetation (around)	Damage by hiking, horse riding etc.
Creation of habitats	Fauna	Upsetting vital areas
Screening of low buildings by landscaped surroundings	Image of landscape	Aggressive building; incongruous elements
Low, due to nearby highway connection	Traffic load	High on guests' changeover days
Creation of new, permanent jobs	Employment	Unqualified jobs; competing with local employment
Taxes and revenues	Local communities	Infrastructure costs; negative cost-benefit
Activity for local builders; increase of revenues for local enterprises; new economic impulse	Regional economy	No local effect at building stage; competition to traditional holiday enterprises
Access to resort for local population	Socio-cultural impacts	Influx of outsiders; 'artificial world'; not enough consultation at planning stage

Source: Büro für Strukturentwicklung (1994), p. 26.

Beyond the opposing 'ecological morality' versus 'job creation' arguments, case studies show that:

- these 'artificial worlds' do not consume much more water than the traditional resorts (about 130 l/day/guest plus 40 for the aquatic centre), but more energy;
- concentrated facilities in these integrated resorts are less damaging for the landscape and the environment than scattered facilities, such as weekend residences or caravans: the average density is higher than in traditional holiday resorts;
- jobs created are about 0.1 per bed (half full-time, often qualified);
- the impact on local inhabitants is positive, adverse reactions are quite limited;
- with suitable screening, the impact on the landscape is better than in most resorts (with higher buildings) or camping sites.

5.5 SPAS AND HEALTH RESORTS

Some of the world-famous spas were the first fully integrated resorts, often developed under the autocratic control of one landowner. Over the last fifty years or more, the popularity of spas has been decreasing and planning proposals are more often concerned with infusing life into existing spas rather than with creating new ones. An exception applies in the developing countries and also to the more sophisticated forms of health resorts.

5.5.1 Markets and resources

The concept of the *kur* (taking the waters) is long established in some developed countries (particularly in central Europe) whilst having limited interest in others (such as in the USA where medical practitioners are extremely dubious about its efficacy). The analyses of various spa waters in developed countries are well known and the bottling and selling of mineral water is often an important part of the spa industry. In Europe there are over 750 established spas and many of the traditional spa resorts have developed sophisticated social, cultural and recreational facilities which appeal to a wide spectrum of visitors. In several countries (such as Germany and France) spa treatment has been supported by state funding through social security reimbursements, but such subsidies are tending to reduce. Whilst the markets for medical spa tourism are generally ageing and in decline, there is a growing interest in health/beauty and fitness tourism with emphasis on revitalization through exercise, tests and treatment, particularly amongst the mature, high income groups.

In developing countries, mineral spas are used widely for medical treatment, although commonly without an adequate knowledge of the water's specific virtues and without medical supervision. 'Watering' is often taken as an opportunity for the whole family to have a holiday. Facilities are usually poor: the source is frequently just one or several large pool(s) with inadequate hygiene control and accommodation provided by renting rooms in neighbouring villages or camping on site. Two levels of development may be considered:

- the provision of cheap but hygienic traditional basic facilities (see 5.5.2 below) with some medical supervision and proper control of standards;
- the development of a modern resort with a range of alternative treatments and facilities.

However, the markets for an international clientele are likely to be limited outside those from neighbouring countries.

5.5.2 Spa facilities

The development of a modern spa represents a heavy investment, combining the cost of a resort with the costs of a clinic.

Treatment may be provided in thermal baths distinct from the hotels or in spa hotels offering both curative treatment and accommodation.

Basic traditional facilities provide fountains for drinking water, collective pools and/or individual bathrooms for immersion, shower rooms, rest rooms with beds, changing rooms and sanitary accommodation, together with the necessary technical equipment and services. This may be adequate in a developing country.

More sophisticated facilities usually include:

- consulting rooms, medical diagnostic and group therapy areas, administrative offices;
- therapy buildings with many collective or, more often, individual facilities for: hydrotherapy, thalassotherapy, mud wraps, fango, massage, aromatherapy, thermotherapy, electrotherapy, heliotherapy, laser treatment, physiotherapy, etc.;
- swimming pools, exercise pools, aeration and jet pools, saunas and steam baths with plunge pools, needle showers, washing areas, showers and toilets;
- rest rooms, sunbathing areas;
- gymnasium, with cardio-vascular rehabilitation and weight training equipment, areas for aerobic and yoga practice, etc.;
- beautician rooms, facilities for chiropody, manicure, hair dressing, etc.;
- cafe/restaurant and lounge;
- staff and service areas, plant rooms.

Space requirements for thermal baths and spa facilities are usually between 20 m^2 and 40 m^2 per patient undergoing treatment in a hotel (including hotel facilities) or an average of 2 m^2 to 4 m^2 per patient for central facilities where patients stay elsewhere in the resort.

Trends: the facilities listed above extend beyond the form of traditional spa treatment. In a modern spa the emphasis is often placed on attracting a widely diversified market by catering for such needs as: weight control, lifestyle changes, detoxification, improvements in health and vitality, stress management, athletic training, fitness and body condition, beauty and pampering.

5.5.3 Non-specific facilities

To broaden the range of attractions, the image of a modern spa is not so much focused on medical treatments but on comfort, culture, leisure and recreation in quiet, pleasant surroundings. Spas cater not just for people requiring treatment or rejuvenation but for their families and other tourist interests.

Depending on the resources, recreational activities may extend to yachting and skiing, but more commonly include tennis, bowls, golf, horse riding and leisure facilities (including all-weather provisions). Patients and convalescents often stay longer than most other tourists and programmes of varied events and activities need to be promoted. Film, theatre and music festivals, casinos and special attractions are usually introduced in addition to other resort facilities such as high class shopping arcades and business facilities. In addition to long vacations, short break and second holidays may be targeted and particular emphasis given to business meetings, conferences and exhibitions, for which the high quality hotels are particularly suited (e.g. Harrogate, UK).

A good environment is of prime importance: parks, gardens, streams, lakes, sun terraces, pavilions and landscaped pedestrian areas providing for relaxation in sunlight and shade with extensive walkways linking areas of interest. Circulation paths in the central area must be designed for use by disabled and elderly but other routes and extended trails are required for fitness training, jogging and walking in the countryside.

Accommodation facilities depend on the location and market segments to be attracted. In developed countries and nearby destinations – where the need is to promote tourism for higher spending clienteles (for example, in Eastern Europe) – most of the accommodation is in high grade or luxury hotels supplemented by some guesthouse facilities. This is generally warranted by the higher standard of personal care and staffing involved. In developing countries the emphasis is often placed on relatively inexpensive but well maintained accommodation of moderate standard with adequate facilities to rent.

5.5.4 Planning spa resorts

In planning a spa resort special attention must be given to:

- defining the hydrogeological 'protection zone' around the water resource;
- creating an attractive, relaxing atmosphere, with sheltered landscapes, interesting parks, gardens and features, attractive approaches and protected surroundings;
- linking accommodation to the spa treatment complex by covered ways (arcades, etc);
- ensuring adequate room for future phased expansion of the resort and for the needs of the residential population (which may be in a separate village);
- eliminating vehicular traffic and other sources of pollution as far as possible whilst ensuring adequate access for invalids.

5.5.5 Thalassotherapy and health centres

In the last twenty to thirty years, thalassotherapy has developed widely in many European and Mediterranean countries (about fifty centres in France). The more medical-orientated centres, usually related to a 3- or 4-star hotel, provide most of the sophisticated facilities of a spa (see 5.5.2) with an accent on seawater, sea muds, seaweeds and sand. Controlled exercise and diets are combined to treat overwork and stress and provide slimming cures. Some centres may have a special clientele of disabled persons.

There has been a shift from purely medically-based treatments to improvement of fitness and beauty care. In order to attract an additional segment of clientele (wealthy 40- to 50-

year-olds: younger than in spas), and to increase the length of the season, many seaside resorts have developed **health and fitness centres**, with:

- hydrotherapy (indoor pools, jacuzzis, underwater massages and physiotherapy, ionizing baths, etc.);
- fitness suites, gymnasium and saunas;
- dietary advice (with the availabililty of special menus if the centre is related to an hotel);
- beauty care (massages, peeling, UV, manicure, make-up, etc.).

Such centres need one director, one dietician, two physiotherapists, two hydrotherapists and one beautician (plus service personnel). They cover an area of about 700 m² and may be feasible in a resort of 3–4000 tourist beds, or less if they attract a local clientele.

Similar health and fitness centres – sometimes smaller – can be developed not only in seaside resorts but in mountain resorts and in holiday parks (see 5.4.4).

5.6 FUN, SAFARI AND AQUATIC PARKS

5.6.1 Categories

Leisure park is a generic term (French: *Parc de Loisir*, German: *Freizeitpark*), and covers a wide range of variations from the attraction and theme parks which are sited and constructed to attract mass markets through to recreation parks which are orientated around the natural environment.

Recreation parks are examined in 5.7.

5.6.2 Attraction and theme parks

These share many similarities and generally involve large-scale commercial investments. As a rule the key requirements are location, accessibility and size. A naturally attractive site is not necessary – flat land being easier to develop – and the area is often extensively altered by the construction and landscaping.

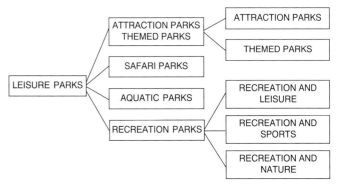

Figure 5.8

Attraction parks. Parks featuring spectacular attractions can be traced back to the seventeenth and eighteenth centuries, often constructed at the whim of a rich landowner, such as Versailles (water features) and Prater in Vienna. Present day attraction parks with their 'white knuckle' rides and range of thrills derive from the nineteenth century, when travelling funfairs settled on permanent sites (Tivoli, Copenhagen, 1843; Coney Island, New York, 1887). They were then called *amusement parks* or *tramway parks*, being sited on the outskirts of the town at the end of the line.

Generally developed by promoters coming from circus backgrounds, attraction parks offer:

- classic funfair attractions: great wheel, toboggans, big dipper, roller coaster, labyrinths, shooting ranges, mirror halls, haunted manor, etc.;
- newer features: water toboggans, river rapids, parachuting, electronic displays, lasers, robots, etc.;
- shows and events: seals and other animals, concerts, stunt men, automates, ghosts, etc.;
- mini-train or overhead telecabin, or monorails for transportation;
- catering, shops and services.

Theme parks. These include many of the elements of an attraction park but present a more specific image based on:

- children's fairy tales and stories: Disneyland (USA), Gluck Kingdom (Japan), Efteling (Netherlands);
- miniature towns: Madudoran (Hungary), Minidom (Switzerland);
- future and science: Futuroscope (France);
- Wild West: Fort Fun (USA), OK Corral (France);
- rural world, flowers, honey: Flevohof (Holland), Mellipark (Belgium);
- TV series: Sesame Street (Japan).

There is no strict barrier between theme and attraction parks: large attraction parks often provide a 'Western' section or a 'Forbidden City' and large themed parks funfair attractions.

Potential markets. Visitors to attraction and themed parks are mainly town dwellers, couples, parties and family groups (with 3- to 15-year-old children). These can be segmented into three main markets:

- *Permanent residential market:* inhabitants of the catchment area (very extensive in the case of large parks) who could be attracted once a year or more.
- *Temporary residential market:* holidaymakers in the catchment area (who represent more that 40 per cent of the local population on the Côte d'Azur for example).
- *Tourist market:* Parks of national importance, to be visited over more than one day, being the main destination of a family weekend (for example, Disneyland in Paris).

An optimum location is generally held to be within two hours' drive time of at least 10–12 million residents and within 15 minutes of a motorway or major trunk road.

The potential size of a fun park depends on its potential market. The tendency to visit is related to the distance from home to the park. Indications of percentages of visitors in the various catchment areas have been provided in Europe for Europa-Park, Germany, in Fichtner and Micha 1987 and DATAR 1986 (optimistic evaluations).

Level	Number of Visitors		Area hectares (including car parking)	Number of jobs	
	Yearly (in millions)	Daily average		permanent	temporary
National	1.5–3.0*	9–12 000	100–150	150–200	500–600
Regional	0.8–1.4	5–8000	70–80	80–150	200–350
Local	0.3–0.5	2–3000	over 50	30–50	80–100

*but up to 14 million in Tokyo's Disneyland and 11 million in Disneyland, Paris

Investment. The creation of a park is a heavy, high-risk investment. Furthermore, a park must re-invest each year up to 10 per cent of the initial investment to develop its attraction in order to bring back previous visitors. The necessary turnover is estimated in Europe at 25–30 per cent of the investment, and at 45–50 per cent in the USA. Many local communities, interested in the creation of employment, have met problems in having to finance the roads, parking, water or electricity supplies or provide grants or guarantees for parks which became bankrupt.

Design of fun parks. Detailed planning procedures are provided in Chapter 6. Special attention must be given to:

- *the entrance area:* parking of cars, access for buses (with control of congestion at peak entry and exit times), ticket stands, controls, pedestrian access avenue with information, shops, etc.;
- *flow of visitors:* each one of the 2000 or 10 000 daily visitors should feel free to go where he or she wants, but the move should flow as continuously and uniformly as possible. The itinerary from one attraction to the next should impose itself without being compulsory. At peak hours of arrivals some diversions should be available at the beginning of the itinerary (opening alternative roads, staging a musical attraction, etc.);
- *public transport system* (e.g. open train) stopping at the main attractions within the park;
- *landmarks:* a high tower or a roller coaster enabling visitors to orientate themselves; a central lake reached several times in the itinerary serves the same role;
- *artificial landscapes:* carefully designed to enhance the setting and attractions, provide transition between attractions, screen services areas and withstand intensive traffic;
- *provision for entertainment:* of the inevitable queues in front of the main attractions: areas for musicians, clowns and other temporary attractions;
- *service roads:* every attraction, shop and restaurant should be serviced individually but the service roads must not cross

visitor routes and where possible should not be visible. In main circulation routes, technical and support services are in underground structures;

- *locations of future attractions* should be considered from the beginning to allow continuous redevelopment;
- *security* is essential: strong fencing, controlled gates, provisions for fire fighting, visitor safety and evacuation, money security and thefts, first aid, lost children, bomb scares, emergency evacuation, and other procedures.

5.6.3 Safari parks

Safari parks range from:

- national, state or private parks supporting stocks of wild animals in their natural environments, such as in Kenya or South Africa;
- modern zoos combining animal welfare, conservation, breeding and educational programmes with enhanced facilities (Chester Zoo, UK);

Chester Zoo, UK

In existence for more than sixty years and operated as a Charitable Trust, the Chester Zoological Garden is a centre of excellence for animal-related education, welfare, benign study and conservation breeding programmes. The grounds extend over 50 ha of landscaped gardens, lakes, islands and spacious enclosures with near natural barriers (moats or dry ditches) where practical. An overhead railway extends over a mile round the site.

In 1994, the zoo accommodated 5640 specimens in 516 species — more than one-third being endangered species. The enclosures are designed to create suitable territorial habitats and include, for example, a large free flight aviary of well over 10 000 m³ for endangered European birds. A children's farm allows close encounters with domestic animals.

Over 800 000 visitors are attracted each year, with over 25 000 on busy days, and 300 staff are employed, half of whom are permanent. In 1994, total operating costs were in excess of £4 million. The zoo has a policy of progressive improvements with phased building programmes.

Chester Zoological Gardens, 1996.

The Eden Project, Cornwall, UK

This project for a huge ecological centre — to be created in a 14-ha derelict clay pit near St Austell in Cornwall — consists of a half-mile long greenhouse enveloping four controlled ecological zones (Mediterranean, desert, rainforest and sub-tropical).

Visitors will arrive by shuttle bus from the car park, descend to a visitor centre, cross a bridge over the pit floor to enter the Mediterranean biome, then the next, with restaurants and service spaces at each junction. In the rainforest section (up to 30 metres high) several paths, some well above ground level, will allow visitors to appreciate the ecologies of different levels.

The high-tech structure, inspired by the Grimshaw/ Hunt TGV Waterloo Station in London, will support a transparent film formed into inflated 'pillows'. The project is supported by major funds from the Millennium Commission.

Architects: Nicholas Grimshaw & Partners
Engineers: Anthony Hunt Associates

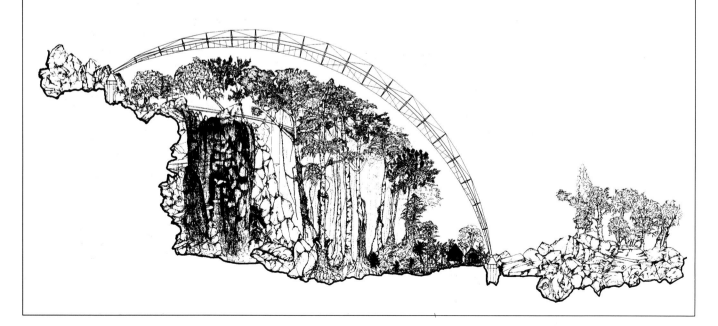

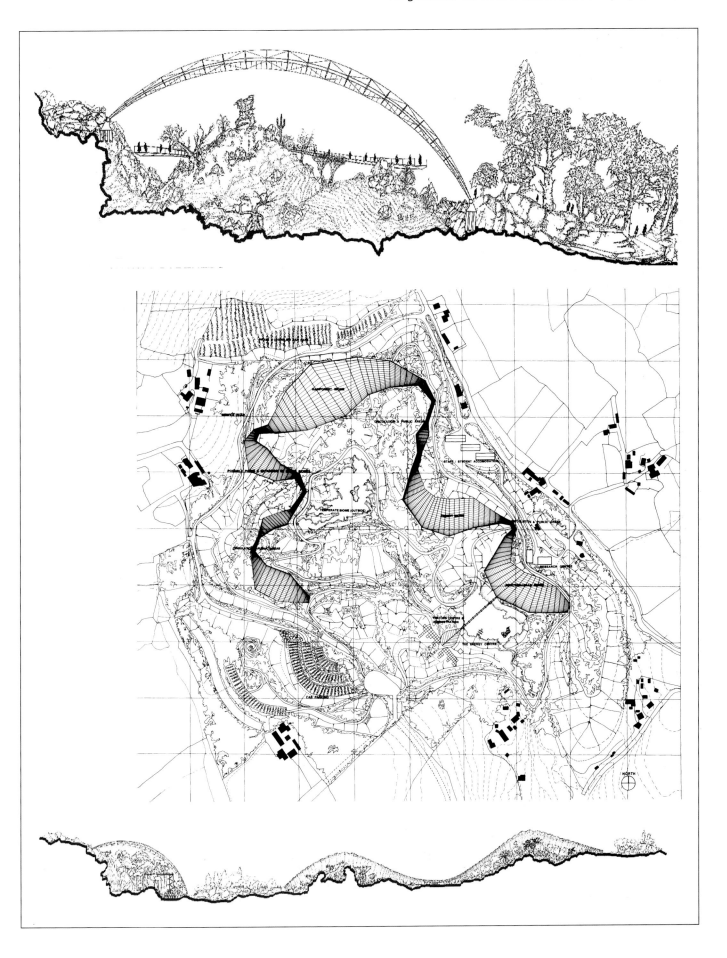

- created safari parks bringing together collections of animals, birds, butterflies, sea life, etc. in sites developed to create near 'natural' conditions.

Created safari parks. Originating from zoos, created safari parks offer suitable habitats with much more space, extending to 100–200 ha with up to 0.5 million visitors per year and more. They often include educational programmes and exhibitions for close animal contact as well as supporting facilities for animal welfare and visitors (catering, shops, rest areas). Visitor circulation may be on foot, in individual cars or organized transport (monorail, train, coach).

Many of the original safari parks created in the 1960s from large private estates have faced difficulties:

- the catchment populations are often limited;
- operating costs have risen significantly;
- visitor interest is usually confined to a few hours;
- repeat visits are relatively few.

  Trends in created parks are towards:

- small (less than 500 000 visitors per year), specialist centres with niche markets (butterflies, endangered species, local wildlife, bees, birds, etc.);
- very large complexes with exotic attractions (such as Sea World, US);
- ecological centres demonstrating the range of diversity – desert, rain forest, sub-tropical, etc. – both in natural settings and enclosures; often these are created from waste ground.

Walt Disney World, Florida, USA

In the 25 years since its opening in October, 1971, Walt Disney World has welcomed more than 500 million visitors and has grown from a single theme park (the Magic Kingdom) and hotel to include the EPCOT and Disney-MGM studios theme parks; Pleasure Island night-time entertainment complex; three water parks; five championship golf courses; 26 themed resorts with almost 22 500 guest rooms and 784 campsites; 55 800 sq m of convention space and hundreds of new attractions and shows.

With 35 000 employees, the complex is the largest single employer in central Florida and extends over a 12 000 ha (30 000 acre) site of which 2840 ha has been developed and 3320 ha dedicated as a wilderness area.

Walt Disney World has a policy of continual improvement and addition. Recent additions in 1996 included the Blizzard Beach water park – a 24 ha, 5000-person capacity water park, complete with ski jumps, slalom runs and chair lifts, which features a dozen different adventure zones.

Walt Disney Company, 1996.

Theme Parks in the UK

Since the first UK theme park opened in 1979, the numbers of parks and visitors has increased dramatically:

	1985	1996
Numbers of parks	7	10
Numbers of visitors (millions)	5.4	10.8
Revenues (£millions)	29	130

This increasing popularity is due to:

- *substitution – for other holidays and leisure time;*
- *investment – £36 million invested in new rides and attractions in 1994 alone;*
- *marketing – aggressive campaigns and media coverage;*
- *opportunity – late-night opening, provision of hotels and more all-weather protection;*
- *quality – increasing sophistication, quality of services and visitor experience.*

Sources: English Tourist Board, Tussaud Group.

Efteling, Holland

Dating from 1954, Efteling is based on a fairy-tale theme set in a forest. Other attractions include thrill rides, boat tours and train rides. Open seven months a year, the park attracted 2.65 million visitors in 1995, generating work equivalent to 574 employee-years.

Since 1966 new attractions have been added practically every year. 1992 saw the opening of Hotel Kaatsheuval, 121 rooms, which achieved occupancies of 61.5 per cent within three years. In 1994 a championship 18–hole golf course (95 ha) was added. With a clubhouse and an average of 5 ha per hole this provides spectator facilities and has a capacity of 60 000 rounds per year, half reserved for a club membership of 400.

Efteling Public Relations Department

Efteling

Trends in theme parks are also towards the use of simulated environments with animated models providing an experience of danger, fear and excitement.

Natural safari parks. Large reserves designated for the protection of wildlife are essentially nature parks (see sections 5.8 and 9.2.1). Animal stocks need to be managed, including culling, protection of endangered species and the reintroduction of animals (or birds) from other areas to conserve depleted herds or flocks. Problems often arise from:

- poaching – requiring international action;
- loss of livelihood and grazing lands, etc. – requiring positive steps to involve and compensate the local communities;
- the costs of management – offset by allocated benefits from tourism, regulated game shooting, and employment in the reserves (direct and indirect – giving priority to local inhabitants);
- tourism saturation – causing excessive disturbance to wildlife and disruption of traditional activities.

5.6.4 Aquatic parks

Indoor pools for competitive swimming and training needs are essentially functional and must comply with standard dimensions. In contrast, leisure pools are designed for fun and adventure in order to attract many types of users, particularly families and young people. These 'water parks', 'aquatic parks', 'aqualands' or 'aquatic paradises' started to appear in Germany in the 1960s, in the 1970s in UK (free-form pool at Milton Keynes, 1974) and elsewhere in Europe in the 1980s. They have been developed as community facilities in many towns, for example:

- Aquaboulevard (Paris): 3.5 ha (water park: 13 500 m²), 22 tennis courts, 22 squash courts, artificial ski slope, bowling alleys, gymnastic and spectator sports; 500 000 visitors annually.
- West Edmonton Mall (Edmonton, Canada): in a commercial centre (46 ha), an indoor attraction and aquatic park (1.6 ha) with wave pool, kayak river, 25 m high flume.
- El Dorado in Wien-Wiesendorf (Austria): glassed dome of 65 m × 65 m, 14 m high, with aquatic landscape, 2800 m² of water, restaurants, 5-star hotel and conference centre.

Others have been created in beach resorts, caravan/camping sites, shopping malls and, on a larger scale, in holiday parks (see 5.4.4).

In hot countries, 'aquatic parks' are essentially sited in the open air for use during the summer season (four to six months) by local residents and holidaymakers. Mostly these have been located in association with the beach in seaside resorts, as an additional tourist attraction, and may cater for up to 6000 simultaneous users in an area of 5 ha or more, having 1 ha of water surface (Gauthier and Breel 1990). Elsewhere, leisure pools are mainly indoor to allow year-round use, sometimes with one or more of the pool basins extending outside. They are invariably designed as 'tropical' enclosures with a mild climate (air and water at 28–29°C) and exotically landscaped surroundings.

Main elements of an aquatic park:

- shaped pools, often 5000 m² or more, designed for play rather than swimming;
- wide range of water activities – pools with beaches and waves, with salted or iodide waters, rivers and cascades, large tortuous flumes, waterfalls and sprays;
- some pools may extend outside, with linked channels and island features, for summer use;
- landscaped areas around the pools with whirlpools, aerated pools, nautical bars, beaches and surrounds with 'tropical' vegetation;
- other facilities – sauna, steam baths, solarium, massage and separate fitness centres;
- spectator viewing areas, with cafes, bars, sometimes with a separate restaurant having musical entertainment;
- controlled access and supervision, changing rooms and toilets, facilities for the disabled, extensive technical plant rooms and service areas accessible from a separate goods entrance;
- the whole enclosed within a large glazed enclosure (domed or pitched roof structure) with artificially assisted daylight.

Feasibility and impacts: Aquatic parks are expensive to build and operate: as a rule they do not reimburse the investment nor cover all operational costs. Typically, some 30 full-time equivalent employees are required for a medium sized aquatic park (excluding catering) and high expenses are incurred in water, energy and maintenance. On the other hand benefits arise from the popularity of this attraction for large numbers of people, available in all weathers and seasons, requiring a relatively small area of land with highly concentrated usage, thereby relieving pressure on other natural resources.

Aquatic parks may be provided by municipal authorities (subsidized as necessary out of public funds), by shopping centres to attract leisure shoppers (West Edmonton Mall, Canada or St-Gall, Switzerland), or by tourist resorts – holiday parks (5.4.4) and other centres.

There is much criticism of the trend towards artificiality, although it can be countered that such facilities are a response to market forces and relieve pressure on the natural resources (see 1.4.9):

Traditional outdoor leisure	Aquatic and recreation parks
Near nature, its fauna and flora	Totally artificial surroundings
Awareness of the seasons, of the weather	All year round controlled climate
Not expensive to develop and operate	Heavy investment and operating costs
Cheap for users	Expensive for users
Without technical infrastructures	High consumption of energy and water
Risk of erosion of natural resources	Visual intrusion in the landscape

Seagaia Ocean Dome, Miyazaki, Japan

Phoenix Seagaia is a 600–ha (1480–acre) property with a 45–storey ocean-view hotel, a convention centre, the Ocean Dome, a golf course, 16 tennis courts and a 2000-spectator tournament court, cottages and condominiums.

The Ocean Dome is the world's largest aquatic park: it measures 300 m × 100 m and holds up to 10 000 people under its sliding roof. The waves (from ripples to 2.5 m waves) reach a marble sand beach. Other facilities provided include: a volcano (erupting several times an hour, with a high-speed body slide), a cinema, 16 restaurants and bars and an adjacent shopping centre. A viewing promenade and terrace are provided at an upper floor around the attractions.

Additional facilities, which extend on both sides of Phoenix Seagaia between the beach and the road, include three hotels, four 18 to 36-hole golf courses, a large zoo, a baseball stadium and hot springs spa.

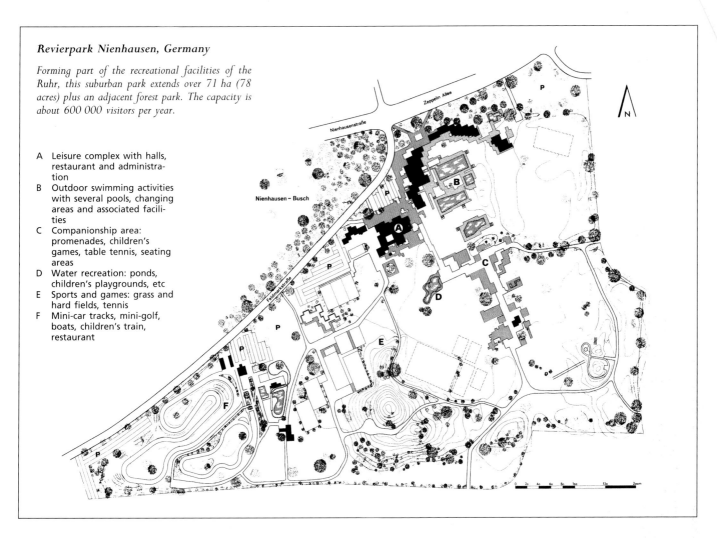

Revierpark Nienhausen, Germany

Forming part of the recreational facilities of the Ruhr, this suburban park extends over 71 ha (78 acres) plus an adjacent forest park. The capacity is about 600 000 visitors per year.

A Leisure complex with halls, restaurant and administration
B Outdoor swimming activities with several pools, changing areas and associated facilities
C Companionship area: promenades, children's games, table tennis, seating areas
D Water recreation: ponds, children's playgrounds, etc
E Sports and games: grass and hard fields, tennis
F Mini-car tracks, mini-golf, boats, children's train, restaurant

5.7 SUBURBAN RECREATION PARKS

Recreation park is used as the generic term for those suburban parks which provide for open air recreation, allowing contact with nature with a limited range of facilities. This term includes the French *bases de détente*, German *Freizeitzentrum* and Dutch *Recreatieschaps*.

Outdoor 'green areas' should be incorporated into the planning of every neighbourhood for the recreational benefit of the homes, schools and workplaces in the vicinity. However, in most cities and towns such quiet open space is at a premium with pressure from traffic, car parking and intensified development of high-value urban land.

The need for recreation calls for the creation of specific areas:

• *urban parks* and other landscaped areas within the city – including the improvement and conversion of existing sites (see Chapter 6).
• *suburban parks* on the outskirts of the city where land is cheaper and more readily available. Suburban recreation parks vary widely in area and character. They may be broadly grouped as follows:

Type	Facilities	Section(s)
Recreation	basic provision for outdoor recreation	5.7.2–3
Leisure	combined with other leisure facilities	5.7.4
Sports	with more sports grounds and facilities	5.7.5
Nature	linked to more extensive natural areas	5.7.6

5.7.1 Favourable sites

Favourable sites for outdoor recreation activities should contrast with urban bustle, noise and pollution and include:

• picturesque, hilly landscapes with views;
• water: lakes, ponds, streams;
• vegetation: with trees, hedges and clearings.

Many areas, such as woodlands, have high visual appeal and privacy, but poor carrying capacity, while grassland looks occupied with relatively few users. A mix of wood and grassland (such as fields with clumps of trees, glades and edges of woods) is preferable.

In some places such sites are still common and allow free access for the inhabitants of nearby towns. Around most heavily populated areas, however, they have disappeared almost completely with industrialization of agriculture, rural restructuring, removal of

Ruhr Area, Germany: Regional planning for outdoor recreation

The Ruhr area, covering 4600 km², is one of the most densely inhabited in the world: 1200 inhabitants per km². In the 1960s, the area planning authority, the Siedlungsverband Ruhrkohlenbezirk (SVR) developed a comprehensive outdoor recreation plan creating:

- Extensive networks of roads, pedestrian and bicycle trails which link towns with the countryside, the forests, and some scattered facilities, and
- A number of major outdoor recreation centres linked to this network which cater for full family leisure. These centres present a variety of types:

	'Revierparks' (leisure complexes)		'Freizeitzentren' (leisure suburban parks)		'Freizeitstatten' (leisure places)	
	ha	acres	ha	acres	ha	acres
area of park	25–30	60–75	200–300	500–750	15	37
adjacent parkland or forest	25–30	60–75	100 and more	250+	100	250
body of water	none	none	100 and more	250+	possibly	
location	central area (1)		peripheral		intermediate	
impact	regional		regional		local	
authority	joint company of public interest under SVR's initiative		both categories		local authorities towns	
facilities	very diversified sport, cultural and recreational facilities designed for heavy use (2)		lighter facilities taking advantage of the presence of a body of water		as Revierparks although usually less developed	

(1) 25–50 000 inhabitants 15 minutes distance by foot and up to 1 million inhabitants within 20 minutes by car.
(2) Very numerous organized social, cultural and sporting events

//// Natural parks and recreational areas
▓   Regional system of green areas
Ⓢ   'Freizeitzentren'
◓   'Revierparks'
▼   'Freizeitstatten'

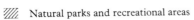

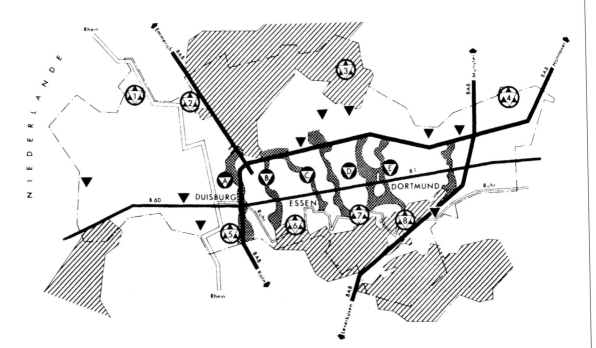

Suburban park in Wienerberg, Austria

This large park (85 ha) has been created on disused clay quarries and brick works which had been used for domestic refuse disposal. Quarrying and deposits have left traces in the landscape which still characterize the site today.

The Wienerberg was designated a forest and meadow belt protected area by the City of Vienna in 1975. At the city's edge, surrounded by satellite towns and lower density residential development, it provides the nearest countryside recreation area for the 160 000 inhabitants living in the south of Vienna.

The contrast between its moist low areas (with a lake of 16 ha) and its dry mounds has been maintained, the existing vegetation retained and extended with mown (12 ha) and natural (11 ha) meadows and reforested areas (14 ha). Today the area is open to pedestrians only (with bicycle trails at the periphery). Amongst the few facilities there are:

*   *paths (a few main paths only being planned and constructed; subsidiary paths and tracks have been created by the users of the park);*
*   *sitting areas, playgrounds and day camping (in boundary areas only).*

Client: Municipality of Vienna
Planners: Marija Kirchner, Dipl. Ing. and Wilfried Kirchner, Ing., Vienna

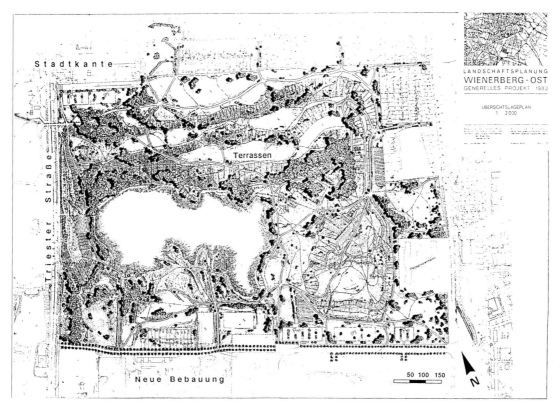

Master plan

General view

Aerial perspective sketch

Spaarnwoude recreation park (Holland)

An example of a park introduced, at the end of the 1960s, in a very densely inhabited area (1.5 million people in the vicinity) between Amsterdam and Harlem, on previous unattractive polders. The park covers 2800 ha, mainly untouched fields, with two equipped recreation areas: Buitenhuizen (670 ha) and Houtrad (160 ha).

Facilities include: aquatic activities, meadows for rest and picnicking, camping and day camps, farms (visits for children), sports fields, tennis courts, riding centre, golf, restaurants and refreshment stands.

More than 1.5 million people visit the park each year. Visitors on peak days total 50 000 in Buitenhuiuzen and 25 000 in Houtrad (75 to 150 persons/ha per day). Access is free (except public golf and day camping). The operating deficit is covered by the state, the province and the neighbouring towns.

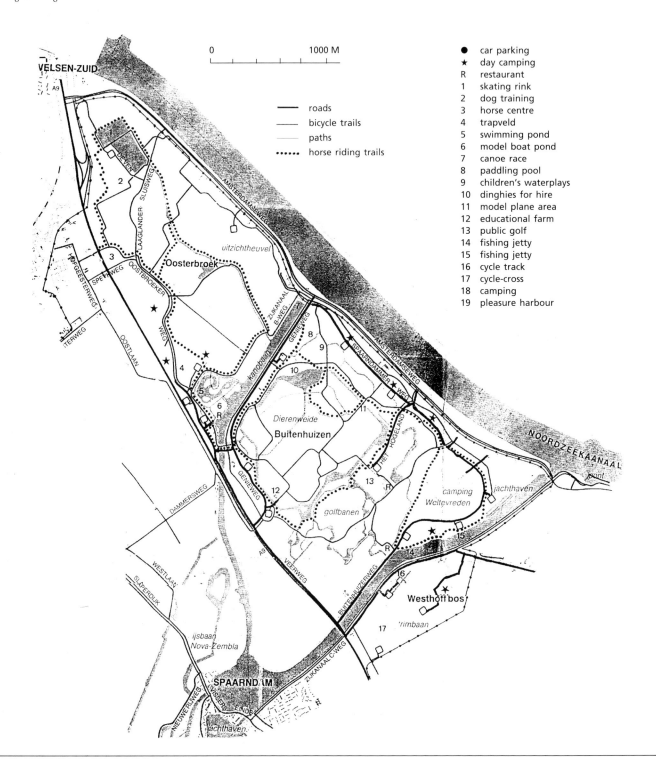

●	car parking
★	day camping
R	restaurant
1	skating rink
2	dog training
3	horse centre
4	trapveld
5	swimming pond
6	model boat pond
7	canoe race
8	paddling pool
9	children's waterplays
10	dinghies for hire
11	model plane area
12	educational farm
13	public golf
14	fishing jetty
15	fishing jetty
16	cycle track
17	cycle-cross
18	camping
19	pleasure harbour

roads
bicycle trails
paths
horse riding trails

0   1000 M

hedges, canalization of streams, and so on – and suburban parks are therefore indispensable.

Often the only sites available are poor or derelict, such as disused industrial areas, gravel or sand pits, or even waste dumps. Such areas have been successfully restored to parks around industrialized towns in Europe and the USA.

5.7.2 Specific facilities

The use of recreation parks depends on many criteria – pressure of demand, location in relation to urban areas, quality of site, facilities provided. Demand is generally highest at weekends, during school and public holidays and when there are special events. Facilities are never planned for the peak demand, but for the 'optimal day', when the demand is typically about two-thirds of the peak figure. Some three to five Sundays each year with an occupancy in excess of the optimum are considered acceptable.

There is a progressive shift towards more intensive use of recreational areas, necessitating increasing reinforcement of the natural environment by artificial features for durability, convenience, increased capacity and easier maintenance.

Basic facilities include:

- *Access area:* Access should be possible by public transport and bicycle trails, by pedestrian paths (from neighbourhoods) and by cars (mainly families, with an average of three persons/car). Parking areas should have stone paving or open grid concrete surfaces in preference to asphalt. Since most visitors come only during sunny weather, cars can be parked on gravel or grass, with reinforced circulation lanes only. For peak days, additional parking on grass is sufficient. Average density: 350 cars/ha (for 1000 occupants).
- *Grassed areas for picnic and games:* Green fields are essential for picnics and informal games and should be within 200–300 m of parking areas. Picnickers mainly come in family and other groups and often bring their own equipment. Apart from nearby sanitary facilities and rubbish bins, no other facilities are normally required – although sometimes fixed tables, benches and firegrates for barbecues are installed. Each picnic group occupies 50–100 m² giving an average density of 100–200 persons/ha.
- *Children's playgrounds:* Some suburban parks provide playgrounds for children (slides, swings, huts, rope bridges, adventure areas, etc.) in a sheltered area near the car park. In nature orientated parks, the trend is towards simplicity with basic equipment.

- *Day camping:* In some countries (for example, Holland and the USA) camping places for one day (sometimes two days including Saturday night) are provided for tents, caravans and camper vans. Basic sanitary facilities are installed. Average density 100–200 persons/ha.
- *Water features:* Water is often used as an element of landscaping, as well as the focus for recreation. This may be in the form of a natural or artificial lake, stream, swimming pool, or water cascades. Fountains, spurts or gushes of water, manually operated non-recirculating spray-pools also provide an opportunity for water play at minimal cost and space. The density around a pool, etc. at any one time (i.e. simultaneous use) is often 500 to 2000 persons/ha equal to 1000–5000 persons/day.
- *Sailing and boating:* If the water area is sufficient a jetty or slip may be installed for boats, sailing, water skiing, etc. with appropriate equipment and supervision. Separate sites may be allocated for fishing.
- *Catering:* Where the intensity of users is high a restaurant/snack bar pavilion may be viable. In other cases, day stands may be set up for peak periods only.
- *Other attractions:* Depending on the environment, these may include:
  - parks for deer and other native animals,
  - children's farm to allow close contact with domestic farm animals,
  - information centre or eco-museum presenting local flora, fauna, etc.,
  - arboretum and botanic or dendrological trails to observation points.
- *Networks of trails:* If the park is large or adjoins woods and other areas of countryside, a variety of signposted circuits of different lengths should be provided for fitness trails, walkers, cyclists and horse riders.

In purely recreation parks, buildings and asphalted areas should be kept to a minimum to retain a natural appearance for the area. However, many suburban parks near large towns and cities are faced with increasing demands for sports and leisure facilities and may be adapted to accommodate these needs (see 5.7.4–5).

5.7.3 Average densities

Recreational nature-based activities tend to fall into four distinct categories, related to the density of use, the activities proposed and the environmental character:

	Density of use			
	Very low	**Low**	**Medium**	**High**
Number of daily users per ha	less than 5	5–50	40–300	1000–2000
Quality of the environment	Contact with nature possible	Large spaces available	Uncrowded to crowded	Very crowded
Examples of activities	Using trails	Picnicking in the country	Organized sites for picnics/camping	Beaches, pools, sport centres
Facilities	Markers. Rest areas	Minimal	Necessary	Very important

Average densities in a suburban park are not significant: large areas (e.g. a forest) may attract a small number of users only; alternatively, users may be highly concentrated in one area, for example around a swimming pool. The effects of concentrated activities on average densities can be illustrated by four hypothetical examples.

Comparable sites (each 50 ha)	A	B	C	D
Forest, lake or pond (no. of ha)	39	18	16	13
Number of users (5 per ha)	195	90	80	65
Grassed areas for picnic/games (ha)	10	30	30	30
Number of users (100/ha)	1000	3000	3000	3000
Beach (no. of ha)	–	–	1	3
Number of users (1000 per ha)	–	–	1000	3000
Car park and miscellaneous (in ha)	1	2	3	4
Total area (ha)	50	50	50	50
Total number of users	1195	3090	4080	6065
Average density (no. of users per ha)	24.0	62.0	81.5	121.5

The maximum number of users is defined in each site by its natural features and the facilities provided. Exceeding this number means damage to the site and deterioration of the quality of the experience, in particular opportunities for contact with nature. Some comparative figures: New York Central Park receives 15 million visitors annually on 340 ha of park: an average of 120 daily visitors/ha, rising significantly on peak days.

5.7.4 Suburban recreation and leisure parks

Located near large towns and conurbations, this type of recreation park has a higher intensity of use and provides for a wider range of leisure interests. In Europe, these are described as:

* *Bases de plein air et de loisirs* (France),
* *Recreatieschap* (Holland),
* *Revierparks* (Germany).

In addition to the basic activities of a suburban recreation park, described above, a number of built attractions are constructed both to extend leisure interest and to provide wet weather facilities for year-round use. These popular attractions are often grouped together to create a nucleus near the points of access and parking places around which most visitors tend to congregate. Nuclear grouping is convenient for access and infrastructure and this concentration helps to reduce pressure on the more sensitive quieter recreation areas (the 'honeypot' effect).

The **range of attractions** provided depends on the extent to which they are available elsewhere in the catchment area – both public and commercial facilities – and the market demand. These may include bathing places, an open air swimming pool, a riding centre, a public golf course, light yachting facilities, a theatre concourse and restaurant/cafe. In cooler climates (and to extend the season of use) many of the facilities are grouped into a built leisure centre enclosing a landscaped pool and other activities (see 4.4.2). The German Revierparks in the Ruhr typically cover 25–35 ha and often include an indoor 'domed' pool with solarium, sauna and other attractions.

A few **trends** are indicated:

* range of attractions extending to all age groups;
* need to include revenue-generating facilities to offset high operating costs (restaurants, cafe outlets, equipment hire, instruction, club facilities, bowling, spectator events);
* educational programmes (aquariums, farm animals, ecology centres).

The **concept** of suburban parks is to offer a range of nature and sporting activities to the inhabitants of the town, at a very low tariff, but with low user-fees they are not feasible. Both the investment and operation costs therefore have to be subsidized, sometimes heavily.

Size and average density. The size varies depending on land availability (usually 20–100 ha). The average density: 25–100 visitors/ha/day rising to 400/ha/day on peak days and where there is a swimming pool.

On a smaller scale **countryside recreation parks** (*bases rurales*) are being developed in France on 20–30 ha, with ponds or other natural bathing places, picnic areas, camping site, 1–2 tennis courts, volleyball, etc., for a dual market:

* holidaymakers in the countryside;
* local recreationists (from towns of 100 000 inhabitants less than 50 km away or market towns of 15 000 inhabitants less than 15 km away).

5.7.5 Suburban recreation and sports parks

Sport orientated recreation parks combine standard sports grounds with more general recreational interests. They result from an evolution of the sporting facilities:

facilities conceived for a single sports club
↓
facilities shared by several sports clubs
↓
facilities shared by several clubs and individual participants
↓
combination of facilities for sport and family relaxation

Sports grounds within a recreational setting facilitate better contacts between club activities, sports enthusiasts and other types of recreational users, which often generates a wider interest and participation in both sport and family recreation. In this regard, the investment is usually more readily acceptable for community support and municipal funding. Often the same sports grounds can be scheduled for regular use by schools, local clubs and competitions. However, the management has to maintain a careful balance between the needs of all types of user.

In addition to the recreation facilities (see 5.7.2) provision is usually made for:

- *standard sports grounds* (football/athletics, tennis courts, etc.) which are carefully landscaped with embankments and trees,
- *services* such as changing rooms, clubhouses, equipment stores and refreshment stands,
- *spectator areas* with raised banks and (possibly) seating.

Depending on the space and resources of the park, a boating/sailing lake, a public golf course or practice range, a competition standard swimming pool, archery ranges and other, more specialized, sports areas may be included.

Circulation planning must take into account the different needs of visitors:

- participants in the various activities;
- spectators with specific interests;
- non-committed visitors seeking general leisure or entertainment;
- families with multiple requirements.

The interfaces between those taking part and others merely looking on require special attention.

Location: Relaxation and sports parks are usually situated very near to the city, with convenient public transport, in order to be used:

- after work on weekdays by sports persons and others taking daily exercise;
- by schools, societies, clubs and other groups;
- by large numbers of users at weekends and on public holidays.

Many parks having a high density of usage tend to become more urbanized, with the addition of:

- extensive indoor sports facilities (indoor swimming pool, sports hall, ice skating rinks);
- artificial sports pitches, courts, tracks and training areas, often with floodlighting, to allow intensive use extending into the evenings;
- covered seating in the main stadium, etc.

5.7.6 Suburban recreation and nature parks

Nature orientated recreation parks are similar to basic recreation areas (see 5.7.4 above), but with a low density of use and backed by an extended nature area: moors, pastures, dunes, marshes, streams, woodland. Often they include artificial features (man-made ponds, lakes, hills, landscapes) to facilitate use. They have been located sometimes around reservoirs and flooded workings (gravel pits, clay workings, etc.). Their equivalents in Europe are:

- *bases de nature* (France)
- *Freizeitzentren* (Kemnade in Ruhr, Germany)
- *large recreatieschaps* (Biesbosch, Bielse Meer, Holland)
- *Naturparks und Erholungsräume* (Austria)
- country parks (UK)

Usual **characteristics**:

- *size*: variable, from 30 to 1000 ha or more (but only a part equipped for visitors)
- location: up to 50 km from town, or more.
- objectives: to provide recreational opportunities during the weekend, in order to reduce pressure of demand on the more vulnerable natural parks.

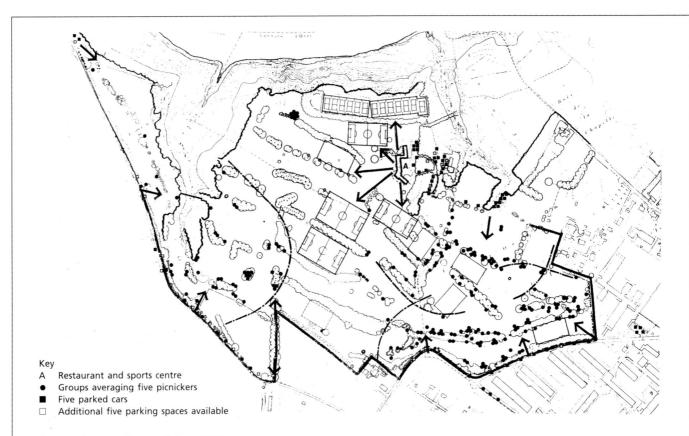

Key
A   Restaurant and sports centre
●   Groups averaging five picnickers
■   Five parked cars
☐   Additional five parking spaces available

Survey of use on Sunday 9 June 1986

Master plan

Picnickers

Athletics track with sunken services

Track services

One of the three toilet blocks for picnickers

Recreation and sports park, Les Evaux, Geneva, Switzerland

Created in the 1970s on land previously used for a golf course (50 ha), this suburban park provided tennis courts, football fields, a restaurant with changing and sanitary facilities, and extensive meadows separated by lines of old oaks and newly planted birches. The site was used by neighbouring communities for children playing, dogowners exercising their pets, by visitors from the town, footballers and families picnicking (up to 2000 people on Sundays). In order to extend the sports facilities – involving additional well-drained football fields and a new athletics track – without jeopardizing the valuable landscape, a study was undertaken in 1986, and implemented in 1995. This involved:

- grouping the sports activities in the middle part of the site (less visited by picnickers) with the track in a less visible remote place, with sunken changing facilities, screened by banking;
- organizing a network of circular trails for pedestrians, horseriders and disabled people;
- building three toilet blocks for picnickers.

Architects/planners: A. & M. Baud-Bovy, Geneva

Master plan

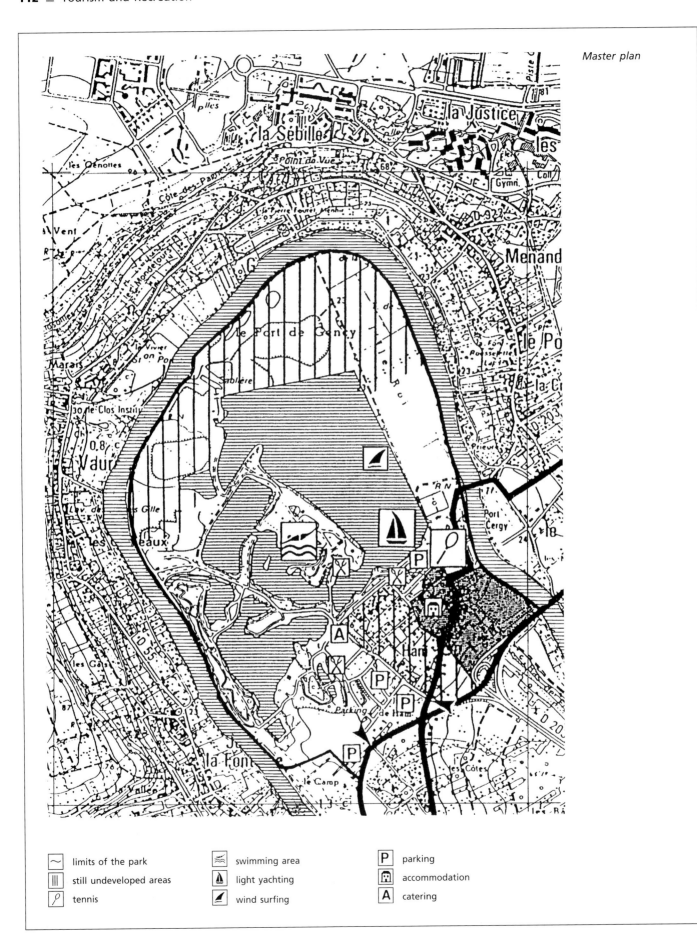

	limits of the park		swimming area	P	parking
	still undeveloped areas		light yachting		accommodation
	tennis		wind surfing	A	catering

Original ponds

Proposed development

Recreation and sports park, Cergy-Neuville, France

This suburban park was projected in 1970 using gravel pits (and ponds) in a crook of the River L'Oise, around which the new town of Cergy Pontoise was being developed, near Paris. The project was conceived around three poles: (a) sports activities, (b) farming activities with a children's farm (not implemented because of high maintenance costs) and (c) nature observation. The base facilities opened in 1979.

By 1996, 150 ha had been developed with 90 ha of water. A further 70 ha (still occupied by gravel pits) and 20 ha (occupied by private houses) are to be added at a future date. The facilities provided include:

- swimming area (10 ha of which 1.6 ha are water), around one of the ponds with a diverse range of attractions (paddling pool, flume, water teleski, etc.);
- boating area with light sailing boats and canoes for rent and a windsurfing area;
- tennis (11 courts) with training courses; mini-golf; a beginners' golf course is also being considered;
- activities for children and young persons;
- picnic areas and a variety of trails, fishing, nature observation, etc.;
- three snackbars;
- a multi-purpose sports hall and accommodation for groups of up to 140 people (in order to increase the out of season occupancy).

Planned in 1978 for 18 000 simultaneous users, the park has received in recent years 50 000 to 70 000 visitors on peak days (up to 2 million visitors annually) coming from the new town (25 per cent), the surrounding area (25 per cent), Paris (25 per cent) and other regions (25 per cent).

Staff (1990): 30 permanent employees and 12 temporary, but during the summer there are usually more than 100 people working, including instructors provided by non-profit-making associations, catering staff, etc. The revenues earned cover about 65–70 per cent of the operating costs.

Miribel-Jonage recreation and nature park, Lyon, France

The site

An island, north-east of Lyon, between two branches (canals) of the River Rhône, with a direct access from the Lyon-Geneva highway:
Island area: 3000 ha of which 800 are cultivated by 20 farmers;
Public area: 2200 ha, of which 800 make up the recreation park (including 300 ha of water);
Diverse landscapes: dry meadows (30 orchid species), alluvial forest, marshes and reeds, botanical garden and rich fauna (beavers, waterfowl).

Development

The SYMALIM, which owns the 2200-ha public area, was created in 1968 by regional authorities, Greater Lyon, the town of Lyon and eleven local communities to:

- regulate the river (part of the park may be flooded);
- protect the aquifer for Lyon's drinking water;
- create a recreation and nature park adjacent to Lyon's suburbs;
- commission studies to develop the park on behalf of SYMALIM;
- maintain and operate the park and its main facilities.

SEGAPAL, created in 1979, and the park operator, consists of 50 permanent employees (six administration, thirty maintenance, twelve sports centre, two security), plus temporary employees and a police force of twenty (on horses or motorbike), during the summer season.
Other facilities are operated by associations (horse-riding centres) or commercial companies (drink stands, restaurant).

Facilities

- Several beaches (accommodating 5000 visitors each) with facilities.
- Picnic sites (with gravel parking) with meadows for relaxation and informal games.
- Bicycle trails (up to Lyon City), pedestrian paths, mountain bike and horse riding trails.
- Fishing and hunting areas.
- Three horse-riding centres.
- A sports centre (15 ha) with water-based activities, six tennis courts (one indoor), fitness hall, sauna, basketball and volleyball courts, restaurant and snack bars, artificial climbing wall, golf driving range, archery butts and other sports, with ten instructors and equipment for rent.
- Holiday centre for 200 children.

The facilities will be extended in the period 1996–8 with:

- the creation of an additional lake;
- rehabilitation of the four existing gravel quarries to make nature trails, ecological banks;
- the extension of a marsh where the river floods, to encourage new flora and fauna;
- maintenance of the natural areas.

Future plans include: a theme park on the environment, an ecological farm, a nature interpretation centre and trails.

The visitors

- 3 to 3.5 millions visitor each year
- 50 000 visitors (17 000 cars) on peak days, most for water-based activities.

Almost half of the visitors reach the park in less than 15 minutes from the nearby suburban 'new town'.

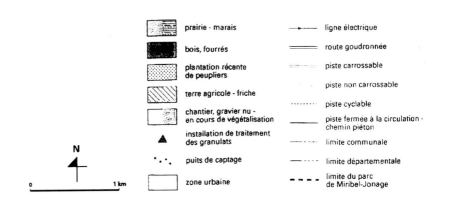

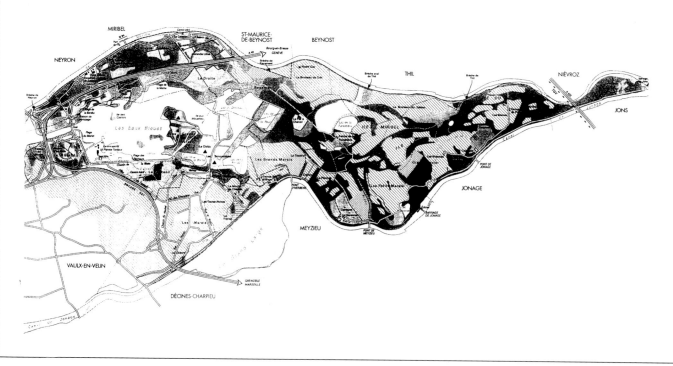

- limits of park
→ access
= road
-- trail
★ reception
P car parking
∩ picnic site
▲ equipped camping site
∧ light camping
⌂ accommodation
△ canoe camping
≈ slipway
∧ canoe facility
△ light yachting
⋯ preservation area
▨ recreation area

Parc de Frontenac, Quebec, Canada

This recreation and nature park was created at the beginning of the 1980s along the large lake of St-François, following studies initiated in 1967. In less than two hour's drive, 1.5 million people have access to the park.

The park (155 km²) is public land (previous public property or recently bought private land) but surrounded by private agricultural properties which have limited its extension. Its main resources are the lakes, maple forests, peat areas and conifer forests on marshy land, and a rich fauna.

The draft development plan of 1985 distinguishes:

- *two preservation areas (access limited to a few trails);*
- *a few intensive small recreation areas with facilities for parking, camping, swimming and sailing;*
- *the rest of the park, essentially for excursions by foot, horse or canoe, with very light facilities only, along the trail system.*

Source: Ministère du Loisir, Chasse et Pêche (1985) Le parc de Frontenac

5.8 NATURE PARKS

Most outstanding natural areas can accommodate a limited number of visitors without detriment and the provision of a few well-designed facilities will invariably add to convenience and enjoyment without loss of the benefits of the surroundings. But the situation changes, often dramatically, when the numbers of visitors or facilities increase beyond a certain threshold:

*   the quality of the visitor experience progressively decreases;
*   facilities begin to dominate the site and (owing to a change of scale or density) lose contact and harmony with the natural scenery;
*   excessive numbers of visitors and/or their activities physically damage the site and its ecology.

These effects are magnified when vehicles (cars, coaches, motorized sports) are involved. Changes in character are usually insidious and only recognized after the event.

5.81 National parks

Protection of important natural areas, of ecosystems which have not been significantly altered by human activity, may be secured by land-use classification as a national park. The usual size of national parks is between 100 and 5000 km² (10 000 to 5 000 000 ha), although varying from 5 km² at the smallest to 9000 km² (Yellowstone, USA) and even 20 000 km² (Tsavo, Kenya). The two fundamental objectives, both calling for staff highly skilled in protection and management are:

*   the protection of natural resources, providing legal protection against all exploitation (including hunting, stock grazing, agriculture, lumbering and mining);
*   the reception, under special conditions, of visitors for educational, cultural and recreational purposes (using guides and rangers).

These rather strict conditions, defined by the International Union for Conservation of Nature, exclude most of the European national parks where:

*   the presence of people has substantially modified the primitive wilderness;
*   human establishments and traditional activities (such as lumbering, agriculture, stock grazing) are accepted and to some extent encouraged;
*   controlled hunting and fishing may even be authorized.

Where the conservation of vast areas appears to be in the national interests, a less restrictive definition may be adopted.

In fact, most national parks have tourist/recreation facilities. Their density and location are largely dictated by circumstances and policies. As a general rule, in countries which are sparsely populated, the main facilities may be conveniently located in the core of extended parks (such as the tourist facilities in African wildlife reserves) but in densely inhabited countries they have to be located at the periphery of smaller parks. In planning terms, this may be represented by the principle of concentric zoning shown in Fig. 5.9.

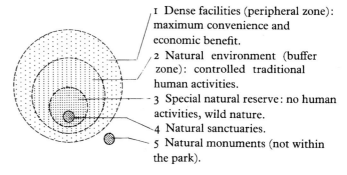

1 Dense facilities (peripheral zone): maximum convenience and economic benefit.
2 Natural environment (buffer zone): controlled traditional human activities.
3 Special natural reserve: no human activities, wild nature.
4 Natural sanctuaries.
5 Natural monuments (not within the park).

Figure 5.9

According to the circumstances, one or more of these zones may or may not be represented and the peripheral zone need not extend all around the 'park' boundaries. A methodological approach for planning national and regional parks is provided in 8.5.2.

Types of facilities appropriate for each zone:

*   **Peripheral zones**: Facilities for tourism and recreation (accommodation, catering, sport, picnicking) including associated buildings (with strict control over siting and quality). Preferably grouped together near access routes and existing settlements). The recreation facilities may be comparable to those for suburban nature parks (see 5.7.6).
*   **Natural environment**: Facilities may include catering and light sports facilities (for swimming, sailing, boating, fishing, skiing etc.), accommodation of a temporary nature: camping and caravan camps or *eco-lodges*. Eco-lodges – or nature-based lodges – are tourist lodges that meet the philosophy and principles of ecotourism: carefully integrated into their environment, offering an educational and participatory experience through nature interpretation, trail hiking, wildlife tours, bird watching, river trips). Of limited capacity (usually 25 to 80 beds with catering and bar), they are built with natural materials, reflecting local traditions and building methods and operated in an environmentally sensitive manner (Hawkins *et al.* 1995).

A park information centre should be provided at the entrance to the zone, giving a complete briefing on the park's significance and resources, and information on activities and excursions (with a reservation system) including nature interpretation trails (centre-guided or self-guided trails), colour coded for different lengths from 0.5 to 3 km (0.3 to 2 miles). Museums of natural history and/or crafts and customs (housed in original or reconstructed traditional buildings) may be provided, and the information centre may serve as an excursion base where individual cars are parked and visitors transfer to public park transport (buses, tramways, cable lifts etc.).

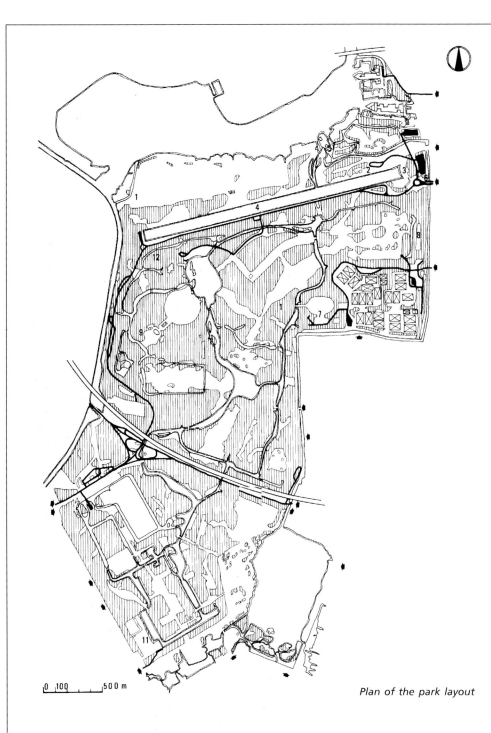

Key

▨ Wooded areas
▢ Grassed areas
⊠ Sports fields
▭ Water
— Main roads for all traffic
▸ Entrance
1 Farm and Forest Park Museum
2 Bosbaan Restaurant and Stand
3 Boat houses
4 Rowing courses
5 Canoe hire
6 Bicycle hire
7 Equestrian centre with manége
8 Pony centre
9 Children's paddling pools
10 The Hill
11 Camping site
12 Open-air theatre

Plan of the park layout

Amsterdam Bos, Holland

One of the first examples, dating from 1928, of a suburban nature park. Constructed out of a polder landscape, with water levels about 4.6 m below sea level, by part excavating, part raising the ground levels, the park extends over 905 ha (2235 acres) with the proportions of water:open spaces:woodland about 1:1:1. Woodland — rare near Amsterdam — was introduced in sections of 20–30 ha to provide a wind screen and natural landscape as a contrast to the urban areas.

Most parts of the park are accessible to vehicles and 5000 parking places are provided, but a number of entrances and paths are exclusive to pedestrians and cyclists. The park receives on an average busy day between 40 000 and 80 000 visitors with peaks of 100 000 visitors/day.

- **Special natural reserve**: No roads, other than essential ones restricted to public transport; organized circuits for nature interpretation, trails for bicycling, walking, horse riding, limited activities such as hiking, climbing, nordic skiing. There are no facilities other than rudimentary camping sites and shelters for mountaineering.
- **Natural sanctuaries**: No access, no facilities.

National parks necessitate public ownership (or at least public control through lease, purchase or other form of acquisition). They may represent appreciable sources of foreign exchange (in Kenya or Tanzania for example) and important assets in tourism promotion and attraction (US national parks).

The policies related to protected areas have evolved (Agee and Johnson 1988) in recent years:

- earlier aims: adequate protection of undeveloped, essentially unmanaged areas within a protected boundary;
- later aims: need for active management within park and wilderness boundaries;
- present aims: refined goals and implementation of cooperative management with the neighbouring landowners.

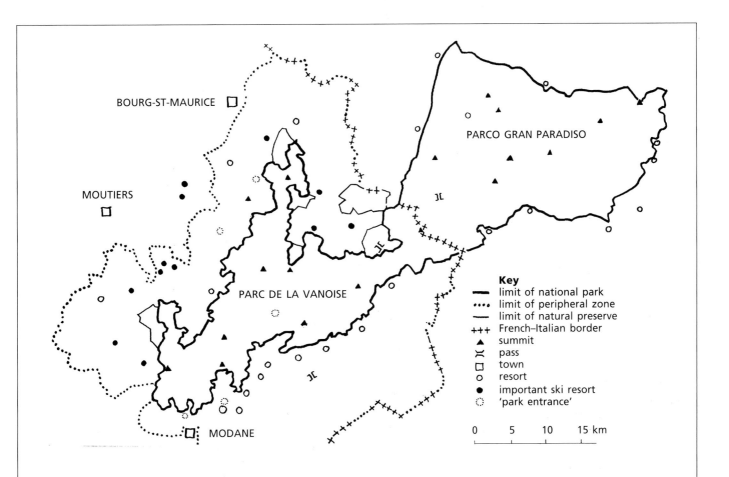

A 'European' alpine park, France-Italy

Over the French–Italian border, two parks have been united:

- *the Italian Gran Paradiso (70 000 ha, 13 parishes, created in 1922)*
- *the French La Vanoise (53 000 + 140 000 ha, 28 parishes, created in 1963)*

With summits up to 4000 m, both alpine parks are aimed at safeguarding unique landscapes, a rich flora and fauna (in particular ibexes, chamois, eagles and vultures).

The creation of La Vanoise caused conflicts with important ski resorts such as Val Thorens, Meribel, Tignes and Val d'Isère). Hence the national park was limited and supplemented with a peripheral zone which includes the main ski resorts and smaller, more traditional, mainly summer resorts. The peripheral zone provides a variety of accommodation, sports and leisure facilities, park information offices and most of the park entrances — including accommodation for special groups and a two-hour nature trail. In the park itself serviced mountain huts are provided; hunting, dogs and mountain bikes are prohibited; camping, pasture and forest activities regulated.

The notion of a peripheral zone did not exist at the time the Parco Gran Paradiso was created: the park is zoned between areas of total preservation and village areas with controlled development.

The park rangers organize guided walks, nature trails, slides and films shows and other educational facilities for schools and interested groups.

Asir National Park, Saudi Arabia

Located in the south-west of the country, the Asir National Park contains 450 000 ha, from the shores of the Red Sea and its coral reefs, to a coastal plain and its wadis, to the foothills and the rim of escarpments, and to the highest part of the country (over 3000 m in altitude) and its juniper trees. On the inland side of the escarpment, several villages are made of stone and mud houses with terraces to capture the water.

The visitor centre in Abha contains exhibits and explains the concept of the park: the visitor, using stairs from the sea to the summit of the cliffs, is able to view the park from the lookout fitted with telescopes. Additional viewpoints, camping grounds, hiking trails, picnic areas, restrooms and catering facilities are provided at several points along the crest.

A five-star hotel, apartments and luxury villas are provided in New Abha, one of the coolest places of the Kingdom. A beach development is envisaged at Al Shuqayq.

Designated in 1976 and developed with advice from the United States National Park Service, Asir has been designed by Wirth and Berger, Idea Center and Consortium West.

Source: Guide to Asir National Park

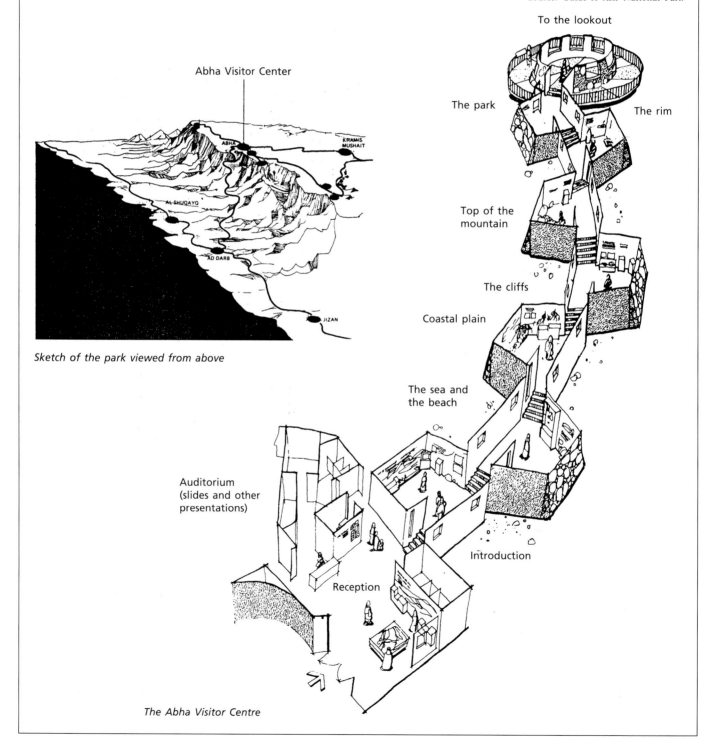

Abha Visitor Center

Sketch of the park viewed from above

To the lookout

The park

The rim

Top of the mountain

The cliffs

Coastal plain

The sea and the beach

Auditorium (slides and other presentations)

Introduction

Reception

The Abha Visitor Centre

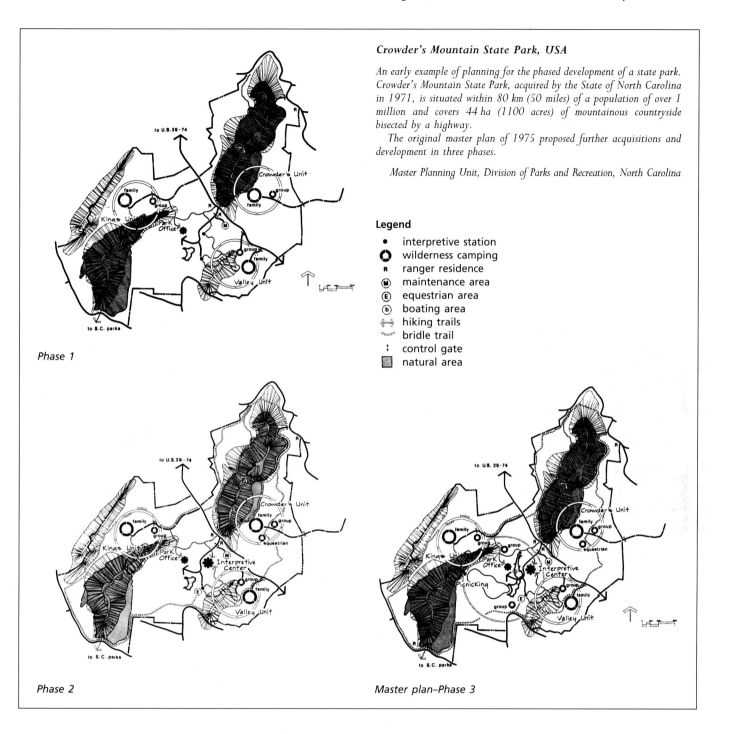

Crowder's Mountain State Park, USA

An early example of planning for the phased development of a state park. Crowder's Mountain State Park, acquired by the State of North Carolina in 1971, is situated within 80 km (50 miles) of a population of over 1 million and covers 44 ha (1100 acres) of mountainous countryside bisected by a highway.

The original master plan of 1975 proposed further acquisitions and development in three phases.

Master Planning Unit, Division of Parks and Recreation, North Carolina

Legend

- • interpretive station
- Ⓞ wilderness camping
- ℝ ranger residence
- Ⓜ maintenance area
- Ⓔ equestrian area
- ⓑ boating area
- ⟷ hiking trails
- °°°° bridle trail
- ⌇ control gate
- ▨ natural area

Phase 1

Phase 2

Master plan–Phase 3

5.8.2 Regional parks

The regional parks (corresponding to UK country parks, US state parks, French *parcs régionaux*, some of the German *Naturparks* and Dutch *recreatieschaps*) are generally of a smaller acreage and under regional, municipal or joint control rather than that of the state. Parks of this type may be established to safeguard an attractive landscape from industrialization and urbanization, preserve examples of the traditions of the country (traditional agricultural methods, old mills, sawmills, old mines etc.) and may develop natural attractions (ponds,

lake, plantations, etc.). They are often located near important population centres and generally offer numerous facilities to visitors: educational and cultural (in particular visitor centres aiming to develop a responsible behaviour amongst visitors) but also strictly for recreation. One of the objectives may be to reduce the pressure for outdoor recreation in the national parks. Typically regional parks receive five to twenty visitors per day per ha.

The size of the German *Naturparks* varies from 4000 to 300 000 ha (average 85 000), covering more than 20 per cent of the former Federal Republic territory:

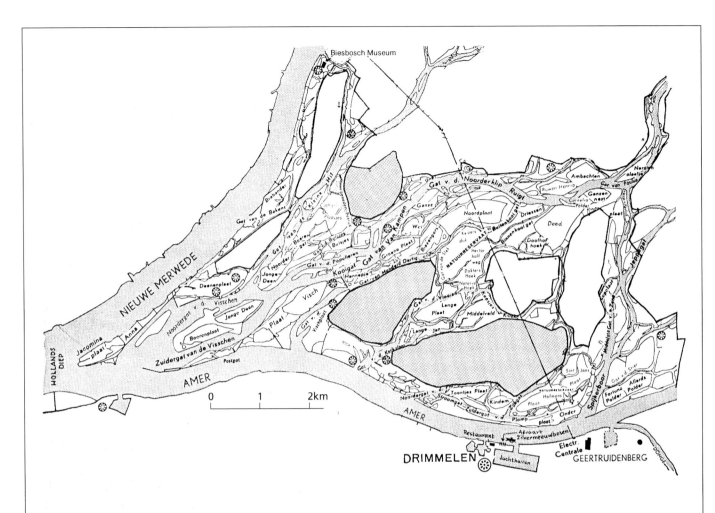

Biesbosch National Park, Holland

South of Rotterdam, the Biesbosch is a large area (6800 ha) with extensive water (two rivers, many little streams, three artificial water reservoirs), natural vegetation (willows, reeds and rushes) and a variety of other plants and birds.

The southern part of the park covers 3000 ha, with an access point in Drimmelen which provides camping and bungalows for rent, a visitor centre, marina and round-trip passenger boats. Canoes, rowing boats or water cycles are available for hire. East of Drimmelen, 5 km outside the park's boundaries, the Kurenpolder recreation centre (80 ha) provides a large pond, light yachting and windsurfing, beaches and day camping.

In the northern part (3800 ha), the recreation park of Merwelanden (200 ha) offers a visitor centre (100 000 visitors/year), paths and bicycle trails, playgrounds, fish ponds, a restaurant, golf course, horse riding, artificial ski track, picnic and informal sports areas, natural swimming pool, day camping and a nature trail of about 5 km visited by 500 000 people each year.

Visits to the park are mainly by boat. Some waterways are open to motor boat traffic, others only to individual visitors with rowing boats or canoes. Some places have meadows for picnics or rest, nature trails or a museum. Other areas of the park and several waterways are strictly forbidden to visitors.

- larger ones, with extended areas providing a high degree of protection, but also offering leisure and tourism activities in other parts, may be considered as national parks;
- smaller ones are quite similar to the French *parcs régionaux*.

They are controlled by associations, joint private–public organizations or local administrations. The regions (*Länder*) and the local communities, provide most of the financing.

The French *parcs régionaux* (Billet 1982), typically covering 100 to 3000 ha, are aimed at:

- preserving natural/cultural heritage and traditions;

- developing traditional human activities (agriculture, forestry, livestock farming, etc.);
- providing tourism and outdoor leisure activities, preferably involving the local community and benefiting the local economy, with accommodation usually provided in farms or in small hotels.

The constraints for the local population (strict controls on buildings and landscape, prohibition of industry or industrial agriculture) are balanced by:

- the presence of a local administration to manage and promote the park;

Map of the national park

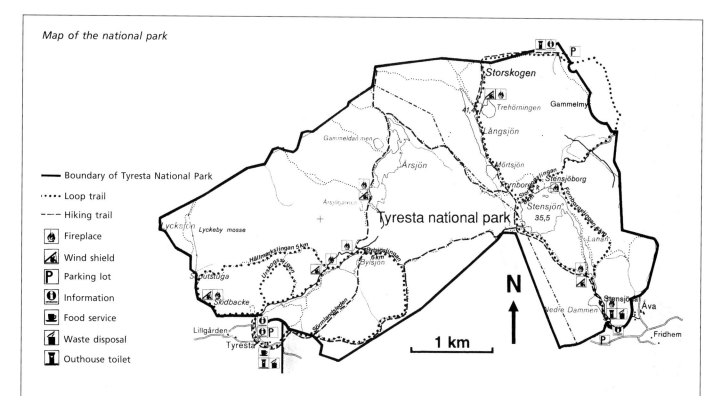

- **——** Boundary of Tyresta National Park
- **·····** Loop trail
- **– – –** Hiking trail
- 🔥 Fireplace
- ⛺ Wind shield
- 🅿 Parking lot
- ℹ Information
- 🍴 Food service
- 🗑 Waste disposal
- 🚻 Outhouse toilet

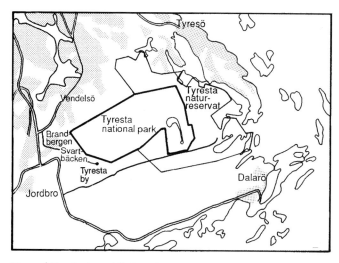

Map of the Park and Nature Reserve

The forest

Tyresta National Park, Sweden

Located only 20 km south-east of Stockholm, this park was established in 1993 and covers some 2000 ha (4900 acres). Its purpose is to preserve a representative fissure valley landscape, with extensive undisturbed, primeval forest (a part of which has been affected by commercial forestry in the past will now be left to develop naturally), wooded pastures and forest lakes. The park provides facilities for camping, picnicking, fishing, bathing and rowing, and trails for skiing, hiking or cycling.

The National Park is surrounded by the Tyresta Nature Reserve, covering almost 2700 ha (6700 acres). This Reserve acts as a buffer zone around the Park, whilst preserving plants and animals less sensitive to disturbances than those in the Park.

Source: Naturvårdsverket –
Swedish Environmental Protection Agency

- creation of cultural facilities: visitor centre, specialized trails, etc.;
- promotion (in particular by the 'park label' which attracts tourists and recreationists);
- rehabilitation of traditional buildings;
- direct subsidies to the local population to meet the added costs of building in traditional styles or for the development of facilities for visitors (accommodation, horse riding centres, etc.);
- other assistance for the development of infrastructures or activities.

The terms and conditions may be stated in a joint agreement between the park authority, the region and a syndicate of the local authorities concerned (the *charte* of the French *parcs régionaux*).

Regional parks consider both the protection of the environment and the development of the local economy. Much more than the traditional national parks, new regional parks play an increasingly important role in many areas of Europe, with trends towards a more environmentally-concerned, traditional agriculture (Weixlbaumer 1995).

Other French *parcs régionaux* or, in Quebec the *parcs naturels de récréation*, which are created in relatively poor natural environments essentially to provide for recreational activities, are considered in this book as *suburban relaxation and nature parks* (see 5.7.6).

5.8.3 Forests and recreation

Now that recreation has moved into the tourist environment, it has collided with the established uses of forest land and caused serious conflicts. Established and necessary uses of forest land are being attacked by recreationists who need more area … Recreation planning will help to make these collisions less inflammatory by pointing out potential conflicts in the use of the land and water before they happen and by suggesting ways of mitigating the impact … Timing of recreation development is very important for providing the optimal mix of facilities with the minimum investment. Much of the total cost depends upon the advanced planning and the direct purchase of land … Management of forest areas requires long-term plans that give the forest manager an outline of the operation to be undertaken in the forest. If recreation planning information were available to the forester far enough in advance, possibly recreation sites could be saved, specially cut, or cut far in advance of the time when they will be needed for recreation.

(Douglass 1982, p. 27)

Forests provide outstanding opportunities for contact with nature and recreation, at minimal cost, both within and outside regional parks. In many countries forests, even privately owned, are open to the public and their use for outdoor recreation is encouraged, particularly where forestry operations are no longer profitable. Indeed, the relevant public authority may impose public access as a condition of grant aid and other advantages for the forest's owners.

Activities are usually zoned:

- *reception areas:* non-asphalted car parking areas at access points;
- *recreation areas:* grassed areas for picnics at the edges or in clearings (with rubbish containers and, possibly, water points and firegrates for barbecues) linked to a variety of trails;
- *reserved areas:* for forestry operations;
- *nature reserves:* with restricted entry.

Access for motor vehicles and camping sites are usually only feasible in larger forests (over 5–10 km^2). Where there is a substantial visitor demand it may be necessary to organize the following (Plaisance 1979):

- *information, education and control* of visitors – with a visitor centre, maps, directions, guided walks;
- *specific sites* – equipped for parking, camping and recreational activities if the forest is sufficiently large;
- *maintenance* – cleaning after periods of heavy use, restoration and reinforcement of damaged areas, paths, etc.

In small forests near large towns, where intensive use may compromise natural regeneration, it is necessary to maintain the area as a *forest park* with a programme of replanting and restoration work. In other cases, the distribution of visitors over a sufficiently large area is important in order to minimize degradation.

5.8.4 Protected natural areas

These are interesting habitats, areas with a valuable fauna and flora, or a characteristic landscape (dunes, lake, pastures, forest, river banks), too small to be considered as national parks but nevertheless worthy of legal protection. According to their uniqueness they may be managed as natural sanctuaries or special nature reserves (see 9.2.1) or both in different parts.

At the same time, similar but less unique sites are often most convenient for outdoor activities and conflicts of interest may arise between total exclusion of recreational use and the loss of legal protection of the ecosystem. However, provision may generally be made for limited use (Lime and Stankey 1979), for example:

- by confining the movement of visitors to defined trails, and opening areas of lesser ecological value;
- by imposing constraints on visitors: zoning in space or time, rotation of opened areas, limitation of numbers and groups, pre-booking requirements or higher fees on peak days;
- by modifying visitors' behaviour by explaining the limitations, by an introduction to the site and its resources through publications or in a visitors' interpretation centre;
- by facilitating the natural recovery process through irrigation, fertilization or reseeding, or locally converting the natural vegetation cover to more hardy species or laying board-walks.

Chailluz Forest, near Besançon, France

The forest extends over 1630 ha, of which 1200 are essentially for forestry and 310 for recreation and leisure in two distinct areas:

- A sports area (access by public bus within 400 m and car parking) with two jogging trails (1100 and 2200 m) equipped with gymnastic stands; picnic facilities; bicycle trails throughout the forest and pedestrian paths.
- A forest park with car parks and
  - a variety of pedestrian trails (dendro/flower trail, fitness trail, etc) and cycle tracks,
  - clearings with picnic tables, benches and firegrates for barbecues,
  - drinking water, toilets and shelters,
  - information centre (combined with forest guard),
  - an animal park with deer, wild pigs and other native species.

Created by Ville de Besançon, operated by Office National des Forêts.

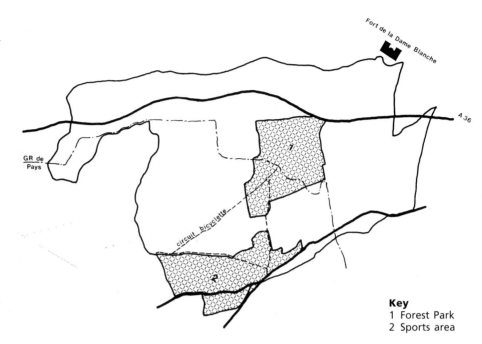

Key
1 Forest Park
2 Sports area

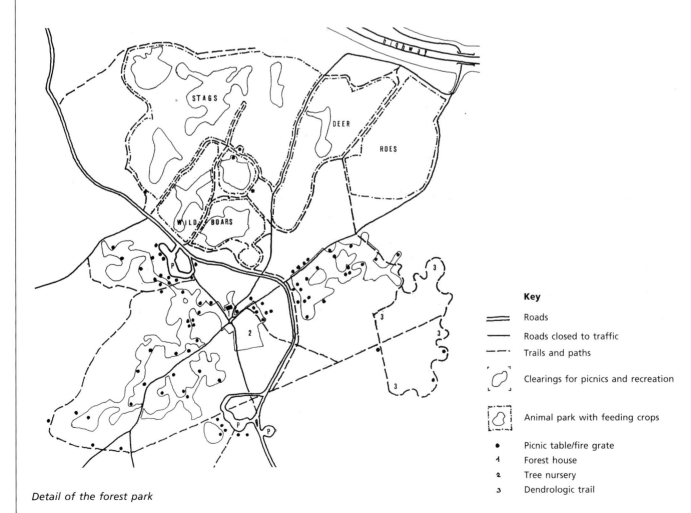

Key

═══	Roads
───	Roads closed to traffic
─ ─ ─	Trails and paths
⬭	Clearings for picnics and recreation
⬚	Animal park with feeding crops
•	Picnic table/fire grate
1	Forest house
2	Tree nursery
3	Dendrologic trail

Detail of the forest park

Corresponding planning principles include:

- *A master plan*, based on surveys of both the ecosystem and the needs of the potential visitors (a kind of advocacy planning), distinguishing between:
  - exceptional habitats considered as natural sanctuaries;
  - special nature reserves with controlled access and activities (e.g. controlled fishing);
  - recreation areas with minimal facilities (picnic areas without tables or benches, but with a water supply and rubbish bins).

- *Reception areas* combining control and education. In large sites a visitor centre may include:
  - background information, museum, library;
  - relief photographs, projected or video-screen illustrations;
  - aquarium, vivarium, herbarium, aviary;
  - identification games (e.g. birds by their songs);
  - botanic or dendrologic trails, etc.

6 Planning tourist resorts and recreation complexes

Whilst individual travel accommodation and other facilities may be located in and around places where there are specific attractions or other market needs (e.g. business travel), most tourist facilities are concentrated into resorts. This pattern of concentrated development is likely to continue with the need to conserve valuable resources. The same can be said of recreation: many new recreational centres encompass a wide variety of both active and passive leisure pursuits within a single complex.

6.1 TOURIST RESORTS

A resort is essentially a place developed for the sojourn of tourists, providing multiple facilities for their accommodation, recreation, entertainment, rest and other needs. Through the concentration of facilities the resort acquires an identity and character: it becomes a specific place to go to and to enjoy in its own right, in addition to serving as a gateway to other resources in the area. Tourist resorts enable the best use to be made of infrastructure and land and of operational services.

6.1.1 Tourist resorts and tourist towns

The term tourist resort, as opposed to a tourist town, applies only where tourism plays a major economic role: where the percentage of tourist beds to inhabitants is very significant. As a rule, the numbers of tourists accommodated in a resort comprise at least half the resident population – as in Cannes or Deauville, for example, compared with towns like Nice in which tourists constitute only about 20 per cent of the population.

Size of tourist resorts, in terms of the numbers of tourist beds, is critical in financing the infrastructure and in marketing.

	Typical numbers of beds
First phase of development	500
Privately-developed resorts (e.g. Club Méditerranée Villages)	800–2000
Small exclusive resorts in unique locations	200–500
Maximum for pedestrian circulation	8000–10 000
Large prominent resorts generating publicity and having an impact on travel patterns	10 000–15 000
Many traditional urbanized resorts (e.g. Rimini)	50 000 plus

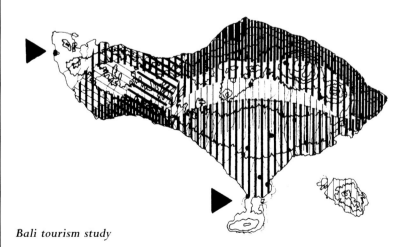

Hatched areas are:
(a) required for other major economic activities (rice growing and other land uses)
(b) not physically suitable for tourism development:
(c) not suitable because of distance from entry points of tourists (airports)

The light coloured are those most propitious for tourist accommodation

▶ airports

Bali tourism study

An early example of approach for the selection of suitable areas for resort development by eliminating unsuitable areas (see key) (Study by SCETO in association with SCET-COOP and SEDES for the UN Development Programme 1970)

Bali: Development of Nusa Dua

The tourism structure of Bali stems from the original Tourism Master Plan, 1971 which identified sites in the south within easy transfer distance of the airport as being Areas of Priority Touristic Interest (APTI). Areas suitable for resort development were originally identified by eliminating those regions which were required for other activities, not suitable for development, or too far from the airport (page 129). Nusa Dua was planned as an integrated resort, with high quality infrastructure financed by the World Bank, and has been developed as one of the world's most exotic destinations with luxury standard hotels.

The Bali Hilton has 544 guest-rooms and suites arranged around a man-made lagoon with an island containing a swimming pool, bar and Balinese theatre. An underground service road extends to the guest and public areas (Architects: Killingsworth Striker Lindgren Wilson & Associates)

Grand Hyatt Bali, opened in 1991, is a cluster of four ethnic villages with 750 guest-rooms and 41 suites set amidst 16 ha (40 acres) of interlinked cascading waterfalls, gardens and lagoons, and includes six swimming pools and a Balinese craft village (Architects: Wimberly Allison Tong & Goo)

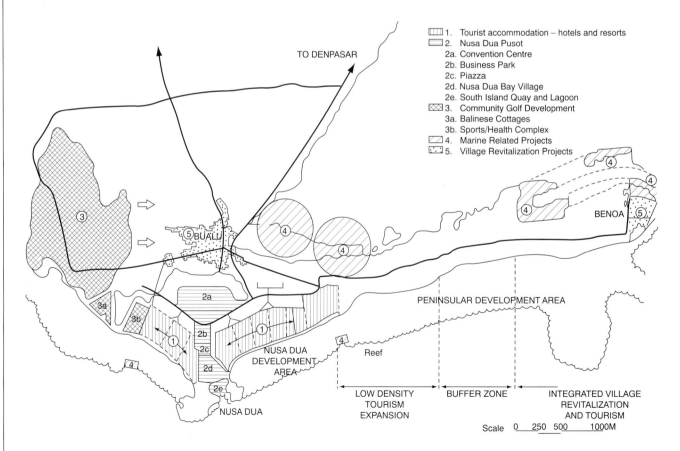

1. Tourist accommodation – hotels and resorts
2. Nusa Dua Pusot
2a. Convention Centre
2b. Business Park
2c. Piazza
2d. Nusa Dua Bay Village
2e. South Island Quay and Lagoon
3. Community Golf Development
3a. Balinese Cottages
3b. Sports/Health Complex
4. Marine Related Projects
5. Village Revitalization Projects

Ovall planning programmes for the area in 1988 provided for golf and associated inland developments, a central core of public amenities, low density tourism expansion, buffer zone and village revitalization projects together with improved road links

Cities of character and culture, such as Paris, Vienna and Florence, and centres of administration and commerce like Washington, London and Brussels, all have an important, even dominant, place in tourism. Invariably, major cities and towns serve as gateways to the country and region, often forming the principal destination for business, entertainment and cultural tourism. Many of the premises and much of the infrastructure and employment in these cities, especially in the central areas, are concerned with providing accommodation and services for foreign and domestic visitors, day visitors and sightseers.

Whilst tourist cities and towns cannot be classified as resorts, many of the principles of resort planning apply, particularly to those areas of the town in which tourists and visitors tend to congregate or in which most of the tourist accommodation, entertainment, and other attractions are located.

Tourism not only generates economic benefits, but enables many facilities and amenities to be made available to residents which would not otherwise be viable. Comprehensive town planning must include sectoral policies to safeguard and enhance the tourism products, for example:

- zoning of areas of tourist and historic interest, together with monument ensembles (monuments in their surroundings) (see 9.2.7),
- conservation of traditional streets, terraces, squares, marketplaces, piazzas and buildings which express character and a sense of place (see 9.2.5–7),
- pedestrianization of areas in which people congregate, retaining a human scale (see 9.2.8),
- cleaning and restoration of key buildings and monuments together with restrictions on encroachment,
- designation and protection of scenic routes for urban sightseeing and access from the airport and/or cruise terminal (see 9.2.4).

6.1.2 Traditional resorts

Up to the end of the eighteenth century, with few exceptions, tourist facilities were limited to the inns, taverns, *auberges* and hospices along the highways and in the main destinations – pilgrim shrines, market towns and ports. Most travellers were accommodated at their destinations by friends or in rented houses and rooms.

In the nineteenth century, coupled with expansion of transport, major development took place, in four types of resort:

- *Spas* for health and entertainment (Baden Baden, Marienbad, Vichy, Bath)
- *Climatic resorts* for treatment of tuberculosis (Menton, and later St Vallier or Leysin in the Alps)
- *Alpine resorts* (Chamonix, Zermatt, Garmisch and other traditional villages)
- *Seaside resorts* for cures and leisure (Deauville, San Remo, Brighton, Bordighera)

In the early twentieth century *ski resorts* were created: in 1920 for the Olympic Games in Chamonix and from 1930 onwards through the growth of Val d'Isère and other areas.

Traditional resorts developed from existing villages and towns, either changing the town itself or growing in its immediate vicinity. The location was largely determined by means of access, and limitations on travel tended to restrict mountain resorts to low or medium altitudes and to concentrate other facilities into relatively few, but often large, seaside and lakeside town resorts accessible to the main conurbations of population. Accommodation in such resorts was almost entirely provided in hotels, boarding houses or rented rooms, often forming characteristic street frontages along the promenades, terraces, gardens and squares.

The fortunes of many traditional resorts have declined as a result of changes in fashion and style of living, in the structure of markets and in the choice of recreation and accommodation. Mostly changes have been brought about by developments in air transport, allowing access to more distant areas able to offer better and more guaranteed climates, new and exciting surroundings and, frequently, more modern and better equipped facilities.

The effects of change and competition have tended to leave the traditional resorts behind, often in a state of increasing neglect, with low-spend visitors and ageing populations. It is possible to introduce new vitality and income by careful planned rehabilitation and orientation towards new market opportunities (weekend breaks, self-catering options, sophisticated entertainment and recreation, conferences, out-of-season training and education programmes). A faded image of a resort may be changed through environmental improvements, such as pedestrianization and the construction of new focal points of interest and activity (marinas, restored historical features, car parks concealed under landscaped gardens and squares). In other cases the existing resort may serve as an infrastructure base for access to new areas (higher ski resorts, regional tours, specialized activity centres). Some recommendations are provided in 6.5.4 Rehabilitating existing resorts.

6.1.3 Post-war developments: uncontrolled urbanization

The growth in opportunities for holidays and recreation since the 1950s, together with increasing accessibility to mass markets, created an apparently insatiable demand for facilities in which to enjoy the sun and snow. For expediency much of the development was speculative and unrelated to the broader and long-term needs of the area or of the community involved. Much of the rapid and, often, large-scale urbanization projects of this period has left a legacy of dominating utilitarian buildings, out of character and scale with their surroundings; vast resorts sprawling out unrestrained along the coast; ribbon development of poor quality holiday homes and motels often spoiling scenic routes; unsightly camping and caravan sites on prominent headlands and plateaux; and, in many areas, overloaded or inadequate infrastructure.

Progressive urbanization with loss of character and environmental attractiveness has direct consequences for both tourism and the local economy. Resorts lose their competitiveness and tourist interests progressively shift down towards mass travel with lower expenditure per capita and narrower margins of profit which, in turn causes further decline in standards of services and maintenance. Specific programmes of resort rehabilitation and environmental improvements are essential if the high commitment to tourism already made – in capital and human resources – is to be safeguarded (see recommendations in 6.5.4).

6.2 NEW RESORT DEVELOPMENT

6.2.1 Integrated resorts

Integrated planning was developed to reduce the drawbacks of the disordered, uncontrolled development of tourist resorts and regions. Integrated resorts are generally built on new sites free from the constraints of previous development: they can be comprehensively planned and programmed – by one single team of specialists – to ensure that all necessary facilities are provided in appropriate places, at the right times, and in the correct scale and character.

The principle of fully planned resorts dates back to the early spa towns developed under the authority of one landowner (for example Buxton, in Derbyshire). However, modern integrated resorts are planned to meet both market and development needs. Among first examples (about 1935) were Cervinia and Sestrières in Italy and Courchevel in France (ski resorts developed at a higher altitude than the existing villages to guarantee a long snow period) and S'Agaro, one of the first developments on the Costa Brava (Spain) and now one of the most exclusive.

Integrated resorts may be located alone or form part of a tourism development area and may be widely different in character, size and type of facilities offered. They may be based on hotel, holiday village or condominium properties or combinations offering a choice of accommodation. Compared with individual units, resorts are able to support a wider range of recreation and entertainment amenities and make better use of the infrastructure.

6.2.2 Developers

Development of planned integrated resorts may be sponsored and coordinated by:

- **Governmental agencies** to attract foreign currencies, to serve as a model for further investment, to develop local or regional economies or to provide relatively cheap holiday accommodation for domestic tourism. Public authorities are also often involved in joint participation (see A.2.7).

- **Tour operators** through negotiations to rent and operate resorts built to their standards. Acquisition and financing of the land and building is undertaken by local authorities or other promoters. This also applies to many of the international hotel groups which generally offer management expertise but only a minority interest in the capital invested.
- **Property developers** involved in speculative purchase of large areas of unserviced land, construction of infrastructure and facilities and sale of plots and/or properties. Sales are generally directed towards private ownership rather than hotel beds.
- **Joint participation** of both public and private interests is common for large-scale development projects. The parties involved generally include:
  - *local community* (municipality, county parish) or a syndicate of local communities responsible for providing the access road, the connecting and distribution infrastructures, the cable lifts and other public services. Much of this provision is financed by state or regional grants and part of the costs may be recouped from charges levied on the developer or later through fiscal taxes;
  - *state-sponsored company or trusteeship* established to provide technical and financial assistance to the local authorities concerned;
  - *private developers*, usually responsible for real estate development, provision of recreational facilities and other commercially profitable services, and for promotion of the resort.

Alternatively, the development may be carried out through the organization of a joint public/private venture company or on the basis of concessional agreements. It is important to determine, in advance, the legal obligations and responsibilities of each of the parties concerned, particularly:

- *land:* availability and regulation of use;
- *infrastructures:* division of commitments between state, local community, utility company and private developer;
- *major developments* (marina, ski lifts, swimming pools etc.): programme, means of financing, implementation and operation;
- *other facilities:* programme and phases of development;
- *property development:* planning criteria, zoning and regulation, types of buildings, enforcement of standards, means of organization and financing;
- *financial aids:* loans, grants, subsidies, guarantees;
- *allocation* of costs and benefits.

6.2.3 Failures and criticisms

Only a few of the recently developed resorts have benefited from *integrated planning*. Many others, in spite of some degree of planning and control, have not measured up to expectations. Common grounds for criticism are over-development; domination of the natural settings; investment in second homes and property speculation rather than tourism; isolation of the local community (having appropriated their resources); and lack of control over quality and benefits. Most of the difficulties have arisen from inadequate organization, from deficiencies in planning – particularly in understanding the real motivations underlying development and their socio-economic consequences – and from maladministration.

An element of speculation is almost unavoidable in private enterprise and commercial investment and this must be directed towards the long-term objectives of a well-planned resort which gains in appreciation and value from its attractiveness. To achieve such ends, strict, almost dictatorial, standards and controls must be enforced.

6.2.4 Operation of resorts

In **traditional resorts** most of the functions are carried out by established organizations:

- Local Tourist Boards (*Syndicats d'Initiative* or *Offices du Tourisme*): information, coordination, promotion, booking and referral services, hotel tax collection, operation of some facilities or services, monitoring performance trends and future requirements.
- Sports representatives, clubs, societies and association (e.g. *Ecole de ski*): operation of sports facilities, teaching and organization of activities.
- Municipalities and local government bodies: municipal services, maintenance of public areas and infrastructures, regulation of building.

Many of the commercial needs of a resort are met by private enterprise, for example, real estate agency, car hire, banking, tour operation. The state (or statutory utility bodies) usually assumes responsibility for undertaking wider infrastructural services such as highways, water supplies, sewerage, telecommunication and postal services, health care, operation of airports and harbours.

In **new resorts**, as part of the planning process, it is necessary to ensure that all the necessary functions are organized prior to opening. These will depend on contractual arrangements with operators of facilities but the following are representative:

- **Resort Board**: Set up to organize promotion, recruitment, training, reservations, general information and some services, boards are usually composed of representatives from the sponsors, developers, operators and local tourist authority.
- **Municipal services**: Depending on location, municipal services and maintenance of public areas and infrastructures may be operated by the Resort Board, by the local authority of a neighbouring town or administrative area or by shared responsibility.
- **Co-owners associations**: In launching a resort the developer will initially exercise responsibility for maintenance of common areas, infrastructures and recreational facilities, for operation of communal services for heating, cleaning and security and for regulation of standards of individual

property care in order to attract sales. At a later stage, this managerial responsibility will normally be handed over to a condominium association of owners.
- **Real estate and renting agency**: Estate agency may be part of the Board's function but is usually a separate role. Services include promotion and sale of plots, apartments, etc., procuring credit for buyers, renting and management of private units (supervision, control, cleaning and maintenance).
- **Sports associations**: Where sport is a dominant feature, as in, say, skiing, sailing, or golf-based resorts, the sporting activities are normally under the supervision of a full-time director with a staff of specialist instructors and service personnel. Sports facilities should be planned, designed and operated to the standards laid down by the international sports federations. Among the managerial responsibilities will be the operation and maintenance of equipment (for example ski lifts, marina facilities, ground irrigation systems), development of new and extended ski runs, sailing routes, golf ranges etc., organization of competitions and instruction, hire and sale of associated equipment, and supplementary services.

6.3 RECREATION AND LEISURE COMPLEXES

The various types of recreation parks and complexes are described in 5.6 to 5.8. Depending mainly on location, local inhabitants may have opportunities to use:

- *nearby tourist resorts* allowing local club membership or charges for facilities (as in ski resorts, marinas, holiday parks, golf resorts);
- facilities provided specifically for community recreation (leisure centres, recreation parks), large complexes such as attraction, theme and aquatic or water parks which rely on wide market catchments of both day visitors and tourists staying in the area.

The main principles and procedures in planning large leisure complexes and most recreation parks are similar to those followed in planning tourist resorts (detailed from 6.4 to 6.6). However, there are a number of aspects which require special consideration and these are summarized below (see 6.3.1–2).

6.3.1 Attraction, theme and aquatic parks

Large complexes of this type (see 5.6.2–4) are invariably planned as a commercial investment and are highly dependent on visitor numbers. The catchment may be increased by providing some hotel or chalet accommodation on site but this must be weighed against the seasonal usage. Particular consideration must be given to:

- *Market research:* extent of catchment areas, demographic and socio-economic profiles, competing destinations, projections of visitor numbers (annual, seasonal, peak), factors liable to affect future demand.

Ground floor plan

Architects: S & P

Leisure World, Hemel Hempstead, UK

Located in Jarman Park, this is an example of trends in non-residential leisure centres which are planned as commercial investments. The Leisure World operated by Rank, provides a balanced mix of facilities with a skating rink, aquatic fun pool, two bowling alleys, eight cinemas, fast food outlets and bars. On the upper floor there is an indoor bowls court and children's play area.

- *Site investigation:* location relative to markets, surroundings, land control, highways and road/rail access, infrastructures, site development works, constraints and costs, environmental and socio-economic impacts.
- *Programme:* definition of alternative themes, facility requirements, cost estimates (capital and operating), financing arrangements.
- *Physical planning:* traffic, circulation and crowd management for the peak numbers of visitors, including diversion attractions and events.

Aquatic or water parks with landscaped leisure pools may form the central element of a holiday resort (see 5.4.4), a distinct park (see 5.6.4), or part of a leisure centre (see 5.7.4). In each case consideration must be given to the market demand and variations in use, the high capital and operating costs and feasibility.

6.3.2 Recreation and nature parks

Suburban recreation parks (see 5.7.4 to 5.7.6) are essentially for community recreation and must take account of local needs – including tourists and others who visit the area. Although recreation and sport are often highly subsidized (see 4.5.3), the trend is to use commercial methods of evaluation to ensure that the best use is made of resources and subsidies.

Specific attention should be paid to:

- *Market study:* quantification of the wide range of demand with segmentation by areas, usage (1–2 hours, daily, weekend, after work, school groups and clubs) and various categories of ages, activities and interests; in each case, the **latent demand** must be considered and the facilities available elsewhere (regional study); market studies enable tentative products to be defined and their feasibility assessed.
- *Site study:* quality of the natural resources (zoning) and landscaping requirements, land control, site access and traffic analyses, resolution of conflicts of interests.
- *Structures and policies:* national and local policies, agreement with other agencies, agreement between the various authorities on location, land allocation, planning, funding and administration issues.
- *Financing and operation:* sources of funding – national, regional, local (taxes, land allocation, sale of other assets); capital requirements; pricing structure, revenues and costs (investment, operating).
- *Special provisions:* for the disabled, clubs, school groups, elderly, etc.

Recreation parks are primarily conceived for the populations of densely inhabited towns. Often the land for recreation parks is only available in the territory of neighbouring authorities and agreement on the development of the park and its financing may necessitate the intervention of a higher authority (metropolitan or regional).

Nature parks (see 5.8) are primarily related to environmental conservation but the type and location of visitor facilities is equally important.

Outdoor recreation in the cities (see 9.3) involves separate issues.

6.4 PRINCIPLES OF DEVELOPMENT (TOURIST RESORT OR RECREATION COMPLEX)

6.4.1 Objectives, ways and means

In addition to providing adequate facilities, the planning of a resort or recreation complex must meet other criteria: to satisfy market and investment needs, to create an attractive image, to harmonize with the environment and to meet social and economic objectives. The following principles apply:

- **To meet individual requirements**: this involves careful zoning and interfacing as tourists and recreationists often seek, paradoxically:
  - tranquillity and rest – but also facilities for entertainment and sport;
  - anonymity – but also the opportunity to meet other people and participate in the social activities of the changing community;
  - contact with nature, with foreign countries and customs, with pre-industrial societies in the case of long-haul tourism – but with standards of home comfort;
  - seclusion and privacy – but with the benefits of security and close proximity to a variety of leisure and recreational facilities.
- **To provide a different experience**: most recreationists and tourists are city and town dwellers, for whom day excursions or holidays essentially mean an escape from urban conditions, high densities, pollution and organized routine lives. To provide a refreshing experience of contrasts, tourist resorts and recreation complexes may be planned as 'anti-towns', offering such features as:
  - quietness, change of pace and opportunities for relaxation;
  - contact with nature, sun, sea, snow, forest and mountain;
  - a human scale;
  - a change in activity, provided by sport and recreation;
  - contacts with other people outside the circles of work and home;
  - discovery of other cultures, and other ways of life (tourism).

a *Theme park and hotel area*

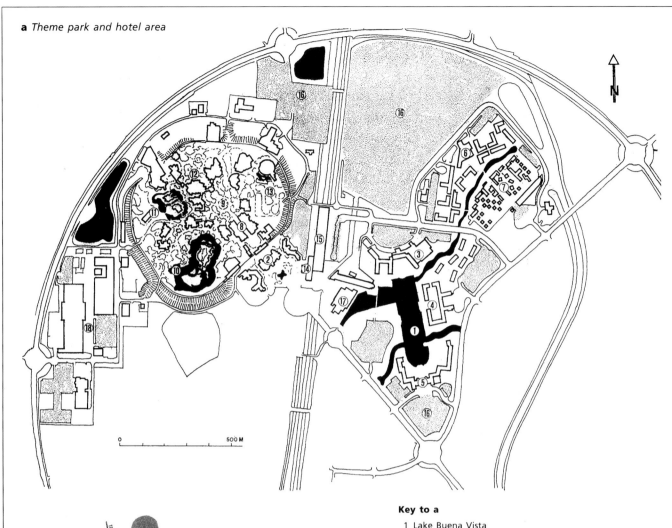

0 ⊢——————————⊣ 500 M

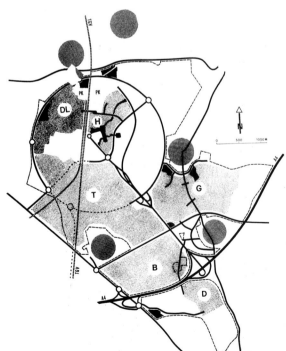

b *The overall development*

Key to a

1 Lake Buena Vista
2 Disneyland Hotel (Walt Disney Company Architects)
3 Hotel New York (M. Graves, arch)
4 Sequoia Lodge (A. Grumbach, arch)
5 Newport Bay Club (R. Stern, arch)
6 Hotel Cheyenne (R. Stern, arch)
7 Hotel Santa Fe (A. Predock, arch)
8 Main Street USA
9 Hub (Central Plazza)
10 Frontierland
11 Adventureland
12 Fantasyland
13 Disoveryland
14 RER Station
15 TGV Station
16 Parkings
17 Festival Disney (Frank Gehry, arch)
18 Theme Park's Service Area

Key to b

DL Existing Eurodisney Theme Park
H Existing Hotel Area
G Existing Residential Golf
D Existing Davy Crockett Ranch
T Proposed Val d'Europe
B Proposed Business Park

▨ existing village
▬ lakes and ponds
—— existing road
····· planned road
⸽⸽⸽⸽ TGV and RER railways
– – – overall development area

Disneyland, Paris

In March 1987 a 30–year agreement was signed between Eurodisney, the French state, the Region, the Department and EPAFRANCE (a regional public development agency) for the creation of the largest European theme park with the participation of both public and private sectors. A 'Porte de la Brive' SAN (an inter-community management agency representing the five communities concerned) is to share with Eurodisney the responsibility of building a new town around Disney Resort.

In 1996, five years after it opened to the public (April 1992), Disneyland Paris received nearly 11 million visitors, half of which were foreigners. The theme park (56 ha) is a small part only of a much larger development (b). Access infrastructures include a trans-Europe railway (TGV–Eurostar) stop, the final station of an RER (regional subway-railway crossing Paris) and the Paris–Brussels A4 highway.

c

The theme park (c) provides a mixture of fairytale characters, futuristic architecture and high technology with 40 attractions and 18 hours of daily live entertainment shows. The visitors entering the park come across a small train driving around the park, walk through Main Street USA (shops, catering, daily parades) and reach the HUB (central plaza); at this point they may select one of the four themed Lands. Fig. 6.6a shows the respective land occupied by:

- the theme park and the related service area;
- the hotel zone (5700 rooms with two convention centres totalling 10 500 m² for up to 5000 people per day and 46 function rooms): each hotel (d to g), built by a well-known architect, presents a different character and category (from 2 to 5-star), including, further away, the Davy Crockett Ranch (family bungalows and indoor swimming pool);
- the Disney Village, a large indoor arena for daily shows and occasional music festivals, with shops and restaurants;
- parking areas for cars and buses.

At the time of publication Phase I of Disneyland Project (b) had been completed. This included the initial theme park, several hotels, 35 000 m² of tourism-related business with a total employment of about 10 000 people, a convention centre, a residential 27-hole golf course and the beginning of residential developments in four of the five communities.

Phase II was launched in 1996 but at the time of publication had yet to be signed. It includes launching Val d'Europa, a multi-purpose regional urban development. It will also include a 90 000 m² international shopping mall, a second RER station, residential housing and an international business park etc.

Theme park's architects/planners; Walt Disney Company's architects; New town's architects/planners: J. Robertson (New York, USA); M. Macary (Paris, France)
Photographs © Disney

d

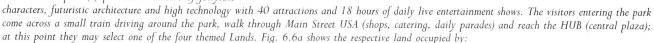

e

f

g

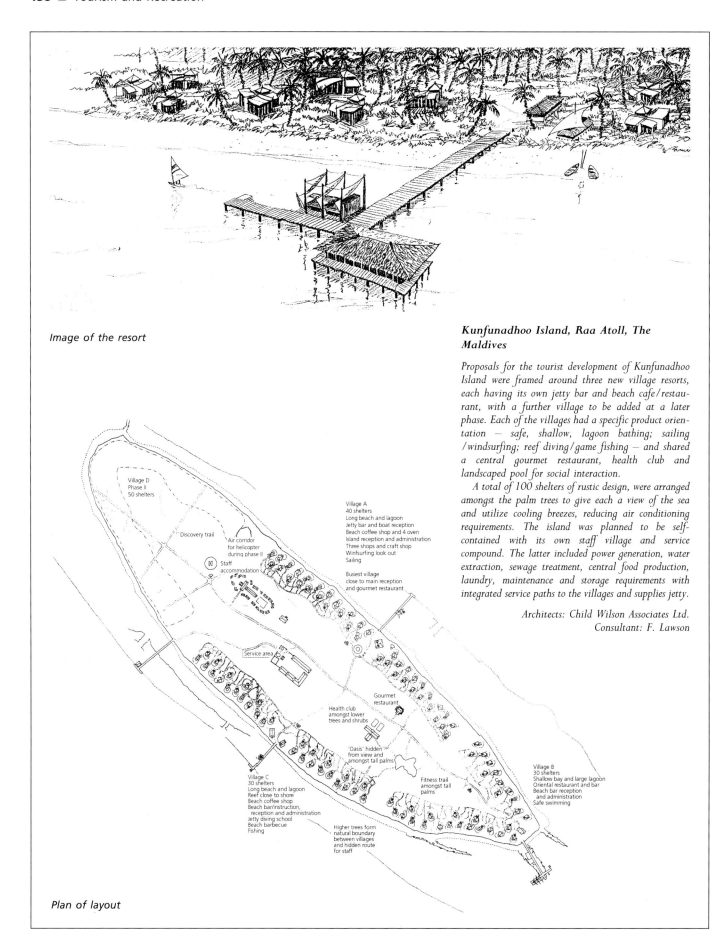

Image of the resort

Village D
Phase II
50 shelters

Discovery trail

Air corridor
for helicopter
during phase II

N Staff
accommodation

Service area

Village A
40 shelters
Long beach and lagoon
Jetty bar and boat reception
Beach coffee shop and 4 oven
Island reception and administration
Three shops and craft shop
Winfsurfing look out
Sailing

Busiest village
close to main reception
and gourmet restaurant

Gourmet
restaurant

Health club
amongst lower
trees and shrubs

'Oasis' hidden
from view and
amongst tall palms

Fitness trail
amongst tall
palms

Village C
30 shelters
Long beach and lagoon
Reef close to shore
Beach coffee shop
Beach bar/instruction,
  reception and administration
Jetty diving school
Beach barbecue
Fishing

Higher trees form
natural boundary
between villages
and hidden route
for staff

Village B
30 shelters
Shallow bay and large lagoon
Oriental restaurant and bar
Beach bar reception
  and administration
Safe swimming

Plan of layout

Kunfunadhoo Island, Raa Atoll, The Maldives

Proposals for the tourist development of Kunfunadhoo Island were framed around three new village resorts, each having its own jetty bar and beach cafe/restaurant, with a further village to be added at a later phase. Each of the villages had a specific product orientation — safe, shallow, lagoon bathing; sailing /windsurfing; reef diving/game fishing — and shared a central gourmet restaurant, health club and landscaped pool for social interaction.

A total of 100 shelters of rustic design, were arranged amongst the palm trees to give each a view of the sea and utilize cooling breezes, reducing air conditioning requirements. The island was planned to be self-contained with its own staff village and service compound. The latter included power generation, water extraction, sewage treatment, central food production, laundry, maintenance and storage requirements with integrated service paths to the villages and supplies jetty.

Architects: Child Wilson Associates Ltd.
Consultant: F. Lawson

Land-use plan

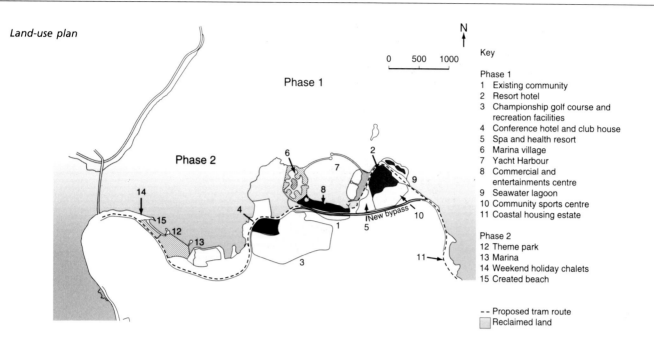

Phase 1

Phase 2

N

0   500   1000

Key

Phase 1
1 Existing community
2 Resort hotel
3 Championship golf course and
    recreation facilities
4 Conference hotel and club house
5 Spa and health resort
6 Marina village
7 Yacht Harbour
8 Commercial and
    entertainments centre
9 Seawater lagoon
10 Community sports centre
11 Coastal housing estate

Phase 2
12 Theme park
13 Marina
14 Weekend holiday chalets
15 Created beach

-- Proposed tram route
▨ Reclaimed land

Southern Seto Nagaura, Japan

Under the Resorts Act, the policy of the Japanese government has been to promote domestic tourism and opportunities for leisure in partnership with regional authorities and the private sector. The first phase in the development of two new resorts on O-Shima Island was started in 1990/91 by Casabella Kowa in a joint venture with the Prefecture of Yamaguchi and the Local Authority of Kuka Town.

The main goals of the development were:

- to provide attractions for domestic tourism and leisure needs in the region;
- to ensure appropriate use of natural resources (with conservation and improvements);
- to protect the interests of the local community (employment, crafts and products);
- to achieve a sound financial investment/balance of accommodation and recreation).

With limitations of a steep, rocky coast and coastal currents, phase one provides for:

- a protected harbour (50 ha for 500 yachts) and enclosed marina basin (200 units);
- the formation and stabilization of artificial beaches (500 m long for 1000 bathers);
- an enclosed lagoon (5 ha) for safe bathing and water sports with a sand beach for 800 bathers;
- a choice of accommodation in a resort hotel (400 rooms), spa hotel and health centre (300 rooms), harbour apartments (430 units), marina (400 units), conference hotel (200 rooms) and fairway villas (320);
- extensive facilities including 20 shops, four restaurant/bars and six entertainment areas together with administration and operational services.

The layout of buildings, roads and recreation areas was dictated by the steep sloping ground and leisure activities planned for this first phase of development include an 18-hole golf course (60 ha), play areas (2000 m²), bowls (5000 m²) eight tennis courts,

A pitch and putt course (5000 m²), 3-hole practice course (8 ha), driving range (5 ha), shooting range (8 ha), riding centre (8500 m² for ten horses), sports centre with enclosed leisure pool and fitness areas and various trails (climbing, trekking, par cours, nature studies).

Sensitive to the needs of the local community the overall development provides for:

- the retention of the existing fishing harbour,
- the installation of boat repair and servicing facilities,
- the development of a local crafts/arts centre.
- by-pass road construction,
- the construction of a large community sports centre with outdoor pool,
- baseball/multi-purpose arena and enclosed sports/social building (8000 m²)

Marina village

Architect: W. S. Atkins International
(Team leader, R Alvey/Landscape architect, K. Farnes).
F. Lawson – tourism consultant. Casabella Co Ltd

Tama forest zone, Japan

The character of a traditional Japanese village in the Akigawa Valley (a) may be destroyed by a massive new school or hotel (b), while, if broken in several elements and built with adapted material (c) to (e), the same building may blend in with the traditional environment, even using contemporary architecture (e).

Source: ACAU+MEIGE, architects-planners, Geneva, 1993

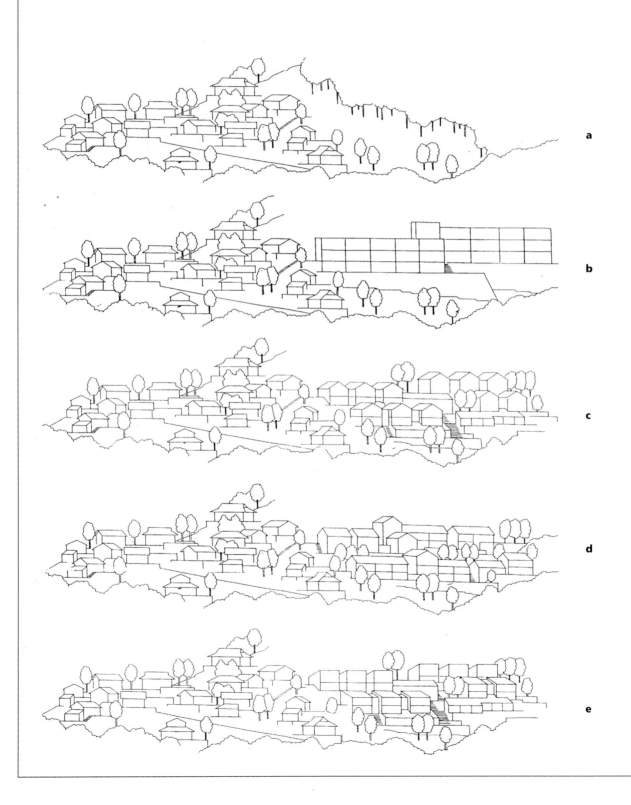

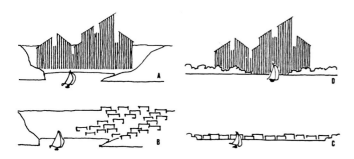

Figure 6.1

the pyramids in la Grande-Motte – (D) – and man-made features of striking interest – e.g. the canals in Port Grimaud.

In many places, the sites have not only a visual value, but a historical one: traditional buildings or man-made landscapes (rice paddies, terraces, vineyards). In such places the future development should respect the present environment and recall the past.

6.4.3 Contact with nature

Contact with nature may be visual, such as a panoramic view from a balcony or terrace, or physical, providing opportunities to become surrounded by, and possibly to touch, the flowers, trees, rocks and other features of the natural landscape. In many situations, both may exist together, contact with the immediate surroundings being complemented by a backcloth of distant views. Physical contact, which is probably more important than visual, is almost impossible to achieve in high rise buildings. Small cluster constructions may provide a better solution, particularly where the site configurations and infrastructure allow flexibility of layout. In many cases, contact between the buildings and the environment may be emphasized by allowing trees and gardens, water (natural or artificial lakes, inlets, rivers etc.) and snow (pistes) to penetrate into or extend through the resorts. In other situations, the resort may be stretched out to take advantage of the views of the sea or mountains, while maintaining contact with the natural surroundings.

The centre of resort activity (such as a promenade, quay or square) should always have direct contact with nature. This is one of the main recreational assets and will be largely responsible for creating the image by which the majority of tourists will identify the resort.

Provision should be made in the layout and design to make the most of the climate, particularly the sun, and to avoid an over-dependency on mechanical systems. Open, sunny beaches and squares in hot climates should be adjoined by deep vegetation, fountains, basins, cool gardens, sheltering streets and deep porticoes. Similarly, resorts in ski areas should allow close contact with the snow and elements, while providing protection against the worst extremes through south-orientated squares or porticoes, large chimneys in the building, etc.

- **To create an attractive 'image'** as original as possible to give the place a personality, an easily remembered character. This may be achieved in a number of ways:

  - by making the best use of the particular resources and peculiarities of the site, its surroundings and climate, using local materials and techniques where possible;
  - by adapting the development plan and the scale and design of buildings to reflect the character of the main activities: skiing, or golfing, horse riding, sailing, surfing or hunting;
  - by providing opportunities for contact with local people, their crafts and customs.

There are no definite recipes for planning tourist resorts or recreation complexes; each situation requires individual appraisal and interpretation. The following paragraphs illustrate some of the principles which may be applied, in particular in tourist resorts.

6.4.2 Environmental integration

There is a need to establish a good relationship between a resort as a whole and its natural environment. Some integration may be achieved through the architecture (vernacular, for example), but is much more a matter of scale, defined in the master plan, building codes, management rules and regulations.

Two main principles are usually involved (see Fig. 6.1):

- Where the environment is attractive with high scenic value, the scale and character of building developments should be subdued, as in Hydra, Mykonos or Positano (B). Strongly profiled, dominating buildings tend to contradict the surroundings (A).

- In an insignificant area without environmental interest, buildings of equally neutral design and arrangement generally produce a poor image (C). The personality of the resort may be deliberately created by buildings of character – e.g.

6.4.4 Increasing value of the resources

The two sketches overleaf (Figures 6.2a and 6.2b) indicate how the main resources may be used to provide extended benefits:

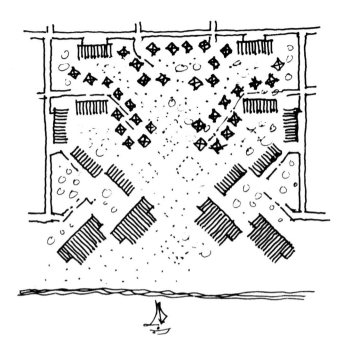

Figure 6.2a *A line of high density, tall buildings, arranged to take maximum advantage of the main natural attractions, e.g. along the seashore (but the same may occur at the bottom of ski slopes), creates a visual barrier to the resort area situated behind and a very few buildings only benefit from a direct relationship with the sea and the beach*

Figure 6.2b *By orientating the building lines at right angles, maintaining a balance of lower buildings and extending the beach area with adapted layout and landscaping, contact with the main resource and attractive visual lines can be extended throughout the resort*

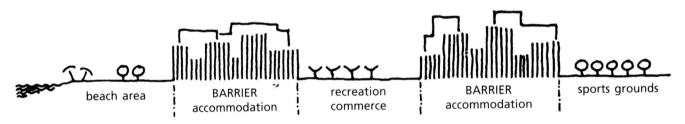

Figure 6.3a *Segregation of activities*

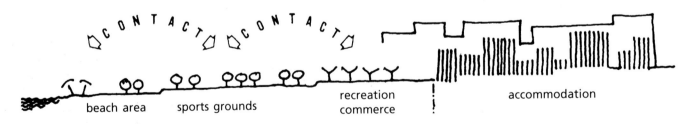

Figure 6.3b *Contact between related zones*

6.4.5 Grouping of activities

Segregation of the main recreational activities into isolated pockets must be avoided. Facilities must be assembled in a way which allows some degree of contact between related zones of recreation: a spillover of excitement and interest from one zone to the next and from these zones to the residential areas. At the same time, there is a need to avoid:

- the overall recreational area becoming too exposed or monotonously large and impersonal;
- conflict between different interests (for example, noisy activity and quiet relaxation).

6.4.6 Landscaping

Good landscaping is of the utmost importance in a resort or recreation complex. Natural features such as rocks, mature trees and running water should be retained, even in the most densely built-up areas and emphasized as components of the landscape design. Steep slopes and rock formations may be incorporated by constructing terraces, steps and even elevator shafts for access.

However, modern resorts or recreation complexes do not always benefit from attractive surroundings. In many cases the location is determined by other market factors (distance, access from airport and main traffic routes, centrality to region etc.). Often only one or two features (sunshine, sea and space) predominate and many resorts have been built on bare lagoons, swamps and rocky plains, many recreation complexes on derelict land, abandoned industrial estates, quarries or waste tips. In these situations an artificial landscape must be created, utilizing the best of the resources available and introducing complementary man-made features and transplanted vegetation as necessary – e.g. recent hotels in Hawaii.

6.4.7 Distribution of buildings and focuses of interest

Uniform distribution of buildings over the whole area (O) tends to produce a large number of small and often uninteresting garden spaces – an exception, perhaps, being where dense introverted buildings extend around patios and atriums creating internal landscapes which link and extend the building activity. Concentration of buildings into specific zones is usually preferable to allow preservation of the most valuable natural areas of the site (B) or (A).

The layout should provide a good vista or compensating features of interest as an outlook for:

- main public areas such as restaurants and bars (profit centres),
- guestrooms which may be disadvantaged in location,
- groups of residences, to add to exclusiveness and value.

Features may be natural (landscaped), created (ornamental), refreshing (water features), or animated (leisure pools, tennis

courts, marinas, ski activities, piazzas), depending on the particular location and style.

6.4.8 Separation of traffic

In the initial stages of resort planning, policies must be determined for the control of traffic, (visitor, service and construction vehicles). Traffic control is usually based on the separation of vehicles and pedestrians.

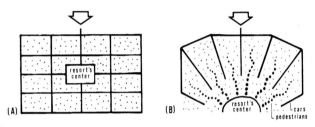

Figure 6.5

For example, instead of routes passing through the resort, Fig. 6.5(A), traffic may be confined to the periphery (B) allowing pedestrian access to the centre without the need to cross any traffic flow. The same principle may also be applied at the scale of individual neighbourhood units. Compared with traditional street layouts, Fig. 6.6(A), cluster type development of residences (B) represents an economy of about 30 per cent in infrastructure costs.

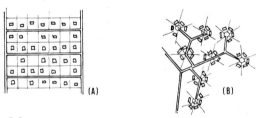

Figure 6.6

In large integrated developments, provision may be made for public transportation, usually free, within the resort area proper. Apart from the benefits of isolating the private car (infrastructure savings, reductions in congestion, noise, fumes, hazards etc.) this often has an attractive novelty value. However, requirements for transient visitors, car parking, reception, luggage handling and transfer, passenger inter-movements, accommodation services and maintenance and the effect of weather must all be taken into account at the initial planning stage. In resorts catering for a wide spectrum of tourists, from groups to individual transient and recreation users, complete segregation of the private car may not be feasible. In this case, it is necessary to identify specific zones of activity to which private and, possibly, service or commercial vehicles will need access and for which local car parks will be required (for example, a marina, sports stadium, or conference hall). Some form of barrier (excavation or banking, trees and shrubs, walls etc.) must be provided to screen major traffic and parking zones. Underground parking areas may be formed below squares, promenades and gardens.

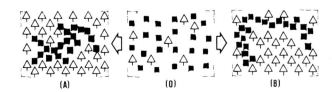

Figure 6.4

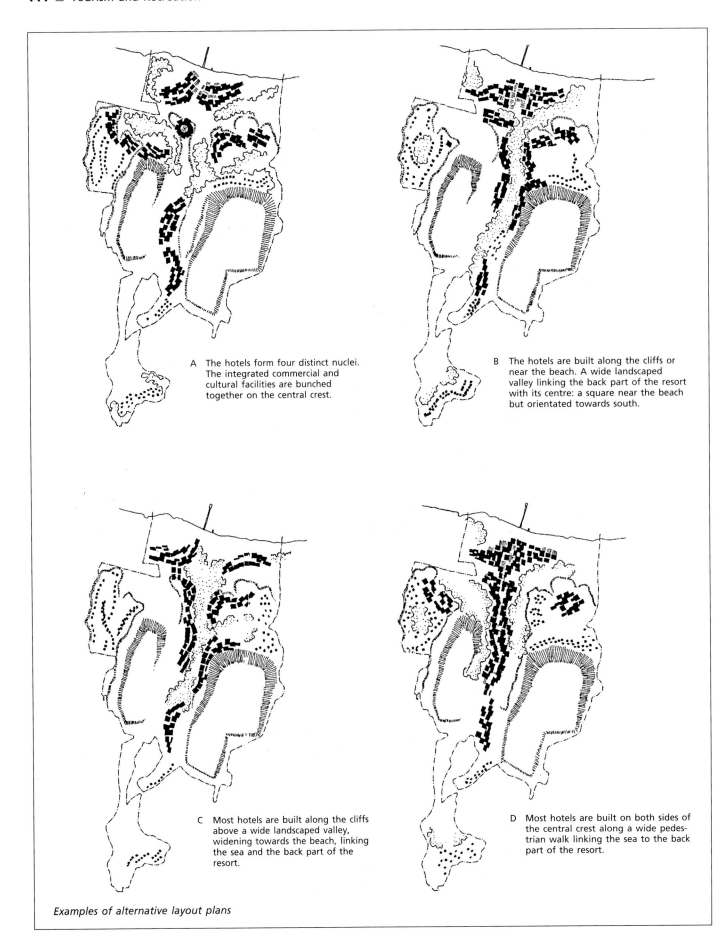

A The hotels form four distinct nuclei. The integrated commercial and cultural facilities are bunched together on the central crest.

B The hotels are built along the cliffs or near the beach. A wide landscaped valley linking the back part of the resort with its centre: a square near the beach but orientated towards south.

C Most hotels are built along the cliffs above a wide landscaped valley, widening towards the beach, linking the sea and the back part of the resort.

D Most hotels are built on both sides of the central crest along a wide pedestrian walk linking the sea to the back part of the resort.

Examples of alternative layout plans

Limni Beach Resort, Cyprus

The resort was planned in 1990 on a site (113 ha) previously used for the preliminary treatment of copper ore, excavated from a nearby mine. Two large tailings, created by the mud deposits of the plant, tower over the whole site. Accommodation capacity was limited to 2200 tourist beds in six hotels or aparthotels and 400 beds in 80 villas. Instead of planning for six independent hotels, each having limited recreation and sports facilities, the whole complex is planned around **integrated facilities**:

- two large outdoor swimming pools (basins 1000 to 1500 m²) and a smaller indoor pool;
- water sports centre and school for sailing, water skiing, windsurfing, diving, with slipway, hoist and dry harbour;
- 18-hole golf course, partly on the rehabilitated tailings;
- tennis centre with ten courts, squash and coach and riding centre (25 horses);
- shopping centre, five speciality restaurants apart from hotels, two dance/nightclubs;
- health, fitness and beauty centre.

Client: Limni Mines Holding Ltd, Cyprus Project: A&M Baud-Bovy, architects/planners, Geneva, in collaboration with J+A Philippou, architects, Nicosia and Giral SA, tourist consultants, Geneva

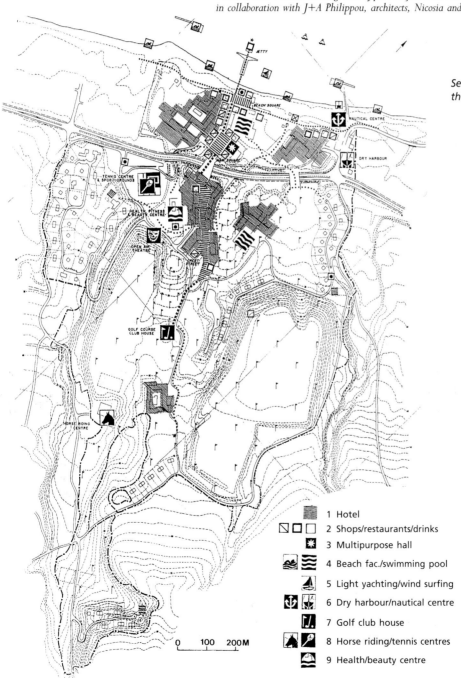

Selected layout plan: location of the main facilities

1 Hotel
2 Shops/restaurants/drinks
3 Multipurpose hall
4 Beach fac./swimming pool
5 Light yachting/wind surfing
6 Dry harbour/nautical centre
7 Golf club house
8 Horse riding/tennis centres
9 Health/beauty centre

0   100   200M

Gaswork Park, Seattle, USA

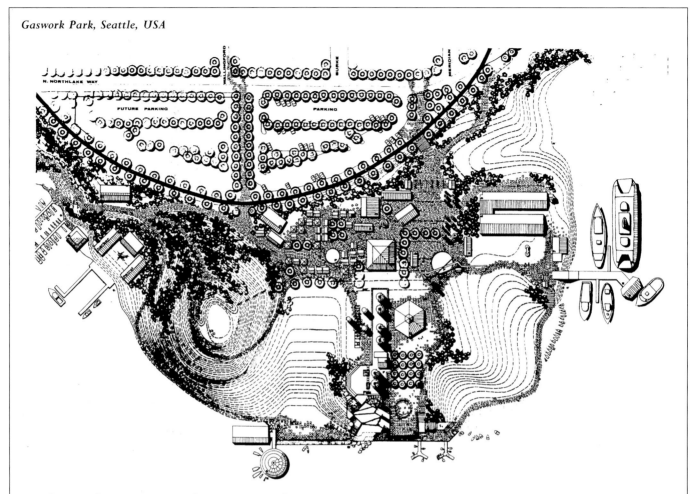

One of the most famous parks resulting from the conversion of an industrial site, the Gaswork Park, designed by R. Haag's, dates back to 1972. The old – and previously considered unsightly – cracking towers have been maintained and carefully landscaped with meadows and mounds. The boiler house has been converted into a picnic shelter (with tables and cooking grills), with the upper floor used for dancing and the mezzanine for musical events. A children's play barn has been formed out of the exhauster-compressor building amongst the old machinery repainted in bright colours.

6.4.9 Quality of construction

The construction of buildings also requires regulation. In many countries the application of general legislation (building codes and regulations) may be adequate as a basis for governing standards of quality but often more specific planning requirements need to be introduced to ensure comprehensive development of the resort towards a distinctive character and 'image'. This may range from stylized modern architecture (La Grande-Motte) to the recreated characteristics of old houses and villages with their narrow streets and small squares. In all cases, it is important to retain a unity of structure, scale, materials and colours, a sense of human relationship which will generate interest and social atmosphere.

6.5 PHASING AND EXTENSION

6.5.1 Phasing development

Resort development usually involves a long-term programme (five to twenty years) of progressive extension and investment. This also applies to:

- large recreation complexes such as attraction and theme parks which are obliged to renew continuously and add to their attractions in order to maintain market share;
- local recreation facilities like golf courses (extending from 9-hole to 18-hole), horse riding centres or recreation parks having a programme of life cycle updating and restoration.

Phased development offers a number of **advantages**:

- initial capital commitments are reduced: later stages being partly financed out of revenues;
- facilities, services and design can adjust to clients' changing requirements, styles and competition;
- proposals are more sustainable enabling changes (in infrastructure, local resources and requirements) to keep pace with development.

Difficulties can arise in ensuring adequate *initial* provision (infrastructure, public facilities, support services), duplication of some costs and disturbance of guests and environments by subsequent works. The number of phases, programmes of work and intervals of time will largely be dictated by marketing and financial considerations but as far as possible extensions should be:

- anticipated in the overall master plan;
- undertaken during low season periods to minimize disturbance;
- timed to coincide with life cycle replacements and maintenance programmes;
- balanced against market demands and resources to maintain standards.

6.5.2 Phases of development

The first phase is particularly critical since this must:

- provide a *conception* of the resort which will establish its image and reputation, with high standards of accommodation and public services, and expressing a highly developed character and vitality;
- be positioned in a part of the site which will allow convenient access and use of facilities *without disturbance* by further building development;
- offer good standard public facilities, including a *reasonable variety of choice*, without excessive initial investment.

The master plan for the resort must show the eventual layout proposed together with programmed phases of implementation. To minimize disturbance and duplication of investment over the many years needed for the implementation of a large resort a number of approaches may be adopted:

- A **spatial layout** conceived for a phased development may take two forms: (a) the resort may be divided into a series of relatively self-contained *polar groups* each developed at a different stage. Polar development involves some duplication of amenities but is particularly suited to condominium developments. (b) Initial development may be located in a part of the site which will allow convenient access (for visitors and services) and use of facilities, with *zones* allocated for future extensions. Disturbance during building works must be minimized by screening (landscape plans) and strict control (noise, work periods, access).
- The **public facilities**, public areas and their associated services must be easily accessible and are often a prominent feature of the resort. The location is strongly influenced by

access requirements (for visitors, goods and services) and capacities are determined by the total numbers accommodated in each successive phase. Typical arrangements:

- – permanent location of service areas (goods deliveries, stores, food production, laundry, employee facilities) with access from a service road and space for future extension and/or addition of equipment;
- – central location of public areas (lobby, restaurants, bars) linked to the service cores with space for extension;
- – duplication of some cafes, restaurants and bars with satellite kitchens supplied via planned service circulations.
- The **infrastructure and technical services**: the technical plant may be largely centralized or localized for each zone of operation. Capacities must be planned to meet phased requirements with space and connections for additional plant installations (including access tunnels/galleries). Road and service main extensions also need to be planned at the initial stage.

Similar principles apply in planning large recreational attractions and parks.

6.5.3 Changes in requirements

Changes in market requirements and recreational interests may affect the design of facilities for future phases. Life cycle replacements also allow for updating and redesign. Most resorts have a policy of continuous improvement to maintain their attractiveness and market shares. This calls for monitoring of performance and visitor satisfaction and market research into trends and competition.

Provision must be allowed for some degree of flexibility in programme, scale, layout and facilities for diversification and introduction of alternatives to meet new demands. The image should, however, be consistent: as a rule it is not feasible or satisfactory to change the basic concept and character of the resort.

Hajdunanas, Hungary

Changes in economic policies in Hungary required a reorientation of marketing to attract more tourists from the European Union, the redevelopment of facilities to the standards required and the creation of new competitive tourism products.

Hajdunanas, in the Plains of East Hungary, was one of the first resorts to recognize this challenge and, in 1991, commissioned a detailed study of the market potential, together with strategies for improvement of facilities and generation of economic benefits.

The main attractions of the resort derive from its hot spa waters and rural surroundings. Recommendations were framed around the reconstruction of the spa facilities, with a phased extension of the resort area in parallel with the provision of support systems and marketing to ensure sustainability. Proposals for the development of integrated products (combining the core attraction, facilities, transport and booking services) covered:

- *spa, rural, farm and nature-based tourism*
- *sailing, fishing, cycling, camper and pony trekking/horse riding holidays*
- *training courses, festivals and events.*

International team: J. Fletcher, F. Lawson, S. Wanhill.

6.5.4 Rehabilitating existing resorts

Redevelopment of declining traditional resorts (see 6.1.2) or of over-urbanized post-war developments (see 6.1.3), perhaps even more than new developed areas, requires survey and appraisal of resources to identify those which should be retained (attractive characteristics) and those which are best removed or modified (unsightly and obstructive structures).

Redevelopment may be primarily:

- within the boundary of the existing resort (the natural configuration may not allow any alternative);
- peripheral to the resort, either as an extension or a separate detached development.

Many of the principles which apply to the development of new resorts are equally relevant for existing resort areas. In many situations, however, there are additional complications:

- delays and frustrations due to multiple ownership of parcelled land and conflicting views on development;
- lack of representation of actual and potential users (tourists, recreationists);
- financial limitations on local authorities who are often involved in supporting the costs of tourism development (public amenities, infrastructure, environmental improvements), without adequate direct benefit (through local taxes);
- difficulties of ensuring that governmental aid is applied only in those areas which specifically benefit tourism and in a way that restricts speculation;
- unsuitability of planning regulations which are primarily directed to community needs rather than tourism;
- constraints resulting from previous development (traffic and parking problems, high costs of developed land required for environmental improvements, condition of ageing attractions and amenities).

The *local community*, representing the interests affecting the area, is the most important of the vested interests but **strategic town planning** should be co-ordinated by the *regional/provincial authorities* on the basis of national legislation: local authorities may be too vulnerable to immediate local – particularly real-estate – interests.

Recommendations for the improvement of resorts with environmental problems have been recently produced by the Tourism Unit of the Commission of European Communities (Econstat 1993), based on analyses of the situation in six European resorts:

- *Implement an integrated approach* relating environment to all the factors involved in the development and taking account of their interrelations, including coordination between the various

departments and with the private sector; medium-term planning for growth development; obligatory assessment of environmental impacts.

- *Strengthen control at supra-local level:* planning at regional level for the protection of the environment; limiting accommodation capacity; improving the quality of the urban environment (green areas, traffic free zones, control of air and noise pollution, garbage disposal).
- *Establish coordination between agencies influencing environmental resources* to protect and improve homogeneous parts – or 'clusters' – of the environmental system (such as beach, or sea, or urban area): creating partnerships with all interested bodies and individuals for each cluster.
- *Level out seasonal peaks* to avoid peaks of pollution and disorder by controlling and limiting tourist arrivals in high season (by increased prices, limitation of private traffic, size of car parking); developing business tourism, conferences and special interest tourism to extend the season; moving towards clienteles supporting environmental improvement.
- *Encourage autonomy* in the production and sale of the tourism products in order to avoid decision-making from outside the area: encourage local entrepreneurs, upgrade local know-how, pursue a self-managed development of tourism.
- *Develop flexible planning* by favouring modular plans and developing networks aimed at different purposes (productive/operative/informative); create local task forces for promoting, upgrading, developing new projects, and for assisting the local government in strategic planning and improvement; provide financial incentives for upgrading.
- *Other possible objectives:* emphasize local identity (local style of building, valorizing local traditions); encourage, through publicity campaigns and incentives, individual operators to adopt environmental measure (e.g. in operating hotels); involve tourists in using and respecting local resources (information, advice); diffuse tourism-environment know-how (through data bank); stimulate environmental competition amongst resorts (periodic merit awards, etc.).

An example of strategic planning coordinated between different authorities

Over the past ten years 'Resorts Contracts' between state, region and resort have been created in France in order to define the actions to be taken for (1) improving services (information, transport, parking, protection of beach area, pedestrianization and parks, rehabilitation of historic buildings); (2) developing attractions and activities, new tourism products (e.g. nordic skiing, artificial snow, dry harbour), and (3) conducting marketing surveys and programmes. The costs of these efforts have been contractually split three ways between state, region and municipality.

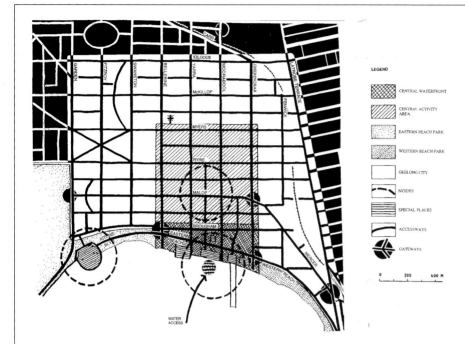

LEGEND

- CENTRAL WATERFRONT
- CENTRAL ACTIVITY AREA
- EASTERN BEACH PARK
- WESTERN BEACH PARK
- GEELONG CITY
- NODES
- SPECIAL PLACES
- ACCESSWAYS
- GATEWAYS

0   200   400 M

Geelong design and development code (Australia)

Geelong (100 000 inhabitants), a provincial city west of Melbourne, has grown since the 1830s from the shores of Corio Bay along a rather strict street grid. One of its main assets is its open waterfront which is a continuation of the urban fabric. The challenge was to convert this waterfront into an attraction for both residents and visitors.

The Geelong Waterfront Design and Development Code of July 1996 sets out guidelines for the design of Geelong's urban waterfront precincts, in an effort to bridge the gap between general strategies or concepts and the physical work required. This provides guidance both for private development and the design of the public environment.

Four main precincts have been defined (Fig. 6.19) and analysed, development principles being drawn up for each precinct. A design framework provides recommendations for the design of accessways, gateways, special places, etc. Street furniture, lighting, paving and so on, are treated as coordinated systems (Fig. 6.20) to help provide a unique character to the place.

Client: Greater Geelong City Council
Planners: Keys Young (Milson Point, Sidney)
in association with Urban Initiatives (Melbourne).

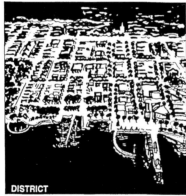

DISTRICT

PRECINCTS:

CENTRAL ACTIVITIES PRECINCT

CENTRAL WATERFRONT

WESTERN BEACH

EASTERN BEACH

WITHIN EACH PRECINCT ARE:

ACCESSWAYS

GATEWAYS

SPECIAL PLACES

EDGES

LANDSCAPE

BUILDING INTERFACE

WITHIN THESE SPACES ARE THE COMPONENT SYSTEMS:

LIGHTING   FURNITURE   PUBLIC SIGNAGE   SHELTERS   WATER   PAVING   ADVERTISING   ART

a *Mmelesi Lodge (photograph, Hollywood Triple K Studio)*

b *Semonkong Lodge: near the highest waterfall in southern Africa (photograph, Hollywood Triple K Studio)*

c *Ketane Village: pony-trekking with overnight accommodation (photograph, Hollywood Triple K Studio)*

Lesotho: Improvement of tourism infrastructure

Lesotho is a high, mountainous country which offers tourism products ranging from life viewing and outdoor activities (pony trekking, climbing, fishing, bird watching, fossil hunting) to more sophisticated facilities in the capital Maseru. The objectives of a study in 1988 for the government by the World Tourism Organization as executing agency for the UNDP, were to recommend strategies to improve the quality and performance of hotel and lodge accommodation and other tourism infrastructures, to create opportunities for the Basotho to play a larger role in operations and management and to draft plans for further tourism development.

The study involved detailed surveys of all the accommodation and facilities, the preparation of specifications for improvement, estimates and programmes for implementation. The main problems hindering the improvement of accommodation and the tourism industry as a whole were identified as:

- *financing difficulties — lack of long-term loans for investment;*
- *security of leases — short leases limiting long-term planning;*
- *operation — lack of external services and managerial skills and experience;*
- *lodges — isolated locations, limited and seasonal demands, high operating costs*

Strategies to deal with each of these aspects included the establishment of a development fund for improvement of facilities, programmes for management and skills training, zoning of future developments in areas of specific attractions and the preparation of specifications for modern lodges based on the traditional Basotho style. Constructed examples are shown in Figs 6.21a–c.

Subsequent reports on the tourism industry have also drawn attention to the financing difficulties. In 1997 the government of Lesotho was working towards providing and adjusting policy frameworks on tourism that would encourage both local and foreign investors to consider investing in Lesotho as a viable venture.

Surveys and planning: F. Lawson

Weston-super-Mare, UK: A heritage and environmental strategy

This study by the Civic Trust, in 1993, was one of many Local Area Initiatives which the English Tourist Board has supported with partnerships of public and private sponsors. The objective was to secure and implement the regeneration of this family seaside resort. The recommendations included a strategy for practical improvements to the architectural heritage and environment of the resort, covering:

- *the approaches – with planting schemes to create green 'gateways' leading to the resort;*
- *arrival – improvements and landscaping of the railway station and car parks;*
- *streetscape – restoration of characteristic street frontages and harmonious shop fronts;*
- *historic buildings – proactive approaches to conserve and restore historic landmarks;*
- *traffic – creation and landscaping of pedestrian routes and pedestrian-friendly areas;*

- *open spaces – recovery and improved design of green areas and 'pocket' gardens;*
- *relationship with the sea – creating attractive approach routes and visual contacts;*
- *information – improvements to signing, street furniture and road surfaces;*
- *interpretation – development of events, exhibitions, linkages and themes.*

English Tourist Board, 1993

Stage	Financing and appraisal	Resort planning and development	Marketing and operation	Consultation and regulations
Broad Concept	Sources of finance Conditions Incentives	Regional survey Draft site survey	Market surveys Competition Decisional centres	Planning policies Socio-economic conditions
	Prepare outlined programme for alternative broad concepts			
	Estimate costs and check availability of funds	Alternative land use plans – check site's carrying capacity	Check compatibility with potential markets	Assess socio-economic impacts and local attitudes
Action: Select one (or more) concepts(s) – buy or control land required for project				
Draft Project		Detailed site surveys Off site infrastructures	Check alternative facilities with markets	
	Prepare alternative programme corresponding to alternative products			
	Draft financing plans Investment needs Initial appraisal	Draft master plans illustrating the alternative products	Market analyses Methods of operation	Cost and benefits Environmental issues Define involvement of authorities (grants etc.)
Action: Select one programme – secure financing and agreements of public authorities				
Final Project			Organizational arrangements Partnerships	Local consultations Labour force Support services
	Prepare alternative programmes for Phase One			
	Financial plans Feasibility analyses Cash flows	Development plan Layout of site Building regulations	Organize promotion and operation	Publication of plans
Action: Approval of public authorities – contractual agreements with 'partners'				
Phase One	Cost planning Stage payments Variation analysis	Construction works Project management Stage completion	Contracts Operational systems Supply arrangements	Local involvement System linkages Regulation
Action: Opening of resort Phase One				
Operation	Asset appraisal Refinancing options Long-term provisions	Maintenance plans Organization Cyclical changes	Monitoring performances and market changes	Review of incentives Land use plans
Future Phases	**According to final project and its evolution (flexibility)**			

Each stage implies:

1.   surveys and collection of additional information;
2.   elaboration of alternatives;
3.   evaluation of these alternatives;
4.   immediate action (if the decision is to proceed).

6.6 PLANNING PROCEDURES

6.6.1 Framework

The planning of resorts or recreation centres is generally more complex than the procedures for individual facilities. It usually involves:

- large sites: often in multiple ownership;
- high overall investment;
- major changes in land use patterns;
- environmental assessment and impact analysis;
- wide consultation and agreement of tourism, planning and local authorities;
- cost benefit analysis in addition to feasibility appraisal;
- infrastructural works: on and off site;
- phased development over long timescales (see 6.5.2).

The procedures depend to some degree on the political structure of the country and the extent to which requirements (surveys, consultation, analyses) have been covered in national or regional plans.

To minimize risk and commitments planning usually involves **five stages of progression** from decisions on the broad concept and site, to draft proposals, detailed plans, contractual arrangements and operational programmes. This systematic approach generally involves parallel consideration of finance, plans, markets, operation and regulation, calling for the participation of a **team of specialists**.

The main phases presented in the table on the previous page are detailed and explained in the following paragraphs.

6.6.2 Broad concept

The type of development and its location is strongly influenced by the provisions of the national, regional and local plans (Chapter 8). However, the character of the resort or recreation complex, its size, clienteles and main activities, with the corresponding facilities, architecture, marketing and operation, depends on the motivations and interpretations of the sponsors and developers. Some of the considerations determining the concept are broadly quantifiable (markets, occupancies, revenues, costs, competition), others involve an entrepreneurial assessment (trends in fashion, aesthetics, attractiveness, image). This first stage aims at **reviewing and comparing alternative global tourism/recreation images and products**: for example, should the site be developed into a marina, a beach resort or a camping site? of which size? with which activities?

Surveys: information regarding potential markets may be obtained by analysing tourism statistics (growth) and by comparing the experiences of similar resorts within comparable distances of the main tourist generating areas (competition). Surveys should examine both existing conditions and planned changes.

Studies	Coverage
Site details	Carrying capacity, main assets and restrictions, regional plans/projects, land ownership, local attitudes, community needs and priorities, available services and accesses, protection.
Tourist markets Recreation markets	By segment: age, individuals/families, spending, place of residence, domestic/foreign, growth rates, activities
Nature of use	Seasonality, average stay, holiday/weekend/other usage
Facilities required	Competitive facilities and products, relative prices, feasibility, accommodation and facilities sought, means of access
Influences on development	Competitive proposals, financial aid, national policy, commercial infrastructure, location of 'local influences' and decision centres

Lack of information – such as in newly developing regions or in introducing new concepts – may limit initial development to organizations able to

- offset the higher financial risk (state, multi-operational groups);
- exercise influence on markets (tour operators, travel clubs e.g. Club Méditerranée).

Alternative concepts: at this initial stage a number of alternative proposals (i.e. alternative broad concepts) may be examined. Some may be eliminated as falling outside the developers' goals, interests or means of finance. Others may not be feasible due to

- inadequate or unsuitable site areas;
- lack of control over access or use of resources;
- season of use being too short;
- disproportionate infrastructure costs.

Alternative broad concepts may include putting an accent on particular activities, variations in sophistication and densities, emphasis on natural or organized activities, targeting specific market flows, balance of revenue-, non-revenue-earning facilities

The possible options are compared by preparing:

- draft plans (1:5000 to 1:1000): alternative land uses and carrying capacity of the site
- preliminary cost estimates and market feasibility
- assessments of socio-economic, environmental and fiscal impacts

Consultation of all parties concerned at conceptual stage: the policies and priorities of various parties having a direct concern in tourism development will have a considerable influence on the type of concept which can be supported

Ocean Park, Bremerhaven, Germany

On a disused dockland of approximately 60 ha (240 acres), where the seaport of Bremerhaven was originally founded, this new development will enjoy a prime location between a major pedestrian zone and the dyke system along the River Weser. Plans include the extension of the inner city to the river side with the right mix of residential accommodation and commercial properties. The highlights of this DM 1.2 billion project, which should be visited by more than 3 million visitors a year, will be:

- *the Blue Planet around the 'Oceanarium' consisting of sea aquariums with a tank volume of 4 600 m³ in a tropical rainforest environment, a multimedia theatre called 'the magic of the Oceans', a hotel with casino, restaurants and shops;*
- *an IMAX cinema;*
- *the Alte Werf an old boatyard, with a replica of a 14th-century medieval boat under construction and children's play area;*
- *the AquamaXX centre for entertainment, fun and leisure activities, with multiplex movie theatre with ten cinemas, bowling alley, pool hall, video arcade, disco, restaurants and bars;*
- *Tropicum, a large Dome with pools, waves and beach in a Caribbean environment;*
- *the Harbour village, a genuine community with 500–600 people living in low houses with romantic hotels, streets cafes, exhibitions, practising old skills and running shops. This will be the link between the city of Bremerhaven and Ocean Park.*

Developers: Ocean Park Entwicklungsgesellschaft, D-17568 Bremerhaven

a *Model of Ocean Park, Bremerhaven, Germany. The Alte Werf is in the foreground and the Blue Planet is behind the Harbour Village.*

b *Model of the Blue Planet*

c *The old docks with traditional vessels and the Blue Planet in the background* and its effective implementation. Meetings and discussions with the local people (not only the officials) are necessary in order to minimize misconceptions on both sides.

Organization	Matters to be determined
State or regional planning authority	Approval and support for development proposed in that location. Conditions which may be imposed. Other major changes planned in surrounding region.
Community, local, environmental, etc. concerns	Position of local people. Socio-economic, fiscal and environmental impacts. Steps required to ameliorate possible opposition, or to obtain financing assistance.
Sources and conditions for finance	Funds available, phasing arrangements returns required. Additional sources of funding, terms, conditions, procedures. Assistance available (grants, loans, guarantees).
Promotion, marketing and operation	Method of operation (partnership, management contracts, rentals or concessions), terms and conditions, agencies
Local building industry	Resources, capacity, need for importation of materials and components (costs, delays).
Manpower	Trained/trainable manpower in region, competition.

Immediate action: once the initial enquiries and evaluations are sufficiently completed, steps must be taken to ensure control over the whole area likely to be required. Later acquisition of additional land is liable to induce inflation and involve higher risk. Alternative policies which allow control of the land within and around the resort may be based on:

- buying all adjacent land suitable for development
- renting land, under long term agreements with or without the option to purchase to reduce the initial capital outlay;
- associating adjacent owners in the overall development as a joint venture;
- giving minority owners shares in the development society corresponding to the value of their land;
- deferring payment by retrocession of part of the land, with infrastructure and defined building rights, in return for placing all the land at the disposal of the developer;
- obtaining the agreement of public authorities to a local land use plan defining restrictions on development (low densities, conditions for sale) of surrounding areas.

6.6.3 Draft project

The **main aims** of the draft stage are to define the character of the tourist/recreation complex, and the selected image(s) and product(s) necessary in order to secure financing from and agreements with public authorities. This implies carrying out detailed surveys of the site, drawing up alternative programmes of the main facilities and drawing up the corresponding draft layout plans, from which cost estimates and financial plans can be prepared.

The surveys cover the site's characteristics, on-site and off-site infrastructures, and the reaction of the markets to the specific products selected in the previous stage.

Coverage	Examples of detailed physical surveys
All relevant physical features	Relief, soil conditions, geology, groundwater and drainage patterns, ecology, vegetation, wildlife, views
In mountains	Snow cover, avalanches, conditions for skiing (see 5.3.2)
At seaside	Erosion, evolution of beaches, characteristics of sea, waves, currents, dune restoration, oceanography, protective measures (see 5.2.1)
Microclimate	Extent of exposure, shelter, screening, orientation, prevailing winds, fog, mean seasonable temperatures and range of extremes, rainfall frequency and intensities, sunshine data.
Additional infrastructure	Both on and off site, roads, water purification and distribution, electricity supplies, telecommunications (with estimates of costs).
Surroundings	Present and possible land use, measures to ensure protection and control.
Environmental surveys	Natural or ecological values, areas of special interest or fragility. Carrying capacity. Impact analysis, steps to ameliorate damage. Conservation measures

Surveys may include aerial photography (including infra-red), multi-spectral scanning and other techniques, land measurements, contouring and ground trials.

The alternative **layout plans** control the implementation of the considered alternative or complementary tourist/recreation products considering:

- *ecological value* of each part of the area; whether this is of primary importance or secondary to the needs of infrastructure, building and other requirements;
- *alternative preferential locations* for the activities considered;
- *variations in costs* of development for different locations including infrastructure costs;
- *functional relationships* between facilities, identifying zones or sectors of accommodation, recreation, sports area, shopping, social interests, rest and relaxation etc.;
- *separation of conflicting activities*: noise and animation from areas of rest and relaxation; children's playgrounds from traffic; provisions for spectators and participants etc.;
- *circulation planning* for residents, day visitors, operational services and maintenance, including provisions for vehicular traffic;
- *phases of realization,* location (particularly of Phase I) and extension.

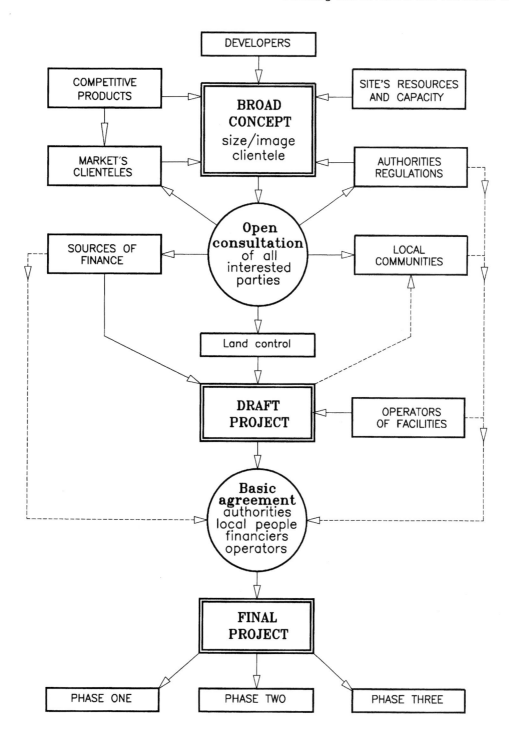

Figure 6.7

Market analyses (target markets, feasibility) and alternative **methods of operating** the facilities may be reviewed in the light of consultations and other changes.

Draft financing plan: financial plans are prepared from the market information, site surveys and layout plans. At the draft stage these should include estimates of:

- total investment needed and investment in first phase;
- annual operating costs;
- value of saleable land based on markets for secondary development condominiums etc.;
- market demands and revenues from the facilities operated by the promoter;

- gross operating profits and other benefits (or losses);
- fiscal or taxation revenues and employment for the local communities which could justify their assistance in financing the project (grants, loans, guarantees);
- relationships between capital investment, turnover and various returns including sensitivity analyses of the effects of modifying any of the crucial variables (such as values, costs, charges, utilization, construction period).

Computerized modelling is required to test sensitivities, compare the financial costs and benefits of the alternatives, project cash flows, analyse possible impacts on the various groups in the community and highlight other details which may need to be analysed further in the final plan.

After selection, the planning layout will enable a land use plan (scale 1:1000 to 1:2000) to be drawn up and a number of perspective sketches to be prepared to show the image the resort or complex will project. The latter is particularly important for promotion purposes following this early stage.

Immediate measures: contacts must now be formally established with the various authorities concerned with the development and financing of tourism. Any outstanding problems of capacity and density must be resolved and any additional land – including access rights – purchased or brought under control. Consideration must also be given to the form of building, materials, techniques, local contractors, types of contract and programmes of work involved.

Formal contracts are also recommended with potential operators (hotel groups, estate agencies, catering companies) and other organizations which might influence the design or programme. Once future operators or buyers for the facilities are found, financing the development is generally made easier.

6.6.4 Final project

This stage is concerned with details, using the draft plan as a basis. It determines the contents of the phased programme, technical requirements, the precise character of buildings and landscapes together with detailed estimates of capital costs. Alternative architectural concepts, building techniques and material may be examined, together with alternative arrangements for infrastructure and phasing of the work. The **programme and layout of Phase 1** is given detailed attention and alternatives are usually considered. Any additional information to complete or update the marketing and financing plans must be taken into account as well as the outcome of negotiations for operating the facilities or sale of the sites when completed.

Final development plans are usually drawn to a scale of 1:1000, giving details of:

- the proposed layout of the site;

- allocated zones for various uses (for example, categories of accommodation, different activities, municipal services, public areas and collective facilities);
- designated green areas, open spaces reserved for recreation (beaches, ski runs, areas of high scenic value, vantage points, etc.);
- potentially dangerous locations (cliffs, avalanches and other hazards);
- road diagrams, parking areas, pedestrian zones, provisions for services and maintenance vehicles, separation of through traffic;
- infrastructure diagrams showing arrangements for water, electricity, telecommunications, district heating (if used), sewerage and surface drainage in phased stages;
- building site plans, alignments, densities, height and size restrictions and specific features;
- landscaping details including planting schedules of trees etc., for screening, shelter, aesthetic benefits;
- longitudinal and cross sections, elevations and other details showing relative heights, slopes, depths;
- models and artist's sketches of the development for presentation to prospective agents and associated organizations.

Planning and building controls should be considered at two levels:

- *Statutory requirements:* planning and other statutory restrictions and conditions must be taken into account from the beginning and formal approval will normally be sought in outline initially, in principle for the final development plan and in detail prior to the construction of each phase.
- *Individual standards:* apart from statutory requirements, more specific rules for building control within the resort must be drawn up by the developer. These will define the authority which is to be in charge of implementation and control, the ownership and maintenance of public areas, infrastructure and common facilities; they will regulate the densities and zoning of development, impose constraints on architecture, materials and other building details, and regulate open spaces, landscaping and parking etc. This control must be sufficiently strict to ensure that the development is properly regulated – both to comply with planning conditions and for the eventual benefit of the resort – while being sufficiently flexible to allow valuable evolution and change.

The **detailed financial** plan provides all the relevant financial details, expanding and clarifying the information gathered during the draft stage, namely

- *estimates of capital costs:*
  - land acquisition and off-site connecting infrastructure (less contributions and subsidies);
  - on-site infrastructures such as roads, parking areas, district engineering services;
  - buildings and facilities provided by the developer;
  - costs incurred in surveys, promotions and administration.

- *operational costs and revenues:*
  - management, domestic and community services, maintenance, security and other services offered by the developers;
  - estimates of receipts from selling plots for development, building rights or actual facilities.
- *conditions:* sources of finance and conditions imposed (rates of interest, extent of participation, period for repayment) and phasing of finance.
- *cash flows:*
  - estimates of total costs involved, discounted by subsidies, taxation and other fiscal benefits as annual or phased payments;
  - benefits to the developer in remuneration and other advantages such as increasing asset value.

Accounting systems such as discounting, Internal Rate of Return (IRR) and sensitivity analysis are generally applied.

As the final plans become available **immediate action** may be taken to:

- have the details ratified by the public authorities concerned, including approval for any grant aid or subsidies;
- establish contractual agreements with the associated parties;
- organize the operational functions – with subcontracting and licensing arrangements as appropriate.

6.6.5 Phase 1 and operational projects

Success or failure of a resort or large recreational complex is highly dependent on the image and performance achieved in the first phase. This should be:

- an exemplary representation of the future resort, with distinctive character and high quality attractions and facilities;
- in the right location with attractive surroundings allowing future expansion without disturbance.

In preparing the final report, various options may be examined, for example to:

- diversify the facilities in Phase 1 in order to test the markets;
- reduce infrastructure costs by phasing work (see 6.5.1–2);
- extend flexibility by limiting irreversible decisions for future programmes (see 6.5.3).

At this initial stage it is also necessary to determine:

- the operational profiles for Phase 1: functions involved in operating the resort, levels of profitability, performance criteria, appropriate methods of operation (see 6.6.2) and agreements;
- the operational requirements: organizational structures, policies, staffing levels, job specifications, recruitment and training, purchasing of supplies, quality control.

7 Framework for tourism/recreation master plans

7.1 INTERRELATION OF TOURISM AND RECREATION

Boundaries between tourism and recreation are indistinct as both often share the same facilities and compete for space and finance (see 1.1.3). Both exert strong pressures on sites and natural resources and call for similar measures of correction and selected improvement.

7.1.1 Aims in planning tourism/recreation development

There are many benefits in planning tourism development at national and regional level. These have been well documented by the World Tourism Organization (WTO 1994) and earlier studies (Baud-Bovy and Lawson 1977). As a summary, planning of these levels should aim to:

- define the objectives (both short- and long-term), policies and implementation procedures for developing tourism;
- integrate tourism development into the overall development plans and policies to establish close linkages with other sectors;
- coordinate development of the various elements to ensure appropriate relationships between the attractions, facilities, services and various tourist markets;
- optimize and balance economic, environmental and social benefits of tourism and their equitable distribution;
- establish guidelines, procedures and standards for preparing detailed plans in areas designated for tourism development;
- institute the administrative, regulatory and financial structures required to ensure effective implementation of the tourism development policies and plans;
- ensure effective measures can be taken to manage, conserve and sustain the attractiveness of tourist resources;
- provide the framework for coordination of public and private interests in tourism investment;
- establish procedures to monitor continuously the progress of tourism development and to make necessary corrections or revisions.

Source: World Tourism Organization

Most of the aims for tourism development apply also to outdoor recreation. Sites suitable for recreational development, particularly those near main centres of population, are subject to pressures from many competitive demands for land. Recreation planning policies must, specifically, give priority to

- measures for land allocation and reservation;
- the implementation of the necessary facilities;
- the protection of the environment.

Developed countries with limited natural attractions for foreign tourists tend to give more emphasis to domestic tourism and recreation while, in newly developing countries, the need for revenues from foreign tourism is usually more critical.

Industrial Heritage and Tourism in Scotland

As part of the implementation of the Strategic Plan for Scottish Tourism, 1994, a review was undertaken of the industrial heritage assets in Scotland. In 1995, there were 82 museums and sites devoted to industrial heritage themes open to the public, the top 20 of which attracted 1.7 million visitors each year. A further 62 mixed sites contained an element of industrial heritage element. In general, it was proposed that:

- *priority should be given to funding existing sites which have a national role and to improving the quality of interpretation and presentation to create wider appeal;*
- *whilst local initiatives were to be encouraged, a coordinated approach was necessary to avoid duplication and subsequent difficulties in preservation and maintenance.*
- *local communities should be involved and the wider impacts of heritage development — in tourism, environmental, economic, social and educational benefits — recognized.*

Industrial Heritage and Tourism In Scotland — A Review,
Scottish Tourism Coordinating Group,
Scottish Tourism Board, 1996
Consultants: Pieda

7.1.2 Differences in planning for tourism and recreation

The major difference in the development of tourism or recreation master plans arises from the fact that the market for outdoor recreation is largely a captive one: recreationists are generally limited to those attractions and facilities at a suitable time–distance from their home. Other differences arise from the way tourist and recreational facilities are marketed, run and financed:

Albania: Integrated Tourism Development Plan for the Coastline from Llogaras to Qeparo, District of Vlora, November 1996

Two broad areas — along the north and south coast and in the interior — have been designated *Priority Tourist Zones* in Albania. Following the approval of a Coastal Management Plan (which was funded by the Mediterranean Technical Assistance Programme, METAP, and administered by the World Bank), an Integrated Tourism Development Plan was prepared for the southern area of coast between Llogaras and Qeparo.

The broad objectives of this integrated plan were:

- to increase the value of tourism and maximize foreign earnings in the region by developing a niche in the international tourism market;
- to develop a sustainable level of tourism and a high quality sector focused on the needs of tourists, encouraging cultural and economic exchange and European integration;
- to respect the social, religious and cultural concerns of the host population, motivate a positive attitude, increase employment opportunities and ensure suitable distribution of benefits;
- to outline necessary amendments to the legal, institutional and administrative frameworks and define a system for education and training of staff and managers.

Detailed recommendations covered:

- carrying capacity recommendations — based on optimum beach capacities;
- marketing strategies — target markets, competing destinations, potential products and images;
- infrastructural development — existing technical services, requirements and improvements;
- education, training and organizational frameworks;
- tourism products and their implementation;
- analysis of the economic, physical and social impacts.

Project funded by the Republic of Austria Federal Chancellery.

A joint venture study by: **t.r.b.**, technik-recht-betriebs-swirtschaft, in association with Horwath Consulting, London.

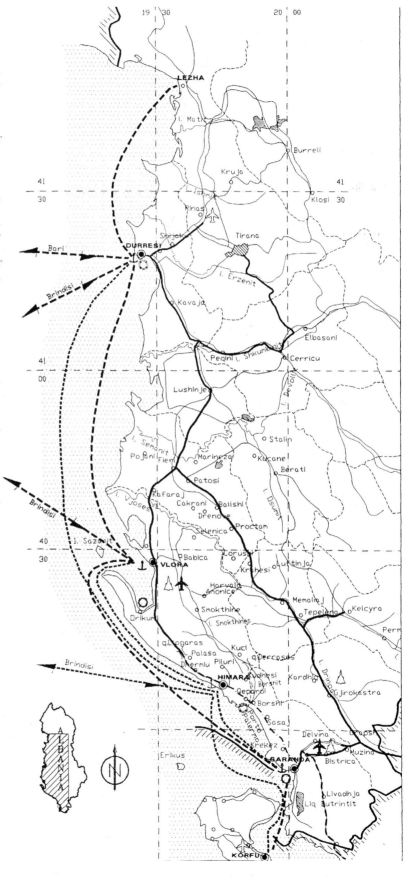

LEGEND

◉	Town
○	Village
——	Road
▬▬	Two lane highway
- - -	Two lane highway proposed
·-·-·	Two lane extension proposed
——	Railway
——	River
- - - -	District border
/////	State border
⋈	Pass
▒	Sea
✈	Civil airport proposed
✈	Civil airport existing
△	Military airport existing
⊥	Harbour proposed
⊥	Harbour existing
◌	Marina proposed
○	Marina under planning
Seaway proposed	Seaway existing

Leisure tourism	Recreation
Affected by policies of foreign governments (i.e. in destination countries)	Determined by policies of local government and municipal authorities
Wide choice of destinations and facilities for holidays	Limited to those attractions and resources within suitable time–distance (i.e. defined catchment areas)
Occupancies generally high over the long holiday season	Occupancies highly concentrated into weekends, public holidays
Private sector investment is normally responsible for facility development	Public sector investment is invariably required to provide public recreation amenities (parks, leisure centres, sports grounds)
Profitability mainly arises from accommodation and food services (exceptionally: gambling).	Most community recreation and sports need some form of financial support.
Leisure facilities subsidized by residential sales	Private clubs and commercial facilities rely on cross-subsidization from memberships and other sales. Profit generating activities involve large numbers in small areas (spectator events) or intensive repeat use (e.g., bowling)
Usually highly dependent on the role of intermediaries (tour operators, travel agents)	Limited use of intermediaries but greater influence of clubs and societies in setting standards and requirements.

> ### Kentucky tourism master plan: A strategic plan for tourism development
>
> In 1995 tourism in Kentucky was worth $7.1 billion, the state's third largest industry and its second largest employer with nearly 145 000 employees. The Tourism Strategic Plan, 1995, issued by the Tourism Cabinet, identified values, a mission and goals together with strategies by which these could be achieved. Detailed strategies covered aspects such as organization, infrastructure, targeted rural areas, conservation of historic structures, beautification of downtown and urban areas, integrated attractions based on themes, marketing, implementation, monitoring and support measures (incentives, bonds, tax credits, joint funding).

7.2 FUNDAMENTAL PLANNING CONSIDERATIONS

7.2.1 Definitions

Planning is an official process established by – or imposed upon – a community, which assesses, decides, implements and controls the allocation of scarce resources between competing demands.

Resources may be physical (such as land and infrastructure), economic, administrative or/and technical. The demands for tourism may be in competition with priorities sought by local communities (for housing, education, recreation, etc.) as well as those of other sectors for commercial, industrial and agricultural development. In sensitive areas there are often counter demands for strict environmental protection by representative pressure groups.

The role of planning is usually to provide the **framework** on which decisions may be based. Decision-making on questions of policy goals, priorities and methods of funding is normally a matter of politics.

In **physical planning**, for example, the aim is to achieve harmonization between the demands for and supply of land in accordance with agreed land-use policies. Economic plans often set other priorities such as the balance of benefits to the community and country.

7.2.2 Governmental structures and policies

Government participation in encouraging and financing tourism/recreation development depends on many factors and may be negative where there are limited prospects for tourism or conflicts with other concerns (security, local antagonism, saturation of resources). The main factors are:

- *Political and economic structure:* extent of centralization (federal or centralized government), division of power and financial control between national, regional and local levels.
- *Government policies:* direct intervention and investment through a planned economy, or free enterprise market economy requiring private sector funding of development and infrastructure.
- *Development needs and priorities:* stages of development, competition for resources, extent of tourism and need for changes.

Depending on the government structure, the basic tourism development plans are developed at national or regional level as shown in Fig. 7.3.

7.2.3 Processes

Planning has promotional, controlling and monitoring roles, and may apply generally, as in development control, or more specifically to one sector of the economy, such as community recreation or tourism.

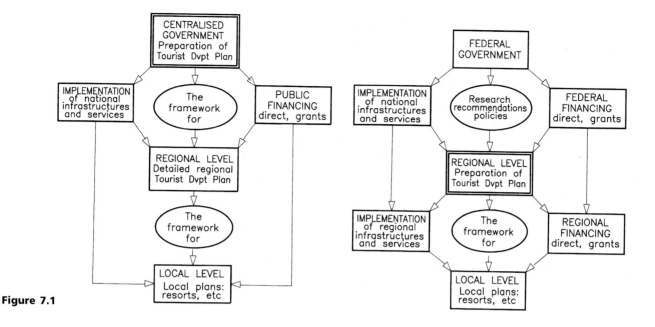

Figure 7.1

Types of measures	Examples relevant to tourism
Promotional measures	
Preparation of development plans	Survey and evaluation of resources and demands
	Assessment of needs, benefits and balances
	Recommendations for optimum use of resources
Strategies for implementation	Enactment of enabling legislation and ordinances
	Establishment of administrative structures and processes
	Determination of priorities and phases
	Designation of land usage areas, zones and optimum densities
Financial provisions	Funding provisions and budget allocations
	Acquisitions of necessary land andresources
	Schemes for incentives and compensation
Controlling measures	
Regulation of development	Requirements for planning approval or refusal
	Control of unauthorized development
	Regulation of building and infrastructure works
Protection of resources	Conservation of environmentallysensitive areas
	Listing buildings of historic/architectural interest
	Preservation of trees and sites of scientific importance
	Protection of monuments and their historic settings
	Designation of parks and areas of natural beauty
Monitoring procedures	
Comprehensive time-series and ad-hoc surveys	Review of demographic and socio-economic changes
	Monitoring of usage of resources
	Surveys of visitor characteristics and patterns of demand
	Analysis of trends for future projections

Cyprus: Sustainability of tourism

In 1993 Cyprus provided 70 000 beds in licensed establishments, of which 53.7 per cent were in hotels and 34.8 per cent in aparthotels. A further 11 200 beds in hotels and apartments were under construction. Tourism employed 35 000 directly and about 70 000 in total (employment multiplier 1:1), i.e. 26.4 per cent of the employed population, and accounted for 40.8 per cent of total receipts for exports, with an import coefficient of 20–25 per cent.

From 1991, following an 18-month moratorium on all new hotel applications in coastal zones, government policy has been directed towards sustainability, improvement of product quality and market targeting of the third age groups, conferences and special interest visitors. The strategies include:

- *slowing down coastal development and obtaining a better mix by banning further aparthotels and hotels below 3-star grade (4-star in main tourist areas) and encouraging higher quality tourist villages;*
- *directing investment to ancillary tourism projects, particularly marinas, golf courses, casinos, health and fitness centres;*
- *introducing small-scale rural, special interest and agro-tourism, nautical tourism;*
- *renovating and landscaping village squares and examples of vernacular architecture;*
- *protecting of archaeological and natural resources, conserving of water supplies;*
- *coastal zone management, control of pollution, adoption of the 'Blue Flag' scheme.*

National Report, Republic of Cyprus.
Euro-Mediterranean Conference on Tourism with sustainable development, 1993

An earlier study of conferences and incentive travel optimized the location and requirements for a new international conference centre leading to the development of the Philoxenia Conference Centre with associated services in Nicosia and nearby resorts.

Conference study: Tibbalds Partnership.
Consultant: F. Lawson

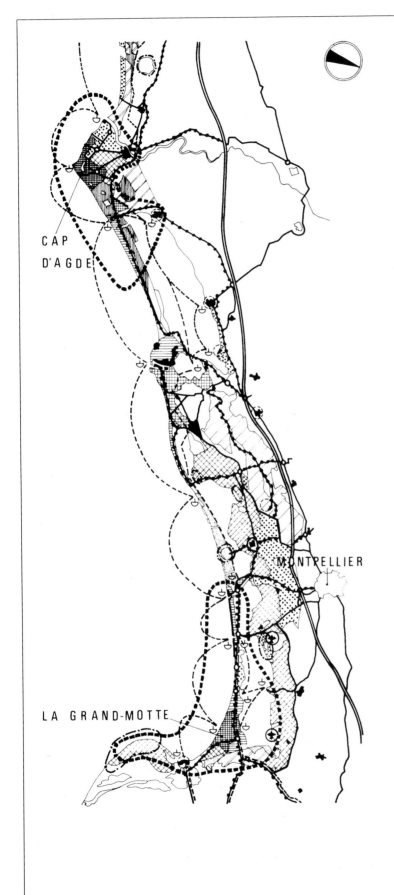

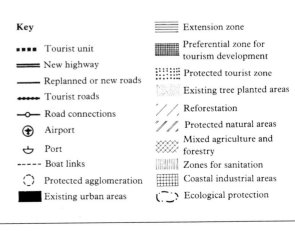

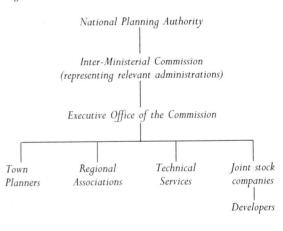

Languedoc-Roussillon, France

One of the very first examples of regional tourism planning, this 200 km coastline was originally a flat desolate area with limited access and mosquito-infested marshes and lagoons isolating the beaches. An Inter-Ministerial Commission was created in 1963 to take under control key areas of land and prepare a regional development plan together with master plans for the six main resorts, concentrated around previous villages and ports. The resorts are separated by zones of agriculture and forestry in which building is largely prohibited. The eastern part of the development plan, including two of the resorts, is illustrated.

The State's direct financial involvement has been in the development of more than ten yachting harbours, highways and roads, water supplies, cleaning and clearing the main lagoons (sewage plants, water protection, dredging, etc), elimination of mosquitoes and reforestation programmes.

The infrastructure of each resort (local roads, parking areas, electricity, gas and water distribution, commercial centres, playing fields, green areas and public buildings) was implemented by a non-profit joint stock company authorized to borrow from the main government credit establishments. The land so equipped was then resold with detailed specifications to public or private developers to build the actual facilities. This large-scale integrated project has served as an international model for many years, inspiring the development of Cancún (Mexico) and other tourist regions.

Organization

National Planning Authority

Inter-Ministerial Commission
(representing relevant administrations)

Executive Office of the Commission

Town Planners — Regional Associations — Technical Services — Joint stock companies — Developers

Key

- ▪▪▪▪ Tourist unit
- ═══ New highway
- ——— Replanned or new roads
- ●—●—● Tourist roads
- —○— Road connections
- ⊕ Airport
- ⚓ Port
- - - - Boat links
- ◌ Protected agglomeration
- ■ Existing urban areas
- ≡ Extension zone
- ▦ Preferential zone for tourism development
- ⸬ Protected tourist zone
- ▒ Existing tree planted areas
- ⫽ Reforestation
- ⫻ Protected natural areas
- ⤬ Mixed agriculture and forestry
- ▥ Zones for sanitation
- ▦ Coastal industrial areas
- ◌ Ecological protection

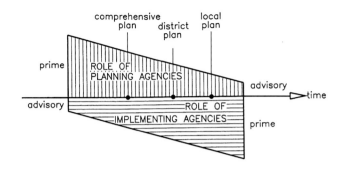

Figure 7.2

During the elaboration and the implementation of any development plan the role of the *planning agency* (or team) progressively changes from prime to advisory, while that of the *implementing agency* increases (see Fig. 7.2).

7.2.4 Scales and levels of planning

The scale of planning ranges from the formulation of broad national plans to the specific requirements of individual projects. National or regional plans provide the framework for development in most countries and usually extend over a 10–12 year perspective with details laid down for 5-year programmes (in some cases 3, 4 or 6 years) to allow for progressive changes.

Level[a]	Main emphasis
National	Framework, environmental, economic and social policies
	Financial and legal provisions and procedures
	National structures, institutions and reservations
Regional	Development strategies, structural plans for region
	Environmental protection, reservation areas
	Regional infrastructures, transport and tourism
Local[b]	Local development plans, allocations, conservation measures
	Zoning of land uses, densities, conditions for development
	Coordination and implementation of policies
Project	Market and financial appraisal, organization of investment
	Site acquisition, facility planning and construction
	Coordination of development and operational needs.

Notes:
(a) Depending on governmental structure
(b) Private or public sector organization

Depending on its relative importance in economic development and on the characteristics of the area, tourism may be treated as a separate sector of planning or grouped with other related issues such as outdoor recreation, environment or travel.

Community leisure tends to fall into two main spheres of interest, sport and recreation or the arts and heritage. Both usually feature in national plans but the forms of development and funding are mainly decided at regional or local level.

7.2.5 Environmental protection and tourism image

More general planning provisions also cover a number of related subjects which can directly affect tourism and recreation; for example:

- *Preservation* of ancient monuments, listed buildings of historical or architectural importance, and of defined trees and woodlands together with grant aid of their maintenance and restoration.
- *Protection* of areas of great landscape value and outstanding natural beauty; sites of scientific importance; 'green belt' areas around large cities and conurbations; conservation areas of groups of buildings, streets and landscapes; common lands.
- *Creation* and management of national, regional and urban parks; visitor and recreation facilities; improved access to the countryside and coast; leisure use of waterways and marginal lands.
- *Control* of external signs and advertisements, particularly in sensitive areas of special control.
- *Powers* to acquire land and buildings compulsorily in order to meet planning objectives (redevelopment schemes, clearance of obsolete buildings, road improvements).

Szolnock County, Hungary

Through the PHARE Programme, which promotes local enterprise agencies and helps with funding, the European Union has been actively involved in setting up local enterprise agencies (LEAs), providing assistance with funding and the preparation of sound business plans and, within that framework, strategies for tourism. Strategies for the development of tourism in this region, in 1994, considered potential markets and products, the steps required to improve the existing attractions and facilities, training and organizational structures, investment costs, feasibilities and economic impacts. Integrated products were centred on:

- *the extensive River Tisza system (cruising, boating, fishing);*
- *cutural interests (interpretative centres, museums, art/craft centres);*
- *touring and transit travel (locations and standards for new hotels/motels and restaurants).*

SRG (Team Leader): J. Fletcher,
Facility planning: F. Lawson

Tourism master plan, Sri Lanka

The ten-year Tourism Master Plan (1992–2001) for Sri Lanka was funded as part of the UNDP Country Programme and prepared by the World Tourism Organization. The primary objective was to formulate a long-term strategic plan for international and domestic tourism development integrated with the country's society, economy and environment. Within this framework, a five-year (1992–6) Tourism Development Programme was formulated for priority areas, together with pre-feasibility studies for four tourism projects. The study was backed by 14 technical reports.

Optimum targets to be achieved by 2001 were set and 14 tourist zones, catering for different tourist segments, were identified in which major integrated developments could be planned and coordinated. Product development was directed at upgrading existing attractions, diversifying the product range, expanding capacity and developing new circuits and product packages inland. In each case, consideration was given to market requirements, carrying capacity (including environmental impact assessment), sustainable operations, control of incompatible development and provision of adequate infrastructure.

Unwata Bay, together with the nearby Galle Fort (a World Heritage Site) was one of the Tourism Action Areas, with proposals for a programme of conservation and phased development to provide two good quality hotels (100 and 150 rooms) on the headland overlooking the bay.

Study team: 10 international and 12 national consultants: Project Director: M. Gerty, Resort architects: M. Pugsley / A. de Vos, Land use planner: J. Hawkes

The project was co-ordinated by Consultative and Steering Committees chaired by the Minister of Tourism.

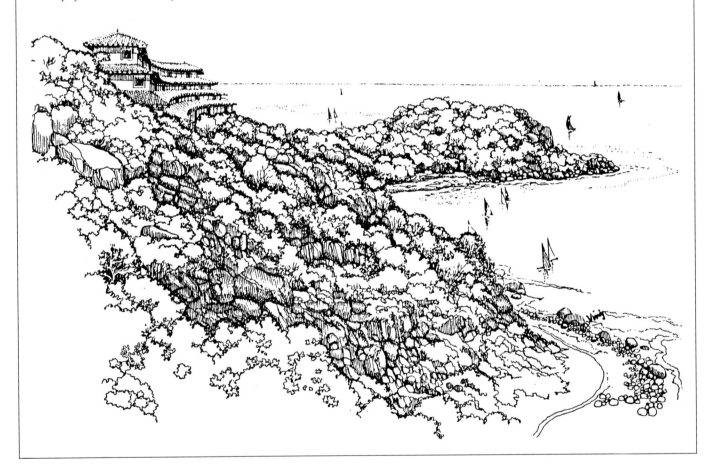

- *Regulation* and enforcement of plans by requiring planning permission for the types of development, including changes in use (with permitted exceptions) and the application of building regulations or (codes) and other legislation standards.
- *Financial provisions* including grants operated through tourist boards, parks authorities, sports councils and other agencies to provide and improve tourist facilities, local amenities and recreation opportunities. Grants and subventions may also be directed to the improvement of declining inner cities, conversion of industrial wastelands and recreational use of surplus farmland.

In contrast to other economic sectors, tourism is highly dependent on the nature and quality of the resources and types of visitors which can be attracted to particular localities. This calls for **sensitive planning approaches** and measures which take account of the particular interests and needs of tourists, including measures to conserve and enhance the attractiveness of the destination. Under those circumstances, creativity has a major role to play.

Implicit in tourism development in the future is change. In recent years, with greater emphasis on nongrowth and environmentalism, change is looked upon with less and less favour. Perpetuation of the

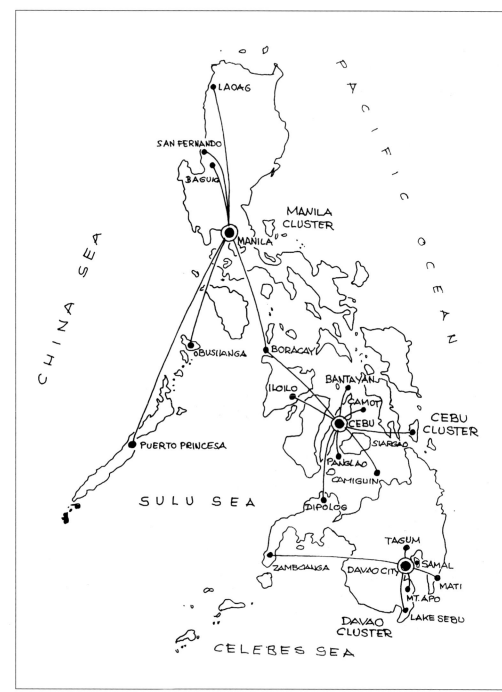

Tourism development in the Philippines

The Master Plan for Tourism Development in the Philippines was prepared in 1991 by Hoff and Overgaard, on behalf of the WTO and the UNDP (WTO 1994) and presented in three parts:

- *Long Range Plan: a policy framework for the development of tourism to 2010;*
- *Medium Term Development Programme (1992–6): corresponding to the goals, objectives and targets of the long range plan;*
- *Destination Areas Plans: providing a specific on-the-ground focus for the medium term programme.*

The Master Plan was characterized by the definition of three international tourist gateways (international airports), corresponding to three cluster destination areas, each providing a gateway to satellite destinations:

- *the Manila cluster: a multi-faceted destination;*
- *the Cebu cluster: resorts and cultural heritage;*
- *the Davao Cluster: exotic wilderness and cultural attractions.*

The draft of the Updated Medium Term Development Plan (1996–8) was produced in December 1995.

same – the same theme park design, the same fast-food business, the same motels – seems to be a strong rule of tourism development. Much of this is fostered by the world of finance that demands evidence that a business type has established records of success over time. It is further supported by government park and recreation agencies that routinely use the same policies and planning concepts year after year. However, the lessons from tourism history well show that markets change, transportation changes, and innovations are regularly introduced in services and attractions. Tourism is dynamic. If the future of tourism is to be served, it will depend as much on creative new expression as upon conformity with past patterns.

(Gunn 1988, p. 279)

7.2.6 Conflicts of interest

In most developed areas, tourism is closely integrated – and may be in conflict – with domestic needs for recreation as well as the day-to-day activities of the resident population (employment, housing, transport).

The economic and environmental benefits generated by tourism are often discounted by the disadvantages perceived by the communities affected (intrusion, increased costs, loss of resources). Land use plans, particularly at local level, are determined more by utilitarian needs and priorities than the

Development of recreation facilities

Special attention to promoting recreational activities in addition to other land uses

Landscapes of national value

'Consolidation areas' where permanent resorts and holiday homes in private ownership should be banned as much as possible

Possibilities for expanding tourism/recreation permanent and temporary accommodation sites

Sailing zones where the number of permanent moorings could be increased

The Netherlands: Structure plan for outdoor recreation

The Netherlands has been one of the first countries to recognize the necessity of a systematically planned policy for the development of outdoor recreation facilities, taking into account the growing integration of the living environment with the recreational environment as well as requirements in the fields of nature and landscape conservation. Since the 1980' the government objectives have been to:

- *safeguard outdoor recreation spaces with a priority in areas of greatest demand;*
- *devote special attention to sectors of population taking little part in outdoor recreation;*
- *develop day-trip destinations as close as possible to towns and urban centres;*
- *increase the intensity of use of recreation areas facing great pressure (Randstad);*
- *promote recreation on public land (forests, military exercise areas, national parks);*
- *distribute facilities for residential recreation throughout the country, except in 'consolidation areas' (priority given to the protection of landscape and natural environment);*
- *designate as landscape of national value areas with a variety of wildlife, different types of countryside, historical or cultural value.*

A nation-wide structure plan for outdoor recreation was introduced as early as the 1960s. It has been carefully monitored and adapted at intervals.

Source: Parliamentary Session 1985–6

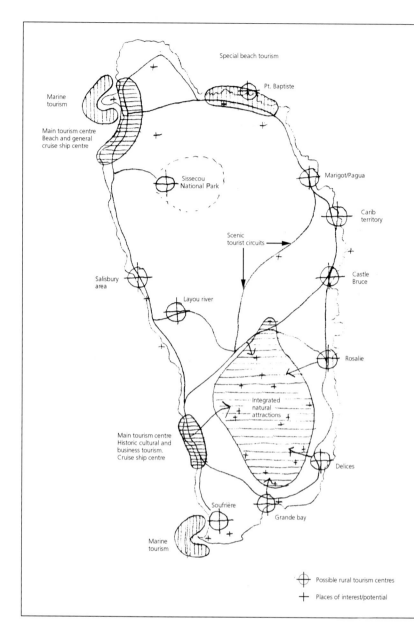

Special beach tourism

Marine tourism

Pt. Baptiste

Main tourism centre
Beach and general
cruise ship centre

Sissecou
National Park

Marigot/Pagua

Carib
territory

Scenic
tourist circuits

Salisbury
area

Layou river

Castle
Bruce

Rosalie

Integrated
natural
attractions

Main tourism centre
Historic cultural and
business tourism.
Cruise ship centre

Delices

Soufrière

Marine
tourism

Grande bay

⊕ Possible rural tourism centres

+ Places of interest/potential

Dominica tourism sector plan

The tourism plan 1991—4 was prepared with finance from the European Union and reflects the government's policy of promoting small-scale developments, integrated as far as possible with the rural community, strong economic links to other sectors, an orientation towards conservation and with tourism set at a level which the island can absorb.

A medium-term strategy framework to achieve these objectives was set out together with a 3-year tourism sector plan having an action programme. The latter included an evaluation of all resources with action to ensure their protection, improvements to existing attractions (including cruise tourism excursions), a dispersed high quality pattern of tourism activity focused on smaller establishments (typically not more than 50 rooms) making maximum use of local materials and products and improved marketing.

Tourism Planning and Research Associates;
Planner: J. Hawkes

sightseeing interests of tourists. Environmental and historic assets may be neglected by lack of funding, sensitive sites allocated to competing developments and agricultural use intensified – causing progressive loss of the features of tourist attraction.

At the other extreme the commercial pressures of tourism development may be equally destructive, with large domineering hotels, leisure facilities and car parks, crowding round beauty spots and obscuring their natural settings, shorelines and vistas.

In developing countries difficulties commonly arise from lack of comprehensive planning or the means of effective enforcement of building control. Often this is shown in the sprawl of ribbon development along access roads and around resorts with unsightly advertising and poor quality shanty buildings lacking infrastructure and landscaping.

7.2.7 Planning for tourism and recreation at local administration level

Local planning for tourism and recreation is generally regulated by the framework (legislation, financial, structural) laid down at national and regional level. Planning guidance is also provided in government circulars and directives. The state usually reserves powers to hold public inquiries, determine appeals and decide large-scale controversial planning applications.

The extent of devolution of planning administration to local areas varies with the structure and system of governance. In most countries local authorities are concerned with:

• representation of local views;
• preparation of land-use plans for the area;

- implementation of the planning provisions.

  Physical plans may take two main forms:

- *Strategic or structure plans* for the region (county, state) or metropolitan areas as a whole consider matters such as traffic, improvement of the environment, tourism and recreation needs in the region and the effects of planning proposals on neighbouring areas.

- *Local or district plans* for each local administrative authority show the manner in which land is to be used. Local development plans designate zones or areas for specific needs including open space and amenities and stipulate nature of use, density of development, setback from the highway, massing of buildings and external appearances.

Local plans are generally framed on long-term (ten-year) trends but are subject to detailed revision every three, four or five years to take account of changing needs. More immediate concerns are covered by provisions such as:

- *action area plans* covering areas where substantial redevelopment – which may also involve compulsory purchase – is to take place within five or ten years;

- subject plans *detailing particular schemes and proposals.*

7.3 APPROACHES TO TOURISM/RECREATION PLANNING

Preparation of **tourism sector plans**, particularly at national and regional levels, involves a study of all the components which will affect the implementation, particularly:

- government policies, goals and priorities for development;
- financial, technical and administrative resources available;
- resources in the locality and their potential;
- markets likely to be attracted and the extent of competition;
- conditions and requirements for development of suitable projects;
- means of monitoring progress and adjustment for changing needs.

Such studies may be undertaken directly by the government departments concerned but are often supplemented by consultancy and/or advisory inputs by the organizations involved in this field. Depending on the nature and extent of the study, these may be tourism specialists (World Tourism Organization, consultancy groups), representative bodies (hotel and tourist associations, sports associations), other departments (transport, environment), etc.

In most countries, comprehensive national and regional plans for tourism are well established and have served to channel new developments into regions and areas suitable for this purpose. Support for such developments has come from international agencies (EU, UNDP, World Bank) and national funds allocated to assist the implementation of infrastructure and other enabling projects.

Recreation sector plans are usually prepared at regional or local levels. Recreation planning in conurbations involves regional and local authorities, possibly represented in a joint board. The Netherlands is one of the few countries which has developed a national structure plan for outdoor recreation.

Examples of planning priorities and goals

Priority	Circumstances	Initial needs	Goals
Demand led development	Destinations offering suitable resources which need to match facility developments to particular market requirements	Market identification Selective development incentives	Economic benefits leading to other development opportunities
Supply led control	Risk of damage to vulnerable environmental or socio-cultural resources by excessive or inappropriate use	Management and regulation of use	Conservation of resources Long-term sustainability of tourism
Diversification of demand	Decline or saturation of existing attractions. Need to create new products or alternative destinations	New product research, design, development and marketing	Extension of economic benefits Establishment of new images
Implementation of new products	Development proposals to implement a network of golf courses, theme parks, etc.	Market identification, evaluation of regional and/or local impacts	Ascertaining attraction and feasibility of proposed facilities
Reduction of leakages	Excessive growth, shortages leading to high importation of supplies	Phasing of development, inter-sectoral co-ordination	Widening of economic benefits Reduction of external dependency
Community recreation	Increasing urbanization, encroachment on attractive landscapes, loss of amenities	Reservation of land, improved public access and facilities	Benefits for local communities and domestic tourism

States in the USA have prepared statewide comprehensive outdoor recreation plans – SCORP (see 8.5.2).

7.3.1 Priorities

Approaches may be initiated by different needs and priorities depending, to a large extent, on the stage, scale and nature of tourism involved.

Whilst priorities may be defined, planning studies must be comprehensive, considering all the issues involved, the marketability and feasibility of development proposals, and the impacts which are likely to result.

7.3.2 Extent of studies

The minimum geographic size of a region to be considered for comprehensive planning of tourism development should:

- include more than one resort (or town) with its immediate surroundings;
- have sufficiently attractive and original resources together with potential for development and promotion as a tourist/recreation destination;
- provide a homogeneous geographical whole whether as a defined area (national park, mountain range) or linear arrangement (river, coast, along a new highway).

A region (such as the Sahara) may be larger than a nation. Where possible the area should correspond to the administrative units of decision-making authorities, but may involve joint authority administration.

Most planning studies are carried out by or on behalf of public sector authorities responsible for land-use administration. Regional studies may be instigated by conurbations, local authorities, local authority joint boards; or by private developers and entrepreneurs for more specific purposes, for example, to determine suitable locations for projects or to gauge the possible impact of development prior to seeking planning approval (environmental impact studies, local attitudes).

7.3.3 Timescales for implementation

The period required for implementation of development plans is often difficult to predict. Accurate projections for market forecasting are generally limited to 3–5 years, although longer-term tourism trends may be discernible. Economic changes tend to produce 5–10 year cycles of investment activity but erratic factors can have immediate impacts on demand (changes in interest rates, taxation rates, inflation and currency values).

Much longer periods are required for the implementation of major tourism development projects, particularly where large-scale infrastructure provision is involved. Whilst there are wide variations – depending mainly on the difficulties of planning, organizing and financing the work – the following periods are broadly representative:

Project: from concept to opening (planning, design, construction, opening)		Implementation period (years)
Medium-sized hotel		2–3
Large hotel complex		3–4
Integrated resort:	main phase	3–5[a]
	later phases	5–10
Large-scale regional development:	main phase	7–10[b]
	later phases	10–20

Notes:
(a) Condominium, marina and real estate developments determined by rate of sales
(b) Including infrastructure provision

Phasing of large-scale development is important in order to:

- maximize the economic benefits from tourism by enabling the infrastructure, construction and supply resources to keep pace with development, thereby avoiding excessive leakages;
- enable progressive training of staff and continuous utilization of training resources (teaching facilities, trainers);
- allow adjustments in facility design and provision to meet changing market requirements;
- minimize investment outlay and ensure a more advantageous flow of capital offset by revenues;
- conserve resources and maintain a sustainable balance in development.

Planning programmes: planning is usually based on a horizon of 20 years with detailed plans and revisions every five years and provision for more urgent action as necessary:

Timescale	Main emphasis
Long range (10–15 years)	Long-term goals for development
	Desired rates of development to ensure sustainability
	Justification of heavy investment (e.g. airport)
	Measures to protect and enhance the resources
	Means of monitoring changes and correcting imbalances
	Measures to control the land necessary for future facilities
Short term (4–6 years) (*Action programme*)	Strategic plans for region (structural)
	Detailed development plans in each area
	Establishing standards and principles
	Ensuring implementation of necessary projects
Urgent action (1–2 years)	Steps to secure land necessary for planning
	Introducing controls to protect resources
	Enforcement against development in default
	Action areas requiring urgent planning

The *action programme* (five-year plan) is the most important period: it defines the priority products, the corresponding facilities and the implementation of the necessary accompanying measures (e.g. an investment code for tourism or a financial fund for recreational facilities).

The long view provided by the long-range programme allows for the protection of resources or for sites for future facilities to be earmarked before any speculation is involved.

7.3.4 Demand analyses

The planning process is dependent on accurate forecasting of future requirements. This involves both qualitative assessments and quantitative projections.

Qualitative analysis is necessary to determine the direction of development in the types and ranges of tourism products likely to attract potential markets. It involves a detailed examination of the various categories of tourists segmented by their main origins characteristics (socio-economic), motivations (interests, preferences) and competitive influences.

Quantitative analysis dictates the extent and pace of development and has a direct influence on the financing, construction and feasibility of individual facilities. Statistics and other data for analysis will be required from several sources (see 8.3.5).

Forecasting requires accurate quantification of sets of homogeneous information over a time series. In tourism (and recreation) difficulties may arise over the classification of variables as well as the comparability of measurements.

Simple extrapolation of historical data is limited to short-term projections – up to three or five years – and naivety should be minimized by examining relationships between the variables and their influencing factors.

Overall growth may be linear or exponential in the initial period following development but is often limited by intensive or extensive parameters (capacity, life cycles, competition) resulting in logistic curves. In addition to cyclical changes, tourism and recreation demands are sensitive to the vagaries of external influences which may affect the destination or market areas.

Forecasts of medium- and long-term changes involve statistics, and mathematical or descriptive methods. Projections may be extrapolative from the present or examined normatively to determine the steps required to achieve future goals. Extrapolation methods include systems analysis, modelling, scenario writing, delphi techniques, morphological research and simulation. Normative approaches may use similar mathematical systems and also relevant-tree and feedback schemes.

7.3.5 Planning models and simulation techniques

Interactive forecasting techniques using mathematical models (gravity, multivariable regression and simulation) are widely employed to evaluate optimum locations and demands for a proposed development as well as the probable impacts on the destination (trip-generation, traffic and visitor patterns, economic, environmental and social changes).

Various forms of both descriptive and behavioural models have applications analysing, forecasting, representing and monitoring information. In particular, mathematical simulation may:

- represent the distribution of resources and forecast levels of demand;
- indicate trends in demand and sensitivity to changes in the determining factors;
- analyse potential conflicts which might eventually arise in the use of resources;
- test the consequences of planning proposals and policies.

Modelling is well developed at micro levels of planning (project evaluation) and in recreation planning where the variables are more easily defined, consistent and quantifiable. At macro level (regional and national) modelling is dependent on the availability and selection of homogeneous data and is commonly used in market forecasting, economic analyses; resource mapping, usages and impact assessment. Static representation is often developed into dynamic analysis using step-by-step progression and feedback corrections. Modelling relies on judgement in the selection of variables and appropriate quantification of the information. The latter may be obtained from

- *measured data* (e.g. demographic and economic statistics, time-distance, market surveys);
- *assessment* (e.g. weighted responses, frequencies or mathematical techniques).

Mathematical modelling techniques offer a number of advantages: they can accommodate complex analyses of many variables and their relationships enabling a wide range of possibilities to be explored. Quantification can also facilitate the updating of information through monitoring systems and the adjustment of policies. Techniques include:

- *gravity productive models* to examine the relationships between attractions, time-distance and population on trip-generation and demand;
- *multivariate regression models* to explain the effects of a range of variables (generators, attractors and deterrents) on tourism flows;
- *presumptive models* such as fuzzy programme approaches, to determine the optimal use of recreational resources and carrying capacities;
- *transfer function models* to reflect changes in the influencing variables affecting time–series data in forecasting market demands;
- *simulation models* to study the flows and distributions of recreationists and tourists in parks, along beaches and other areas;
- *analytic hierarchic process* (Monthino 1992, p. 19–30), a modelling device allowing the decision-makers to be

Oman: implementation of development

This development is of a large resort hotel–conference centre–leisure complex, with an associated village for employees, near Muscat in Oman. Its implementation, in a previously undeveloped coastal area, involved the installation of all infrastructures – including an access road through the mountains – construction, furnishing, landscaping and introduction of operational services, all within a 24-month period before the sixth Summit Conference of the Gulf Cooperative Council.

Work was scheduled using computerized planning programmes and included parallel working, off-site and on-site prefabrication – with supplies being brought by sea – and continuous critical path analyses. HM, the Sultan of Oman, and the Coordinating Committee of Ministers headed by HRH Sayyed Fahd bin Mahmood Al Said, took a personal interest in the careful representation of Islamic design throughout. The completed Al Bustan Palace Hotel, operated by Inter-Continental Hotels, has been described as one of the most splendid hotels in the world.

Architects: J. + A. Philippou
Project Managers: Valtos, UK & Oman,
Consultant: F. Lawson.

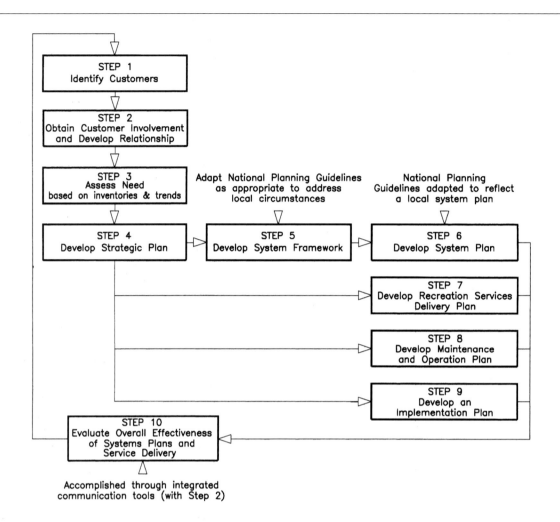

NRPA – National Recreation and Parks Association (USA): Guidelines for parks, recreation, open spaces and greenways

Present trends:

*   *Increasing demand for based recreation and open space preservation (especially for less active leisure activities, nature, etc.).*
*   *Growing recognition of ethnic and cultural diversity and needs, as well as the importance of citizens' participation.*
*   *Financial difficulties of many park agencies: increasing demand, decreasing financial capacity and resources.*

Hence the importance of establishing level of service standards which are needs-based, facilities-driven and land-measured.

*A **system planning model** has to be an integral part of the land-use guidance system, integrated into planning decisions and strategies for housing, transportation, education, environmental management, etc. (see 1.2.1). It is summarized in the diagram above, with the following definitions:*

*   *Strategic plan (or comprehensive plan): objectives, goals and strategies (practical alternatives, proposals, action programme and implementation tools).*
*   *System framework: parameters and guidelines for a given community, based on national planning guidelines and LOS (see below).*
*   *System plan: the physical plan for open areas, greenways and facilities (location, classification, detailed information for individual sites.*
*   *Delivery plan: the mix of recreation programmes (sport, swimming pools, senior centres, etc.) to be offered to the customers, and the strategy for providing services.*

*The **level of service (LOS) guidelines** is a ratio expressed in acre/1000 population representing, for a given community, the population needs in terms of land, facilities and programmes. It is calculated by determining the*

*   *park classification for which LOS applies;*
*   *recreation activity menu for each park classification (amount of space for each facility);*
*   *open space size standards for each park classification for which LOS standards apply;*
*   *present supply of these recreation activity choices;*
*   *total expressed demand for these recreation activity choices;*
*   *minimum population services requested for these recreation activity choices;*
*   *individual LOS for each park class;*
*   *collective LOS for the entire park and recreation system.*

Source: James D. Mertes and James R. Hall (1995) Parks, Recreation, Open Spaces and Greenway Guidelines, 163 pp., NRPA, Alexandria (VA)

responsible for major inputs into the model in the form of 'What if' procedures.

- *rule-based models* (Monthino and Curry 1992, p. 17), establishing 'if … then' relationships between factors relevant to site location decisions;
- *LOCAT model* (Monthino and Curry 1992, p. 21) to measure a site's attractiveness taking account of accessibility, catchment area, uniqueness of product, etc.

7.3.6 Comprehensive planning: approaches by alternative plans

This plan formulation technique, proposed by Inskeep (1991) and favoured by some of the international funding agencies, is to prepare alternative plans in outline format. Each alternative shows a different approach and different types of recommendations. The alternative plans are then evaluated to compare how well each

- satisfies the plan objectives;
- reflects the development policies;
- generates the desired economic benefits at an acceptable cost;
- minimizes negative environmental and socio-cultural impacts and reinforces positive ones;
- is realistic to implement.

But alternative plans, based on the same data, are often very similar and the evaluation of a matrix in ranking alternatives requires careful judgement. This procedure does not take into consideration, in detail, the difficulties of implementing specific products (see Figure 7.3).

7.3.7 Comprehensive planning: the PASOLP approach

Much of the conceptual theory used in tourism and recreation planning originates from the Products Analysis Sequence for Outdoor Leisure Procedure (PASOLP) developed in the 1970s (Baud-Bovy and Lawson 1977) (see Figure 7.4).

PASOLP is a progressive process which has five main steps:

- **Surveys and analysis** of the factors which affect tourism and recreation, namely:
  - existing and potential markets (measured as segmented 'flows'),
  - resources of the country or region (considered as usable 'products'),
  - the country's structures, policies, priorities and goals for development.
- **Definition of alternative products** for tourism or recreation,
- **Recommendation of the needs and priorities** for tourism and recreation development by evaluating each

product against the market flows which could be generated, taking into account:
- relative attractiveness (compared with competing destinations),
- feasibility (for investment, support and operation),
- possible impacts (environmental, economic, social),
- comparisons with the goals for development.
- **Preparation of plans** for the tourism and recreation sectors including:
  - designation of main sites, their nature and extent of use,
  - additional facilities, infrastructures and improvements required,
  - detailed evaluation of the potential impacts from development,
  - determination of the conditions for sustainability and other safeguards.
- **Implementation of the development** including:
  - measures for effective implementation (legislation, finance, administration),
  - procedures for monitoring progress and correcting imbalances,
  - action plan for first phase of development,

PASOLP is equally appropriate for *demand-led* approaches to determine how resources can best be utilized to maximize benefits, and *supply-led* requirements to identify appropriate markets and the feasibility of development.

This approach has **advantages** in that it:

- takes full account of the players and mechanisms of the system;
- enables the effects of problems and bottlenecks to be simulated;
- allows direct comparisons with other competing products in other destinations;
- provides details of the impacts of each product;
- enables comparison with the impacts of similar investment in other economic sectors (agriculture, industry, handicraft, etc.).

A similar PASOLP approach may be used for recreation planning (see 8.5.2).

7.3.8 Monitoring system

Planning is a continuous process: a plan has to be permanently controlled, supplemented, corrected, modified, re-adapted. An essential part of the planning process is the introduction of a system for monitoring development and its resulting impacts. The PASOLP system provides for permanent monitoring and subsequent correction of deviations.

The diagram in Fig. 7.5 includes:

- **A permanent monitoring system**:
  - recording the outputs of the tourism or recreational activities through statistics of arrivals and facilities provided, a budgetary control of the tourism industry and of the protection of the tourism/recreation sites,

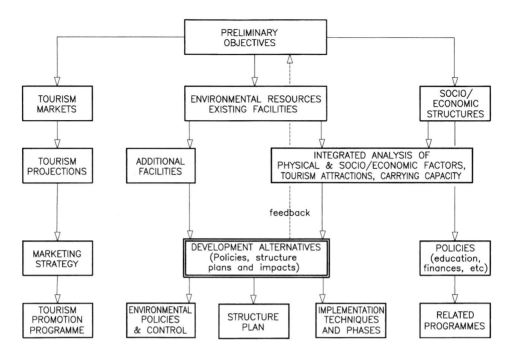

Figure 7.3 *Alternative development plans approach*

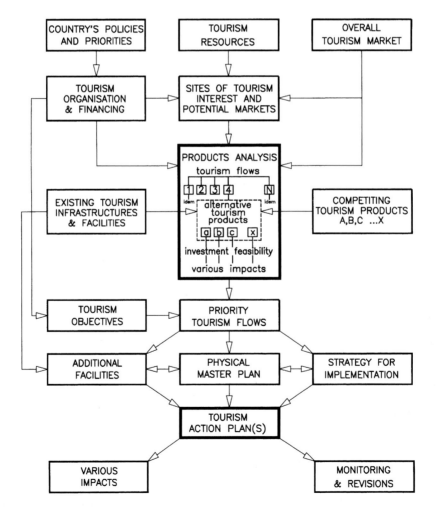

Figure 7.4 *PASOLP for tourism*

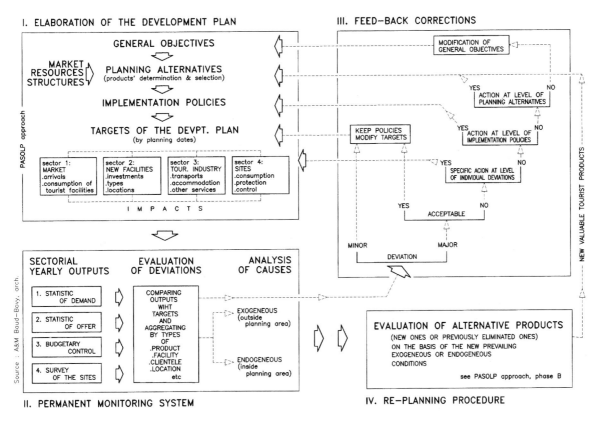

I. ELABORATION OF THE DEVELOPMENT PLAN

III. FEED-BACK CORRECTIONS

Figure 7.5

— comparing these inputs with the corresponding goals and targets of the development plan,

— evaluating the deviations between the intended goals and the actual inputs, aggregating them by products, clienteles, regions in the country and types of facilities,

— analysing the causes (endogenous or exogenous) of these deviations.

• **Feedback correction opportunities** at the various levels to be considered according to the importance of the deviations: targets, incentives, implementation policies, planning alternatives or ultimately development objectives.

• **Re-planning procedures**: taking account of new conditions in generating or competing areas, of changes in the country objectives and priorities, new products are to be considered and introduced in the development plan.

7.3.9 Flexibility in planning

Whilst plans are formulated with a four-, five-, or even ten-year horizon (see 7.2.4), flexibility is essential. Changes over this time are almost inevitable in markets and development requirements, in the benefits desired from tourism and/or measures for control. In order to avoid large investments in

non-adaptable facilities which may have a limited or saturated market or are too marginal or too original in concept, preference should be given to facilities and product allowing progressive modifications and adaptations, and attracting a number of market flows (at different times and seasons, from several sources, etc.).

Programmes for phased implementation are provided by action plans which identify priorities and specific provisions to meet the evolving requirements of the market and changes in the tourism industry.

An example of an Action Plan for Tourism: India 1992

In 1990 foreign tourist arrivals in India were 1.71 million and domestic tourism estimated at 62.5 million. The tourism industry generated direct employment of 5.5 million with indirect employment for another 8 million and was a major contributor to foreign exchange earnings. The Action Plan proposed an improvement of the tourism infrastructure with increased incentives and assistance for special areas, circuits and destinations, for 1–3 star hotels, and for conversion of palaces into heritage hotels. Measures to facilitate domestic tourism included the development of camping sites, affordable hygienic accommodation and pilgrim centres. To facilitate the diversification of products, assistance was provided for craft villages, fairs and festivals and zonal cultural centres as well as improvements in tourist coach, train and water cruising transport. To promote convention tourism the government proposed to set up an integrated convention city.

Source: Government of India,
Ministry of Civil Aviation and Tourism, 1992

7.4 PRELIMINARIES FOR A MASTER PLAN

7.4.1 Terms of reference

In broad terms, requirements for preparing plans may be defined by statutory obligations and relevant government directives. Precise Terms of Reference form the basis for costing and organization of the work, including contract arrangements for consultancy outputs. They should identify:

*   objectives for studies, goals sought in planning;
*   activities to be undertaken in preparing plans;
*   inputs to be provided by the different public authorities;
*   outputs to be represented in the plans;
*   timescales for preparation and approvals;
*   resources (and, in some cases, methodologies) to be employed;
*   constraints and conditions to be observed;
*   measures for implementing of the plans and monitoring subsequent changes.

An example of Terms of Reference: Seychelles Tourism Master Plan 1998–2007

*Economic activities and development in the Seychelles have tended to remain concentrated on the narrow coastal plateau of the three main islands, particularly Mahe, which has 87 per cent of the population. Prior to the introduction of the Town and Country Planning Act, 1972 and Building Regulations, 1975, development had often been indiscriminate and haphazard and the need for a comprehensive land-use plan was recognized in the National Development Plan, 1990–94. The development objectives of the Tourism Master Plan 1998–2007 were 'to generate socio-economic benefits for the people of the Seychelles through a carefully planned and controlled development of tourism which will increase the economic contribution of tourism to the economy while preserving the environment, protecting the culture and enhancing the image of the country'. To achieve that end the **Terms of Reference** for the study set out 14 Immediate Objectives, each with a number of outputs and activities. These covered such aspects as:*

*   *review and formulation of objectives and policies,*
*   *indentification and evaluation of existing and potential resources,*
*   *identification of present and potential markets,*
*   *preparation of a national tourism development structure plan,*
*   *standards and design guidelines for tourism facilities,*
*   *economic cost-benefit, environmental and social impact analyses,*
*   *manpower and training requirements, marketing strategies,*
*   *institutional arrangements, legislation for quality standards and incentives,*
*   *specification of priority development areas, projects and improvements,*
*   *promotion, implementation and monitoring.*

Source: Seychelles Master Tourism Plan

7.4.2 Planning objectives

The planning objectives will depend on the level of planning involved and may be broad-based to identify new opportunities for tourism and recreation development, or specific to particular situations and conditions. They may concern:

*   coverage: national, regional or local concerns,
*   nature and extent of tourism which already exists,
*   stage of development in country and region,
*   political policies and goals for future development,
*   resources to be allocated or potentially available.

Objectives are usually first identified as a preliminary guide and refined by the results of surveys and detailed investigations. Particular considerations may be stressed as necessary requirements such as the need for sustainability, minimization of environmental and/or social impacts and realization of socio-economic benefits.

7.4.3 Organizational framework

In addition to providing guidance on planning requirements and the Terms of Reference, the responsible authority will normally need to structure the work, i.e.

*   appoint a steering committee,
*   select a technical team,
*   organize study activities,
*   establish procedures for reporting progress.

8 Tourism/recreation master plans: surveys and formulation

8.1 RESOURCES SURVEYS

Three main fields:

- surveys of resources (8.1.1–5)
- market assessment (8.2.1–3)
- assessment of structures and policies (8.3.1–5)

must be investigated at the same time; exchanges of information are profitable: each field may reorientate the research in another. A common mistake is to spend too much time in irrelevant surveys: experience plays an important role.

8.1.1 Principles in surveying resources

The attractiveness of a location will vary with different market segments of tourists and recreationists, largely being dictated by their particular interests and activities. Requirements may be highly dependent on specific geophysical conditions and confined to particular areas (skiing, surfing, spas) or be more broadly-based (camping, golfing). Resources need

- to be judged in relation to their interest and attraction for identified groups of tourists and/or their suitability for recreational use. Particular sites must be appraised in terms of their potential rather than the existing conditions and this requires a vision of the opportunities offered by appropriate development;
- to be evaluated diachronically, taking account of changing conditions: trends, changes (daily, monthly, long-term), tendencies, factors in action, risks of erosion, etc.;
- to be weighted in a homogeneous way for the whole territory, and evaluated against similar resources in competing destinations;
- to be presented as clearly and as visually as possible.

General considerations	Particular aspects
Features of outstanding attraction	Vulnerability to development or change
	Measures for protection
Detrimental factors	Difficulties and costs of remedial works
Alternative uses	Value and importance for the local economy
Infrastructure requirements and availability	Limitations, difficulties and costs of provision
Size and characteristics of available sites	Carrying capacity without diminution of the tourism experience

8.1.2 Methodology and stages

Surveys of resources and their usage require careful preparation to ensure effective coverage and provision of comparable and quantifiable results within the set time and cost constraints.

Framework	Considerations
Information required	Essential and supplementary data; selection of areas and methods
Limitations to studies	Time, costs and technical resources; need for authorizations, joint studies
Existing sources	Existing maps, reports, records, surveys; local information; utility services
Method of survey	Satellite images and interpretation; aerial, land and coastal surveys; equipment, interviews, tests
Representative conditions	Timing of surveys; seasonal variations; samples; adverse conditions and effects; recent evolution and trends
Survey organization	Skills, number and local inputs required; instructions (for homogeneous results); standardization of data

The use of satellite imagery (SPOT) and digital image processing have made considerable progress possible:

- Many studies use a Geographical Information System (GIS): analysis and evaluation of tabular or graphic data.
- Synographic Mapping (SYMAP) compares and visualizes information through maps produced by computer (relative values of resources, densities of use, etc.).
- Software using GIS information allows computerized representations which can be integrated with computer-aided design (CAD): e.g. converting two-dimensional GIS maps into a three-dimensional CAD model, generating a landscape of three-dimensional objects from two-dimensional data maps, laying a landscape of architectural objects over a three-dimensional surface model, etc., with the possibility of viewing these landscapes from any angle (Erwin 1996).

Surveys of resources are usually carried out in several stages:

- Preliminary examination: To classify areas for further study; usually desk work (maps, records, reports); preparation of draft maps or GIS.

- Field surveys: To evaluate features, products and development options. May be combined with analyses of air photographs or satellite imagery. Preferably one surveyor covers the whole study area for one (or several) categories of resources.
- Detailed surveys: To evaluate more precisely potential products related to some segment(s) of the market.

8.1.3 Existing features and activities of potential tourist interest

- **Land use patterns**:
  - land ownership: patterns and tenure, relative values
  - existing uses: compatibility with tourism, economic importance
  - planning control: existing classification, zoning
  - land availability: and access rights around main resources (e.g. shores)

Key issues: Degree of priority for existing uses. Compatibility with tourism and recreational use. Problems of ownership, access and control.

Northern Ireland: Tourism study of north-eastern area

The north-eastern area of Ireland has a number of key attractions including the North Antrim Coast, Giant's Causeway and several established resorts. This study proposed a strategy for developing tourism based on:

- *tourist zones with clusters of attractions;*
- *touring bases for the region using accommodation in resorts;*
- *coastal and glen trails through sites of interest;*
- *entry points with visitor centres and information.*

PIEDA report for the Department of the Environment

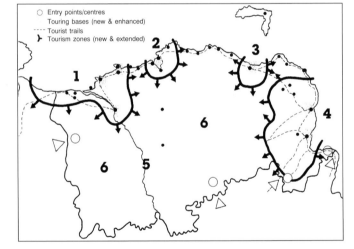

Strategic master plan for tourism development in Romania

Financed by the European Union PHARE programme, a master tourism plan was prepared in 1994 following a decline in tourism in Romania. The plan addressed the need to increase foreign exchange earnings and the contribution of tourism to the economy by product upgrading and diversification, positive image creation and active marketing and promotion. Targets for future growth in markets were drawn up together with recommendations for appropriate product development, including investment in upgrading and restoration.

In the first phase (short- to medium-term) – Fig. 8.4a – action was focused on priority tourism areas to avoid the dispersal and dilution of resources, priority being given to improve and consolidate the products in areas that were most popular with international tourists and where tourism facilities and infrastructures already existed.

The long-term proposals – Fig. 8.4b – extended and linked these areas.

Strategic recommendations also covered:

- *upgrading airports, transport corridors linking key attractions and tourist circuits;*
- *setting up a tourism upgrading/investment fund and incentives for priority projects;*
- *implementation of laws and procedures to facilitate privatization of assets;*
- *extension of training at all levels;*
- *restructuring the Ministry of Tourism to participate in land use and urban planning;*
- *creating a Romania Tourism Corporation for marketing, promotion and collection of statistics;*
- *encouraging the involvement and participation of local authorities and communities;*
- *changes in legislation to allow registration, classification, safety and regulation;*
- *legal provisions for protection of areas (including the Danube Delta Biosphere Reserve), conservation of monuments and historic assets, control of National Parks;*
- *encouraging the cultural enhancement of tourism products through networks of tourism villages, exhibitions, interpretation facilities, festivals and events;*
- *introduction of an implementation programme and monitoring system.*

Planning team: London Office of Horwath Consulting, SRG (Director: J. Fletcher), Physical planning: J. Hawkes, Facility design: F. Lawson

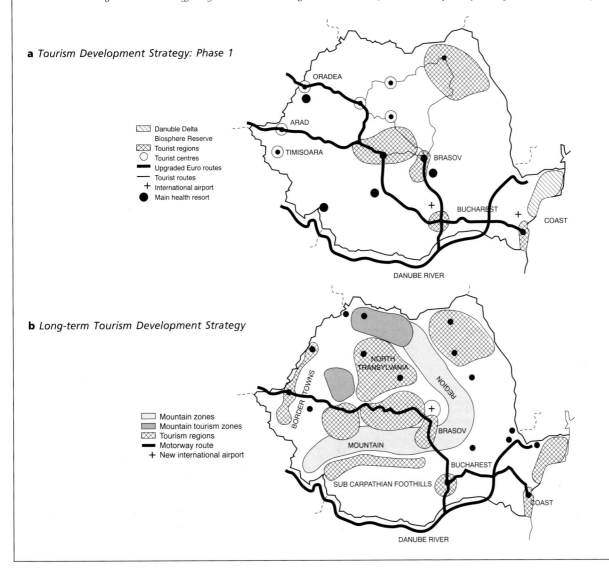

a *Tourism Development Strategy: Phase 1*

Danuble Delta Biosphere Reserve
Tourist regions
○ Tourist centres
━ Upgraded Euro routes
─ Tourist routes
+ International airport
● Main health resort

ORADEA
ARAD
TIMISOARA
BRASOV
BUCHAREST
COAST
DANUBE RIVER

b *Long-term Tourism Development Strategy*

Mountain zones
Mountain tourism zones
Tourism regions
━ Motorway route
+ New international airport

BORDER TOWNS
NORTH TRANSYLVANIA
REGION
BRASOV
MOUNTAIN
SUB CARPATHIAN FOOTHILLS
BUCHAREST
COAST
DANUBE RIVER

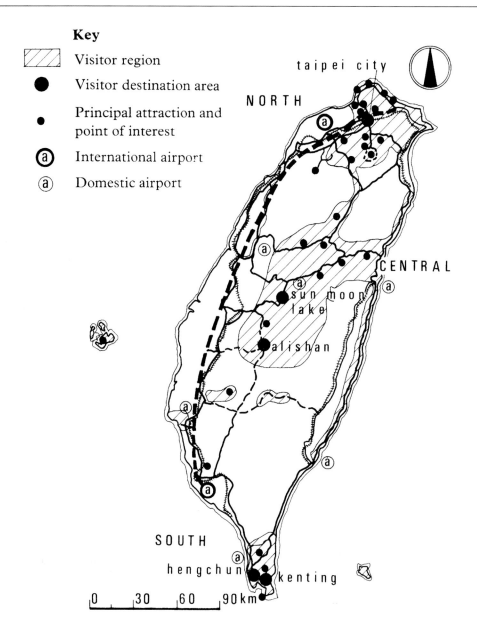

Key

- /// Visitor region
- ● Visitor destination area
- • Principal attraction and point of interest
- ⓐ International airport
- ⓐ Domestic airport

Taiwan: general plan for recreation/tourism system, 1992

Tourism has been long recognized as a vital part of the national economy of Taiwan, Republic of China. The general plan, 1992, provided medium- to long-term guidelines for development and promotion over the next decade based on forecasts of demand for international travellers and domestic trips (49 per cent of domestic demand is for hostels).

In addition to an analysis of the recreation resources, the plan laid down specific development goals and strategies. Thirty-six recreational systems were identified grouped into eight categories:

Urban systems – within 1–2 hours of urban centres, focused on culture, amusement, intensive use
Cross-island highways – with mountain and river scenery, forest recreation, farm tourism
Rugged terrain – concentrations of attractions within daily trips of metropolitan areas
Touring corridors – scenic transitional routes between destinations
Coastal systems – important sites in coastal zones within two hours of metropolitan centres
National Park systems – outstanding scenic, natural and wildlife features
Outlying islands – marine activities and aboriginal villages combined with conservation
East Coast and Huatung Valley – isolated areas linked by scenic highways

Tourism Bureau, Ministry of Transport and Communications, 1992

a *Preferred destinations for long-haul tourists (excluding businessmen). The resources analysis revealed that, in addition to the archaeological attractions from antiquity and Islam, there were many interesting traditional cultures, reflected in the architecture of villages, costumes, handicrafts, folklore, etc. Another aspect was the absence of attractive seaside areas which could compete with foreign destinations*

b *Concept for long-haul international tourists: (a) to develop the destinations for groups of sightseeing tourists by creating a number of additional circuits including accommodation facilities of a local character; (b) to add to the present main destinations (Teheran, Esfahan and Shiraz) two key tourist centres in Mashed and Kerman; (c) to diversify the present tourist products, for instance by increasing contacts with the variety of traditional cultures in Iran*

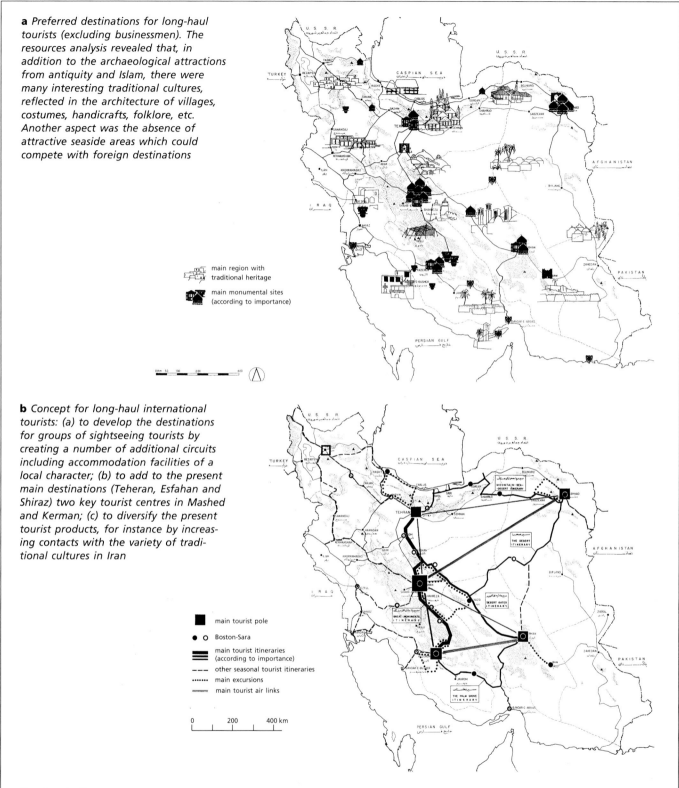

Tourism in Iran

The master plan for the development of tourism in Iran, drawn up in accordance with World Bank recommendations for the Iranian National Tourist Organization, was one of the most comprehensive tourism plans prepared in the 1970s.

The two maps are examples of a strong relationship between resources and development plans. A similar approach was provided for domestic tourism.

Tourist consultants: ACAU, Zanganeh (1974), Master plan for the development of tourism in Iran
Project manager: M. Baud-Bovy, tourism planner

Tourism development master plan, Niger

The master plan for this small African country was prepared on the lines of the PASOLP procedure (see 7.3.7). Identification, evaluation and selection of priority tourism products (see 1.3.2) was followed by 20 recommendations for their implementation, covering such aspects as the protection of resources, preparation of local development plans, financing and control of tourist facilities, training tourist manpower, organizing travel agencies, defining air transport and marketing policies, etc., together with an evaluation of impacts.

Source: M. Baud-Bovy (1980), Plan de mise en valeur touristique du Niger, for UNDP and the Government of Niger, 220 pp.

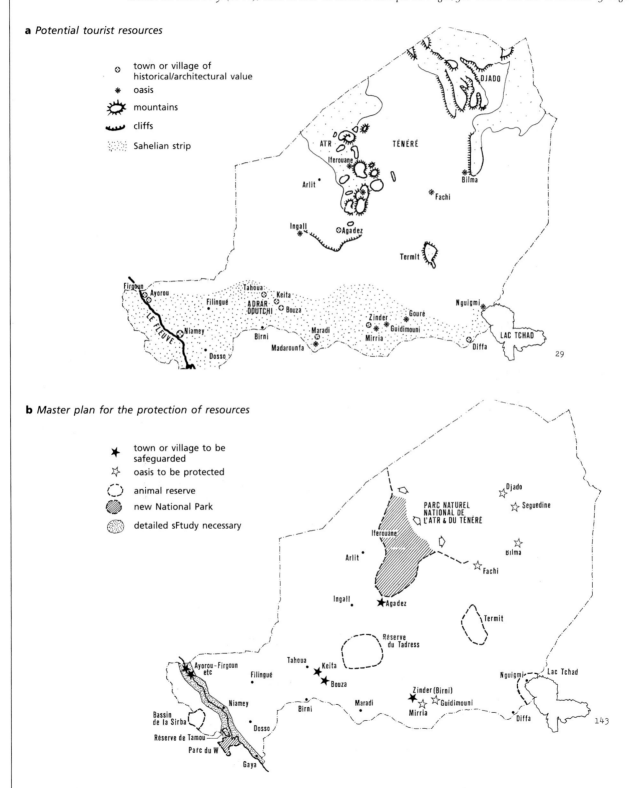

a Potential tourist resources

b Master plan for the protection of resources

c *Master plan for new facilities*

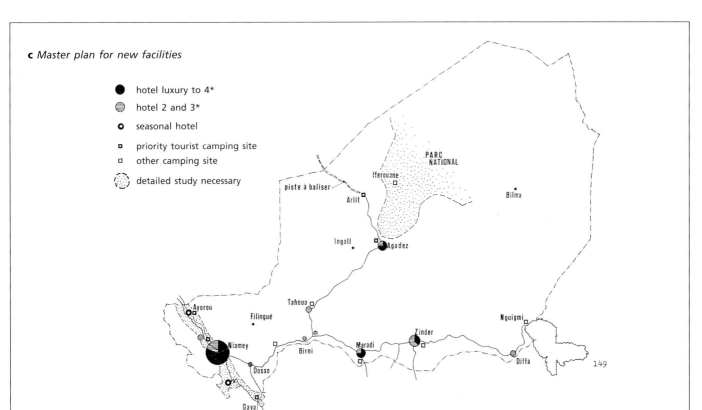

● hotel luxury to 4*
⊜ hotel 2 and 3*
◉ seasonal hotel
▫ priority tourist camping site
▫ other camping site
⊙ detailed study necessary

d

e

f

- **Natural resources and environmental quality**
- **Climatic conditions**:
  - comfort charts: temperature and humidity ranges, monthly variations
  - rainfall: main periods, duration, intensities
  - sunshine: mean daily duration, radiation intensity
  - snow cover: conditions affecting skiing and other uses
  - wind direction: prevailing favourable breezes, uncomfortable winds
  - extremes: frequency of storms, flooding, drought

  Key issues: Extent to which climate may favour or restrict tourist activities to certain areas or periods of the year. Record studies to determine the main climatic zones.
- **Geomorphology** in relation to:
  - local climate: orientation, microclimates affecting use
  - tourist activities: climbing, trekking, skiing
  - scenic attraction dramatic or gently changing, extent
  - specifications: vantage points, volcanoes, caves, defiles, dunes etc.
- **Vegetation cover**: to assess the extent to which it provides:
  - recreation opportunities: e.g. forests for recreational activities
  - characteristic species: cedars, palm trees, maple forests
  - visually attractive landscape: e.g. rice paddies or vineyards
- **Hydrology**: and in particular the presence of water for
  - recreation resources: sea, lake, river activities, quality of beaches
  - development: possibility of creating ports or marinas (see 5.2.4–7)
  - visual value: lakes, waterfalls, lush vegetation
  - basic supply: freshwater source, thermal waters
- **Wildlife**:
  - viewing: photo-safari, national parks, protected sites
  - sport hunting and fishing: in favourable areas existing stocks can often be improved by positive management policies

  Key issues: To identify the main places which have attractive characteristics and potential for development as composite sites and those areas which need special protection.
- **Historic and socio-cultural resources**
- **History, archaeology and religion**:
  - monuments: individual and grouped monuments and their settings
  - museums: including open air museums, industrial and folklore museums
  - historic sites: preserved towns, castles, religious shrines

  Key issues: The potential of historic sites should be considered in terms of the tourist experience – which is enhanced by the 'atmosphere', presentation and surroundings.
- **Traditional lifestyles**:
  - ethnic cultures
  - traditional character
  - picturesque villages
  - local handicrafts

Key issues: Tourist interests are reflected in 'sightseeing' and 'lifeviewing' of traditional activities and events; it is important to understand the local culture and to avoid the introduction of socially unacceptable or morally offensive practices.
- **Entertainment, cultural, social and shopping facilities**
  - large metropolitan cities: Paris, Bangkok, San Francisco, Hong Kong
  - centres of culture and art: Florence, Venice, St Petersburg
  - preserved small town: examples of local architecture and urban patterns
- **Technical achievements, industrial archaeology**
  - impressive constructions: unique buildings and structures
  - centres of technology: space centres, power stations
  - industrial archaeology: potential for interest and utilization
- **Cyclical and specific attractions**
  - cyclical attractions: fairs, carnivals, large pilgrimages, festivals
  - organized events: exhibitions, races, games, promotions

  Key issues: Specific events may be established in the area or elsewhere and may require temporary provisions for accommodation, etc.
- **Negative features**: drawbacks or difficulties affecting tourism potential must also be considered.
- Natural deterrents:
  - geographical features: flat plains, swamps, mangroves
  - development risks: storms, cyclones, flooding, earth movements
  - dangers to health: mosquitoes, endemic diseases
- **Man-made dangers**:
  - large extractive industries: mines, forestry, sand and gravel workings
  - polluting activities: industrial etc. discharges to air, water, ground
  - existing development: mundane housing, shanty buildings, industry

  Key issues: In assessing developmental risks the probability and seasonality of occurrence, nature and difficulty of preventative works and alternative uses should be considered. Many deterrents may provide scope for recovery or reuse under the sponsorship of tourism and recreation investment, for example:
- **Land reclamation/insect control**: as achieved in Languedoc-Roussillon or Fort Lauderdale.

8.1.4 Recreational attractions

Similar categories of resources form the basis for planning recreation but with different degrees of importance. The main tourist attractions (unique monuments, spectacular features, dramatic landscapes) do not make such a strong impression on local residents – except those opposed to development. For

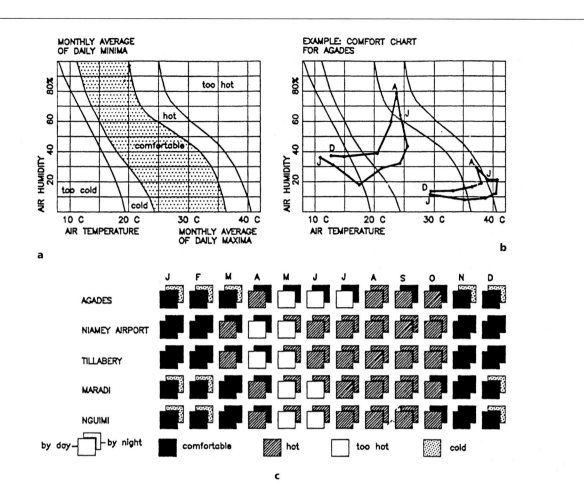

Climatic comfort charts

The use of 'comfort charts', based on a combination of the temperature and humidity of the air, can be used to determine the climatic comfort of places, according to the seasons. The information provided by such charts may be presented in a variety of ways, as for example above.

Source: Baud-Bovy (1980) Plan de Mise en Valeur Touristique de Niger

countryside recreation it is important to consider the availability of places to park and view, to picnic and practise activities such as swimming, sailing, fishing or golf. The main resources for this purpose are:

- edges of water and forests: sea, lake, river, canal, reservoir, woodland;
- glades and undulating landscapes, with road access and minimal visual intrusion,
- marginal land with broken slopes (gradient of 15° to 250°) having limited agriculture value.

Suitable resources are increasingly scarce in the vicinity of cities and conurbations from which the main demands for recreation originate:

- attractive sites face competition from housing and other developments;

- industrialization of farming has extensively modified landscape diversity and attraction;
- informal woodlands and marginal lands are often commercially reforested,
- ecology interests often limit or prohibit public access in order to protect the remaining natural sites.

Hence, surveys of recreation resources must also consider alternative ways of creating recreational sites, for example:

- improvements to lakes, ponds, reservoirs, river banks and works for flood or storm-water control to provide accessible recreational land near water;
- utilization of disused quarries, sand/gravel workings, derelict industrial sites;
- innovative landscaping, including screening (groups of trees, undulations, rock outcrops, etc.) to minimize visual intrusion and exposure.

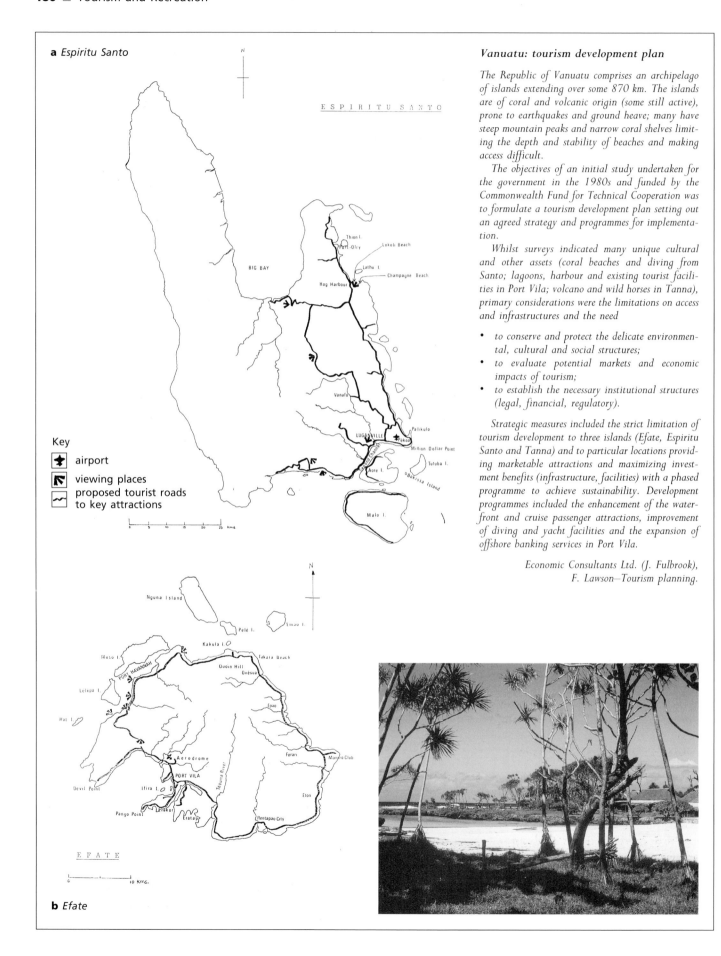

a *Espiritu Santo*

ESPIRITU SANTO

Thion I.
Port-Olry
Lokoli Beach
Lathu I.
Champagne Beach
BIG BAY
Hog Harbour

Vanafo

Palikulo
LUGANVILLE Pekoa
Million Dollar Point
Tutuba I.
Aore I.
Bokissa Island

Malo I.

Key

✈ airport
↖ viewing places
〰 proposed tourist roads
to key attractions

0 5 10 15 20 25 Kms.

b *Efate*

Nguna Island
Pelé I.
Emao I.
Kakula I.
Muso I.
Takara Beach
PORT HAVANNAH
Quoin Hill Onésua
Lelepa I.
Epao
Hat I.
Aerodrome
Forari
Mangro Club
PORT VILA
Devil Point
Ifira I.
Teouma River
Eton
Pango Point Erakor
Eratap
Rentapao City

EFATE

0 10 Kms.

Vanuatu: tourism development plan

The Republic of Vanuatu comprises an archipelago of islands extending over some 870 km. The islands are of coral and volcanic origin (some still active), prone to earthquakes and ground heave; many have steep mountain peaks and narrow coral shelves limiting the depth and stability of beaches and making access difficult.

The objectives of an initial study undertaken for the government in the 1980s and funded by the Commonwealth Fund for Technical Cooperation was to formulate a tourism development plan setting out an agreed strategy and programmes for implementation.

Whilst surveys indicated many unique cultural and other assets (coral beaches and diving from Santo; lagoons, harbour and existing tourist facilities in Port Vila; volcano and wild horses in Tanna), primary considerations were the limitations on access and infrastructures and the need

- to conserve and protect the delicate environmental, cultural and social structures;
- to evaluate potential markets and economic impacts of tourism;
- to establish the necessary institutional structures (legal, financial, regulatory).

Strategic measures included the strict limitation of tourism development to three islands (Efate, Espiritu Santo and Tanna) and to particular locations providing marketable attractions and maximizing investment benefits (infrastructure, facilities) with a phased programme to achieve sustainability. Development programmes included the enhancement of the waterfront and cruise passenger attractions, improvement of diving and yacht facilities and the expansion of offshore banking services in Port Vila.

Economic Consultants Ltd. (J. Fulbrook),
F. Lawson—Tourism planning.

Canary Islands: mapping technique

This type of representation was based — more than 30 years ago — on the principles employed in present-day mapping techniques using added layers of information. It enabled four sets of different characteristics to be superimposed simultaneously.

A&M Baud-Bovy (1964), Développement touristique des Iles Canaries, OCDE, Paris.

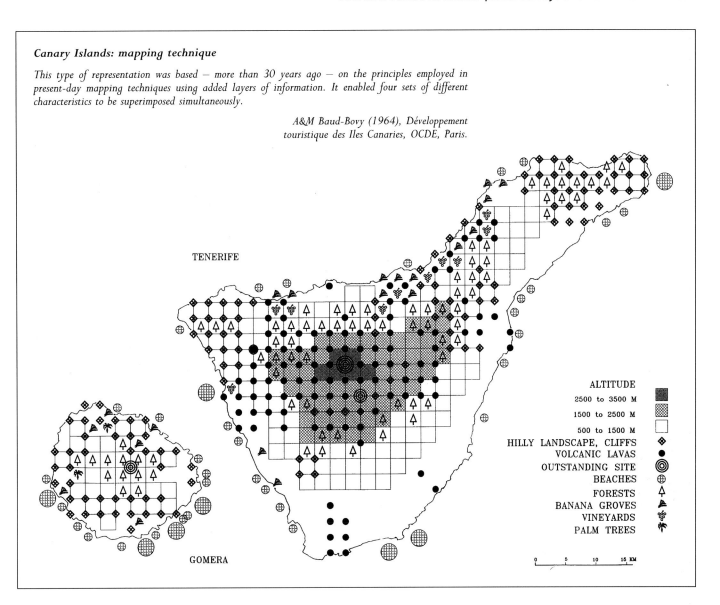

ALTITUDE
2500 to 3500 M
1500 to 2500 M
500 to 1500 M
HILLY LANDSCAPE, CLIFFS
VOLCANIC LAVAS
OUTSTANDING SITE
BEACHES
FORESTS
BANANA GROVES
VINEYARDS
PALM TREES

Green plans for cities or metropolitan areas 8.5.3–6 necessitate detailed surveys of

- present vegetation, degree of greenery;
- structure and uses of the various categories of outdoor open spaces;
- main deficiencies and opportunities.

More detailed research of potential recreation areas include both fieldwork surveys and studies of regional trends and motivations. Surveys are not only concerned with recording physical features but will take account of the psychological and social factors associated with landscape evaluation (perception, screening, security, durability, capacity, intrusion of noise etc.).

The time-distance between competing attractions and each main centre of population generating demand for recreation plays a decisive role and may be expressed in the form of gravitational models (see 7.3.5).

8.1.5 Facilities and infrastructures

Both existing and planned facilities must be examined, the latter including the proposed time schedules for completion and the extent to which the proposals are flexible. Details must include:

- **Tourist facilities** (including facilities for recreation use such as accommodation, food and drink services, sports and recreation):
  - *actual facilities:* specific location, location relative to other resources, size capacity, age and characteristics, standards of quality and service provided
  - *clientele:* market origins, characteristics and variations in seasonal and daily demands, trends
  - *operation:* ownership, tariffs, staffing and purchasing arrangements costs of provision and operating expenses, feasibility of further investment

 — *local and regional impact:* employment, purchases, multiplier effects, local use, contribution to regional tourism and commercial development, indirect needs for business facilities, investment opportunities in condominium and holiday accommodation
 • **Present tourist products**:
   — *characteristics:* main destinations of tourists, duration of stay, means of transportation, average range of expenditure, facilities patronized, preferences etc.
   — *organization:* tour operators involved, scale of business, extent of promotion, scale of demand and trends compared with other destinations and markets, feasibility of development
 • **Transport facilities** and in particular:
   — *means of access:* capacity of airports, ferries and associated handling facilities, regional and local road networks, seasonal variations in use, proposed improvements and extensions
   — *transport infrastructures:* main modes of transport, travel patterns, effects of changes in major highways and by-passes, comparative costs and conditions of transport services
   — *relative inaccessibility* of areas and zones: feasibility of alternative methods of connection including mail and cable links
 • **Technical infrastructure**:
   — *water supply and resources, electricity, telecommunications etc.:* availability, reliability and quality of systems, total capacity, extension potential, alternative resources, costs of provision and operation
   — *sewage and garbage disposal:* means of control, standards effectiveness, extent of public facilities, feasibility of conversion
 • **Service infrastructure: employment patterns**:
   — *hierarchy* of main towns, resort centres and other market towns providing services
   — *social and demographic structure*
   — *manpower available* for tourism services, training facilities provided and planned, standards, outputs of trained personnel, restrictions on expansion
   — *supporting services and facilities:* availability and quality of local agricultural products, souvenirs, hotel supplies, property construction and maintenance services.

8.2 MARKET ASSESSMENT

Market research and sectoral organization studies must be carried out at the same time as resource surveys to enable interchange of information. Market studies will depend on the finance and time available, the difficulties of obtaining representative information (on prospective markets) and the degree of precision required to meet planning objectives. Marketing must also be regarded as a continuous process,

monitoring changes in market conditions and trends to enable suitable adjustments to be made in later phases of planning.

8.2.1 Outdoor recreation activities

A market study is necessary for determining the recreation activities to be developed. At a local level, participation in a survey by the potential users within a locality may be quite effective (see 9.3.8). At regional or national level, market research requires a good knowledge of current outdoor recreational activities (see below). Surveys conducted in different countries indicate similar rankings.

Survey American Outdoors 1986
Ranking of outdoor recreational activities

 1 Walking (+)
 2 Car excursion, sightseeing
 3 Picnicking
 4 Swimming (+)
 5 Visiting parks, cultural, sports events
 6 Outdoor games and sports
 7 Fishing
 8 Boating
 9 Bicycling (+)
10 Camping
11 Watching nature (+)
12 Hunting
13 Horse riding
14 Golfing

The practice of some activities has increased (+) since the US Outdoor Recreation Resources Review Committee report (1962)

 −   decreasing
 − − decreasing steadily
 +   increasing
 ++   increasing steadily

Survey in Germany by LOGON-Institut
1 Walking
2 Car excursion, sightseeing
3 Gardening
4 Swimming
5 Outdoor games and activities
6 Outdoor sports
7 Improving one's mind
8 Visiting cultural events
9 Weekend house

Survey in France by BIPE

(Comité Régional du Tourisme 1989; p. 139)

1 Walking
2 Picnicking
3 Events and excursions
4 Parks and other areas
5 Individual sports (++)
6 Jogging (++)
7 Fishing (−)
8 Weekend house (− −)
9 Team sports (+)
10 Hunting (− −)

UK

In the UK similar surveys, conducted between 1986 and 1991 (Williams 1995), may be broadly synthesized as follows, so far as outdoor activities are concerned:

1 Visiting parks and open spaces
2 Walking (+)
3 Excursions
4 Cycling (+)
5 Outdoor sports and games
6 Swimming (+)
7 Golf (+)
8 Fishing
9 Horse riding
10 Visiting theme parks

Evaluating the latent demand (see 8.2.2) is more difficult. For example, the *American Outdoors* survey asked the question, 'Which activity would you like to practise?' with the following ranking of answers:

1 Yachting
2 Golf
3 Horse riding
4 Winter sports

Clearly for most of the respondents the costs and lack of ability would make such wishes impossible to fulfil.

These surveys reveal a relation between sport and leisure: one may take part in the same sporting activity (such as cycling, swimming or skiing) either in order to improve performance or to compete, or simply for recreational enjoyment. The graph in Fig. 8.1 shows the relationships between sport and leisure, which range from primarily sport-motivated, to mixed sport and leisure interest (in 'unstructured sport' or 'sport for all'), to sole leisure use.

It has been argued (Jay-Jaton 1983) that:

> The amateur-sport of today, with its stadia, gymnasia, swimming pools, its tracks, contents and compulsory regulations, is becoming out-of-date and is reconsidered almost everywhere. ... The concept of 'Sport for All' may slow down the process but not stop it as some people believe. The more policies are directed towards open spaces, the less society will need sport grounds, supervisory staff, security standards and expensive regulations.

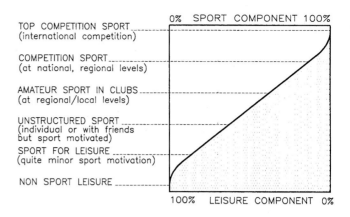

Figure 8.1

8.2.2 Specific aspects of the outdoor recreation markets

Assessment of demand involves similar, but different, approaches for both recreation and tourism. The recreation patterns of demand are influenced by environmental opportunities (existence of a lake or a forest), by the provision of facilities and by social inducements (fashion, education, examples, mass media, etc.).

The recreational market is a captive one, usually characterized by excess demand and dominated by the existence or non-existence of adequate facilities at a reasonable cost. The existence of the required facilities allows *participation* in the desired activity, but if the desired facilities are non-existent:

- alternative facilities may cause a *substitution* of activity, or
- the creation of a *latent demand* – the potential demand deferred by lack of opportunities, facilities or inducement.

This latent demand must be considered in detail (see Fig. 8.2).

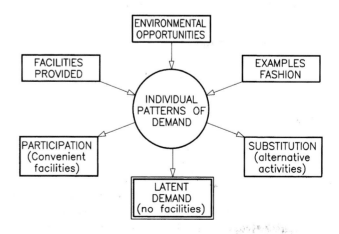

Figure 8.2

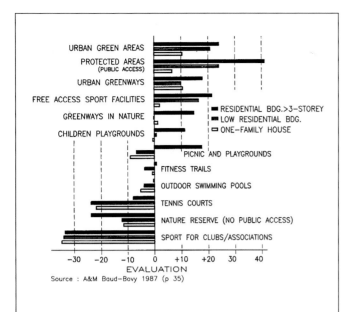

Source : A&M Baud-Bovy 1987 (p 35)

Survey

A survey was conducted in 1987 in three Swiss towns: 'Which kind of recreational facilities should be developed?'. Illustrating Cordell's opinion, the survey revealed a strong discrepancy between the existing facilities offered and the demand of the 'silent majority' of the inhabitants: parks, non-sports activities, green areas were preferred to sports activities (already well-developed in fact due to the strong pressure exerted by the sports associations). The results were similar, whichever town or age was considered; there was a strong correlation between the priority for outdoor recreation facilities and the type of housing: much higher by people living in apartments than by those living in cottages (with their own garden).

Source: A. and M. Baud-Bovy 1987 (p. 35)

The evaluation of the latent demand is necessary although
- recreational interests are difficult to quantify,
- many activities (picnics, excursions, etc.) are scattered over a large area,
- surveys do not generally reveal the degree of personal involvement in activities such as swimming, bicycling or rambling,
- fashion phenomena may induce rapid over-development of particular facilities (e.g. tennis courts),
- most recreationists do not benefit from representative organizations.

Recreationists' interests are not organized to be effective in presenting the case for outdoor recreation budgets, incentives, legislation and policy. Effectiveness in this context has many dimensions, including coalitions, credible and believable analyses, influential people willing to 'take up the flag' and 'standing' where money and political power confer entitlement to share in decision making. (Cordell 1989, p. 146)

Outdoor activities vary from place to place with the environment and the facilities provided, and market study implies an

assessment of the current demand for recreational activities involving:

- segmentation of the various users groups, with their respective socio-economic characters: time budget, recreation patterns, user preference, satisfaction, causes for non-use of facilities, etc.;
- identification of the main categories of existing and potential recreational activities;
- analysis of present participation: by ethnic origin, age, activity, socio-economic profiles, disabled people, school groups, etc.;
- analysis of trends and future requirements for each category of activity.

methods chosen might include a combination of focus group workshops with scientifically drawn samples of both users and nonusers; well-published 'unstructured' neighbourhood meetings to generate themes and issues in a non-threatening, informal setting; and a scientific survey involving interviews of a random sample of citizens by telephone or mail. Front-end focus group meetings are helpful to obtain a quick pulse of the community, as well as citizen views and values as a basis for structuring an appropriate needs assessment strategy.

(Mertes and Hall 1995)

The *future market development* is highly dependent on the availability of further facilities:

- either provided free of charge by local or regional authorities as needs-based services,
- or considered as user-pay services and provided by private enterprises,
- or mixing both systems through public subsidies or other financial arrangements.

More than in tourism, in recreation the **supply mainly creates the demand**.

Methods used in forecasting tourism demands (time/budget analysis, attitude surveys or in-depth interviews) may be applied. More sophisticated approaches (see 7.3.5) can be used (see Gold 1980, pp. 145–209, and Fisk and Hatry 1979, pp. 180–99). The influence of socio-economic factors can be indicated in systems modelling and multivariate regression analysis.

8.2.3 Specific aspects of the tourist markets

Very few destinations attract only one category of tourist. In most situations it is necessary to segment various groups or flows, for example by country of origin, main motivations, level of spending, type of travel (individuals, inclusive tour groups, chartered tours), main destinations and types of facilities used.

Market flows	Domestic tourists		International tourists from[b]		
	Staying in the country	Going out of country[a]	Neighbouring countries	More distant countries	Remote countries
Business/conventions	●	●	●	●	●
Transit tourism[c]				○	●
Visits to family/friends	●	○	○	○	○
Holiday sojourns[d]	●	●	●	●	○
Sightseeing/touring	●	●	●	●	●
Health/spas	●	○	○	○	
Education/students		○	○	○	
Pilgrimages etc.	●	●	●	○	
One-day excursions[e]	●	○	○		
Daily leisure	●				
Weekend tourism[e]	●	○	○		

● usually primary flow
○ usually secondary flow

Notes:
(a) Considered in terms of economic loss and the need to provide attractive alternatives within the country.
(b) May be separated by the main countries of origin.
(c) Including stop-over breaks.
(d) May be separated by specific motivations, e.g. sailing, camping, walking, riding/pony trekking, angling, skiing.
(e) Important near large urban areas. Often use same facilities as holiday tourists. Direct planning towards particular markets, for example, to attract higher spending tourists, business travellers, domestic tourists who normally take vacations abroad.

A distinction should be drawn between:

- business flows, where growth is related to a country's development, and
- other tourist flows (holiday, sightseeing, etc.), where rate of growth is determined by the quality and pricing of products, the existence of competing destinations and economic factors affecting the tourists' disposable income.

Planning should be directed essentially to these non-business flows, for example, to attract higher spending tourists, domestic tourists who normally take holidays abroad and incentive travel.

Existing tourist flows may be analysed according to:

- volume: seasonal and growth patterns, influences and trends (over 10–20 years);
- socio-economic characteristics: professions, ages, marital status etc.;
- main motivations: and extent to which these are met in the destinations;
- consumption characteristics: way of access to the country, duration of stay, preferential destinations, facilities patronized, frequency patterns, level of spending, elasticity;
- competitive destinations offered: location, relative prices, distribution circuits;
- commercial organization of present products: roles of intermediaries, influences.

Data for planning purposes is usually obtained from several sources (see 8.3.5). More specific studies and interviews may also be required, particularly to identify motivations and preferences. Surveys must aim to provide information which is relevant, reliable, practical and capable of being analysed for comparison across the range and over time. They must give special attention to:

- analysing similar tourist products provided in competing destinations (attraction, pricing, characteristics of customers, seasonality, etc.);
- soliciting opinion about potential tourism products from tourist market specialists (e.g. tour operators) with detailed illustrations and pricing of these products.

Methodologies for surveys are well documented and may be conducted at points of entry/exit, during transportation, in main destinations and/or at main selling points. Market studies may also be conducted in the country of origin of the main tourist flows and/or in a number of potential market areas.

8.3 ASSESSMENT OF STRUCTURES AND POLICIES

Whilst tourism development will depend mainly on the resources and market, the economic, political and administrative organization of the country and region will have a decisive influence. For instance, in a free enterprise market economy, it may not be feasible to implement detailed and strict limitations on land-use whilst, in a country having strong central government direction, major contributions from the private sector may be lacking. The planning proposals must be within the mainstream of political policies.

8.3.1 Socio-economic surveys

Socio-economic surveys are necessary to define:

- the main economic resources of the country and its region;
- the demographic structure, manpower engaged in tourism and secondary industries;
- education, health, municipal and other services;
- existing training programmes, resources invested;
- the level of urbanization, relative values of properties and land, building costs and organization of the construction industry;
- the present role of tourism and associated economic sectors – transportation, infrastructure, local craft industries, food supplies;
- economic sectors where development could or would compete with the development of tourism, and their degree of compatibility.

8.3.2 Survey of the implementation framework

Main decisional structures responsible for implementing and operating tourism/recreation:

- state, regional and local administrations, their respective powers and base policies;
- roles of the parties interested in development of tourism/recreation (administration authorities, private developers, trade unions, community groups, non-profit-making organizations, specialized clubs and institutions and associated sectors of the economy);
- identification of foreign and domestic businesses, public or private companies who may be interested in running, operating or franchising the facilities planned (carriers, tour operators, hoteliers, food service operators etc.);
- structure, aims, powers, resources and extent of regionalization of the national organization for tourism and other bodies associated with outdoor recreation;
- sources of finance for tourism/recreation development at local, regional, national and international levels and from public or private funding;
- legislation for land control, protection of resources, valorization of national heritage.

Egypt

Tourism has been the fastest growth sector of the Egyptian economy, with accommodation increasing from 24 000 rooms in 1985 to 47 000 rooms in 1991, and is one of the top government priorities. A Tourism Development Authority (TDA) was established in 1991, under the auspices of the Ministry of Tourism, to administer a national strategy for tourism development, including an improved climate for investment with tax exemptions, reduced import duties and the right to repatriate profits and invested funds (extending law 230, 1989).

Priority areas for planned development were centred on the Gulf of Aqaba and Red Sea zone (for winter sun, beach and diving tourism), Nile cruise tourism (floating hotels increasing from 176 to 300 by the year 2000) and yachting tourism.

Coordinating with other agencies, the TDA has also taken steps to research and control the environmental impacts damaging to the coral reefs (caused by land infilling, dredging, garbage trapping and sedimentation) and increased use of the Nile waterway.

Egyptian State Tourism Office, 1996.

An earlier extensive study, funded by the World Bank, investigated the problems involved in financing and constructing hotels and other tourism facilities, with a view to:

(a) reducing the costs of investment and operation;
(b) achieving a more optimum balance between market demands and the supply of tourist accommodation in Egypt.

This involved a detailed examination of hotel design, construction programmes, operations and cost factors, in parallel with market forecasts and economic analyses, and led to the preparation of models for future planning requirements.

International team: F. Lawson, J. Beavis, R. Kotas, S. Wanhill, with national consultants.

8.3.3 Survey of existing development plans

Surveys must also include detailed studies of current and recent plans and provisions for related sectors which could influence tourism and/or recreation development:

- plans for the *economic and physical development* of tourism, housing, agriculture and industry and infrastructures in the country and region concerned (content of plans, programme for development, method of implementation, investment involved, authorities responsible etc.);
- provisions for *environmental protection and redevelopment* of derelict areas – to enable these to be integrated with tourism and recreation planning. Many of the most interesting and valuable recreational projects have stemmed from the reclamation of industrial wasteland, financed by regional improvement grants;
- proposals for *secondary recreational/tourism use* of resources developed for other purposes – forestry, water supplies, inland navigation, highway improvements.
- *current resources for education and training* and plans for expansion of facilities at various levels.

8.3.4 Development goals and policies

The second stage in planning involves a more precise definition of the objectives in developing tourism or recreation, in accordance with the nation's/community's structures and policies. Specific information must be obtained on numbers, quantities and values, for example: what forms of tourism are preferred, what main benefits are sought, what rate of growth is expected, how is the development of tourism or/and domestic recreation to be funded, what proportions of the population and for which social groups is provision to be made? Goals and priorities for tourism development are identified by comparing the detailed objectives with information obtained about the potential markets and resources.

8.3.5 Sources of data

A number of methods must be applied to ensure adequate coverage and reliability of the information. For projections and trends it is necessary to analyse consistent time series statistics. Examples of the statistics and other information, which is generally available on markets, resources or structures, are outlined below. For specific studies, such as conference and exhibition tourism, reference will need to be made to other sources (Lawson 1981).

8.4 FORMULATION OF TOURISM DEVELOPMENT PLANS

A comprehensive plan for tourism development at national or regional level usually consists of five parts:

- recommended objectives and priorities;
- a physical development plan detailing the main resources, areas to be developed or protected, main tourist resorts, programmes of additional facilities needed, means of access, road networks and technical infrastructures;

Sources of data	Examples
Demand	
International agencies[a] (WTO, OECD, EU, PATA, OAS)	Global and regional tourism patterns and trends. Economic data, subsidies, employment, developments
Government: tourism authorities[b]	Visitor surveys, tourist segments, patterns of demand. Destinations, facilities used, hotel occupancies, prices
Government: social and economic surveys	Demographic patterns, socio-economic trends. Economic indicators, trends in employment and trade
Tour operators, travel agencies	Profiles of tourists, main origins, destinations and facilities used, preferences, expenditures, trends
Transport authorities[c]	Air traffic data, carriers, prices, airport capacities and constraints. Road traffic counts, origins and destinations highway plans. Cruise and ferry traffic, harbour facilities, yacht berths, demands
Recreation and sports, etc., associations	Recreation and special interests, market profiles, participation rates, preferences, competition, contract sources
Supply	
Government: education and training	Resources, types and levels of courses, planned changes. Outputs of trainees, employment prospects, trends
Government: youth and sports	Organization, facilities, financing
Tourism organizations, hotel associations	Registration and grading requirements. Numbers of beds, in various categories of accommodation, location, prices
Facility representatives	Planned new developments and improvements, costs
Community level	Policies for parks, green areas, outdoor facilities and corresponding budgets
Construction and associated supplies	Industry profiles, outputs, employment, trends. Price indices, sourcing of supplies, new developments
Statutory and utility undertakings	Extent of supplies, resources, reserves, levels of demand, system capacities, plans for development, charges

Notes:

(a) World Tourism Organization, Organization for Economic Cooperation and Development, European Union, Pacific Area Tourism Association, Organization of American States, as examples of international agencies.

(b) Tourism authorities at national, regional and local (visitor and convention bureau) levels.

(c) Data on traffic flows and demand as well as facility supply and planned extensions or improvements. Representative associations (e.g. International Air Transport Association, IATA) and some operating companies also publish statistics.

Mauritius: National Physical Development Plan

As part of the National Physical Development Plan (NPDP), a strategic and coordinated approach to the planning of tourism activities was adopted. Projected growth rates from 1995 to 2010 indicated a 72 per cent increase in tourist arrivals and bed-nights which would require a 53 per cent increase in rooms provided. These were allocated to three existing tourist zones with limits on the extent of shoreline development and the retention of distinctive features.

Strategies included the strengthening of inland tourist attractions with improvement of scenic routes, protection of green natural areas, and creation of a National Park and nature reserves. A conservation plan for coastal areas and lagoons proposed the establishment of marine parks and reserves.

Ministry of Housing, Lands,
Town and Country Planning,
Mauritius, 1996
Draft National Physical Development Plan, 1993

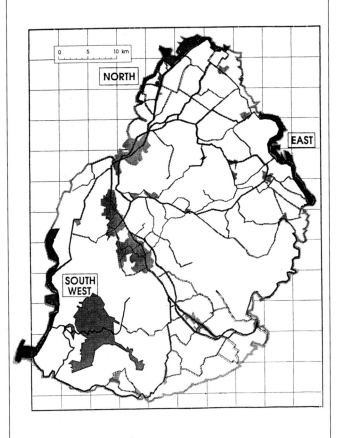

Key

▬	Scenic Routes
┅	A Roads
┈	Other Roads
▒	Settlements
▓	National Park Area as defined at February 1993

- evaluation of economic and environmental impacts and proposals for beneficial improvements and sustainability;
- strategy for implementing, coordinating and financing the development;
- action programme and mechanism for monitoring the changes and their effects.

Methods of assessing the development objectives in accordance with the markets, the resources, the existing or potential products and the country's policies and priorities have been presented in 7.3.6–7.3.7. The following sections summarize:

- the elements usually provided in a physical tourism development plan (8.4);
- the elements usually provided in a physical development plan for recreation at regional scale (8.5);
- the strategy for the implementation of a tourist or recreation plan (9.1);
- specific measures for protection of resources (9.2).

Reference should also be made to 7.3.8, Monitoring system.

8.4.1 Additional facilities needed

Accommodation usually represents more than half of tourism investment and is often the most critical factor in determining the financial feasibility of commercial development. The market studies should indicate the types of accommodation required and quantify the demands expected to be generated by each tourist flow. The total numbers of beds required for each product, for each flow may be estimated by various formulae, the simplest being:

$$B_f = \frac{T_y \times S_n}{365\ O_f}$$

where

B_f = total number of beds required for a specific tourist flow or product
T_y = forecast number of tourists per year
S_n = average duration of stay (nights)
O_f = occupancy rate (expressed as a factor)

This type of formula, although useful in preliminary estimates, requires qualification:

- *average annual occupancy rate* (O_f) must at least equal the break-even point determined by analysis of the projected revenues and costs (operational and fixed costs);
- *seasonal distribution of demand* must be examined for an indication of peak demand conditions with maximum occupancy ($O_f = 1.0$)

$$B_{fm} = \frac{T_m \times S_n}{31\ nights}$$

where:

B_{fm} = maximum beds required during peak months
T_m = expected peak monthly flow of tourists

South Antalya tourism development project, Turkey

This is the largest, fully-integrated tourism development in Turkey which incorporated planning, programming, financial and operational stages from the beginning. It covers a coastal area extending 80 km south from the new Antalya Port to the Gelidonya headland and is entirely within a national park. Within the project area are seven villages, including Kemer, and three ancient cities. Planning studies started in 1974, the Master Plan was prepared in 1976, followed by a World Bank loan of $26 million. In 1978 a list of priority projects was started, including major coastal road, water supply, sewerage and electricity infrastructures, a yacht marina and training hotel and school. Revisions to the Master Plan were incorporated in 1988 and 1990. The current plan aims for a total bed capacity of 65 500, plus two 18-hole golf courses and additional facilities to attract visitors inland.

To attract domestic and foreign investors, the state provides financial aid and other incentives, a high quality infrastructure and long-term (49-year) leases of sites. The state is also responsible for protection of the natural and historic environments as well as providing social facilities (health centre, tourist offices, hotel training centre, municipal buildings). Socio-economic benefits include the creation of some 20 000 new jobs, US $450 million generated annually in foreign exchange, swimming, recreation and entertainment provided for over 200 000 people daily and advanced infrastructure and health services for the local communities.

In 1991, 58 areas had been allocated providing the following accommodation: 5-star hotels – 5244 beds, 4-star hotels – 2103 beds, 3-star hotels – 1485 beds, 1 and 2-star hotels – 186 beds, first-class holiday villages – 14 644 beds, camping – 2212 beds, pensions (bed and breakfast) – 164 beds.

A World Bank project
Director of the project: Seyhun Ors, Deputy Under Secretary, Ministry of Tourism
General Information: Ministry of Tourism 1991.

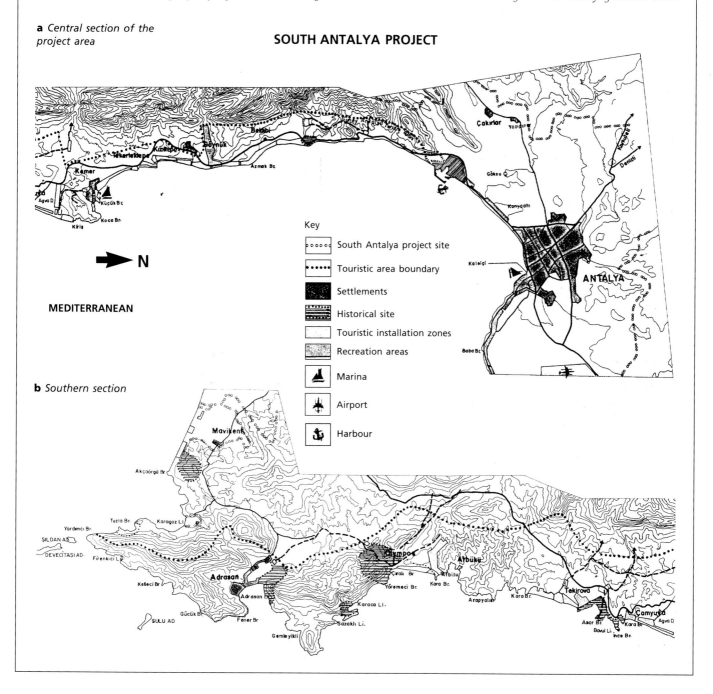

a Central section of the project area

SOUTH ANTALYA PROJECT

b Southern section

Key
- ∘∘∘∘∘ South Antalya project site
- ••••• Touristic area boundary
- ■ Settlements
- ▤ Historical site
- ☐ Touristic installation zones
- ▦ Recreation areas
- ⛵ Marina
- ✈ Airport
- ⚓ Harbour

MEDITERRANEAN

N

a *Paro dzong (castle-monastery)*

b *Paro hotel – first phase*

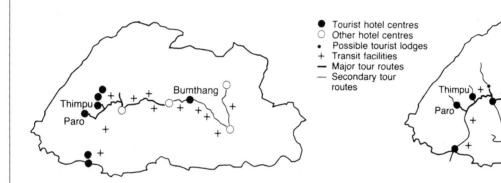

c *Medium-term tour facilities*

d *Long-term tour facilities*

Bhutan

Tourism was only introduced into the remote Kingdom of Bhutan (population 650 000) in 1974 and has been subject to strict control. A national tourism development plan was adopted in 1986 following a UNDP and WTO study which identified three zones of potential:

Himalayan: mountain climbing, professional high-altitude trekking
Central: unique cultural tours and trekking
Southern foothills: wild life, in conjunction with Indian winter tourism

   The aim was to maximize the economic and social benefits from tourism without jeopardizing the rich cultural and spiritual heritage (a,b) and natural environment. The development strategy laid stress on control, training and conservation with a phased progressive extension of excursion routes focused around tourist service centres in the main areas of potential (c,d). Maximum annual targets for tourists in the medium term (1991–5) were set at 3000 increasing to 5600 in the long term (post 1995). Tourism marketing has been limited and restricted to pre-arranged, package tours with a high daily expenditure and carefully monitored. To enable Bhutanese personnel to participate in tourism at all levels from the beginning, a purposely designed training centre was provided in the Bhutan Hotel in Thimphu and overseas courses arranged for managers.
   Since 1990, in response to the religious sentiments of local people and the need to protect the pristine condition of the mountains and peaks, mountaineering activities have been disallowed. The hotel and tourism industry was privatized in 1991, the training needs now being coordinated by the Tourism Authority of Bhutan. An EU assisted South Asia Integrated Human Resource Development Programme (SA-ITHRDP) is now being implemented in the region.

UNDP/WTO Master Plan. Study team: J. Hawkes (leader), A. Fitch, M. Heraty, C. Jest, M. Kohli, F. Lawson.
(Reference: WTO, National and Regional Tourism Planning: Methodologies and Case Studies, Routledge, 1994)

St Lucia: tourism development strategy

Following a recession in major tour operations in the 1980s, an assessment was made of the existing and prospective tourist markets, appropriate projects and actions to improve the tourism potential of St Lucia. As tourism was already established, emphasis was given to strategies that would widen the range of facilities and services available, remove existing constraints on growth and enable St Lucia nationals to retain a higher share of tourist expenditure whilst avoiding the dangers of excessive development, pollution and damage to the natural attractions.

Undertaken on behalf of the government of St Lucia and the Commonwealth Fund for Technical Cooperation this was an example of integrated physical and economic planning.

Among the projects identified and appraised were an expansion of accommodation (particularly small-scale hotels and low-cost guest houses) and the improvement of transport services and cruise ship facilities (featuring a new craft market), restaurant and recreational attractions, training and institutional structures.

These projects have since been implemented and, in 1997, St Lucia's policies with regard to tourism were unchanged from those outlined above.

Economic Consultants Ltd., B. H. Archer, F. Lawson

Original tourism development plan for Cyprus

This master plan — one of the first national tourism development plans to be prepared in the world — organized the transition from traditional forms of tourism concentrating on hill resorts for a regional clientele (Egypt, Israel) to the present seaside resorts for European tourists.

Beaudouin, Baud-Bovy, Tzanos (1962), Cyprus Tourism Development Plan, SCET, Paris.
Project manager: M. Baud-Bovy, tourism consultant

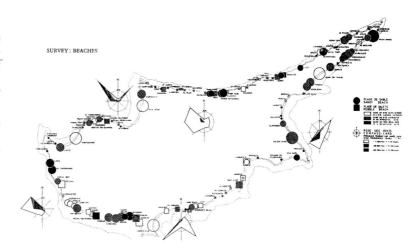

a *Survey: beaches. This graphic representation showed the respective sizes of the beaches, their material (sand or pebble) and the value of the surrounding site*

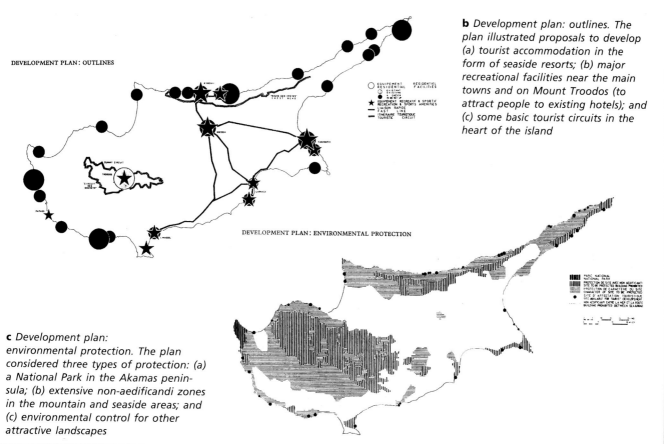

b *Development plan: outlines. The plan illustrated proposals to develop (a) tourist accommodation in the form of seaside resorts; (b) major recreational facilities near the main towns and on Mount Troodos (to attract people to existing hotels); and (c) some basic tourist circuits in the heart of the island*

c *Development plan: environmental protection. The plan considered three types of protection: (a) a National Park in the Akamas peninsula; (b) extensive non-aedificandi zones in the mountain and seaside areas; and (c) environmental control for other attractive landscapes*

	Tourists	Excursion/ touring	Religion	Business	Confer- ence	Health/ conval- escence	Seaside vacation	Mountain vacation	Rural vacation[a]	Total beds
				Tourists/travellers segmented by motivation						
Hotels	•	•	•	•	•	•	•	•	•	C_1
Motels/motorhotels	•	•		•						C_2
Holiday villages							•		•	C_3
Camping caravans	•	•					•		•	C_4
Social tourism		•	•				•	•	•	C_5
Individual properties[b]						•	•	•	•	C_6
Total beds (by motivation)	M	M_t	M_r	M_b	M_c	M_{th}	M_{sv}	M_{sm}	M_r	M/C

Notes:

(a)   Including themed resorts

(b)   Condominiums apartments, villas, second houses: for sale or rent

•   = main motivations determining demand for categories of accommodation

M, M_1 etc. = subtotals of tourists categorized by motivations

C, C_2 etc. = total number of beds required in each type of accommodation

M   = total tourists

C   = total beds

B_{fm} and T_m may need adjustment (by price, preferential booking, etc.) to maximize the annual occupancy. Monthly analysis is also useful in quantifying direct costs and options for the low seasons (closure, alternative products).

The corresponding number of rooms depends on the market analysis of the product selected. For leisure tourism a high proportion of rooms will be two-bed rooms (with typical occupancies between 1.5 and 1.8) whilst business tourism may warrant a greater proportion of single rooms. For family use, units may include both living rooms (convertible) and bedrooms, often with self-catering facilities. Chalets, apartments and condominiums are invariably designed for flexible multiple occupancy. The types of accommodation sought by different categories of tourists will be closely related to their motivation and interest giving a range of distribution for the estimated demand (B_f). See table above.

At this stage, consideration must also be given to specific needs affecting the location, the scale and character of the development. These will determine the minimum thresholds of scale (i.e., numbers of tourists) for the developments proposed:

- *infrastructural improvements* (airport developments, harbour conversion, marina construction, highway diversion/extension, major environmental changes);
- *specific products* (international standard golf courses, winter/summer sports centre, yacht harbour, conference centre, casino);
- *scale of development* (individually-managed small- or medium-sized hotels or large-scale international standard hotels and resorts);
- *character* (integrated resort or individual plot development, low-rise villa/cottage style or high-rise hotels and apartment buildings).

8.4.2 Means of access

Proposals for developing or improving routes of entry include consideration of:

Facilities/ Resources	Provisions considered
Airports	
Capacity	Runway, terminal and control capacities (types of aircraft, numbers of passengers), expansion proposals
Locations	Regional airports within 1-2 hours' travel distance of major resorts, transit/transfer facilities
Regulation	Legal framework, schedules and charter agreements, flight paths
Infrastructure	Technical infrastructure and support services, housing for personnel, hotel and commercial developments
Integration	Coordination with highway and public transport systems
Seaports	
Ferry terminal	Easy access and high quality parking/waiting and drive on/off facilities, separated from commercial cargo handling areas
Cruise ports	Development of free ports and concentrated local attractions for cruise passengers (see A4.8)
Yacht harbours and marinas	Focuses for recreational attraction, conservation of traditional harbours, quays, building of historic interest, complementary features (see 5.2)
Coach and rail termini	Integrated system of public transport provided to the major resorts (see A4.5–6) taxi services at the major termini regulated by licensing

The point of access provides tourists with their first contact with – and often a dominating impression of – the country or region. It is important that there should be no frustrating restrictions or unnecessary delays (inadequate access, space or facilities). Facilities must be planned to make formalities (customs, security, control, waiting, inter-circulation) easier; directions and information must be clear and precise.

In hub airports with important transit traffic, the transit lounge may be considered as a shop window for the country's tourist products.

8.4.3 Resources: hierarchy of development

Distinctions need to be drawn between resources which are to be protected and those to be developed – with various degrees of priority and intensity (see 9.2):

Category	Priorities
Protected resources	Areas having severe or partial restrictions on access and few tourist facilities (in carefully selected locations). These include national or regional parks, natural areas of high scientific interest and outstanding beauty and sites of monuments or of archaeological value. Conservation objectives come before tourist development.
Resources for priority development	Areas of utmost importance for tourism in which tourism (recreation) is or will become the major activity and in which many facilities will be provided exclusively for this purpose.
Resources of great tourism (recreation) interest	Areas in which tourism or/and recreation will rank along other economic activities and may be appropriate for a few concentrated facilities (such as a resort). As a rule, however, the facilities will be minor and scattered. Development of the natural environment is usually carefully controlled.
Resources of secondary tourism (recreation) interest	Areas in which the extension of tourism will depend on the opportunities offered by the development of other economic activities or will be delayed in time with limited environmental control. Local recreation facilities (leisure centres, public parks) may be integrated with other developments.

8.4.4 Priority areas for tourism and recreation development

The suitability of regions (at national level) or sites (in regions) for tourism and recreational use will depend on the specific resources of each site and the degree of difficulty in developing them.

Sites or regions

Facilities	1	2	3	4	5	6	7	8	9
Integral conservation	■					■		●	○
High conservation	■						■		○
Large resort		●	■	○	△				
Small or medium resort				●	○				
Individual facilities					●			○	
Sightseeing facilities	○					■	■	●	○
Game reserves (hunting)	●							○	
Harbour, marina					○				
Boating, swimming etc.				○	●				
Skiing facilities							△	■	○

■ necessary
● favourable
○ possible
△ difficult

A similar table may be created relating the sites or regions to various tourist products.

An analysis of this kind must:

- take into account the availability of land in the sites/areas and, if necessary, introduce a policy of land control to ensure its reservation for tourism and recreation;
- consider the extent of development and the changes which will result against the sensitivity of each site and its carrying capacity;
- guarantee the full conservation of unique sites of natural, archaeological or historic interest and protection of valuable sites;
- ensure there is a choice of alternative sites and reserve those of lower priority for future development;
- relate the potential attractiveness of the site when developed to the costs involved.

8.4.5 Main tourist resorts

Development proposals need to consider current tourist destinations and changes required in existing resorts (improvements, new facilities) as well as other areas offering attractive features. New resorts may be based on existing settlements (fishing ports, disused docklands, mountain villages) or created in areas not previously developed. Resorts will present a wide diversity of characteristics depending on their location, climate, seasonality, traditional architecture, scale, clientele, range of facilities provided, standards of quality and sophistication and images projected.

The concentration of numerous facilities into a few large resorts presents a number of tourism and planning advantages:

- facilities of large scale and high standard are warranted (large swimming pools, convention halls, entertainment

Development of Corsica

The protection of sites has been an early concern in tourism development plans. Designated zones for protection covered both stretches of the coast and a central regional park. Areas identified for development included corridors in order to extend tourism interest inland.

*Mission Interministérielle pour
L'Aménagement et L'Equipement de la Corse (1972).*

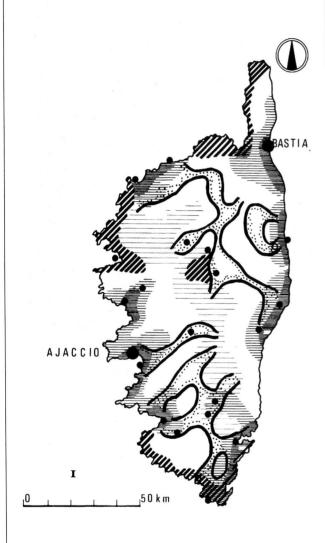

Key

1. Proposed zones of seaside development which will also stimulate development of the hinterland.
2. Zones of extended development linking mountains and coast.
3. Sites designated for protection.
4. Regional natural park.

complexes, speciality restaurants, nightclubs, casinos, ice rinks etc.);
- problems of acquiring or regulating land are restricted to a few defined places
- public services and infrastructures are more economically provided;
- control over non-developed areas is more easily exercised;
- marketing is generally more effective (scale, out of season, conventions, packaging), access and transfers of tourists more easily organized.

On the other hand, the heavy concentration of investment involves higher risk; discriminating and often high-spending tourists may be deterred and the resort may tend to become a tourist enclave isolated from its hinterland (in economic, social and employment benefits). Planning proposals may endeavour to lessen these drawbacks by developing local craft industries and agricultural products and by incorporating traditional properties, streets, villages etc. (restored and conserved) as part of the resort character.

8.4.6 Towns and urban centres

The extent to which tourist facilities are developed varies widely from one town to the next depending on the location and character. Towns and cities serve as 'gateways' to tourist regions and may also be major destinations in themselves. In recent years, 'city tourism' (weekends in historic towns, short holidays for sightseeing or shopping, packages) has been developed at a higher rhythm than any other form of tourism in European countries, becoming a major source of revenues in many cities: historic districts may bring more income than industrial parks.

In general, town facilities are an important feature in tourism development plans, usually achieving a good return on investment because of the diverse market (local, business and tourist), developed infrastructure and local employment.

The tourist attractions of towns will be considerably reduced if facilities are of poor quality, out of character, inconveniently situated or patronized by incompatible clients. Specific zones of tourist attraction centred on the main resources (monuments, urban parks, squares, rivers, promenades) must be identified and protected. Most large tourist centres offering a wide range of services and facilities have developed from traditional towns (Nice) or longstanding resorts (most spas, Brighton).

Historic towns with valuable historic districts may be exposed to overcrowding conditions, with negative impacts on the site and the local population (see 9.2.8).

A tourist centre of any size needs all-year-round occupation and a balance of employment. It tends to complement the resources of the region by offering a wider choice of hotels, restaurants, entertainment, shopping and local tours. In areas of high scenic attraction (national parks) local towns are particularly important in providing the support services and wet-weather facilities.

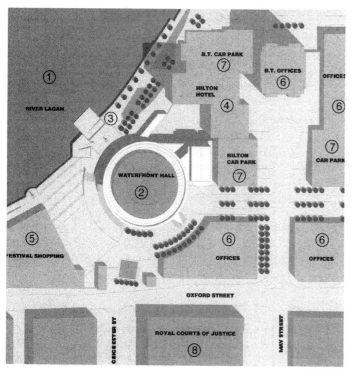

Belfast: Redevelopment of Laganside, Northern Ireland

Following changes in the quayside and industrial areas bordering the River Lagan through the centre of Belfast, a concept plan for riverside improvement was prepared by Shepheard, Epstein & Hunter and BDP Belfast in 1987 as an input to the Belfast Urban Area Plan by the Department of the Environment (NI).

A key element in the tourism revival of Laganside is the new Waterfront Hall (Fig. 8.25), a multi-use conference centre and concert venue which has provided a catalyst for the associated development of a hotel, restaurants and cafes, office building and riverside recreation.

The site extends over an area of 0.7 ha forming part of a 6.1 ha redevelopment zone by the Laganside Development Corporation (LDC). Seating 2000 to 2500 in the main hall, with a supplementary hall for 500, the Waterfront complex opened in January, 1997, the cost of £32 million being met by the City of Belfast with the help of grants from the LDC and EU.

Architects for the Waterfront Hall:
Robinson McIlwaine, Belfast,
Tourism consultant: F. Lawson

Key

1 River Lagan
2 Waterfront Hall
3 Riverside promenade
4 Hilton Hotel

5 Festival shopping
6 New office buildings
7 Car parks
8 Royal Courts of Justice

Foreground: Place du Caudan with food courts, background: city centre (photo: H. Rogers)

Le Caudan Waterfront, Mauritius

Conversion of the old harbour in Port Louis, Mauritius involved the dredging of the Bassin des Chaloupes and Ruisseau du Pouce, installation of turbine pumps to renew the stagnant water and construction of a new marina. The derelict warehouses have been renovated and converted to provide a theme casino, museum, 70 speciality shops, handicraft market, three cinemas, seven restaurants and cafes, a food court, and office space grouped round a lively piazza and promenade along the quays. A new de

luxe business hotel, the Labourdonnais Waterfront Hotel, completed in December, 1996 has been constructed in complementary style.

The Labourdonnais has 109 de luxe rooms and suites with harbour, marina and mountain views. In addition to an elevated outdoor swimming pool and health centre, the hotel provides a business centre and conference facilities.

Developers: Caudan Development Ltd.
Architects: Maurice Giraud, ZAC Associates
Structural and Civil Engineers: Sigma / Ove Arup

8.4.7 Road networks and circuits

Roads serve two very important functions in tourism and outdoor recreation:

- As a means of access, transport and communication between tourist or recreationist attractions and facilities. Hence the need for a suitably development network of roads with vehicle and motorist services.

- As a way of sightseeing and discovering a country, requiring the planning of a road to extend beyond its width to the view seen from the road. This must include the control of roadside development, landscaping and screening. Provision must also be made for the appropriate siting, design and signing of tourist facilities: viewing points, parking zones, information kiosks, attractive picnic and rest/recreation areas, well-designed restaurants and cafe bars, suitable toilets and garbage collection.

Roads used by tourists can be broadly classified in three categories:

- **Main through routes**: These link main destination areas and correspond to the national network of highways and major roads. Changes in the highway infrastructure affect accessibility (time–distance, convenience, extended catchment area) for day excursions and weekend recreation often leading to pressures on national parks and vulnerable coastal resources.
- **Tourist roads**: Secondary roads and avenues of concrete or asphalt (macadam) construction or even gravel, providing access to specific tourist facilities: resorts, isolated hotels, restaurants, monuments or recreation attractions (beach, cove, rivers),
- **Tourist circuits**: Sightseeing circuits providing interesting scenery along a selected road (e.g. Corniche d'Amalfi, Italy) and between tourist attractions. Difficulties arise in reconciling the attractiveness of a scenic route (narrow winding roads blending with the landscape) and created demand (greater capacity, speed and concentration of traffic). Some means of restriction, control and management are required including diversion of through traffic. Prepared waiting areas with facilities for picnicking etc., should be provided at all main vantage points. Scenic routes are important products both for tourism and recreation.

Scenic byways in the United States

Federal programs
Schemes to designate and manage scenic byways have been developed by the Bureau of Land Management (BLM), through its network of Back Country Byways, and the USDA Forest Service (USFS). By 1996 the USFS had designated over 7000 miles of scenic roads through national forests throughout the country in addition to managing nine parkways and numerous park roads.

The National Scenic Byways Program
Established under the Intermodal Surface Transportation Efficiency Act, 1991, this provides for two types of designation:

- *National Scenic Byways – which must possess one or more intrinsic qualities (scenic, historic, cultural, natural, recreational, archaeological) and have a corridor management plan;*
- *All American Roads – representing the finest examples of scenic byways in the country, having at least two of the intrinsic qualities mentioned above, providing an attraction in themselves for domestic and international travellers. Management plans are required.*

The Indiana State Byway scheme is an example of this policy, recognizing three levels of designation – State, National and All American. The State byways are generally shorter and of more local or state interest whilst National routes allow a continuous direction of travel over longer distances.

8.4.8 Isolated facilities

Most tourist facilities are concentrated in resorts and towns. Some, however, will need to be dispersed along routes and elsewhere to provide local services and shelter, such as:

- motels, camping sites, viewing places, cafes and restaurants, bars, garages and service stations along main highways and tourist circuits;
- isolated hotels, mountain shelters, hunting lodges, refuges, picnic areas and information/orientation centres in the vicinity of popular sites of attractions;
- ports, shelters and service stations around lakes and along rivers and other waterways.

Circuits: The location of individual facilities may be deliberately planned to provide an *integrated network* over a tourist region for activities such as pleasure driving, sightseeing circuits, hillwalking, youth hostelling, pony trekking and horse riding.

Conservation design: Facilities in sensitive areas of high scenic attraction must be specifically designed to complement their surroundings and strict control over signposting and advertisements is essential. The most appropriate buildings are generally those which are constructed of local materials in the traditional style of the area and one of the benefits of tourism is the opportunity it provides for preserving, renovating and reusing old farmhouses, castles and monuments – examples being the *Relais Châteaux* (France), *Paradors* (Spain), *Pousadas* (Portugal).

8.5 FORMULATION OF REGIONAL RECREATION PLANS

Even some recent regional physical plans are limited to traffic and other infrastructures, housing, trade and industry, sometimes forestry, agriculture and environmental protection, but without specific provisions for recreation. Recreation planning should always be an integral part of regional planning. Some countries recognized this need as early as the 1960s (The Netherlands' national structure plan for the development of open air recreation) and in the 1970s (introduction of the SCORP procedure in the USA: see 8.5.2).

8.5.1 The struggle for sites

As the demand of towns dwellers (see 9.2.8) for outdoor recreation has grown, the number and quality of sites suitable for this purpose have usually decreased, not only around but within towns (see 9.3).

Many inner cities suffering from disinvestment and decay have large tracts of waste ground which allow provision for outdoor recreation and amenities to be included in redevelopment plans. In other places, derelict land may be landscaped

Building a Metropolitan Greensward for the New York region

The green areas are one of the five 'major campaigns' proposed by the recent New York – New Jersey – Connecticut Metropolitan Regional Plan (together with urban centres, transport, manpower and institutions). The Metropolitan Greensward is a vision of a system of protected open spaces, greenways and rural landscapes that distinguishes the cities and suburbs of the metropolitan region. By implementing them, the region will conserve:

- *its critical natural resource systems (ecosystems and watersheds);*
- *its recreational opportunities (hiking, picnicking, swimming etc. for 7 million households);*
- *the working landscapes of farms and forests.*

Together, these protected open lands will help shape future patterns of growth.
To construct the Greensward, it is recommended that the region should:

- ***establish nine regional reserves*** *(plus the Atlantic seashore and working farmland throughout the region), which encompass the region's most important scenic, biological and water resources and which are now threatened by urban sprawl:*
  - *new plans and regulations through local initiatives, state planning framework, regional commission*
  - *funds by state-level initiatives targeting consumption of natural resources*
- ***reinvest in urban parks, public spaces and natural resources***:
  - *new public spaces, redeveloping urban waterfronts, creation and restoration of parks in deprived urban neighbourhoods, improvement of the region's urban forest resources*
  - *implementation through citizen initiatives, public action, etc.*
  - *credible funding strategies (targeted user fees, community management, etc.)*
- ***create a regional network of greenways and green spaces***:
  - *that protect and enhance individual rivers, trails, ridgelines and urban open lands*
  - *by establishing state-level coordination and support for local initiatives, through programmes and grants.*

Author: Robert D. Yaro, Executive Director, Regional Plan Association (1996)
Reference: Robert D. Yaro and Tony Hiss (1996), A Region at risk, the third regional plan for the
New York–New Jersey–Connecticut metropolitan area, Island Press, Washington DC

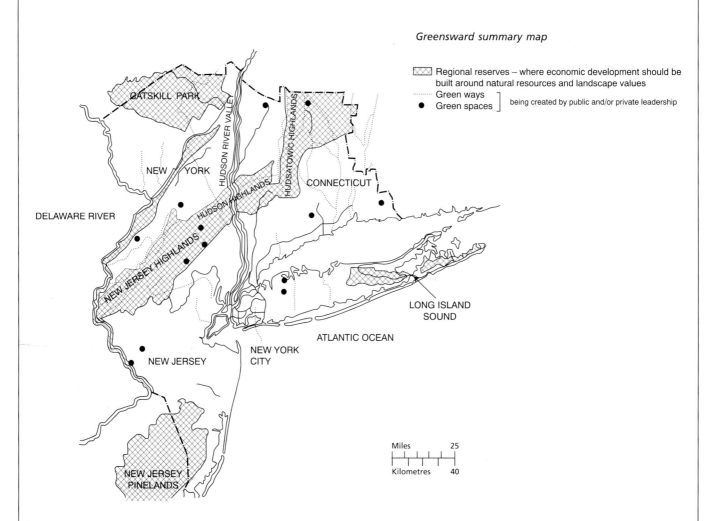

Greensward summary map

'Land Between the Lakes' and the Tennessee Valley Authority, USA

The Tennessee Valley Authority (TVA) was created in 1933 for reclaiming an eroded region, creating hydroelectric plants for power for economic growth, and using the recreational potential of its reservoirs. The TVA has developed more than a hundred state, county and municipal parks, national wildlife refuges and numerous state fish and game wildlife management areas.

Located in western Kentucky and Tennessee and managed by the TVA, the 'Land Between the Lakes' (LBL), a sparsely populated region, was designated a National Recreation Area in 1963 by President Kennedy. His vision was to use LBL to demonstrate how 'an area with limited timber, agricultural and industrial resources can be converted into a recreation asset that will stimulate economic growth in the region'. Today LBL encompasses, between two dammed lakes, 170 000 acres (69 000 ha or 690 km²) of rolling forested hills abundant with wildlife; more than 300 miles (185 km) of undeveloped shoreline; 200 miles (125 km) of trails; numerous lake access areas; campgrounds; and interpretive and educational facilities including the Home Place (an 1850 living history farm), the Nature Station (an environmental education centre) and the Golden Pond Planetarium. In 1994 LBL hosted close to 2.5 million visitors: 40 per cent local, 35 per cent regional (100–300 miles) and 25 per cent national.

In 1995, TVA presented five alternative use plans for LBL with a range of possible annual visitation levels, from an estimated 750 000 in a 'scaled down' LBL, to as many as 4 million in the most developed version (presented here), with lake-front property development, additional wildlife and historical attractions, more accommodation for overnight stay (6000 beds) and additional food and other visitor services.

Source: TVA (1995), LBL, what is the shape of our future?, Golden Pond, Kentucky

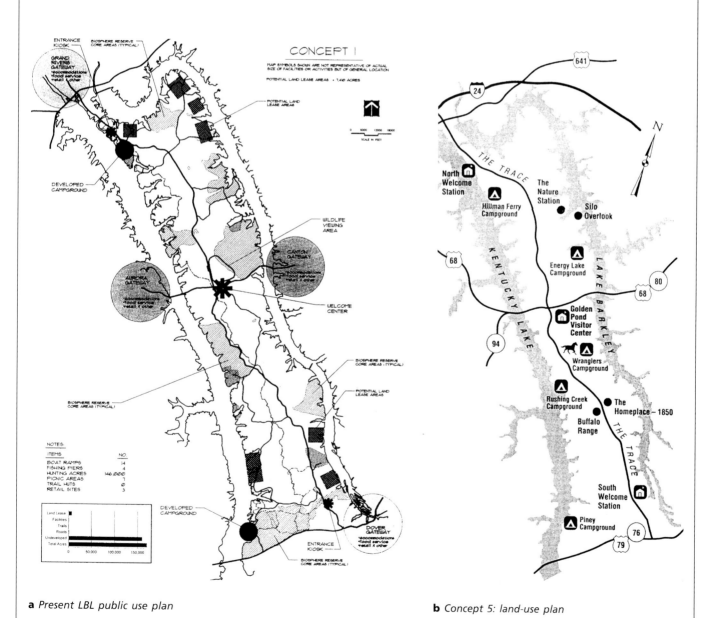

a *Present LBL public use plan*

b *Concept 5: land-use plan*

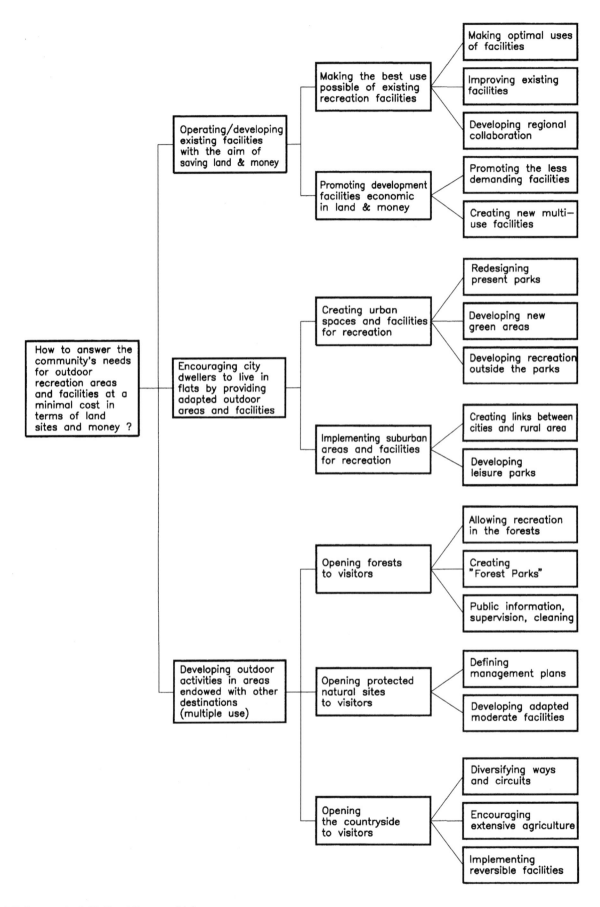

Figure 8.3 *Source: A. & M. Baud-Bovy, arch/planners*

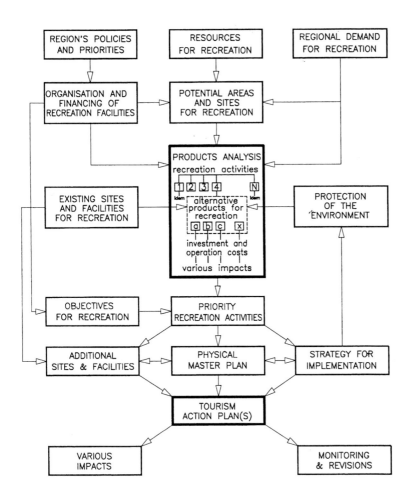

Figure 8.4 *PASOLP for recreation*

for leisure activities.[1] Usually, however, the high cost of urban land precludes such use and it is necessary to consider other approaches (as detailed in the graph in Fig. 8.3):

- making the best use of existing sport and recreation facilities (increasing their use, carrying capacity, range of activities, etc.) and developing new inexpensive facilities, 'the community use of leisure facilities provided by local education or other public authorities, but presently under- or unused, was frequently condemned. Some delegates asked for a legislative remedy whereby public providers would be required to offer their facilities for public use unless the cost of conversion or management was demonstrably disproportionate to the benefits or involved matters of safety' (Sports Council 1983);
- developing parks and other pedestrian zones in the inner city and its suburban area (see 9.3);
- developing multiple uses for land, including dual recreational use of farmland, forestry, reservoirs, etc., in each case with suitable safeguards.

8.5.2 Extent, methodology and content of a master plan for recreation

A regional master plan (structure plan) for outdoor recreation includes parks, open spaces and green networks as integral elements and is always related to environmental protection. It may be either:

- a section of an overall regional development plan (besides transportation, housing, economic development, etc.), or
- a specific document, as most regional 'Green Plans'.

This must include the area around the town accessible to day visits and may include areas which attract regular weekend recreationists. Recreational areas vary with the size of the town, extending up to 100 km and more around large cities. Regional planning is able to take an overview of urban needs and resources to provide for recreation even when this crosses municipal boundaries. For densely populated areas and conurbations, planning should cover the whole region.

Approaches. At local level (district, small town) recreational plans may be based on:

- standards for green areas or outdoor facilities per inhabitant (see 9.3.2), adapted to local conditions;
- catchment areas of the various categories of facilities (see 9.3.3): using mapping to show under-equipped areas;
- the most apparent deficiencies or imbalances between demand and supply: often favouring the organized groups and associations.

Many cities have established in recent years, or are planning, an urban network of parks, other open areas and greenways: the US and UK Green Plans, the French *Maillage Vert*, the Swedish *Grönplans*, etc.

At the scale of a whole region, for extensive structure plans, more comprehensive approaches are recommended. Originally developed for tourism planning, the PASOLP approach may be applied, with slight modifications, to recreation planning (see Fig. 8.4)

Main phases of a master plan for recreation

- *examination of the roles of the various regional authorities* in organizing and financing the implementation of recreation facilities, taking into account their individual objectives (see 9.1.1 and 9.1.2);
- *assessment of the regional demand for recreation* (see 8.2.1). Overall quantitative demand assessments are often lacking in local areas facing a huge latent demand with limited recreation resources. In this case, the regional plan aims to earmark outdoor recreation areas, the facility requirements being defined at a later stage of planning at a more local level;
- *inventory of resources and existing recreational products* (see 1.3.2), usually in conjunction with their environmental value and functions (air pollution control, flood control, aquifer preservation, ecological diversity) and a statement of the main deficiencies by planning units;
- *evaluation of alternative recreation products* (see 1.3.2) with programme standards, cost estimates per user and design criteria;
- *decision on priority recreation activities*, taking account of the overall demand, the main deficiencies, the resources available; and defining the characteristics (in terms of land use, environmental impact, investment or maintenance costs and social benefits) of the corresponding recreation products;
- *development plan* (in this chapter);
- *strategies for implementing, coordinating and financing the plan* (see 9.1);
- *protection of resources* (see 9.2), with environmental policies for limiting critical environmental damage or to improve endangered or contaminated areas;
- *impacts evaluation* (on public welfare, local economy, environment, etc.);
- *monitoring and continuous planning* (see 7.3.8 above): this is an important aspect and may involve the creation of an observatory for monitoring, possibly using satellite imagery and computerized mapping, to show the extent of use and evolution.
Main elements of most physical development plans:
- outdoor recreation areas in the city: parks, riverbanks, pedestrian areas (see 8.5.3 and 9.3);
- green belt with suburban parks and facilities (see 8.5.4);
- rural area outside the green belt with some other facilities (see 8.5.5);
- green corridors linking the centre of the city to the green belt and its facilities (see 8.5.6).

8.5.3 Outdoor recreation areas in the city

A regional master plan for recreation must first consider the recreational areas which are available or could be provided within a city. Urban parks and gardens provide immediate benefits to their neighbourhoods as evidenced by Central Park, New York, Regent's Park, London, Jardin du Luxembourg, Paris. Many other outdoor areas are also highly suitable for recreation such as lakesides, river banks, pedestrianized areas and networks of paths and trails, both within the city and extending out to link suburban parks and green areas (see 9.3.4–6).

The regional master plan should include proposals to balance the typically uneven distribution of green areas in less favoured districts:

- Metropolitan Paris: 10 m^2/inhabitant
- Central Paris: 3 m^2/inhabitant
- several Parisian districts: 1 m^2/inhabitant

The main strategies are outlined in 9.3.3, namely:

- opening to the public existing private or semi-public green areas;
- remodelling existing parks for current needs and uses;
- creating new parks on derelict land;
- improving access to suburban parks, river banks, etc.;
- developing pedestrian areas and other public spaces, e.g. pocket parks.

Quite often, the central city boundaries do not include land which could become outdoor recreation areas at a reasonable cost. The necessary green areas and other recreation facilities have to be implemented on the territory of neighbouring communities which are not necessarily interested in these developments and visitors. In such a case, regional master planning is vital.

8.5.4 The green belt

Olmsted's concept for the *Emerald Necklace of Parks* in Boston (USA) dates from 1883. In 1898, Eugen Fassbender's general regulatory plan for Vienna (Austria) proposed 'the exclusion of a 600-metre wide zone on the city periphery from any form of construction and its provision with vegetation' in order to serve 'as a high-quality air reservoir for the spreading metropolis and as a necessary place of recreation and amusement for millions of its inhabitants'.

Still today, green belts are an essential element of regional planning around major towns and cities. They form a peripheral area, with limited infrastructure, in which changes of use are restricted, thereby reducing land speculation and urbanization, and are instrumental in providing other benefits:

- restricting urban sprawl and creating towns and cities which have distinctive boundaries and a sense of identity;
- protecting 'green' natural surroundings, agriculture, forestry and the ecology of the region;
- providing opportunities for recreation in the countryside relatively near to urban communities – both in suburban parks and for more specific interests in sport (golf, fishing, sailing, etc.).

To reach these objectives requires appropriate zoning of agriculture, housing, industry, forestry, outdoor recreation, valuable ecological sites, sensitive areas with high landscape value, etc.

Following the establishment in 1944 of the London Green Belt, similar plans have been implemented in more recent years for Paris, Tokyo (Minra area), Portland (Oregon), San Francisco, Chicago, the New York metropolis and other major cities. However this concept equally applies to smaller cities and towns.

> The 'greenbelt' is largely a US planning device by which cohesive activity areas of various types are separated and buffered. Ideally, the green swaths are planned to form an interrelated nature preserve which follows the land forms and incorporates woodlands, streams, and the natural drainage ways. They provide not only separation, but birds and animals habitat, and 'breathing room' as well. Often there is sufficient area for agricultural lands, community gardens, many forms of recreation, and paths of interconnection.
>
> (Simonds 1994, p. 163)

To provide for these various needs, it is usually necessary to introduce a system of zoning. In England, where 'green belts' occupy 12 per cent of the land area, countryside management (Bucknall 1993) has been proposed to resolve potential problems between the interests of farming and those of visitors seeking recreation (Elson 1993).

The green belt provides opportunities for implementing **suburban recreation facilities** (see 5.7 to be attended:

- on a daily basis (after working hours) by the inhabitants of the neighbouring district(s);
- on a day-trip or weekend basis by the other inhabitants of the town.

The size of a green belt is related to the population of the town: the width of the ring varying from a few hundred metres to tens of kilometres. The convenient sites may be earmarked for future (even distant future) uses for recreation and to avoid to speculation on land values. It is usually possible to buy woods and forests at a low price (low yield).

8.5.5 The rural area

Recreation demands from large cities and conurbations are not confined to local areas. Townspeople on day trips, excursions or simply driving for pleasure, travel longer distances to the market towns, historic centres, quaint villages, forests, coast and countryside, often creating traffic congestion and excessive demands on the local resources.

Recreational provisions in these areas must take account of the needs of both local residents and visitors. At the same time, the recreational areas must be related to the scale and character of their surroundings with emphasis on the retention of natural features. Facilities should include screened car parks with public toilets, country parks along river banks, carefully sited picnic places, cafes with lawns and terraces, landscaping around monuments and the utilization of waste ground for recreational use.

The master plan should consider specific matters, such as:
- the protection of the landscape and of the environment (sensitive areas, classification, strict application of environmental regulations, protection of habitats, etc.);
- the possible creation of nature preserves (partly) accessible to visitors, or of regional nature parks (see 5.8.2);
- the organization of landscaped circuits and itineraries (pedestrian, horseback, bicycles, cars, etc.).

8.5.6 The greenways

> A greenway is a linear open space established along either a natural corridor, such as a riverfront, stream valley or ridgeline, or man-made overland feature such as abandoned railroad rights-of-way, canal, scenic road or other route. They may be located within urban and rural areas, and provide public access to the unique, scenic and natural lands and waters of North Carolina.
>
> (Coleman (1994), p. 5)

This definition may be extended to distinguish two main functions:

- *urban greenways* within town centres (see 9.3.7) which also link the suburbs and the suburban parks and recreational areas,

(continued p. 215)

Regional green plan for Ile-De-France (Paris region)

This recent Green Plan (IAURIF 1995) covers all scales of planning, from the town itself to the whole surrounding region. The main proposals may be summarized as follows:

The Urban Green
To create in central Paris (12–15 km around Notre-Dame – 60 000 ha, 6 million inhabitants):

- *new major parks (such as la Villette, Parc Citroën or Parc de Bercy);*
- *green ways of regional interest (along waterways, perimeters, etc);*
- *green promenades of local interest.*

The Green Belt
To create at the periphery of the conurbation (between the radii of 10 to 30 km around Notre-Dame – 300 000 ha – 5 million inhabitants – green, agricultural or wooded areas on 60 per cent of this territory):

- *protection and development of green and wooded areas;*
- *new public green areas (suburban parks, recreation and nature parks, allotment gardens, etc.);*
- *protected agriculture and landscape.*

The Rural Area (see 8.5.5)
To combine in this further remote area (900 000 inhabitants – 1.2 million inhabitants – mainly rural with several towns):

- *agricultural production;*
- *protection of valuable natural areas, forests, water resources, etc.;*
- *extraction of building material.*

The Green Valleys and Greenways
To facilitate the creation of attractive pedestrian, cycle and riding greenways and trails of regional or local interest:

- *along rivers and valleys;*
- *along or above new TGV-railways or other regional infrastructures;*
- *at a local level.*

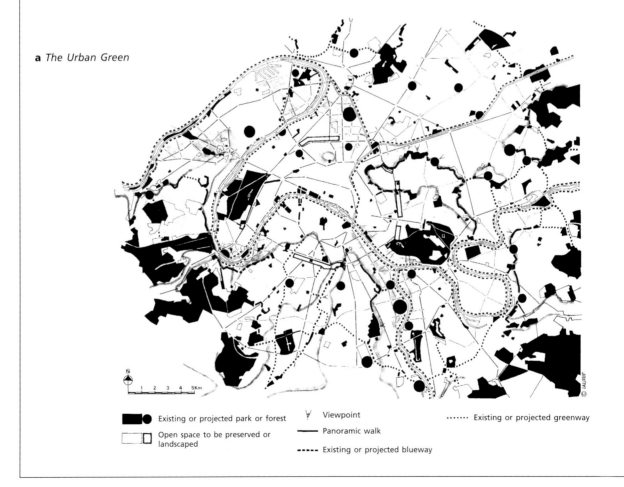

a *The Urban Green*

◼● Existing or projected park or forest   Ⱶ Viewpoint   ······· Existing or projected greenway

☐◻ Open space to be preserved or landscaped   —— Panoramic walk

- - - - - Existing or projected blueway

b *The Green Belt*

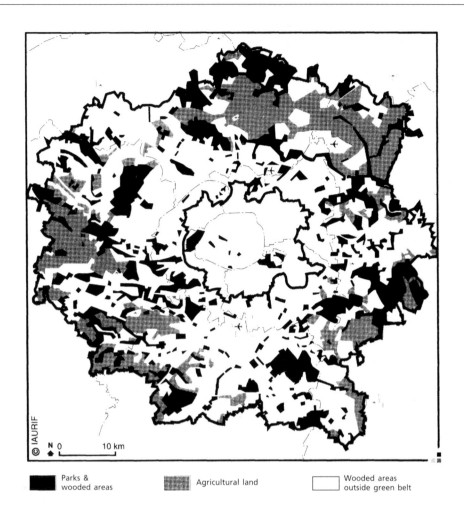

Parks &
wooded areas

Agricultural land

Wooded areas
outside green belt

Exterior border of green belt (=EB)
Existing park
Projected park

c *The Rural Belt and the Regional Parks*

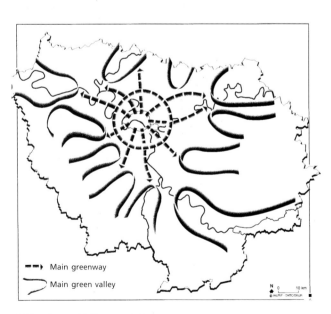

Main greenway
Main green valley

d *The Green Valleys and Greenways*

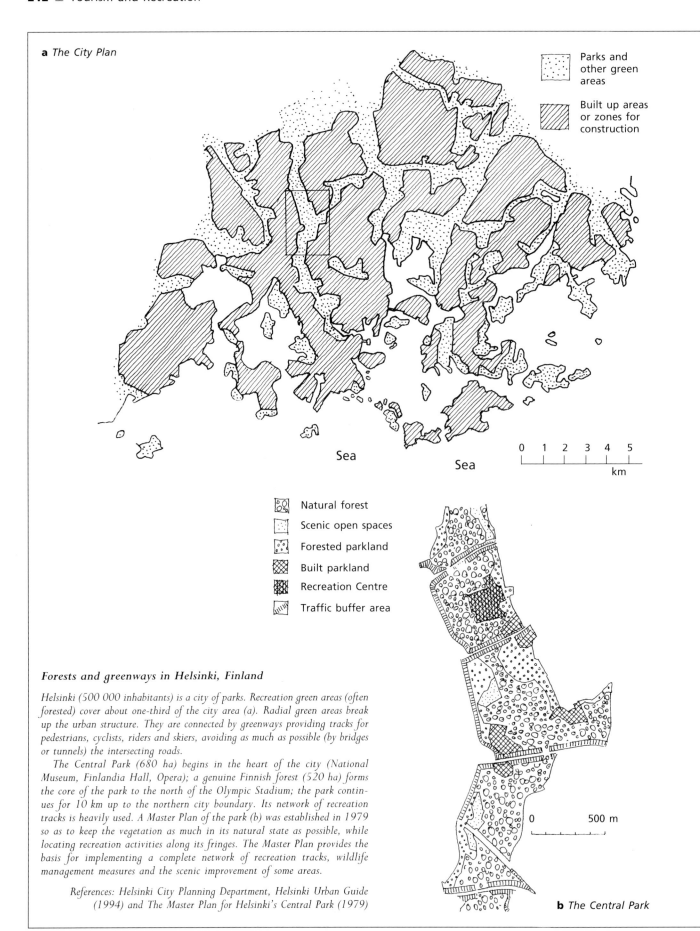

a *The City Plan*

Parks and
other green
areas

Built up areas
or zones for
construction

Sea   Sea

0 1 2 3 4 5
km

Natural forest

Scenic open spaces

Forested parkland

Built parkland

Recreation Centre

Traffic buffer area

Forests and greenways in Helsinki, Finland

Helsinki (500 000 inhabitants) is a city of parks. Recreation green areas (often forested) cover about one-third of the city area (a). Radial green areas break up the urban structure. They are connected by greenways providing tracks for pedestrians, cyclists, riders and skiers, avoiding as much as possible (by bridges or tunnels) the intersecting roads.

The Central Park (680 ha) begins in the heart of the city (National Museum, Finlandia Hall, Opera); a genuine Finnish forest (520 ha) forms the core of the park to the north of the Olympic Stadium; the park continues for 10 km up to the northern city boundary. Its network of recreation tracks is heavily used. A Master Plan of the park (b) was established in 1979 so as to keep the vegetation as much in its natural state as possible, while locating recreation activities along its fringes. The Master Plan provides the basis for implementing a complete network of recreation tracks, wildlife management measures and the scenic improvement of some areas.

References: Helsinki City Planning Department, Helsinki Urban Guide (1994) and The Master Plan for Helsinki's Central Park (1979)

0   500 m

b *The Central Park*

Paris Green Belt

The Plan Vert Régional d'Ile-de-France (Octobre 1995) defines a green belt as that area between the two radii of 10 and 30 km from the centre with the following zones:

- existing woods and forests;
- agricultural areas;
- declining agricultural areas (near urban zone) with special protection, to be turned into green areas if agriculture is no longer viable;
- urban parks (in built-up areas);
- leisure and nature parks (with sports and recreation facilities, such as golf courses, suburban parks, riding centres, etc.);
- unsightly areas (e.g. quarries, gravel, sand or gypsum pits) to be considered for environmental improvement.

The following actions are proposed:

- to reinforce the public forests by progressively integrating private woods and fields at their edges: usually by defining a sensitive area of natural value;
- to control private forests through the existing regulations;
- to enlarge the network of suburban parks and leisure complexes;
- to improve and utilize disused waste grounds, mineral workings, etc.;
- to open to the public (semi-private estates and parks;
- to facilitate the access of the neighbouring population to the suburban parks and leisure complexes;
- to redevelop allotment gardens;
- to avoid speculation on agricultural land and facilitate the creation of extended specific areas dedicated to garden produce, tree nurseries, etc.;
- to preserve agricultural land (buffer zone enclosures) where compromised by the pressure of urban development;
- to restore the use of certain fallow lands, sprawls, etc., encouraging dual use for production and farm visits;
- to acquire the most endangered agricultural land and to act elsewhere through regulatory measures and normal aids to agriculture;
- to improve the landscape along transit roads, at urban fringes, etc.

Source: IAURIF (1995), Plan Vert Régional d'Ile-de-France

Proposals for 2010

- Existing forest or green public space
- Projected green public space
- Potential green public space
- * Relaxation centre
- Existing facility with green care
- Private woods or gardens
- Agriculture

PUBLIC GREEN SPACE
- Project to be implemented

- Proposed acquisition of woods or creation of a forest park
- Proposed leisure zones (golf, riding, games)
AGRICULTURAL SPACE
- Safeguarded agricultural space
- Protection and improvement of rural hedge
- Urban zone

- Waterways and ponds

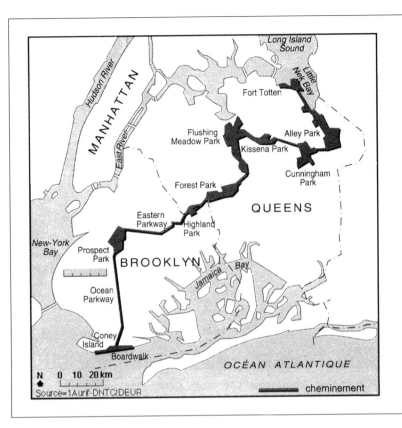

The Brooklyn/Queens Greenway, New York

This is a 40-mile (64 km) bicycle/pedestrian trail running from Coney Island to Long Island Sound through the two most populated boroughs of the most densely developed city of New York. It connects 13 parks, two botanic gardens, two environmental education centres, three museums, the New York Aquarium, National Tennis Center, Shea Stadium and numerous baseball, football fields and tennis facilities, as well as three lakes and a reservoir. The full spectrum of recreation opportunities in New York city is available to users of the Greenway. The idea was launched in 1987 by a small non-profit organization, the Neighborhood Open Spaces Coalition, and studied by Trowbrige Associates, landscape architects. Over 90 per cent of the Greenway was already in place in 1996, using linkages which connect outdoor resources and facilities along the trail. Proposals have been advanced to overcome the key obstacles along the route, in particular for sections which lack adapted traffic crossings.

Reference: IAURIF-DNTC/DEUR

ADMINISTRATIONS INVOLVED / GREENWAY OBJECTIVES	Parks	Recreation	Planning	Sanitary	Storms	Transports
1 Promote the strategic use of flood prone lands for an open-space corridor system.	●	○	●	●	●	○
2 Establish a linear park network, left primarily in its natural state.	●	●	●	●	●	●
3 Complement the existing and future park system through the introduction of a linear park network which will accommodate recreation desires which are now unmet.	●	●	●	○	○	○
4 Enhance private development by giving a common structural system to the elements of urban amenity.	●	●	●	○	○	○
5 Introduce a trail system which connects compatible land uses.	●	●	●	○	○	○
6 Buffer conflicting land uses.	●	○	●	●	●	○
7 Give alternative to automobile for short commuter trips by developing a safe passageway for bicycles and pedestrians.	●	●	●	○	●	●
8 Retain natural ecological functions in the urban environment.	●	○	●	●	○	●
9 Allow more effective planning for future urban growth.	○	○	●	○	○	○
10 Elevate the livability of urban environment.	●	●	●	○	○	○
11 Stimulate the more beneficial expenditure of public funds through multiple use of public property.	●	●	●	●	●	●

(Sewers spans Sanitary and Storms)

● *Directly involved*   ○ *Indirectly involved*

The Raleigh Greenway System, North Carolina, USA

A Report to the City Council on the benefits and methodology of establishing a Greenway System in Raleigh was presented in 1972 as his master's thesis by William L. Flournoy, now acknowledged as having produced the earliest comprehensive greenway system, describing how to implement such a system (using swamps and floodplain zoning, acquiring easements, taking advantage of fiscal aid) and its potential effects on city planning, conservation of ecological systems or provision of outdoor activities.

Raleigh Greenway objectives and their implementation (Flournoy 1972)

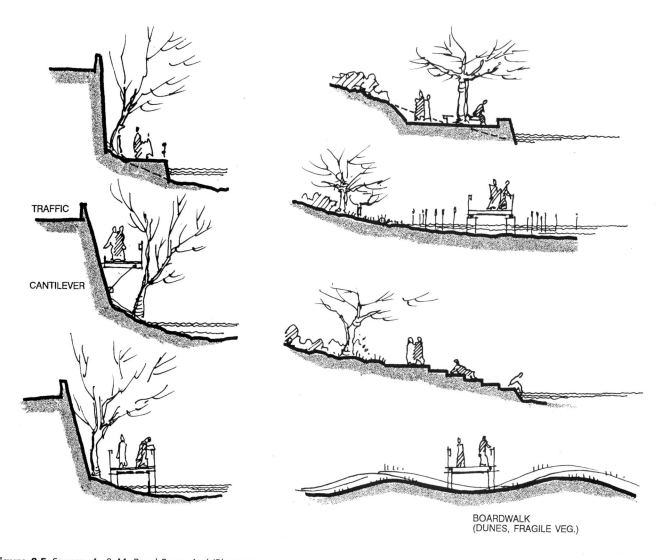

TRAFFIC

CANTILEVER

BOARDWALK
(DUNES, FRAGILE VEG.)

Figure 8.5 *Source: A. & M. Baud-Bovy, Arch/Planners*

- *hiking greenways:* rural paths, trails and routes which often extend over long distances across the countryside, mountains and coast (for example, the Pennine Way, UK).

Urban greenways should form networks, linking parks, schools, residential and commercial areas, and points of access to public transport, enabling pedestrians and cyclists to move through the town in attractive surroundings protected, as far as possible, from traffic and pollution. They may be reduced to a path, increased to a road or extended into a series of recreational areas forming a linear park. Linear parks are often framed around river valleys providing opportunities for both land- and water-based activities:

> ... linear open space has significantly more perimeter or edge than traditional consolidated parks. This edge may be used to buffer competing land uses and soften the urban image. Linear open space can connect traditional parks and other activity centres such a schools and shopping centres. They can also accommodate popular recreation activities, such as jogging, walking, bicycling, and canoeing which are linear activities [...]. When associated with streams [...] the open space allows flooding to occur without damage to buildings, or disruption of the local economy or individual lives. Environmentally, linear open space acts as a vegetated buffer along streams to protect water quality and fragile natural ecosystems such as wetlands. Finally, these areas function as wildlife corridors, allowing a great diversity of animals to travel through and survive within urban areas.

> (Flournoy 1989)

> The [...] weaknesses of an environmentally based linear park movement can be addressed as a single issue: structural leadership. It is not being provided by the government or private sectors in a manner that encourages the development of environmentally sound linear parks. No entity is planning for, or guiding resources to broadscale linear park system development. The educational programs necessary to support the movement are not universally available. Coordination among the numerous participants may not even know they are part of the movement. Clearly the linear parks movement has not been institutionalized, but it must become so if it is to reach its potential for environmental, social and cultural benefits.

> (Flournoy 1993)

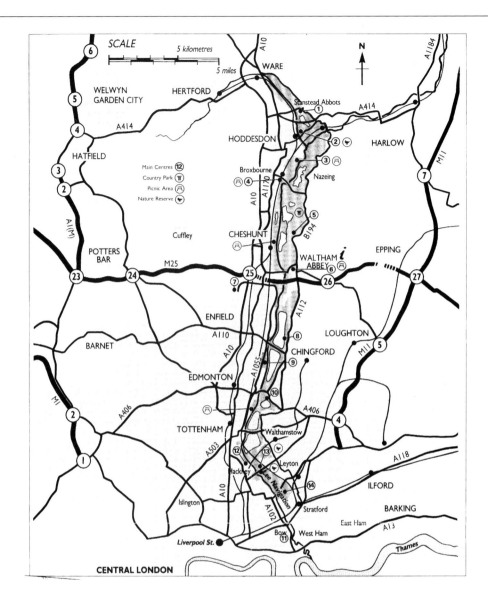

The Lee Valley Park, England

Established in 1967 by Act of Parliament, the Lee Valley Park Authority administers a linear park which covers 4000 ha along the Lee waterway from the Docklands in East London extending 30 km through the areas of 14 local authorities.

In addition to the river towpath, a dual use path for walkers and cyclists provides a 90 per cent traffic-free link between the green spaces and recreation facilities in the park. This will also form part of the London Walking Forum's 2000 km network of walks. Access to the park is provided by parallel rail and road networks, with train and bus services to the major centres. All facilities are designed to meet the needs of disabled people.

In addition to a country park and several nature reserves and picnic sites the main centres shown above are:

1 Marina
2 Historic house
3 Caravan park
4 Boat hire/chalet holidays/leisure pool
6 Waltham Abbey/market town/countryside centre
7 Historic gardens

8 Campsite
9 Leisure complex
10 Watersports centre
11 Historic mill
12 Marina
13 Riding centre/18-hole golf course
14 Campsite/cycle circuit/cyclo-cross and mountain bike trails

The park is supported by levies on 35 local authorities in the region plus local taxpayers. In 1995/6 this amounted to £16.4 million. Expenditure in operating the leisure facilities was £9.177 million compared with an income of £3.829 million. Other costs were expended in maintaining the countryside areas, properties, administration and other services, capital interest charges and repayments of loans.

Lee Valley Annual Report 1995/6

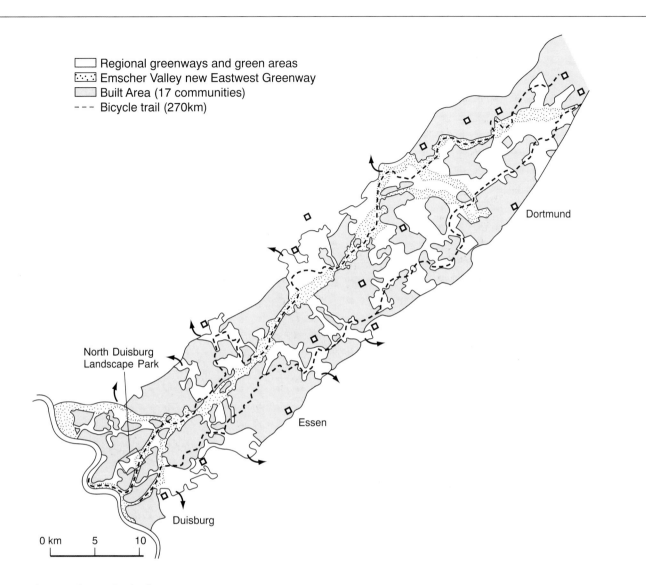

Regional greenways and green areas
Emscher Valley new Eastwest Greenway
Built Area (17 communities)
- - - Bicycle trail (270km)

Dortmund

North Duisburg
Landscape Park

Essen

Duisburg

0 km   5   10

The Emscher Landscape Park, Germany

The International Building Exhibition (IBE) Emscher Park is less concerned with architecture (as previous IBEs were) than with the ecological and urban renewal of the northern Ruhr district (about 2 million inhabitants), one of the most densely populated areas in Europe (1200 inhabitants/km². With the decline of the coal and steel industries it is an economically weakened region with a ravaged landscape. Widespread ecological renewal must precede any lasting economic renewal.

The idea of Emscher Park, extending over 17 urban communities (with major towns such as Duisburg, Essen, Dortmund, etc), was launched in 1988; 90 projects are presently being actively developed or realized in five key fields:

- *regenerating the Emscher River system (running throughout the region to the Rhine);*
- *creating attractive sites for the location of business and service industries;*
- *developing housing and an integrated urban district;*
- *creating new uses for industrial buildings, some of them with a high conservation value;*
- *creating the Emscher Landscape Park, the main unifying theme of the IBE: some 300 km² of land are to be protected, regenerated and linked together by new paths and bicycle trails.*

The seven north–south regional green corridors between the main agglomerations were first proposed in the 1920s. The idea was revived in the 1960s when the Siedlungsverband Ruhrkohlenbezirk (SVR) – now Kommunalverband Ruhrgebiet (KVR) – developed a comprehensive outdoor recreation plan with a network of paths and trails and a number of outdoor major recreation centres of several types. Taking up the earlier idea, the individual north–south corridors are being expanded and linked to a new east-west corridor to form a complete park system of European significance (Fig. 8.37a). Linking up the individual 'green stepping stones' to form a large strip of countryside is still (in 1997) the central task of the next few years. The implementation of the park is happening through a succession of individual projects developed by the local authorities and in some cases private companies or pressure groups. Finance is provided by the region and the communities, with regional aid programmes and structural development aid from the national government and the European Union.

Master planning and source: Kommunalverband Ruhrgebiet (KVR), Essen (see KVR 1996).

Greenway for Chattanooga, USA

Greenways are not considered for large cities or regions only: the goal here is to develop a greenway along the lower eight miles of a creek before it reaches a dam where the Tennessee Valley Authority has developed recreational facilities. The greenway will constitute the developed open spaces needed by the small city of Chattanooga (40 000 inhabitants); protect the stream corridor from flood hazards and urbanization; preserve woodland; protect wildlife habitat; provide opportunities for fishing and canoeing, a system of pedestrian and bicycle trails and several recreational facilities. The acquisition of the land is occurring primarily through the use of individually negotiated conservation easements.

Source: Hixson Chamber of Commerce (1989), North Chickamauga Creek Greenway Master Plan

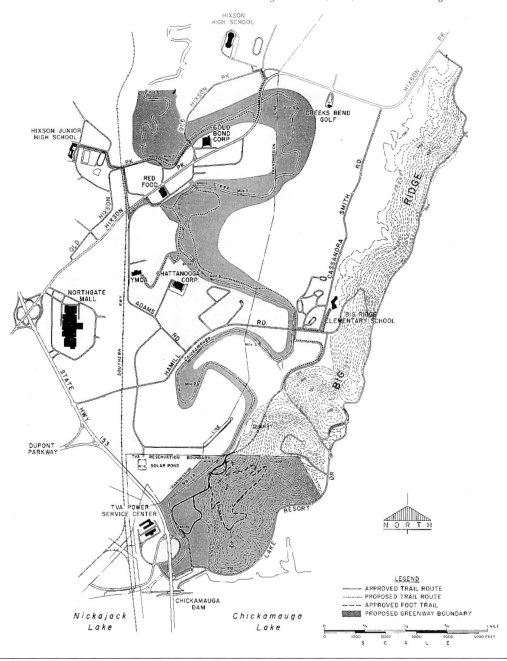

Other examples of park development from wasteland

1. Hedeland (Denmark) is a 1200 ha area of gravel pits being developed as a park, 30 km west of Copenhagen, with horseriding grounds, motorbikes tracks, ski-lifts (on 45 m high mounds) and a golf course.
2. Tommy Thomson Park (Toronto), on 360 ha of building material from the city's urban renewal projects: wilderness section, marina for 1200 boats, beaches and recreation areas, pedestrian paths and bicycle trails, etc.

9 Tourism/recreation master plans: implementation, protection of resources and outdoor recreation in the cities

This chapter contains more details and advice about some phases of the working out of a master plan: the necessary measures for implementation, and in particular for the protection of resources and the creation of areas for outdoor recreation in towns.

9.1 STRATEGY FOR IMPLEMENTATION

Tourism plans are essentially tools for development. Their implementation will depend on the responses from many public and private interests in this and other sectors of the economy. The study of these interests and the ways by which they can be activated, coordinated and controlled is usually an essential part of tourism planning at national or state level and often calls for new measures and rules (legislative, financial, administrative) to be introduced.

At regional and local level the situation is different. Regional planning may, in some countries, include responsibilities for establishing policies but is usually concerned only with applying the measures decided at higher levels.

Recreation planning involves other considerations. Whilst tourism is a major national economic sector, community recreational needs are determined largely at regional and municipal levels, albeit with state influence and financial assistance. The following sections distinguish those policies and procedures which are particularly relevant for tourism development from those which apply to recreation.

9.1.1 Involvement of other economic sectors

The **benefits of tourism** are maximized by supplying products and services from other sectors of the economy, thereby reducing the economic leakage (importation of goods and services), increasing indirect and induced employment and creating outlets for local products. This involves consultation with other government departments, agencies and representative bodies (trade associations, cooperatives) to identify opportunities and difficulties.

Potential difficulties may arise from inadequate quality, variety or reliability of supply and call for improvements in production, organization, marketing and quality control,

whether through government action (standards, licensing, incentives, training) or private initiatives (company investment, cooperative organization).

Sectors which can directly benefit from – and be highly dependent on – tourism include:

- construction and associated industries (buildings, equipment, furnishings, maintenance);
- agriculture, fishing and food processing;
- manufacture of souvenirs, sports equipment, specialized clothing etc.;
- transportation (national, local);
- retail and distributive trades (shops, restaurants, inns);
- entertainment and the arts (cinemas, theatres, art galleries, museums).

The **development of recreation** relies on many other socio-economic sectors, at national, regional and local levels (see 1.2.1):

- *educational authorities* may make available playgrounds and sports facilities after school hours and participate in sports and recreation programmes (e.g. visitor centres or accommodation facilities in a regional park, used for school visits during the week);
- *cultural institutions* may finance open air theatres and visitor centres;
- *sports councils and youth agencies* may finance facilities or provide support for youth organizations and non-profit-making associations;
- *forestry, agricultural and water undertakings* may allow use of their resources for recreation and cooperate in management of national parks;
- *environmental agencies*, such as the Countryside Commission (UK), may finance and administer measures to protect and improve the environment, facilitate public access to the countryside and recreational uses;
- *planning authorities* regulate land use and development, including action plans to improve damaged areas;
- *public works and utility undertakings* may provide recreational facilities directly (marinas, public parks) or as a consequence of other work (road diversion, reconversion of quarries, etc.);
- *real estate developers* may finance golf courses, parks, landscaping, etc. to improve the value of sites.

If they do not already exist, it is essential to organize national, regional and local **bodies to take responsibility for recreation** and conservation of resources. Examples include:

- the UK Countryside Commission, which approves and grant-aids proposals by local authorities for the creation of parks, picnic sites and other quiet recreation areas;
- the French Région Ile-de-France (around Paris) which determines the policies related to green areas, forests and greenways, acquires forest and green areas or participates in the acquisition and development of such areas by local communities, produces surveys and studies, makes agreements with the owners of private parks and gardens (financial incentives for opening to the public), etc.;
- government departments (Forestry, Natural Resources, Youth and Sports, Social Welfare, etc.) responsible for planning and implementing facilities, sometimes in conjunction with the local authorities.

9.1.2 The need for a coordinated strategy

Tourism development requires coordination between its numerous components. It will be immediately and severely affected by failings – even temporary – in any of them: lack of hotels or other necessary facilities; delays in completion of construction or infrastructure; insufficient trained manpower; unsuitable promotion; unresolved air transport or packaging arrangements, etc. The repercussions stemming from such deficiencies include:

- *adverse publicity abroad* including damage to relationships with tour operators and travel agents (legal obligations, financial losses);
- *transferred effects of bottlenecks* on other facilities, hotels and services (frustration, loss of goodwill, custom and confidence).

Recreational development is less sensitive to such delays and deficiencies since this is generally seen as a community service – often highly subsidized – rather than a commercial investment. Furthermore, the response to actual provision of recreation facilities is relatively rapid and direct.

Coordination of **tourism and recreation** with other sectors of the economy at national level may be attained through:

- overall economic and/or land-use development plans, including sector plans for tourism and recreation (see 1.2.1);
- permanent planning and day-to-day coordination through the offices of:
  - *national authority* (Ministry, Department of Tourism or specific agency);
  - *inter-professional council* (to provide links between public and various private sectors)
  - *a public agency* to implement state financed tourist or recreation projects.

Land-use plan for Algarve, Portugal

The 1990 Regional Land-use Plan for Algarve (on the south coast of Portugal and its main tourist destination) takes into consideration all aspects of regional development: tourism, urban development, industry (including fishing), agriculture, traffic and other infrastructures, environmental preservation, etc.

The Plan has been enforced through Regulations passed by the Council of Ministers (December 1990) aimed at providing a balanced socio-economic development, defining principles for a rational use of the territory (detailed zoning regulations) and promoting the protection of resources and the quality of life of the population.

The Regulations consider the following zoning:

- *urbanized zones, distinguishing between urban and tourism zones;*
- *zones of natural resources and environmental balance, distinguishing between priority zones (protection of the aquifer system, agriculture, protection of nature) and preferential zones (forested, agro-forested, attractive landscape, conservation of resources etc.).*

Reference: Comissão de Coordenação da Região do Algarve (1990), Plano Regional de Ordenamento do Território do Algarve, Faro (Portugal).

The extent of involvement of **regional and local authorities in tourism** planning will depend on the administrative structure:

- authorities with major powers of decision: consultation at the initial stage and again when the tourism sector plan is drafted and when steps for its implementation are considered;
- authorities with minor powers of decision: consultation at the formative stage to take account of views on local impacts, services, employment, infrastructure etc.

At **local level**, good coordination between public and private sectors is essential to define who does what in terms of local infrastructure or financing. Contractual procedures (public–private agreements defining common objectives, respective roles, responsibilities and consequences in case of non-fulfilment) provide useful and flexible tools to facilitate implementation.

The roles of **regional and local authorities in recreation** are vital. Agreements may be necessary between neighbouring municipalities and in densely populated areas a regional authority may be created, such as the Randstadt (The Netherlands), the Ruhrkohlenbezirk (Germany) or the Région d'Ile de France, (Paris).

Depending on the administrative structure, policies and financial resources of a country, one or more authorities may take responsibility for:

- undertaking and financing a regional recreation development plan;
- compiling a regional data bank;
- financing the acquisition of forests or other land;
- implementing regional facilities such as green areas, public tracks or others;
- helping or encouraging other administrations (e.g. Forests,

Agriculture, Youth and Sports, Environment, etc.) to implement facilities for outdoor recreation;

- establishing, where necessary, inter-municipal authorities for major projects;
- collaborating with the voluntary sector (clubs, associations, etc.), in particular for operating facilities provided by public bodies (towns or regions);
- informing and consulting the local population, etc.

At **local level** one (or two) independent 'leisure and recreation sections' should be created to take the responsibilities which are otherwise considered as minor concerns with the Education, Sports or Social Departments.

Examples of the roles of regional and local authorities

The **US President's Commission** 1987) proposed a Tool Box for Shaping Growth:

- *Identification of critical open spaces, unique habitats, and sensitive areas so that both private and public sectors can make informed decisions about where the growth should occur.*
- *Zoning and other regulations that limit developments in hazardous or environmentally sensitive areas.*
- *Acquisition of critical land and water which need complete protection, including purchase of development or use rights in lieu of full fee-simple acquisitions.*
- *Land trusts that can employ the full range of land protection tools, including acquisition of land, rights or easements, voluntary landowner agreements, monitoring and stewardship.*
- *Preferential taxation to owners of private farms and forest lands when they commit to keeping their lands free of development.*
- *Impact fees and mandatory dedication ordinances which require developers of land to provide for recreation and other facilities essentially linked to new residential, commercial or industrial developments.*
- *Transfers of development rights are a relatively new tool based on the concept of land ownership as a complex bundle of rights including personal use, physical access, minerals and the right to further development.*

In Norway, the **State Council for Open-Air Recreation** *(1957) is responsible for:*

- *development and progress of open-air activities in the whole country,*
- *collecting information,*
- *measures for promotion, co-ordination with counties and municipalities,*
- *elaboration of standards and operating instructions,*

in relation with the County or Municipal Open-Air Recreation Boards.

Fritid Stockholm, *the Recreation Office of Stockholm, is the organization concerned with leisure activities in the city:*

- *building, running and maintaining parks, sports grounds, fitness centres, skating rinks, swimming pools, marinas, dog parks, leisure centres, school playgrounds, etc.,*
- *renting out premises,*
- *organizing recreation, sport and cultural activities for all ages.*

Its budget (an important percentage of local taxes) allows for supporting (through grants, etc.) private associations, clubs and societies, besides its own activities.

Community involvement in recreation planning, may be facilitated by:

- publicity (press, reports) on benefits, goals and safeguards for development;
- public debates (exhibitions, information centre, publication of draft plans).

This involvement is particularly developed in the US towns for the creation of pocket parks and other green areas, in order to programme something corresponding to the real needs of the people concerned and to involve them in the maintenance (see 9.3.3).

9.1.3 Adapting financing techniques

Methods and sources for finance are indicated in Appendix A2 – Investment in tourism and recreation. As a rule the public sector and utility undertakings finance the infrastructure and municipal services whilst the private sector usually provides finance for revenue-earning facilities – often with state assistance. Aid of this kind, together with land-use control, is probably the most efficient method by which the state can induce private developers to follow the guidelines of the tourism sector plan.

The following **principles for aid** apply to both tourism and recreation:

- financial aid has to be integrated into both tourism planning (sharing the same objectives) and management of public finance (obtaining the maximum multiplier effect);
- there is a preference for incentive measures – such as loans and subsidies to reduce interest rates, or investment provisions – rather than direct public investment;
- fiscal exemptions or relief from specific taxes (e.g. customs on imported goods) may be quite effective;
- state aid may vary according to region (for example, in a new as opposed to existing tourist area) or according to categories of facilities (depending on their profitability and priority);
- some revenue-earning facilities may need to be fully financed by the public sector if low profitability forecasts deter private developers (for example, a first hotel in a new tourist region, uneconomical restoration of historic buildings, hostels for youths or social tourism, or recreation facilities with too short a season);
- even in these cases, the state should give managerial responsibility to the private sector, if sufficiently skilled and capable, by providing, for example, fully equipped facilities at a low or nominal rent;
- the allocation of state aid to a project should involve two successive stages:
  - appraisal of tourist interest (compliance with objectives of the development plan) to be dealt with by the tourism authorities,

– appraisal of the financial standing of the borrower, devolved to a financial authority, usually a public or semi-public bank specializing in tourism development.

A precise investment code summarizes these measures and offers guarantees to the **tourism developers** as far as fiscal matters, transfers of revenues and financial assistance from the state are involved.

Financing recreation facilities. Most recreation facilities are not profitable, being:

- free of charge (access to parks, trails or playgrounds);
- low-priced in order to benefit the local community (tickets to a swimming pool);
- limited by a short season, irregular occupancy, etc.

In some cases private companies may also invest in non-profit-making facilities, such as a company for its employees, a trade union for its members, or a large commercial trust supporting public amenities for promotion purposes. Usually, however, public funds are necessary at least as capital investment, the operation of the facilities being as much as possible handed over to:

- non-profit-making youth, sports or leisure regional or national associations;
- a local group of people interested in running a single facility (for example, a tennis club);
- a private enterprise, selected through tenders, private management being usually cheaper, to operate if not profit-generating.

In many cases the cost to local authorities in subsidizing the operation and maintenance of recreation facilities represents a significant part of their budget, whilst many sports facilities and playgrounds may be under-utilized and benefit only a small percentage of the population. Recreation monitoring and evaluation may help local authorities to make the best of their financial resources for outdoor recreation.

Trends. In a political climate of privatization and deregulation in many countries, and in a farming crisis, there is a trend toward recreation areas where visits are to be paid for: reservoirs with water sports, fishing ponds, golf courses, horse centres, theme parks, recreation centres, etc.

9.1.4 Implementing and controlling facilities

In market economy countries most **tourism facilities** are implemented by the private sector. For *large-scale developments* (resorts, holiday/recreational complexes), modified procedures may be adopted to ensure more direct and effective control.

- The responsible authority controlling the land may draw up plans and specifications for developing the area and subsequently invite bids from one or more nominated developers.

- The authority may participate in a joint stock company with public, semi-public and private investors.
- A specialized single or multi-purpose organization may be created to undertake the development.

Individual facilities, whether in resorts or isolated sites, must also satisfy operational criteria:

- the building plot (not only its geographic location) must be favourable for the purpose;
- the architecture must satisfy the needs of the clientele (facilities, attraction) and the operators (efficiency, profitability) as well as any planning restrictions.

Standards of individual facilities will depend not only on the initial market planning and investment criteria but on the quality of management, adequacy of skilled operational staff and continual maintenance. The tourism sector plans should provide a framework of standards as a guide.

Where a system of tourism standards does not exist, their introduction will involve three main areas of administration:

- *classification:* comprehensive lists of detailed requirements for accommodation, food services, entertainment and recreation;
- *verification:* periodic examination to ensure continued compliance with original standards;
- *supervision:* continuous monitoring by qualified inspectors, the customers (through efficient channels for complaint) and tour operators.

Controls must be supported by effective means of enforcement including, in the case of non-compliance, sanctions and other coercive measures (reduction in grading and in authorized tariffs etc.).

Standards for outdoor recreation. Standards for sports facilities are laid down by the relevant sports federations at national or international levels, giving precise details for dimensions and other requirements. More general guidelines have been laid down for children's playgrounds, parks and urban green areas but these and other recreational requirements vary widely depending on local situations and needs.

9.1.5 Training tourism manpower

In countries with a developing or expanding tourism industry the lack of trained manpower is one of the main difficulties experienced. As a summary, the overall policy for tourism planning should determine:

- *training objectives:* numbers of jobs to be created by development phases; by professions (hotel and food service staff, guides, recreation and supervisors) and by hierarchical levels (managerial, supervisory, craft);
- *concepts for vocational training:* including training of teaching staff and instructors (priority); curricula, practical

instruction, programmes of study, standards, monitoring, fees and costs/trainee;

- *characteristics and location of training schools:* scale (student numbers, size and range of classes); locations (with hotels providing practical experiences), teaching and laboratory facilities, financing costs.

On a broader scale, larger programmes of education are often launched particularly in developing regions or centrally-planned countries to prepare the local population as a whole for contact with foreign tourists.

9.1.6 Transportation

Reasonably priced access to the country (in relation to its attractions) is a prerequisite to any tourist development. Access may be by road or rail in countries and regions not too remote from the main tourist generating areas.

Ferry links, including car transportation on short sea routes, are also crucial in intra-continental travel and the development of offshore islands and isolated peninsulars. Depending on distance, traffic and conditions, transport may be by ship or hydrofoil and promoted as part of the holiday experiences.

A system of vocational training

The International Labour Organization (ILO) has developed over the years the following system of vocational training known as Modules for Employable Skills. These define the levels of skill required for various occupations and the 'modular tasks' involved in each aspect of the operation, broken down into 'steps of work'.

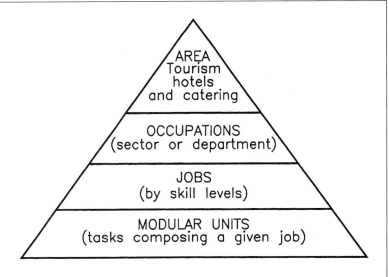

A system of vocational training. Source: International Labour Office, Geneva

Department	**Skill levels**				
	I Managers	II Middle management	III Supervisors	IV Skilled workers	V Unskilled workers
Administration	Manager	Chief Accountant	Storekeeper	Clerk	—
Front office	—	Front Office Manager	Head Receptionist	Receptionist	Porter
Housekeeping	—	Head Housekeeper	Laundry Supervisor	Housemaid	Cleaner
Food and Beverage	—	Restaurant Supervisor	Headwaiter	Waiter	—
	—	Bar Supervisor	Barman	Bar waiter	
Kitchen	—	Chef	—	Cook	Dishwasher
Maintenance, etc.	—	—	—	Plumber Electrician	—

Example of a 'Modular Unit'
(tasks composing a job):
Front office:
1 Preparing for guests' arrival
2 Dealing with enquiries
3 Giving information, etc.

Example of 'steps of work':
1. Preparing for guests' arrival:
(a) checking correspondence
(b) sorting it by alphabetical order
(c) preparing rooming lists
(d) adjusting for unconfirmed bookings
(e) preparing registration forms, etc.

Cruising is in a different category since the cruise-liners and the facilities they offer are in themselves the main tourist products. Nonetheless, ports of call on the primary cruise circuits benefit from the derived tourist markets for goods, entertainment and services.

When destinations are more distant from the main originating countries **air transport** and its cost become key factors in competitive tourist development. Reductions in scheduled airfares are made possible by the interaction of:

- chartered flights or non-scheduled flights organized by tour operators;
- IT (inclusive tours) on scheduled airlines with reduced fares for small groups;
- liberalization of air service agreements and free market competition.

A liberal policy towards cheap group travel is essential for large-scale tourism.

Chartered flights have to be operated as a regular chain: the aircraft which brings new tourists must take back those who arrived one or two weeks earlier to ensure high payload factors. This characteristic may have repercussions on the design of airport facilities, the demands on local transportation, reception and catering services, the organization of tour circuits and capacities of hotels.

Aircraft capacities and flight patterns determine important thresholds in developing tourism. Many of the restrictions on scheduled traffic do not apply to chartered flights which may use any international airport: see appendix A4 – Tourism transportation, recent developments and trends.

The time-distance from the destination airport to the holiday resort is a critical element in tourism planning. As a rule tourist groups will not accept more than one or two hours of coach transfer to the resort. Air transfer by smaller aircraft using short runways near a resort is generally too expensive to make a competitive product. Hence a new airport will set a new threshold in tourism development and open up a new destination.

Within a tourist country or region an organized reliable transport system by air, train, bus, taxis and/or rented cars is important in providing a wider distribution of tourist interests and revenue and in extending the scope of employment in tourism over a wider catchment area.

Transport is also responsible for many of the problems in planning: the congestion on roads leading to popular resorts and local beauty spots, on restricted local roads in mountains and valleys, and around historic cities and towns, is often the result of tourist and excursionist traffic. The use of private cars may be discouraged by the development of group excursions:

- by lake steamer, river or canal boat;
- by train – with bicycles available at the destination;
- by coach – for sightseeing and to attend events;
- by bus – to recreation areas and town centres.

Some alternative forms of transport should also be considered where access to a destination is difficult (narrow, dangerous,

roads etc.) and local parking restricted. This may include novel solutions which are, in themselves, a tourist attraction, adding to the interest and image. For example:

- shuttle service bus, electric truck
- mono-rail, overhead cable car
- track-rail, cog-rail and other forms of train system with electric, diesel or steam engine (restored or reproduced)

In these cases, convenient parking must be provided near the point of embarkation.

Public transport and recreation. It is important for community recreation areas to be served by public transport in order to minimize the use of private cars (traffic, air pollution), and to ensure facilities are accessible to all people in the area.

Outdoor recreation facilities must be located:

- as near as possible to the main areas generating demand (including pedestrian/bicycle linkages with parks and green areas);
- with public transport to suburban parks, leisure centres and places for walking in the countryside (including, where practical, arrangements for transporting or renting bicycles).

9.1.7 Organizing and promoting tourism and recreation products

Implementation of planning proposals is mainly concerned with making available and marketing suitable tourist products. This involves organization between the tourist authorities, the tour operators, the transport agencies and other sectors of the tourism industry (hoteliers, travel agents, etc.): the engagement of many suppliers to provide specific tourist services and facilities for a definite period, in a definite quantity at a definite price. Competitiveness stems from the principle of selling more at a reduced price, cutting down margins by increasing turnover and guaranteeing high rates of occupancy.

Together with the implementation of products, it is necessary to define **sales policies**, to encourage sales campaigns and establish a reliable central service of information distribution and booking. Whilst facilities and services may be sold direct (particularly to domestic and business travellers), promotion activities generally call for:

Marketing requirements	Examples
Large-scale resources to finance marketing and reservation systems	Chain hotels, franchises, airlines
Intermediaries to organize and facilitate arrangements	Tour organizers and operators, travel agents
Cooperation to extend promotion by collective representation	Tourist convention bureau, referral and marketing agencies

The main objectives of **advertising** are:

- to make the tourist products known;
- to create a favourable image of the country or region, or
- to correct mistaken impressions

Efforts have to be concentrated on the main markets (classified by segment), countries selected for the main promotional effort, and countries in which interest has to be built up progressively. Differential levels and stages of promotional information and appropriate media must be selected for the various audiences targeted:

- *tourist groups* identified by age, income, profession, socio-economic class, specific interests, business needs, organizations etc.;
- *intermediaries* such as tour operators, travel agents, journalists, guide compilers.

The continuity, homogeneity and regularity of messages conveyed through advertising are important and campaigns must be strictly scheduled, coordinated, carried out by specialists and the results monitored.

Promotion of recreational products. Details of the diverse range of opportunities for recreation should be made known by:

- information in the local press, TV, radio, on activities and events;
- published maps, leaflets and guides promoting trails of discovery;
- guided tours and excursions;
- open-air training and orientation courses, achievement grades, etc.;
- school educational trips, invited family days, festivals and events.

9.1.8 Land control for tourism and recreation development

A physical plan may be self-defeating: by indicating the areas and sites best suited for development it may induce:

- speculation in land values making implementation impractical;
- division and parcelling of land so that major coordinated developments cannot be effected;
- changes in the use and character of valuable sites intended for conservation as part of the tourism resource.

The **intervention of state or region** may take several forms:

- *Purchase of land*. Costs are dependent on the scale of development and on how far ahead this is envisaged. The main hurdle is often in setting up the purchasing agency.
- *Restrictions on building rights*. Where tourism or recreational facilities are considered, but not in the near future, large areas may be designated for agricultural use or light environmental conservation with virtually no building rights.

Subsequent reclassification into zones of development extends this control by attaching conditions.

- *Control over technical infrastructure*. Provision of connecting infrastructure financed by a public authority may be limited to regulated developments.
- *Regulation and inducement*. Coercive administration and planning regulations may be applied, balanced by the granting of financial loans and/or subsidies for approved projects.

The first approach is most effective, the second and third are practices at minimum cost whilst the last is recommended where development is imminent.

Examples of state or regional intervention

In the development of **Languedoc-Roussillon** (France), the initial, amicable and virtually secret purchase of 1500 ha (3700 acres) of land in six strategic points fixed the base marketing price for all subsequent purchases.

The '*Verein zur Sicherstellung überörtlicher Erholungsgebiete in den Landkreisen um München*' – Association for Safeguarding Recreation Areas around Munich – was created in 1966 by the city of Munich and surrounding districts including 50 municipalities around the town and funded by contributions related to the size of their populations (but higher for cities than rural communities). The Association acquires sites (mostly around lakes and forests) and implements facilities (bathing places, light yachting, trails, rest and picnic meadows).

Created in 1976, the '*Agence des Espaces Verts de la Région Parisienne*' – Green Areas Agency for the Paris Region – is funded by the Regional Council. It develops a regional policy, acquires and makes available for the public forests and other green areas, subsidizes local communities developing natural preserves, rivers banks, other trails, etc.

The **National Conference on Recreation and the American City**, co-sponsored by the President's Commission on the American Outdoors and the US Conference of Mayors, in Baltimore in May 1986, concluded:

- *Stable sources of funding for development, renovation and acquisition of remaining open space are critical to most communities. Participants indicated strongly that state and federal governments should have a continuing role as stimulator of local investments.*
- *Better planning and citizen involvement is essential to integrate recreation into the overall urban fabric of economic development, housing, historic preservation, health, transportation, and related concerns.*
- *Stronger inter-agency and public–private partnerships are also critical for the survival of urban recreation systems. Coordination of programs between school and recreation agencies was the most frequently cited example, but better linkages to state and federal conservation and development programs are also a major concern.*
- *Joint efforts with neighborhood residents, nonprofit service agencies and environmental groups are needed to involve citizens in direct stewardship of their parks and recreation programs.*
- *To increase partnership with corporate America, public officials must also increase their understanding about how private investment can help them reach their open space and recreation goals.*
- *Recreation managers must continually adapt to the needs of changing populations to ensure provision of services to the many special people concentrated in cities.*

Regulation may be applied by using the framework of existing town and country planning legislation (green areas, forests, environmental protection, etc.). Where such powers do not exist new legislation must be introduced ahead of development schemes.

Regulation of areas allocated to tourism or recreation is useful for the few areas earmarked for major facilities (new resorts, marinas, recreation parks, etc.). In these areas, regulations must be applied to:

- ensure priority is given to tourism or recreation requirements (although not exclusive of conservation or other activities);
- provide strict environmental control in its broadest sense (extending to all characteristic features);
- extend if possible and useful the area to include land necessary for green belts, forests, nature reserves around the future tourist or recreation centre;
- guarantee the possibility (through compulsory acquisition if necessary) of acquiring all land needed to create an integrated resort or recreation centre of high standard.

In the case of a large area exceeding the dimension of the site convenient for the implementation of a resort or recreation centre, it is recommended that an integrated area development plan be prepared showing boundaries for extending towns and villages, zoning of various uses, location of major tourist facilities (harbours, beaches), boundaries of future resorts, location of technical infrastructures, etc.

9.2 PROTECTION OF RESOURCES

Conservation of resources is an integral part of planning to safeguard the quality and sustainability of tourism. The following sections consider how to classify and protect resources and, where appropriate, to improve their value. Detailed planning procedures are summarized in Chapter 6.

Tourism and recreation development can exert both detrimental and beneficial influences on the environment. The negative impacts are well documented (see 1.4.1) but visitors can also stimulate interest in and an appreciation of the value of the environment leading to measures for its protection, management and enforcement. The economic advantages of tourism can justify and help to finance the enhancement of resources, restoration of historic cultural assets, control and limitations over pollution (air, groundwater, sea, lakes and rivers, waste disposal) and other environmental improvements which also benefit the local communities.

9.2.1 Nature parks

The tourism or recreational master plan may propose the classification of important natural areas as nature parks. Such a classification must be preceded by a detailed ecological and economic analysis of the area, preparation of plans for conservation and, if necessary, the introduction of enabling legislation.

The terminology differs from country to country and the following definitions are proposed for clarification:

- **Natural sanctuaries** – or scientific reserves, or strict nature reserves, or total preserve areas etc. – are areas of total preservation with no access for visitors except scientists. They are created on totally virgin, publicly-owned land or forest. Their essential objectives are the conservation of unique sites and ecosystems, scientific research, protection of threatened species. One (or more) natural sanctuary is often included in a national or even regional park.
- **National parks** (see 5.8.1), including islands and marine parks, wildlife preserves, etc. are vast virgin, or almost virgin, areas providing various interesting natural features or ecosystems (vegetation, wildlife, lakes, rock formations etc.).

To conserve the scenery and the natural historic objects and the wildlife therein and to provide for the enjoyment of the same in such manner and by such means as will leave them unimpaired for the enjoyment of future generations.

(Statement of National Park Purpose, US Park Service Bill, 1916)

- **Regional parks** (see 5.8.2) are generally of smaller acreage and under regional, municipal or joint control rather than that of the state. The parks safeguard an attractive landscape from industrialization and urbanization near to important population centres and generally offer numerous facilities to their visitors: educational and cultural but also strictly for recreation or relaxation.
- **Natural monuments** are isolated natural attractions (lake, waterfall, curious rock formation, volcano etc.) preserved with their immediate surroundings. In principle these have no facilities except trails, viewing places etc. Some 'monuments' may have a linear extension such as featured rivers, canals, historic trails (Indian or trappers' trails in Canada) etc.

For information on the planning of a natural park and the facilities to be provided, see 5.8.

9.2.2 'Sensitive areas' of environmental control

Many regions don't offer exceptional or unique natural resources. They are unsuitable for major tourist development and usually support other economic activities such as farming and forestry. Nevertheless, these regions often contain interesting features, attractive landscapes and examples of traditional lifestyles. They are often crossed by tourist routes to destinations, or excursion and sightseeing routes, and require some measure of protection to maintain the quality of the environment whilst accepting the needs of other users.

Such regions should be defined as regions of *environmental and tourist interest* – similar to the *'protected landscapes'* of the

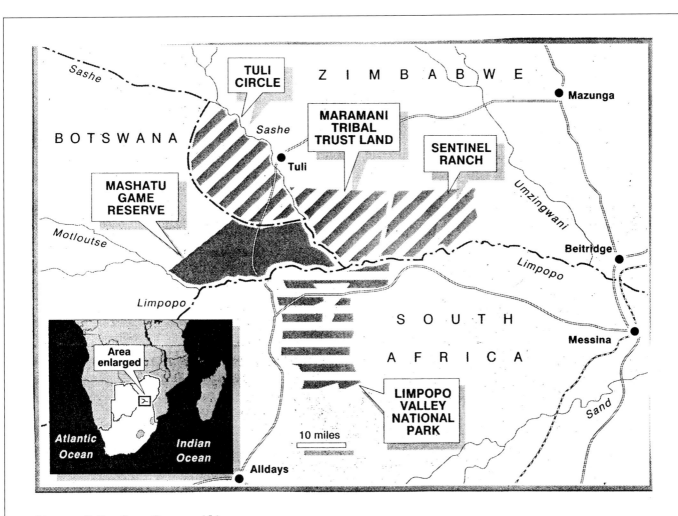

Limpopo Valley Game Reserve, Africa

This vast new transfrontier game park is the latest and one of the largest to be created in Africa. Based on the river Limpopo, it extends over 4093 sq km (1581 square miles) and combines the Mashutu and Tuli Game Reserves – private and state owned – in Botswana, the Maramani Tribal Trust land which, at present is only capable of supporting subsistence agriculture, and the Sentinel Ranch in Zimbabwe and the Limpopo Valley National Park in South Africa created by De Beers Consolidated Mines. The combined areas offer big game watching, spectacular scenery and South Africa's most important archaeological site in Mapungubwe.

Source: 'Travel', The Times 3 August 1990

World Conservation Union (IUCN) – in order to apply conditional controls, through relevant planning legislation (2.1.5). Measures for environmental control may include:

- maintenance of traditional agricultural husbandry, forestry and stockrearing (with incentives and assistance);
- preservation of woodlands and trees for amenity and recreation (preservation orders, planting schedules);
- conservation of historic buildings, characteristics of villages and farmsteads (listing of buildings, creation of conservation areas);
- definition and adaptation of boundaries limiting the extension of existing urban areas (including 'green belt' surroundings to large conurbations and resorts);
- specific measures to protect areas of outstanding natural beauty and vulnerable flora and fauna;

- restrictions on advertisements, signs, overhead cables, unsightly fences;
- consideration of aesthetic criteria in development proposals; adapting design and landscaping of roads and parking.

As a rule, the tourist interest, although considered, does not take precedence over conservation needs or developments of social and economic importance.

The size of environmentally sensitive areas varies widely, being extensive in many lightly inhabited areas (such as forests, moors, pastures, dunes, fjords, savannas and swamps). Environmental protection may also apply over the whole region, such as around all lakes and river banks and to zones of the coast.

Cariboo-Chilcotin Land-use Plan, British Columbia

This region, located in the south-central part of British Columbia (Canada) and dominated by high mountains, is endowed with extensive forest of economic value. The main objectives of the plan are:

- *protection of resources, doubling the area of the parks;*
- *greater security for industry and workers;*
- *promotion of tourism growth.*

Measures for implementation included the establishment of a Regional Resource Board, educational centres, grazing enhancement fund and reforestation. The plan is of interest for tourism/recreation planning in the combination of conservation and socio-economic development, and the characteristics of the different zones, described below:

- ***Enhanced Resource Development Zone*** *(40 per cent of region): land with high intensity of usage where economic benefits and jobs will be increased through intensive resource management and development in all fields: (forestry, mining, cattle grazing, tourism, agriculture, wild/agro-forestry, fishing, trapping, hunting); Government aids for intensive reforestation and other developments.*
- ***Integrated Resource Management Zone*** *(14 per cent): sustained integrated resource use, but local conditions do not warrant enhancement activities; management objectives are social plus environmental plus economic.*
- ***Special Resource Development Zone*** *(26 per cent): area with low intensity of usage, recognizing the sensitive nature of certain lands outside protected areas, with measured resource development activities; full access to mining, agriculture, tourism, wildcraft, agro-forestry, fishing, wildlife and recreation.*
- ***Protected Areas*** *(12 per cent): set aside to protect the province's diverse natural and cultural heritage and recreational values; inalienable; industrial extraction, mining, logging, hydro dams, oil or gas development are not allowed in protected areas.*

The protected areas are divided into five categories presented in the table below with their objectives and management guidelines.

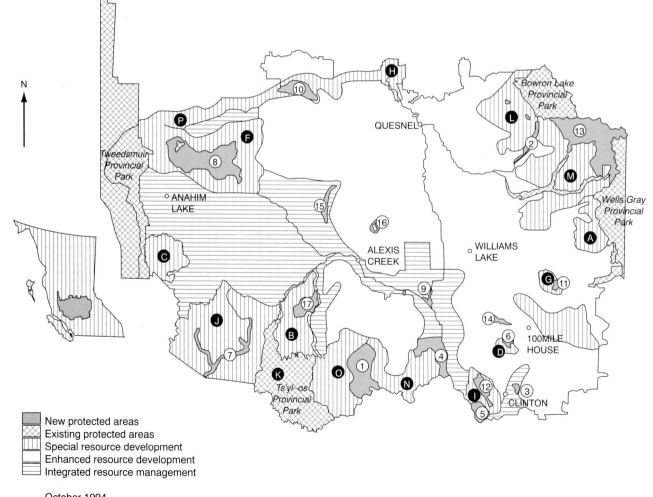

New protected areas
Existing protected areas
Special resource development
Enhanced resource development
Integrated resource management

October 1994

The Cariboo-Chilcotin Land–use Plan

9.2.3 Planning nature parks and sensitive areas

The procedure is similar to that proposed for regional planning (see 8.5.2) with priority given to the protection of resources. The phases are then as follows:

- *Assessment of the present situation:*
  - park's resources and capacity, existing infrastructures
  - possible conflicts (e.g. between conservation, forestry, hunting, recreation, etc.)
  - regional survey
  - market survey (existing and potential)
  - socio-economic local conditions
  - planning objectives and policies
- *Consideration of alternative products*, testing desirable/acceptable level of tourism/recreation activities in the park according to alternative privileged objectives:
  - conserving natural resources and bio-diversity
  - creating employment opportunities through sustainable development in local communities

- developing environmental education amongst tourists/recreationists
- *Selection of the most appropriate products*, i.e. the desirable number and activities of visitors in the park's region; usually, a set of workshops – with representatives of conservation, tourism and recreation sector, local communities and other key partners – will highlight a balance between the many objectives mentioned above and define agreed conservation/use standards
- *Elaboration of a master plan*, with an evaluation of its impact, the strategy for its implementation, the creation of a monitoring system (see 7.3.8) with visitors statistics and surveys.

Specific requirements in planning nature parks have been identified by the Ecotourism Society (Lindberg and Hawkins 1993, FNNPE 1993), including:

- organizing an ecotourism committee for the park (members of the workshop mentioned above);
- building visitor facilities (e.g. an interpretative centre), trails (see 4.3. etc.);

Cariboo-Chilcotin categories of protected areas:

Category	Objectives	Management guidelines
Strict preservation *Outstanding ecosystems, features, fauna, flora, etc. Normally free of human intervention. Highest degree of protection. May appear as a separate zone within another category*	*Protection to ensure perpetuation of genetic material and natural ecological units. Providing opportunities in improving and understanding of natural process*	*Scientific research/environmental monitoring. Public use (where permitted) limited to education and nature appreciation activities (nature study, hiking). Natural process (fire, diseases, etc.) allowed to continue unimpeded. Not allowed: activities mentioned in text, or roads, hunting, fishing, grazing*
Wilderness *Large areas of natural character unaffected by human influences. Opportunities for solitude and personal interaction with nature. Travel within the area by non-mechanized means*	*Protection of large representative ecosystems, natural/scenic areas for scientific, educational and recreational uses. Travel/camping opportunities for unstructured exploration to the extent compatible with preservation*	*Recreational uses: non motorized, low intensity dispersed recreation (backpacking, trail riding, canoeing. Fishing (sometimes hunting) permitted. Minimal facilities. Natural process allowed to continue unimpeded. Not allowed: activities mentioned in text, or roads, commercial fishing, grazing*
Heritage areas and natural/cultural sites *Generally small, with little or no present human activity, of outstanding natural, historical, archaeological, cultural or spiritual significance*	*Protection and opportunities for education. Stewardship with native peoples and continued traditional cultural uses*	*Facilities limited to those needed for education, interpretation, protection. Fishing (sometimes hunting) permitted. Direct intervention in natural process may occur for protecting the area. Not allowed: activities mentioned in text*
Natural environment-based outdoor recreation sites *Protected significant/unique natural ecosystem; landscape for education and recreational enjoyment. Recreation opportunities of direct interaction with the natural environment. May vary substantially in size*	*Protection. Variety of recreation opportunities and services. Full range of interpretive and educational programmes. Unstructured individual exploration to the extent compatible with preservation.*	*Potential permissible uses (may be restricted): auto-accessible camp ground and day use areas, (powered boating, hiking, trail riding, skiing, snowmobiling, aircraft landing, shelters, cabins and lodges, corrals. Fishing (sometimes hunting) permitted. Natural processes unimpeded. Not allowed: activities mentioned in text*
Intensive recreation and tourism sites *Generally small. Natural surrounding providing variety of outdoor recreation and nature-orientated learning opportunities. Emphasis on provision of corresponding facilities. May appear as a separate zone within another category*	*Extensive outdoor recreation opportunities. Protection of outstanding recreation resources such as beaches and of small local/regional significant natural features*	*Diverse recreation/tourism activities of an intensive nature with emphasis on those interacting with the natural environment. Facilities as above plus commercial and staging area services. Fishing permitted (hunting dangerous in densely used area). Direct intervention may be allowed to control natural process may occur. Not allowed: activities mentioned in text*

Source: Government of British Columbia, the Cariboo-Chilcotin Land-use Plan, October 1994

- training guards in visitor management;
- hardening sites to reduce damage from visitors (e.g. with boardwalks or suspended walkways over fragile grounds such as sand dunes);
- developing a handicraft cooperative involving the local communities;
- establishing an entrance fee;
- selecting specialist tour operators.

9.2.4 Protection of roads

Outside the places visited, what most tourists see of a country is what may be seen from its roads. One of the main attractions of touring is the discovery of beautiful and interesting scenery. Tourist routes may be classified into:

- the main areas of circulation (from the airport, frontiers, gateway cities etc.);
- feeder roads to tourist attractions and resorts;
- scenic routes through areas of tourism interest.

Main highway areas are dictated by traffic demand factors and technical considerations, including costs. However, these routes of entry to a city or region establish initial impressions and, to some extent, attitudes. Control of ribbon development, urban sprawl and advertisements is important in addition to good signing, road landscaping and maintenance of the verges.

Routes used primarily by tourists, such as from cruise ports or regional airports to resorts, require specific attention and should be treated in the same way as scenic drives.

Scenic roads must be identified as part of the planning surveys and given special protection if necessary, by introducing regulations. These provisions should include:

- constructing attractive viewing and picnicking places with parking and well-designed amenities;
- appropriate landscaping of verges and maintenance;
- banning advertisements and confining signs and directions to approved designs discreetly located near junctions;
- controlling the number, siting and architectural character of gasoline service stations, restaurants, motels and other roadside facilities;
- establishing 'scenic easements' along the verges of roads prohibiting any construction within, say 100 m, of the road or greater if there are important views (of a lake, seashore, valley etc.).

It is usually necessary to by-pass the narrow streets of villages and towns to preserve their character and historic interest. Where possible the by-pass should provide a view of the town, with nearby parking and convenient pedestrian access to the centre.

9.2.5 Tourists and historic monuments

The average tourist is not a specialist: visitors are generally impressed by the totality of the scene; the precious material found in the natural setting; the aura created by the approach and surroundings; routines and activities still practised; the uniqueness of the site or the fact that the visit takes time ('there is much to be seen'). Hence the list and ranking of monuments of tourism interest may be different from those of archaeological importance and will be influenced more by the way monuments and artefacts are presented, including reconstructions, interpretations and interactions with the past. This applies equally to engineering and scientific achievements (historic and present day) in which interpretation and discovery are an important part of the educational experience.

Visitor attractiveness may be enhanced by:

- *orientation centres* presenting an illustrated account of the history, interactive displays, reproduced scenes, descriptive interpretation
- opportunities to *experience* the sights, activities and conditions of the period with actors or animated tableaux, ('living' museums), *son et lumière*
- *reconstruction* of ruins to illustrate the monumental scale of the original with separate museum to house delicate exhibits
- *visitor centre* including souvenir shops, information and general facilities.

Listing monuments is a relatively simple step: protecting them from deterioration involves many more difficulties. The best way of conserving a monument is to use it, either by guaranteeing the continuity of its original function (religious, political), or reassigning it to new contemporary activities, with temporary (festival, etc.) or more specific permanent use (museum, youth hostel, tourist centre, hotel).

As with natural resources, tourism demands on monuments may be excessive. In the Kyoto Palace, Acropolis, Versailles, or Sistine Chapel, for example, the quality of the experience at peak times is marred by crowds and noise.

The general measures outlined in 9.1.8 to 9.2.8 apply to both natural and man-made resources. These may be supplemented by specific provisions:

- control and management procedures (such as visits limited to guided groups, following planned sequences and routes, off-site general briefing, shuttle systems to various sites etc.);
- diversification of the itineraries and of the items visited by the different groups (as at Versailles);
- multiplication of the point of interest (such as showing the Liberty Bell outside Independence Hall), or drawing specific attention to lesser known features;
- replacing a part of the actual visit by a detailed briefing, 'processing' of the visitors in a separate structure, with maps, brochures, models, slides, even films etc. (as in Williamsburg);
- diversification of the point of interest by the creation of a separate museum, shopping areas, exhibitions, special cultural events;
- limiting access partially (restriction on group tours) or totally, when the risk of irreversible damage occurs.

9.2.6 Isolated monuments

A tourism sector plan must list all the monuments classified under appropriate legislation – which may exist or be introduced when the plan is implemented. Besides protecting valuable sites and monuments from destruction, the classification is intended:

- to draw attention to their value (educational aim);
- to entrust an authority with the responsibility of protection;
- to give a legal basis for the allocation of funds for maintenance or restoration;
- to define the limits of the monument: the protection should extend to the surrounding area from which the monument is viewed or which is viewed from the monument itself;
- to allow control (with intervention where necessary) over monuments, balancing the restrictions imposed by classification with possibilities of revenue generation.

Important **out of town isolated monuments** will generally need (apart from restoration works) some provision to facilitate visitors: access road, parking area, shelter for the attendants, toilets. If the monument is a major attraction a small information room (or museum) and some refreshment and accommodation facilities may be added.

A correct balance of scale and relationship is essential: the monument must not be dominated by its museums, nor isolated from its true surroundings by ornamental gardens, parking places etc. Improvements should always be very discreet and complementary:

- keep the access road as narrow as possible (5.5 or even 3 m wide) and, unless part of the original design, avoid a rectilinear approach straight to the monument (an element of surprise and discovery is important);
- hide as far as possible the necessary facilities (parking places in particular) which should not be visible from the monument;
- modify the natural scenery and character as little as possible;
- protect the surroundings, which form part of the composite image, from major changes and especially from the intrusion of buildings;
- organize individual and group visits.

Urban isolated monuments which are not part of a monumental ensemble (group of monuments) (9.2.7) may be of two main categories:

- originating as an urban monument, i.e. always surrounded by the fabric of the town. The approach through the traditional network of narrow streets and squares should be preserved as far as possible, as well as the size and proportion of surrounding buildings (if not the buildings themselves);
- built outside the town but surrounded since by the town's extension: where possible, the original character should be retained by including such monuments in a small clearing, garden or larger park.

9.2.7 Monument ensembles

This notion, underlined in the 1950s by UNESCO, recognizes that a monument loses its significance when detached from its surroundings, small buildings and features which in themselves are of secondary importance or little value, but which have always been there. A well conserved ensemble is much more attractive than individually isolated monuments (even if these are interesting) and has enormous value in creating a tourist image.

Monument ensembles belong to three main categories:

- **Major out of town archaeological sites** which include a number of monuments, or which can be brought into the same ensemble, such as within a national park.
- **Typical villages** which very often are one of the main tourist attractions of a country, for their picturesque appearance and for the opportunity they may provide for visitors to experience original surroundings, local traditions, ways of life, folklore, handicrafts etc. Their conservation may be difficult, especially in countries where building materials are poor. Various policies may be considered according to the particular circumstances:
  - total classification and protection as for archaeological monuments,
  - controlled modernization and development avoiding foreign materials and alien forms of building but allowing the adaptation of houses to present standards and needs,
  - re-assignment for tourist accommodation (as hotels or for renting of rooms) with careful internal remodelling and renovation,
  - planned salvage, transportation and reconstruction of remaining traditional buildings onto a protected site, complete with craft industries and farming as a living museum (folk museum).
- **Urban monument ensembles** often meet the same problems, aggravated by high land value or traffic problems and by dominating presence of tall buildings around if not in the centre of the area considered. Measures for classification, protection and improvement may have to be considered individually, building by building, following comprehensive surveys.
- **Tourist and monument zones** provide a positive framework for developing tourism in town centres. Ancient buildings and, even more, the historical 'character' will be increased in value and appreciation. Tourist activities will be concentrated there, using old buildings as far as possible, generating economic and social benefits.

A comprehensive scheme for the development of town centres will usually necessitate the introduction of compulsory purchase, joint private/public projects and inducements for improvement of individual properties. Traffic management and pedestrianization of the zones is invariably required, contributing to both conservation and enjoyment.

An example of the conservation of traditional villages

*Attractive villages attract tourists. In France, 135 villages are classified **Most lovely villages of France** attracting 28 million visitors annually, and ten to fifteen of them attract more than 600 000 visitors annually (AFIT 1996). Their selection is based on:*

- *a population of less than 2000;*
- *a recognized heritage (classified monuments or sites);*
- *overall quality and legal protection of the village and its environment;*
- *a quality tourism offer (accommodation, catering, local products and handicrafts).*

9.2.8 Towns and centres of culture

Existing towns, even if poorly endowed with tourist attractions, play an important role in tourist development:

- as intersections of main axes of communication;
- as suppliers of tourist facilities (hotels for businessmen, shopping, catering, various services etc.);
- as urban centres of domestic demand for tourism and leisure.

In most towns there is scope to develop a few interesting, well townscaped and traffic-free areas in which the tourist facilities and basic town services can be located. Such sites can take advantage of any interesting features, a river, a park, an attractive view, the vicinity of a museum or of a monument etc. A scheme indicating the tourist features which could be utilized and improved may be prepared as part of the tourism development plan and integrated into the overall town planning programme.

The problem is different in the **Villes d'Art**, in the towns which are important centres of history, culture and art, and as such, major tourist attractions. The maximum density or 'tourist capacity' for tourist towns is difficult to quantify in precise terms. Even in towns where the overall ratio is low some parts may be so overcrowded by tourists that the original image of traditional calm is lost and a new image of bustle and vitality created in its place (for example in Plaka, Athens).

> The more important the tourism activity becomes in terms of numbers of tourists, claims on public space, landmarks in the built environment and visibility in the daily urban scenery, the more the urban community needs to find ways of coping with the stress of tourism. The 'social acceptance' of tourism activities in the daily life space can be measured in many different ways … although it remains most difficult to indicate in a quantitative way the 'social carrying capacity' of a historic-tourist city. In historic cities where tourism activities are determining the daily and seasonal rhythm, and the quality of daily life in the urban environment, the question arises how to manage people and especially visitors. The development of *visitor management policies* is now indeed a priority on the political agenda of many historic-tourist cities.
>
> (Jansen-Verbeke 1995)

The maximum number of tourists to be encouraged is essentially a political decision: whether the local inhabitants wish to conserve the valuable environment of their town or prefer the benefits brought about by an increased tourism. It must be noted, however, that large tourist flows generally result in many pressures which are difficult to control or alleviate: pressures resulting from traffic (larger parking areas, congestion in the centre), from numbers of sightseers (overcrowding of attractions), from demands for more and more accommodation (larger modern hotels) with resulting loss of character and increasing imbalances in jobs and housing. Progressive deterioration of standards may finally lead to the higher-spend tourists going elsewhere and a loss in the real value of tourism.

Three directions of action may be considered when facing an excessive pressure of visitors:

- to accept the pressure, taking fiscal measures in order to indemnify the residents suffering from the tourism pressure;
- to influence the offer: by increasing the capacity or the intensity of use of the tourist facilities and resources; by diversifying destinations and itineraries (promoting certain elements);
- to influence the demand: selecting categories of visitors, reducing possibilities of access (parking places), increasing tariffs or introducing voluntary or compulsory reservations.

Example: A Venice Visitor Card?

Venice is the typical example of an overcrowded ville d'art, which is trying to restrict the numbers of visitors in the peak season, particularly the crowds of daily excursionists. Unlike traditional tourists who use the 11 500 beds available and usually book in advance (about 2.5 million nights/year), the flow of day visitors (more than 6 million per year) is unpredictable and unmanageable: even the limitation of car parking and closure of the bridge link with the mainland has proved an insufficient deterrent (Van der Bord 1995).

One solution being considered is the use of a dated 'Venice Card', sponsored by the tourism industry, issued in advance and in controlled numbers to improve the quality of the experience (including access to places otherwise closed to the public, price reductions or free elements in local transport, shops and other tourist facilities). Residential tourists would receive a card together with the reservation of hotel accommodation, but the total number of cards issued would be equal to the most restrictive of the different carrying capacities of the centre of Venice, which seems to be the socio-economic one. The card could help to limit peak pressure and extend the length of the season.

9.3 PLANNING OUTDOOR RECREATION IN THE CITIES

Most cities and large conurbations suffer from an ever-increasing lack of outdoor recreation space. The **increasing demand** of the inhabitants of most cities for more outdoor recreation and parks (see 1.1.4) is met by a **reducing offer** in terms of number and quality of sites for green parks and outdoor recreation. Higher densities of building, escalating land costs and the progressive conversion of garden areas into building sites and parking spaces increase this difficulty. The usual solutions are to move to the suburbs or to make excursions (weekend, public

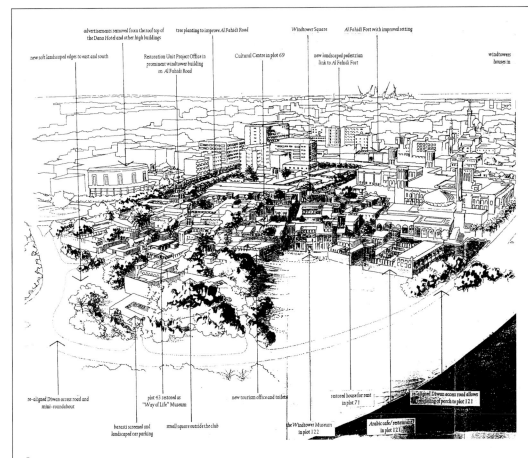

advertisements removed from the roof top of the Dana Hotel and other high buildings

tree planting to improve Al Fahidi Road

Windtower Square

Al Fahidi Fort with improved setting

new soft landscaped edges to east and south

Restoration Unit Project Office in prominent windtower building on Al Fahidi Road

Cultural Centre in plot 69

new landscaped pedestrian link to Al Fahidi Fort

windtowers houses in

re-aligned Diwan access road and mini-roundabout

plot 43 restored as "Way of Life" Museum

new tourism office and toilets

restored house for rent in plot 71

re-aligned Diwan access road allows rebuilding of porch to plot 121

barasti screened and landscaped car parking

small square outside the club

the Windtower Museum in plot 122

Arabic cafe/restaurant in plot 121

a

Bastakia Conservation Study, Dubai

Bastakia is a unique survivor of 'old' Dubai – dating from 1925 – and the only remaining significant area of wind tower houses in the United Arab Emirates. Since the 1980s this area has suffered from decline and demolition of many of the finest buildings.

The strategy for restoration and reuse involved a detailed study of the architectural quality, restoration and potential for sensitive reuse. Ten key projects were implemented by the Municipality in 1997 to set quality standards for later work by the private sector.

This led to a physical plan grouping clusters of attractions in 'nodes' linked by visitor routes through the sikkas and squares (Fig. 9.4b) whilst other areas remained residential. Changes were also proposed to improve the outer edges of Bastakia (Fig. 9.4c). Key projects included 'Wind tower' and 'Way of life' museums, a Tourist Centre, Arab cafe/restaurant, small souk and multi-use cultural centre. Steps have also been taken to upgrade paving, landscaping and services, including concealment of unsightly equipment.

Study and project design: Llewelyn-Davies, for the Municipality of Dubai.

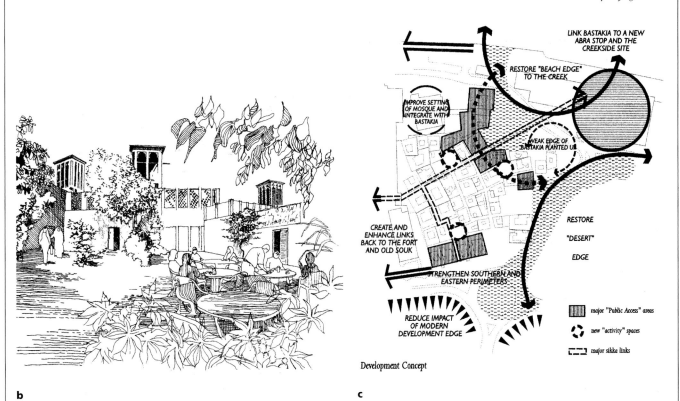

LINK BASTAKIA TO A NEW ABRA STOP AND THE CREEKSIDE SITE

RESTORE "BEACH EDGE" TO THE CREEK

IMPROVE SETTING OF MOSQUE AND INTEGRATE WITH BASTAKIA

WEAK EDGE OF BASTAKIA PLANTED UP

RESTORE "DESERT" EDGE

CREATE AND ENHANCE LINKS BACK TO THE FORT AND OLD SOUK

STRENGTHEN SOUTHERN AND EASTERN PERIMETERS

REDUCE IMPACT OF MODERN DEVELOPMENT EDGE

major "Public Access" areas

new "activity" spaces

major sikka links

Development Concept

b

c

New Lanark, Scotland

Currently nominated as a World Heritage site, with all buildings listed Grade A and in an Area of Outstanding Natural Beauty, New Lanark was created in 1784 as a complete mill town powered by water and later run by Robert Owen as a model village. The mills closed down in 1968 and the decaying properties were rescued by a Trust with capital funds for on-going restoration work provided by a number of agencies including the European Regional Development Fund (ERDF). Now a top Scottish attraction, the village has a community of 160 and attracted 400 000 visitors in 1995, much of the revenue funding being generated by the Visitor Centre and associated business activities.

New Lanark Conservation Trust.

holidays) into the countryside but at the cost of traffic congestion and urban sprawl.

> [The Regional Plan Association's] 1995 Quality of Life poll indicated that for 60 per cent of the region's residents who have moved to the suburbs, outdoor recreation was a primary consideration.
>
> Over the past 20 years, New York City park spending has dropped by more than one third. ... This disinvestment is felt in many ways. The number of street trees is declining at a rate of 2,000 a year. And only 35% of the city's parks are deemed to be in acceptable condition. As a result, city residents flee to the countryside seeking environmental quality, fueling the demand for new homes and businesses.

(Yaro and Hiss 1996, p. 72).

In this context, town planning must address a number of questions: how to make the town or city itself an attractive environment, how to integrate natural elements into urban design and how to develop appropriate links between the town and the countryside? These topics are presented in two sections:

- individual elements (standards and planning procedures): in this chapter, 9.3;
- their implementation at the level of a whole city, which calls for the preparation of a 'Green Plan' as a reference document for planning strategies: see 8.5.

The Green City Concept perceives urban development as based on comprehensive understanding of natural features and ecological processes. In the green city the organization of the green and built spaces provides an interface between human and natural systems, its urban landscapes integrate native plant species and its urban design is used to influence micro-climate patterns by increasing air quality. The green city requires the integration of human and natural processes in a mutually beneficial relationship: human development activities and technology contribute to the preservation of community, place and home in harmony with nature and human culture.

(CHS 1995)

9.3.1 Principles

In planning open spaces for outdoor recreation particular attention must be paid to:

- *diversity of the population* concerned and their respective needs, taking into account:
  - family structures and age groups – in particular young children, the elderly and disabled,
  - preferred activities, either active (running, jogging, bicycling, etc.) or passive (enjoying natural scenery, water, sunshine, street scenes),

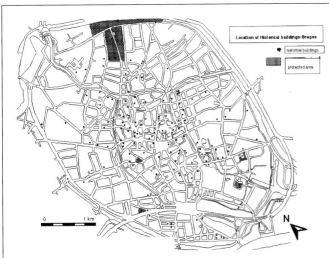

a Location patterns of historic buildings of interest, indicating the tourist zone (From the study by Professor M. Jansen-Verbeke)

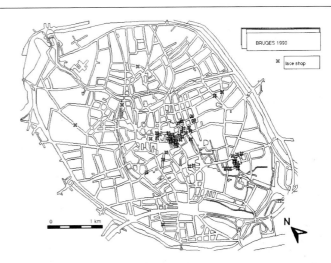

b Location patterns of 'lace shops', indicating the process of touristification in the inner city (From the study by Professor M. Jansen-Verbeke)

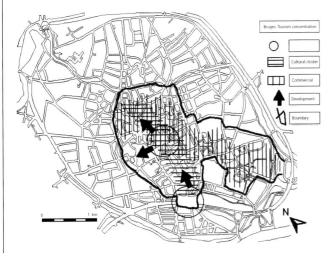

c Concentration model (From the study by Professor M. Jansen-Verbeke)

Bruges, Belgium

The famous Flemish historic city has reached a critical stage, not in its development as such (numbers of tourists are still growing) but in terms of sustainability and carrying capacity. The limits of carrying capacity have been measured – in a study undertaken in 1990 by Professor Myriam Jansen-Verbeke (commented in Jansen-Verbeke 1995) – in terms of:

- *physical impact of tourism activity on public space, traffic, etc,*
- *social acceptance of tourism activity by the local community*
- *management capacity : resource and visitor management issues.*

The social carrying capacity (see 1.4.5) was investigated by means of a survey among opinion leaders and decision makers. Indications that the critical point has been reached are: a decline in the number of overnight visitors, a growing absence of the original target groups, an overcapacity in hotels (leading to price dumping), a loss of quality of the offer, a decreasing interest in the city from project developers and sponsors of events, an indifferent or even antagonistic attitude of the locals towards tourism and tourists.

It was indeed the social irritation among the local community which made the underlying pressure of tourism become more evident, although the real problem was a lack of urban management and policy instruments to control further development.

The survey defined the characteristics of the tourist area (monuments, shops, itineraries, etc.) and proposed new tourism products, a tourism monitoring system, visitor management policies and methods, and two alternative development models:

- *a concentration model based on the development of a hard tourist core in the inner city, a pedestrian area, strict parking and traffic regulations, a stop to hotel building/conversion in particular areas and a much stricter control on the development of commercial activities, in order to prevent a further invasion of tourism in residential quarters of the inner city (conservation of their authentic physical and social characters);*
- *a model of concentrated dispersion extending the tourism activity in other parts of the inner city; it is, however, unlikely that this extension would release the pressure in the areas which are now the top tourist attractions; furthermore, this model would require extensive planning and conservation control.*

Public spaces in Lyon, France

Re-sew agglomerations that have been torn asunder, construct places to be lived in and not vacuums, conceive the city of today, with its multiple evolving uses, founding it on existing patrimony, these are the issues at stake today for our cities. Likewise, these issues should determine urban art, understood as the art of designing city spaces and their constituent elements while incorporating the different functions to be found therein…

(Translated from Jean-Pierre Charbonneau, 'Plaidoyer pour l'art urbain', Le Moniteur-AMC, September 1996)

Created in 1969, Greater Lyon is a 'metropolitan community' of 1 200 000 inhabitants living in 55 original communities: from the historic town at the confluence of the rivers Rhône and Saône, to small villages, from very dense urban areas to the countryside. The master plan (implemented in 1989 on the initiative of Henry Chabert, assisted by J-P. Charbonneau) provided an opportunity to introduce the concept of public open spaces throughout the whole metropolitan area.

Approach

Steps, taken in parallel over a range of scales, included:

- an overall master plan for public spaces;
- specific overall concepts for green areas (Green Plan), riverbanks (Blue Plan), night-time illumination (Lights Plan), rehabilitation of the historic centre, etc.;
- study and implementation of local projects;
- maintenance and control of local projects;

Each scale benefited from and contributed information to the others

Principles

- Solidarity between the different areas, with the simultaneous implementation of projects, worked out by the same team with the same highly qualified designers, in the historic centre, the modern town, the densely populated (and sometimes semi-dilapidated) suburbs, and the villages.
- Contemporary design, every project aimed at reflecting modernity, with selected artists, planners, architects and landscape architects.
- Unity of expression through the definition of a 'vocabulary of public spaces', with specified – often traditional – materials for kerbs, sidewalks, paved areas or porous soils, parking spaces, and selected designs for benches, bus stops, lighting masts incorporating the circulation signs, etc.

Organization

This unitary approach called for the horizontal collaboration of all interested parties: transport, housing, public lighting, sewers and parks authorities, private developers and local communities. The contracting authority within Greater Lyon was:

- the Public Space Section of Greater Lyon Department of Urban Development for large projects and global studies (e.g. urban furniture),

- the Local Departments (e.g. social urban development or town planning) for smaller projects, with the assistance of the Public Space Section.

The comprehensive studies and preparation of strategic plans were carried out by the Greater Lyon Planning Agency (Agence d'Urbanisme de la Communauté Urbaine) with the participation of planners in the private sector (selected directly through competition). The contracting authority designated a project manager to be responsible for each project, coordinating with other official services and the local communities and elaborating detailed terms of reference. Detailed design work and project implementation was carried out by private sector planners and landscape architects.

Political framework

The Council for Greater Lyon appointed a Steering Committee for Public Spaces (CCPS), made up of the heads of the various public administrations, the mayors concerned, project managers and conceptual designers to consider each project. The office and staff of the Deputy Mayor of Lyon, responsible for the planning of the town, performs a similar function in the urban community.

Sequence of studies

Under the authority of the Public Space Section the following sequence was undertaken:

- designation of the project manager,
- technical analyses of each site and its uses,
- consultation with the population (needs and proposals),
- proposed programme submitted to and approved by the CCPS,
- elaboration of the project by the conceptual designer,
- presentation of the project to the CCPS and renewed consultation with the population,
- implementation.

In six years, about 130 sites have been implemented, making Lyon a 'test bed' for similar urban schemes.

The Green Plan

- Protection of agriculture and natural areas.
- Redesign of the main urban squares and creation of pedestrian malls,
- Redevelopment of four large parks and of neighbourhood parks (within 500 m of residences)
- Restoration and improvement of open spaces in the densely inhabited suburbs
- Planting of trees on squares and streets.

The 'Blue' Plan

- Review of 250 km of river banks in Greater Lyon.
- Extension of riverside parks and green areas.
- Rehabilitation of pedestrian quays with cycle trails.
- Creation of a network of small landing stages.

b–c
Redevelopment of open spaces in La Darnaise, with enclosed public parks and car parking under tree-planted alleys (A. Chemetoff, landscape architect)

a *Renovation of Place de la Bourse (with underground parking): a major urban space with individual 'niches' for rest (A. Chemetoff, landscape architect)*

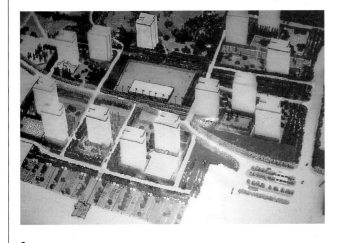

c

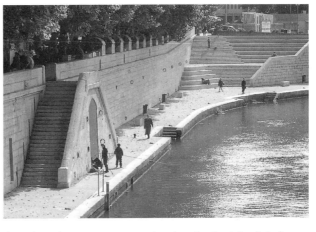

d–e *Blue Plan: new access to the river bank at Quai de la Pecherie and cafés at the landing stage of Quai Carrie (M. Desvigne and C. Balkony, designers)*

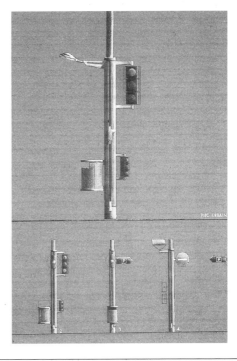

e

f *Urban furniture: a multifunctional street light (J-M. Wilmotte, designer)*

Lyon (cont.)

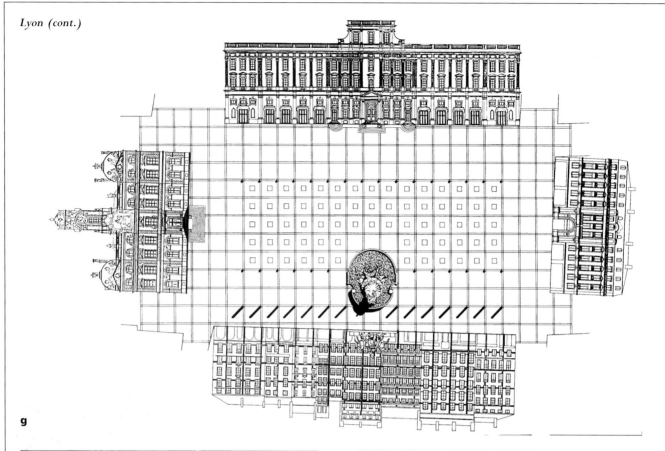

g

h

i

g–i *Renovation of Place des Terreaux: strict control over underground utilities, access to underground car parking by side streets (C. Drevet and D. Buren, designers)*

j

j *Renovation of Place de la République, with underground parking (A. Sarfarti, designer)*

Baltimore, USA: 20-year strategy

Since its decline as a commercial port, the inner harbour area of Baltimore has undergone extensive redevelopment, with environmental improvements attracting large-scale reinvestment. In 1990, following lengthy consultation, the strategic plan for the next 20-year phase was announced.

Growth over this period is expected to require 1.1 million m² of new offices, nearly 0.1 million m² of retail space, 2700 new hotel rooms, 4000 new residential units and 4.2 million additional visitors in the 480 ha (1200 acre) area of Downtown Baltimore.

The vision of Downtown Baltimore in 2010 is that of a place for people, reflecting the character of the city and its citizens, a place of opportunity for economic activity, trade, technology and services, a centre of culture, entertainment and recreation, a harbourside community in which people want to live, with an attractive environment, small parks, plazas and pedestrian walkways extending throughout to link the attractions and areas.

As the first step to achieving that vision, the area was divided into six districts, each with distinctive characteristics, a defined mission, strategy and work plan. In all districts, the work plans included steps to designate and conserve valued buildings and areas, to improve safety, and to encourage community involvement in improving the environment.

The latter covered aspects such as 'Friends of the Park' programmes, landscaping of undeveloped lots, provisions for flower boxes and sidewalk planters, replacement of above-ground lines and creation of new public open spaces by closing narrow neighbourhood streets.

The Mayor and Strategic Management Committee, City of Baltimore,
The Renaissance continues – A 20-Year Strategic Plan for Downtown Baltimore, 1991

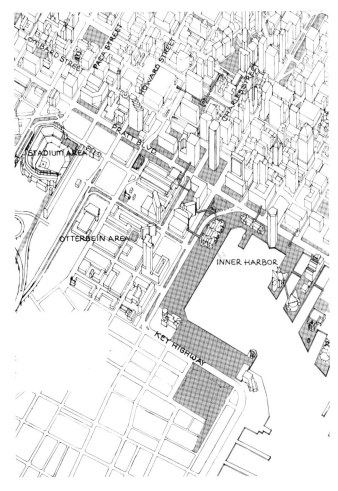

Inner harbour district

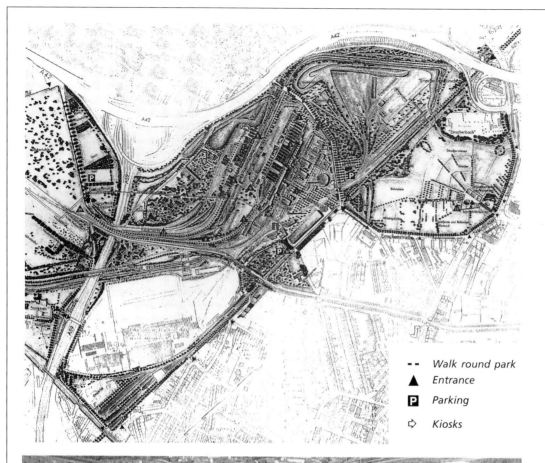

-- Walk round park
▲ Entrance
P Parking
⇨ Kiosks

a

b

Duisburg-North Landscape Park, Germany

Already partly in use, this 200 ha park should be completed in 1999 as a part of the Emscher Landscape Park (see p. 217). The heart of the park is a disused (since 1985) Thyssen steelworks, with abandoned blast furnaces, coking plant, railway embankments, canals, polluted dumps and a growing vegetation cover. The park presents a potential for natural history: retaining the vegetation typical of industrial wastes and showing the stages of its colonization.

Taking account of the existing roads and railway structure, the park is being developed in several zones linked together at special points; it includes:

- railway lines becoming railway malls, relinking district centres and park, with others being used as footpaths or bicycle tracks;
- the blast furnaces, now places of calmness, converted to many uses: playgrounds, meetings, theatre, festivals, exhibitions, even deep diving in the old gas tank now filled with water;
- a water park, created by feeding an originally polluted stream with on-site rainwater;
- an education farm with farm-gardening for schools; community gardens;
- large open spaces for lawns and picnic places, a few sports grounds;
- cafe, kiosks and toilets, which remain mobile and can be driven to various locations;
- permanent and occasional car parks.

A visit to the site is facilitated by a signposted industrial history route (2½ hours).

Developed by the Town of Duisburg and LEG-Landesentwicklungsgesellschaft Nordrhein-Westfalen GmbH

c

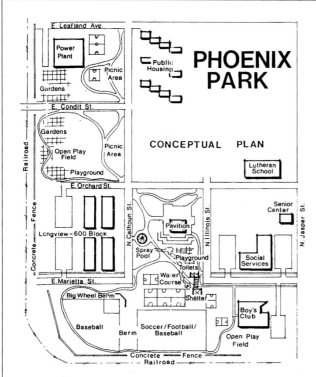

Master plan

Phoenix Park in Decatur, Illinois, USA

The following process was adopted in planning a neighbourhood park in Decatur, with a low-income majority Black population and high unemployment:

- *Gathering and assessing* **information about needs and preferences** *(through census-tract data, block by block telephone random survey, interviews with key individuals).*
- *Identifying* **design output criteria***:*
  - *an image: traditional lawns, trees and flowers; belonging only to the neighbourhood; well maintained; with swimming pool;*
  - *a concern for safety: worries about drinking, gambling, drugs;*
  - *selected facilities: including open-air pavilion for music, dancing, movies, picnics, farmers' market; basketball courts (two of them undersized for younger children!).*
- *Designing a* **conceptual plan** *with the following elements:*
  - *manually operated, non-recirculating spray-pool (the swimming pool being too expensive);*
  - *planting of mature trees (for protection against vandalism and stronger visual impact);*
  - *guaranteeing safety (residents should assume the 'ownership' of the park): participation of residents in the implementation of the park (painting walls, planting trees, etc.); no car parking (people coming by foot or bicycle will be nearby residents); spray-pool under visual control of residents nearby; all activities within easy public view; circulation paths, wide and not too numerous, raised for visibility; 'hanging out' will occur despite all efforts to limit it, but in an area where it would not disrupt other park users (basketball court to the far north, under easy surveillance from the street).*
- ***Testing against set criteria*** *and annotation of the master plan: design intentions.*

Housing Research and Development Programme,
University of Illinois, Salogta,
Bradley, Likins & Dillows, Architects

- ethnic ratios, size of groups and education levels,
- financial resources;
- *distribution of green areas* and other recreation spaces – which are often scarce in the densely inhabited districts with the greatest needs;
- *security*, facilitated by adequate visibility, good maintenance and supervision balanced against the need for free access;
- *maintenance costs*;
- *increasing interest in the environment*: natural or ecoparks being introduced with native vegetation, natural grass instead of lawns, naturalistic open spaces, urban 'bioscapes' (see 9.3.3).

A 'democratic' public space, inviting access, encouraging use and participation by all ages and ensuring the security of children and women is generally well respected and appreciated by its users.

9.3.2 Urban parks standards

Green space functions are multiple:

- social: spaces for meeting and playing in contact with nature;
- structural: urban design and landscaping;
- ecological: regulation of the urban ecosystem by
  - improving climate: humidification, dust filtration, microbial purification,
  - lowering psychological perception of urban noise,
  - attenuating climatic difference and slowing downs winds,
  - regulating rainwater and floods,
  - maintaining vegetal and zoological diversity.

One setting to which little research has been devoted is that of urban parks and recreation. In this area, especially, there seems to be a strong need for applied research. The components of quality and the appropriate mix of opportunities for various urban publics is a particularly vivid issue. Much of the work completed has described users, external benefits, and the distribution of benefits. But knowledge of which factors affect quality for the many urban publics is inadequate.

(Cordell 1988).

Parks must answer the needs of the whole community, including the 'silent majority' mentioned in 8.2.2. Standard sports fields, pitches and stadia, which may share some of these green space functions, are restricted to the members of sporting clubs and associations. They are not presented in detail in this book as other excellent sources of information exist (John and Campbell 1993).

In most countries target standards determine the size, character and hierarchy of city parks and some examples are given below:

Recreation standard concept for Jackson County, Michigan, USA

This plan shows a conventional application of the National Recreation and Park Association's standard to a community.

Source: Seymour M. Gold (1980), Recreation Planning and Design, McGraw-Hill Inc., New York

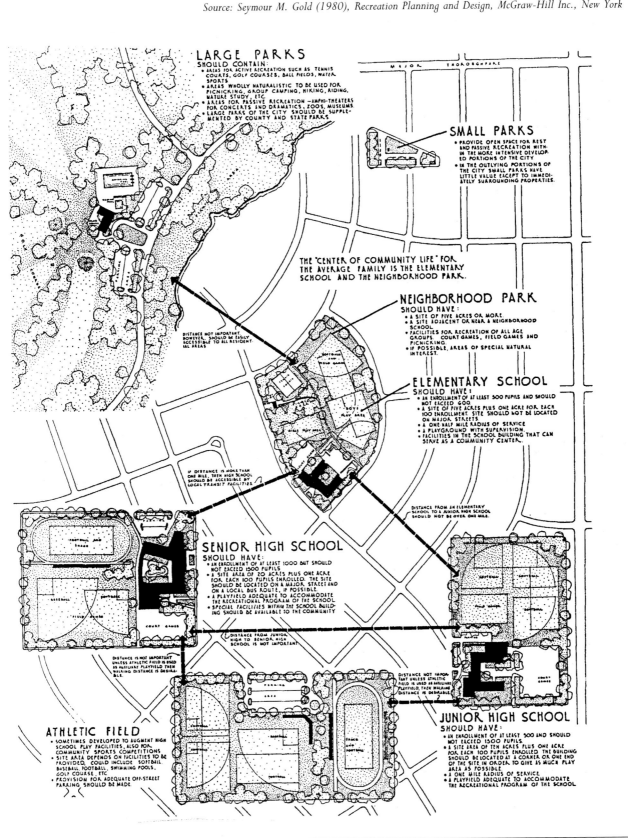

US National Recreation and Park Association proposals (Mertes and Hall, 1995 p. 93):

mini-parks or playlots (not more than 400 m from residences)	2500 to 4000 m^2
neighbourhood parks: 2000 to 10 000 inhabitants (400–800 m from residences)	15 000 to 40 000 m^2
community parks: 10 000 to 15 000 inhabitant (800–5000 m from residences)	100 000 to 200 000 m^2
large urban and metropolitan parks (50 000 inhabitant)	200 000 to 400 000 m^2
sports complexes	150 000 to 300 000 m^2
regional parks	additional 1 000 000 m^2

The urban/metropolitan park areas recommended together represent about 25 m^2/inhabitant compared with the traditional higher standard of 40^2/inhabitant (4 acres/1000 inhabitants)

Ex-USSR recommended standards (Rietdorf and Baeselen 1979, p. 86):

parks according to number of inhabitants	– 6 to 10 m^2/inhabitant
district green areas	– 5 to 10 m^2/inhabitant
total according to number of inhabitants	– 11 to 20 m^2/inhabitant

French 'new towns' standards (Cahiers IAURIF 87/8 (January 1989), p. 116):

parks	– 25 m^2/inhabitant
other green areas	– 25 to 50 m^2/inhabitant

UK National Playing Fields Association standards (Department of the Environment 1991):

adults and young people	16 to 18 m^2/inhabitant
children's playgrounds	2 to 3 m^2/inhabitant
occasional/informal use	4 to 5 m^2/inhabitant
6 acres open space per 1000 inhabitants	20 to 22 m^2/inhabitant

Dutch standards (Rietdorf and Baeseler 1979, p. 88):

proximity parks (1 ha)	4 m^2/inhabitant
neighbourhood parks (6 to 10 ha)	8 m^2/inhabitant
district parks (30 to 60 ha)	6 m^2/inhabitant
urban parks (200 to 400 ha)	32 m^2/inhabitant
total in the city	50 m^2/inhabitant
suburban parks (1,000 to 3000 ha)	65 m^2/inhabitant
total urban + suburban	115 m^2/inhabitant

Swedish standards (Flodin *et al.* 1983):

playlots (at less than 50 m from home)	25–30 m^2/apartment, minimum 1500 m^2
proximity parks (at less than 300 m from home)	about 0.5 ha
neighbourhood parks (at less than 1000 m from home)	about 10 ha
urban parks (at 3000 to 5000 m from home)	over 100 ha

Canadian standards 4 ha per 1000 inhabitants 40 m^2/inhabitant

In fact, most cities do not reach these high standards (area shown per inhabitant):

Calgary (Canada)	53 m^2	Berlin (Germany)	13 m^2
Montreal (Canada)	18 m^2	London (UK)	9 m^2
Ottawa (Canada)	14 m^2	Rome (Italy)	9 m^2
Vienna (Austria)	25 m^2	Paris (France)	10 m^2
Brussels (Belgium)	26 m^2	Lille (France)	18 m^2

Standards are easy to apply but should in fact vary from site to site. Usually described as 'guidelines' they too often rapidly become 'absolute' objectives, ends rather than means. Their application should be replaced by a more sensitive approach taking account of the needs and behaviour of local people.

9.3.3 Park planning principles

Planning green areas and open air facilities on a citywide scale is dealt with in 8.5. For individual parks the planning procedures outlined in 9.3.9 apply with the following specific principles:

- *observe accessibility and present uses* of the site to be developed, as well as uses in similar areas and parks;
- *define the character*, the distinctive personality, the individuality of each park, with regard to its environment and community needs;
- *avoid over-design*, over-planting and over-equipping, except for fixtures allowing variation in uses at different times;
- minimize the ecological impact, maintaining biological complexity, returning drained surface waters to the ground, etc.;
- *develop multiple use facilities* (lawns, alleys, hard surfaces, etc.), avoiding facilities catering for one only clientele (such as permanent standard sports fields, tennis courts, etc. in a park of relatively modest dimensions). Too many parks – in US cities, in particular – are crowded with standard sports grounds; newer concepts are combining active leisure with passive uses;
- *avoid high maintenance costs*, of such elements as due to extended flowerbeds, numerous small grass areas, non-vandal resistant park furniture (benches, lighting), replacing, for example, decorative fountains with manually operated, non-recirculating spray pools;
- *consider accessibility* for catchment areas within (IAURIF 1995, p. 39):
  - 250 m for urban parks of up to 10 ha (proximity parks)
  - 500 m for parks of 10 to 30 ha (local needs),
  - 1000 m for great parks of 30 to 100 ha (multiple needs)
  Those distances, resulting from users' surveys, may be compared with the distances mentioned in 9.3.2 for the

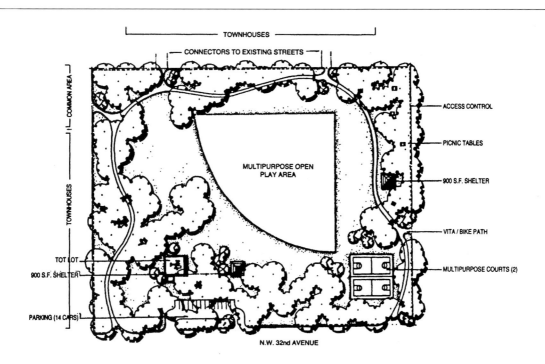

Neighbourhood park standard for Dade County, Florida, USA

This is the minimal National Recreation and Park Association's standard for a neighbourhood. It illustrates the NRPA's concept of mixing the active (sports grounds) and the passive (lawns and pedestrian alleys) recreation forms.

Metropolitan Dade County Park Recreation Department.
Source: Seymour M. Gold (1980) Recreation Planning and Design, McGraw-Hill Inc., New York

USA (NRPA) and Sweden, or with the London Planning Advisory Committee standards (1988) (quoted in Williams 1995, p. 162):
– 400 m for small local parks of 2 ha (including local play space),
– 1200 m for district parks of 20 ha (including outdoor sports and informal pursuits),
– 3000 m and more for metropolitan parks of 60 ha,
– up to 8000 m for weekend regional parks of 400 ha;
• *answer the expected use pressure:* lawns and other green areas are more difficult and expensive to maintain with a high density of users than 'mineral parks' with extended hard ground; the latter may require higher initial investment, but ongoing relatively low maintenance costs. Most 'pocket parks' are mineral parks;
• *select versatile sport facilities* rather than permanent standard sports fields or tennis courts: using more user-friendly, multi-purpose play equipment (skateboard areas, climbing wall, cycle tracks, fitness trails, concrete slabs for table tennis, temporary nets for tennis or volleyball, etc.);
• *organize community planning*, meetings with representatives of all interested parties (designers, managers, sponsors and especially representative cross-section of future users) inviting participation in:

– the selection of suitable activities and features,
– resolution of matters such as safety, security, vandalism,
– implementation,
– maintenance: being involved in decisions on management, organizing and running the different activities, having some control over the maintenance decisions.
– This is often an effective way of limiting vandalism and reducing maintenance costs.

9.3.4 Creation of new urban parks

The creation of new urban parks from scratch faces two main difficulties: convenient areas in densely inhabited districts are generally scarce and, when available, the cost is usually prohibitive. Alternative possibilities need to be considered:

• *Remodelling existing traditional parks* for present day needs and uses. Many of the present parks were conceived as ornamental Victorian parks with expensive flower beds and access-forbidden lawns. Fundamental changes may be indicated by surveys and consultations.

Battery Park City open spaces, New York, USA

Battery Park City (BPC), located at the southernmost tip of Manhattan, is a 36 ha (92 acre) landfill project comprising a business/residential development extending over the disused Hudson River piers. It provides a prime example of public open spaces being used to promote a real estate development while at the same time being supported by it.

Linked by a bridge to the World Trade Center (WTC), the World Financial Center (WFC) winter garden opens to a plaza and a small harbour. Almost 14 ha (35 acres) of parks and other public open spaces were implemented between 1985 and 1995, from Rockfeller Park in the north to the old Battery Park and Castle Clinton in the south, for the 20 000 affluent residents of BPC, mixed-income residents of adjacent neighbourhoods in lower Manhattan, office workers in BPC, WFC, WTC and the Wall Street area, and students from nearby colleges, etc.

Completed in 1992, Rockfeller Park was planned by Carr, Lynch, Hack and Sandell as a predominantly green, pastoral park but with a full range of both active and passive uses and includes:

- *a linear promenade along the river with regularly spaced benches and lamps and a curved railing at the water's edge;*
- *extensive lawns for informal games (Fig. 9.15a), bounded by a mix of deciduous and evergreen trees;*
- *a quiet sitting area with game tables and sculptures (Fig. 9.15b);*
- *a children's play area (3–5 and 6–9-year-olds) and a terrace for play by older children and young adults: swings, handball or practice tennis court, multi-use hard area (Fig. 9.15c).*
- *a park house with space for recreational and maintenance staff, public restrooms, work and storage areas.*

The North Cove is used as a yacht harbour in front of the WFC. The harbour is surrounded by paved open plazas (Fig. 9.15d), with some lines of trees and by a more densely planted park. Partly built on piles, the Esplanades (Fig. 9.15e), planned by Hanna/Olin Ltd, Eckstut and Cooper, provides a linear green park for pedestrians, joggers, bicycles and rollers, heavily planted on the landward side, sunny and bright along the river. At the southern end of the Esplanades, the South Cove (Fig. 9.15f–h), designed by Child Associates and Eckstut, provides images of a natural cove. All these elements took into consideration the high winds, sea sprays, stormy climatic conditions, loading and artificial soil constraints.

For detailed methodology and planning sequence see Carr 1992, pp. 314–26

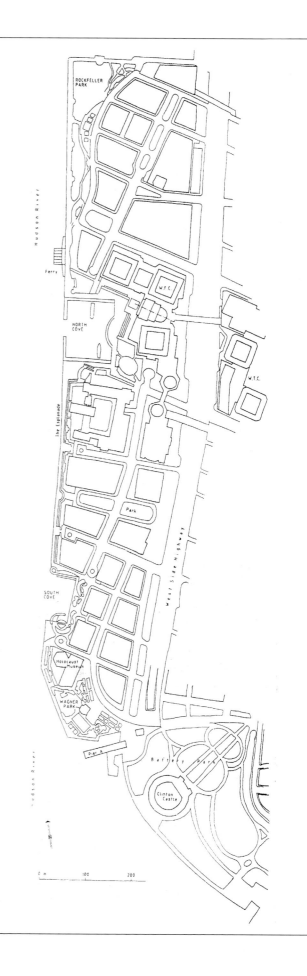

a

b

c

d

e

f

g

h

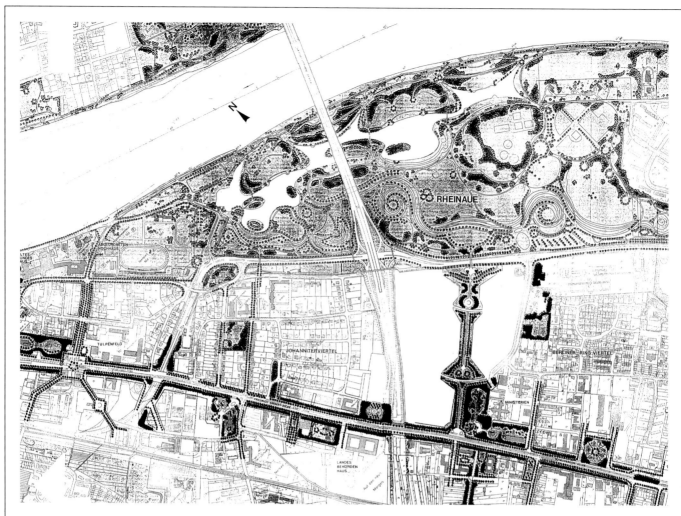

Rheinaue Recreation Park, Bonn, Germany

This large suburban recreation park in the city of Bonn (280,000 inhabitants), was created in 1979 on 160 ha (400 acres) along the River Rhine, for the National Garden Exhibition and to prevent any further development on the site. It is formed on three levels:

- *an upper terrace merging urban spaces and car parks with foot and cycle paths (the new Parliament has been built since the completion of the plan);*
- *a middle terrace for relaxation, games, field and water sports;*
- *a lower terrace at river level as a natural flood basin, with a towpath walk.*

The park is an example of the trend towards the use of extensive green spaces requiring limited maintenance costs (fewer than thirty gardeners). The main elements are:

- *extensive grassed areas for relaxation, informal games and picnics, with few added facilities (such as benches, tables, children's playgrounds, etc.);*
- *small lakes for rowing (hiring facilities), windsurfing or skating (15 ha);*
- *wooded areas (25 ha), almost all the trees having been planted in 1979;*
- *extended networks of pedestrian ways and paths, cycle trails, etc. (45 km);*
- *limited sports facilities (football, a few tennis courts and an athletics track);*
- *a Japanese garden;*
- *restaurant and refreshment bar.*

As many as 50 000 visitors per day use the park in good weather and for special attractions (festivals, concerts, etc.).

In the vicinity of the park, Government Avenue – connecting Bonn central district with the administrative district, the museums and foreign embassies – is a good example of tree-planted areas providing a continuous spatial entity extending over previously irregular streets and influencing the siting of recent buildings.

- *Re-landscaping* the 'green' areas found in many dormitory districts built in the 1960s and 1970s on the edges of towns. The participation of local communities in deciding the content and character is essential.
- *Creating new parks and 'green' areas on derelict land*, reclaimed from disused industrial areas, quarries and mineral workings, railway lines and waste ground (e.g. Gas Work Park).
- *Restoring landfill sites* used for solid waste disposal as parks and recreation areas: sealing with clay cap and/or synthetic membrane, controlling leaching (percolating liquid) and gases, covering with loam and substrate soil: average thickness between 0.6 and 1 m (but varying from 20 cm for turf, to 4 m for high trees).
- *Taking advantage of large shows and festivals* (especially national garden shows like the UK Garden Festival, the German biennial *Bundesgartenschau*) to provide a permanent park (50 to 100 ha) when the temporary buildings are removed.
- *Combining with major civil engineering works* (e.g. highways) necessitating extensive land acquisition and earthworks, which can be used to create new green areas and natural habitats for wildlife.
- *Opening semi-public or private parks* to the public: possibly for periods and subject to conditions.
- *Upgrading public spaces and community facilities* (schools, markets, etc.) by limiting traffic and parking, and creating landscaped street and squares.

- *Using urban interstices* (200 to 4000 m^2) to create small playlots, pocket parks and planted areas.
- *Developing old cemeteries* into public green areas.
- *Defining building regulations* and planning standards for new urban developments requiring the creation of green areas and recreation spaces (see 9.3.8).
- *Earmarking land* for recreation prior to development.
- *Requiring property owners* to provide recreation benefits, such as public access to a shore, riverside or park, as a condition for development approval (the UK 'planning gain').
- *Inviting donations* of public spaces against fiscal or other advantages.

In cities where whole districts are derelict or declining, real estate developers frequently provide private parks and landscaped grounds to make the property attractive. This often creates exclusive rights for the occupiers to the exclusion of the community generally (for example: London Docklands). The loss of public amenity space may be limited if the initiative remains under local authority control, for example through joint development of public parks. In some cases the costs of upkeep for a public square or park may be financed by the development of some 15 to 25 per cent of its area, with the added attractions of cafes, restaurants and boutiques: this approach has been applied on a large scale with the proposed Brooklyn Bridge Park, a park which should 'pay for itself'.

Chestnut Pocket Park, Philadelphia, Pennsylvania, USA

Converted from a parking lot in 1979, this is one of the best examples of pocket parks. Located in a business district, it is closed and locked at night.

The Delta Group, landscape architects

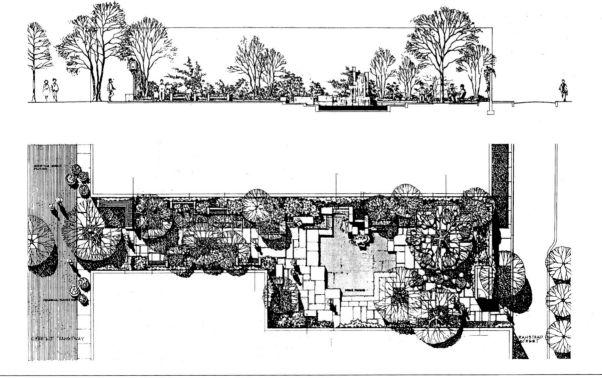

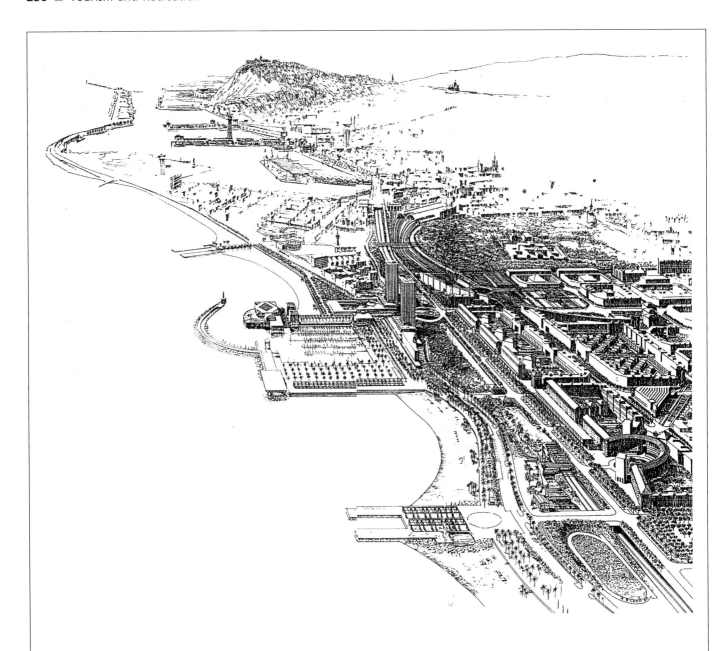

Regeneration of a seafront: Barcelona, Spain

Barcelona, the capital city of Catalonia, had been separated from the sea by a zone of declining industries, railway goods yards, obsolete urban areas and a sewage treatment plant. Two railway lines at ground level created an additional barrier between the centre of the city and the coast.

The 1992 Olympic Games provided a unique opportunity to develop a new relationship between the city and the sea by rehabilitating this large area, which includes over 1 km of beach between two stormwater outfalls and extends over 140 ha (of which 47 were set aside for the Olympic Village).

The objectives of the project were to:

- *extend Barcelona's urban structure of closed city blocks and corridor streets (the famous Cerdas orthogonal grid of 1859);*
- *organize the transport system: a new underground railway line and a new ring road with sunken lines for rapid circulation at a different level from the local traffic;*
- *develop seaside facilities for the whole metropolitan area in a new recreation zone: 17 ha of parks, hotels, commerce and leisure pursuits between the ring road and the beach;*
- *continue the pedestrian route, (paseo marítimo), along the coast;*
- *create a new harbour with almost 1000 moorings.*

Based on the original Cerda grid, the master plan recognized major local features (harbour, railway), localized open spaces and public buildings and defined the most important volumetric characteristics at the scale of 1:500.

Architects-planners: J. Martorell, O. Bohigas, D. Mackay, A. Puigdomènech in Barcelona.

9.3.5 'Eco parks'

Parks of a more ecological character are being planned or implemented in several countries, Holland in particular, usually on large areas (often derelict land) with a limited use pressure. These 'eco parks', 'nature parks' or 'alternative parks' provide unstructured wild gardens with native trees and flowers, more attractive for children than more formal parks, and richer in fauna. They are defined by the nature of the site, the soil, the native vegetation, the biological surroundings, their location in the city, the expected use pressure, etc. They offer to their users a more substantial contact with nature.

Infertile soil usually provides a diverse plant community with few undesirable species: the construction costs of an 'eco park' decrease since importation of topsoil and fertilizers become undesirable; the majority of trees may be planted as very young tree saplings, at a low cost (Spirn 1984, p. 196). They may be combined, especially in arid climates short of water, with the recycling of wastewaters in treatment ponds, basins or lagoons.

A detailed planning procedure is necessary in order to define the 'bioscapes', protect the soil, plant and modify the vegetation to suit the required use. The landscape establishment of an 'eco park' may extend over a long period (ten years or more), during which time the management and maintenance costs are high (less if local residents participate) but subsequent costs of upkeep (mainly rubbish removal and occasional mowing) are lower. As a rule 'eco parks' cannot tolerate a high intensity of use but hard areas may be included for this purpose. 'Eco parks' may also be developed in sections of traditional parks to provide habitats for native plants and small animals. The concept of more natural green areas, with native self-developing vegetation rather than carefully mown lawns, providing habitats for small animals, is developing outside 'eco parks', in sections of traditional parks or other urban green spaces.

9.3.6 Lakesides or seasides and stream banks

Water is fundamental for recreation. Lakesides provide open views of water-based activities; rivers bring nature to the centres of most cities and provide a link with the countryside beyond; canals have shaped whole Dutch cities.

In Paris the quais, which form busy highways along the banks of the River Seine through the heart of Paris, are given over to public recreation on Sundays. From 1000 to 1530 hours, some 5.4 km along the Right Bank, linked by a footbridge and continuing for a further 3.2 km on the Left Bank, are banned to traffic. This allows use by cyclists, rollerskates, pedestrians and quiet riverside relaxation. These traffic-free routed provide access to popular green areas (including the Tuilerie Gardens) and many of the key tourist sights (Eiffel Tower, Hotel des Invalides, Palais du Louvre, Île de la Cité).

Linear waterways provide benefits from:

- the calm coolness of water (unless polluted);
- retention of native vegetation and wildlife in natural surroundings;
- opportunities for long footpaths and trails, often separated from traffic;
- attractive links between neighbourhoods and between the town, its suburbs and the countryside.

Linear waterways must include at least a pedestrian path and may have a cycle track and rest areas. If sufficiently wide the surrounding land may form a linear park with opportunities for both water- and land-based recreation. Drainage easements, prohibiting building, in flood plains can be turned into linear parks for summer use. Creekside parks may be created by liberating a stream (or surface rainwater) from its underground pipe and landscaping the area alongside.

Examples of parks beside linear waterways

*The **North Saskatchewan River Park** extends over 12 miles and 47 ha outside Edmonton (Alberta, Canada), partially on land subject to flooding: 36 ha have been developed as 'natural areas' mainly with local self-seeding vegetation and trees. The park includes several landscaped 'activity centres' (picnic areas, restaurants, sports centres, look-out posts, etc.) linked by pedestrian paths and bicycle tracks.*

*On the **Boise River** in Idaho (USA) inner-tubing developed spontaneously in the 1970s with a 7-mile float trip in inner-tubes, rafts or another mean. A higher number of users (up to 3000/day) called for the creation, and the later extension, of an access park to the river, with parking areas, etc. An unstructured activity appealing to people of all ages at minimal cost for the community.*

Many *maritime cities and ports* of earlier times have vast areas of disused docks and warehouses which provide opportunities to acquire land at reasonable cost for parks, open spaces and frontages featuring water attractions (marinas, berthed historic ships). Pedestrian pathways along waterfronts can provide links with historic and landscaped centres (trails of discovery and leisure interest): examples include docklands in London, Gothenburg, Barcelona, San Francisco, Sydney, etc. Environmental improvements of this type provide a stimulus to regeneration and inward investment.

9.3.7 Pedestrian squares, areas and networks

A city centre is the heart of urban community life, serving as a 'downtown' place to which people go to meet, congregate, shop, socialize, relax and enjoy the throngs of day time activity and nightlife. Many older European cities are privileged with historic districts, wide boulevards (Ramblas, Barcelona) and large traditional squares or piazzas (The Navonna in Rome,

Sydney's Darling Harbour, Australia

Conversion of 54 ha of redundant waterfront and railway goods yard, adjacent to Sydney's business district, to public recreation space of an urban character. Developed in three years only (1985–7) with the following organization:

- Darling Harbour Authority: determination of land uses, decision on designs after advice of a Quality Review Committee,
- Design Directorate (director: Barry Young): development strategy, master plan and design guidelines, design concept and brief for public sector buildings, design development of public environment, design parameters for private sector buildings,
- Managing Contractor: project management, programming, contract preparation and supervising, design development and documentation for buildings (utilizing consultant teams).

For each $1 spent by the public sector, $2 have been spent by private developers.
Main elements:

- new urban park on the valley floor, with water 'stream' and lake, extending under the shadow of the highway structures,
- new people-orientated harbour in Cockle Bay, surrounded by a waterfront promenade,
- maritime and power house museums, aquarium, exhibition and convention centre seating 3500, festival market-place and existing 12 500-seat entertainment centre.

The new area attracts about 10 to 14 million visitors annually, up to 250 000 on peak days, most of them using public transport and local monorail. Impact: redevelopment of adjacent areas, continuing today with the extension of the pedestrian precinct to nearby sections of the city.

Design Directorate: Keys Young, Research, Planning and Urban Design Consultants,
McConnel, Smith and Johnson, Sydney.

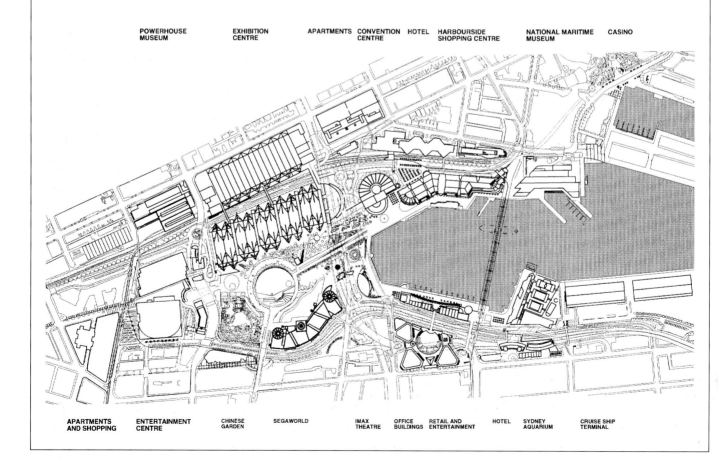

POWERHOUSE MUSEUM   EXHIBITION CENTRE   APARTMENTS   CONVENTION CENTRE   HOTEL   HARBOURSIDE SHOPPING CENTRE   NATIONAL MARITIME MUSEUM   CASINO

APARTMENTS AND SHOPPING   ENTERTAINMENT CENTRE   CHINESE GARDEN   SEGAWORLD   IMAX THEATRE   OFFICE BUILDINGS   RETAIL AND ENTERTAINMENT   HOTEL   SYDNEY AQUARIUM   CRUISE SHIP TERMINAL

DARLING HARBOUR 2000
SYDNEY   AUSTRALIA

SYDNEY
HARBOUR
BRIDGE

SYDNEY
OPERA
HOUSE

DARLING
HARBOUR
BOUNDARY

NATIONAL
MARITIME
MUSEUM

HOTEL
APARTMENTS

SYDNEY
AQUARIUM

HARBOURSIDE   COCKLE

DARLING
PARK

SYDNEY
CONVENTION
CENTRE

IMAX THEATRE

APARTMENTS

DARLING WALK
SEGA WORLD

EXHIBITION HALLS

TUMBALONG PARK

CHINESE
GARDEN

DEVELOPMENT
SITE FOR SYDNEY
EXHIBITION CENTRE
EXPANSION

POWERHOUSE
MUSEUM

CARPARK

ENTERTAINMENT
CENTRE

UNIVERSITY OF
TECHNOLOGY
SYDNEY

APARTMENTS

Strategy for the River Thames, UK

This study examined the 50-km stretch of the Thames from Hampton Court to Greenwich with the aim of promoting a high quality of design and landscape along the river. The design strategy drew up recommendations for:

- *focal points to act as magnets for activity and river transport (a);*
- *building scale, massing and relationship with the river (b);*
- *landscape strategy to integrate buildings and urban frontages;*
- *pedestrian access and river crossings, lighting and security;*
- *corporate signage, use of public art and lighting to produce drama;*
- *a strategy for planning guidance.*

Planners, architects: Ove Arup Partnership (Michael Lowe, Corinne Swan)
The Government Office for London

a

b

Landscape

The River acts as a unifying feature linking the green spaces along it, like beads on a necklace. These vary from informal woodland in the quieter upstream sections, particularly between Hampton Court and Kew, to the planted edges associated with the formal embankments in the metropolitan core. The Arup strategy suggests that a stronger landscape framework should be established to raise the quality of civic space along the riverside. This would be particularly appropriate for integrating areas of mixed architectural style and quality, as on the Southwark riverside (Fig. 5). This approach would not, of course, be appropriate where old warehouses and their modern counterparts rise vertically from the River edge, as in parts of Docklands.

Pedestrian accessibility

There are stretches of the River with very limited access between banks. The Arup strategy highlights the potential for new bridge links between Charing Cross/Embankment and the South Bank Arts Centre, and between St Paul's Cathedral and Bankside Power Station (in its new incarnation for the Tate Gallery). There is also scope for improved pedestrian access in the Kew Gardens-Brentford area, possibly by ferry. Access from Brentford, Hammersmith and Wandsworth town centres could be enhanced too, as well as from the office centre at Canary Wharf.

Enhancement Opportunities

1. Hampton Court Park
2. South of Kingston Road Bridge
3. Ham Lands
4. Kew Gardens
5. Brentford
6. Duke's Meadow
7. Mortlake
8. Corney Reach
9. Hammersmith
10. Barn Elms
11. Fulham Palace Gardens
12. East side Putney Bridge
13. Gargoyle Wharf Site
14. Fulham
15. Wandsworth
16. Nine Elms
17. Tate Gallery
18. Albert Embankment
19. South-Bank Centre
20. St Paul's frontage
21. Bankside
22. West side Tower Bridge
23. Wapping
24. Millwall
25. Deptford Creek

Legend

- Focal Points of Activity - Existing
- Focal Points of Activity - Proposed
- Potential for increased River Activity
- Buildings up to 3 storeys (approx 10m)
- Buildings up to 6 storeys (approx 20m)
- Buildings greater than 6 storeys (20m+)
- Key Landmarks - Action Required
- Key Landmarks
- Public Open Space
- Informal Woodland - Solid / Informal Woodland - Partial / Formal Planting
- Enhancement Opportunities
- Increased Accessibility Desirable
- Thames Path - Significant Missing Links
- Working Wharves

c

Manchester, Salford and Trafford, Tourism Development Inititative (TDI), UK

Manchester is one of the largest conurbations in England with more than 7 million people within one hour's drive and over 14 million within two hours' drive. The city has major sports, cultural and entertainment attractions. For tourism and recreation, the primary needs were to improve pedestrian linkages and to enhance and use the existing canal networks to provide more leisure opportunities.

The TDI partnership concentrated on the linear water corridor through the heart of the city, formed by the Manchester Ship Canal and River Irwell, treating the area as a whole to develop a cohesive urban fabric, rather than as isolated, individual parcels of land.

North West Tourist Board, 1993.
LDR International: Urban Design & Development Consultants.

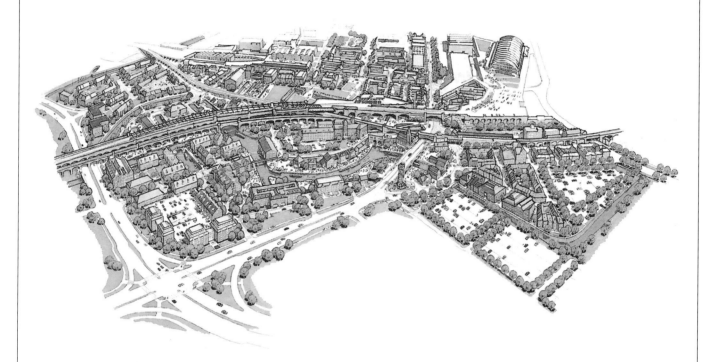

Continuous promenade to be created along the canal

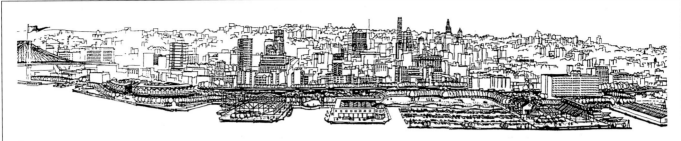

a

The Brooklyn Bridge Park, New York, USA

The project for this new park occupies 74 acres (30 ha) and 1.5 miles of waterfront, south of the Brooklyn Bridge, with a sweeping view of Manhattan. The area, until the 1970s, a cargo marine terminal, belongs to the New Jersey and New York Port Authority. The programme consists of a regional waterfront park of 50 acres (20 ha), 3000 underground parking spaces, commercial and recreation facilities. Its objectives, supported by the Brooklyn Bridge Park Coalition (of community and civic groups), are:

- *to create recreation facilities and open spaces in one of the most populous New York boroughs;*
- *to enhance Brooklyn as a place in which to live and work, attracting tourists with museums, a major world-class conference centre hotel and executive retreat, a working boat-yard and shallow draft maritime centre, and a variety of restaurant and food halls.*

This project has been widely promoted and publicized as a typical example of a self-sustaining park that would 'pay for itself' through long-term leases to private builder/operator 'concessionaires' whose rental payments would cover operation and maintenance expenses of the park, the land remaining in public ownership. According to the Schnadelbach Partnership, landscape architects in New York and authors of the project:

- *parks that pay for themselves should be planned as self-sufficient from the beginning;*
- *commercial uses should be park-related and scattered;*
- *only as much commercial development as is needed should be sought (possibly 25 per cent of area);*
- *facilities that charge user fees should be open periodically to the general public.*

At a time of scarce public funds, this new formula is attractive and should justify the transfer of property from the Port Authority to the city and the Coalition. However, federal, state or local funds are still necessary for repairing the piers and developing the park; in 1996, the Coalition experienced difficulties in attracting potential investors and the Port Authority was considering having to dispose of its land.

b

c

d

Grand Place in Brussels). Large pedestrian squares have also been constructed as a feature of cities in other areas (Portland, US or Yokohama, Japan). Pedestrian shopping centres and malls have reintroduced the features of the nineteenth century arcades and there is a renewed interest in street markets and open air events.

Most cities have introduced traffic diversion schemes to enable whole central areas of historic or commercial interest to become fully or partly (at times) pedestrianized. In many residential areas traffic calming or exclusion has followed the Dutch *whoonerfen* (which date from the 1960s) with residential streets

- being restricted to limited traffic at slow pace;
- giving priority to pedestrians, opportunities for children to play, etc;
- physically restructured (speed bumps, breaks in alignment, bollards, cobble strips, tree planting, benches, etc.).

In other cases large roads have been closed to traffic on Sundays, allowing, many alternative uses – an economic and dynamic solution which involves whole community participation (Laurie 1983).

Many cities and new towns provide integrated bicycle routes and pedestrian networks (see 'trails' in 4.3.3) allowing people to walk or cycle along routes largely separated from traffic, and often in pleasant surroundings, from residential areas to schools, parks and places of work. This network may also link the city with 'green' suburban areas.

9.3.8 Neighbourhood recreation areas

> The green structure has not been regarded as an overriding element of the environment in the city, on an equal footing with buildings and infrastructures. It has rather been considered as 'left over' land and land resources that could be used to solve urgent tasks of development. This attitude will have to change if the city development is to become sustainable. The green structure in a city is intended to meet people's need for recreation and their need to have part of nature in their immediate neighbourhood. (CHS 1995, Addendum 2)

The private gardens of villas, semi-detached or rows of houses, extensively developed in many Anglo-Saxon towns, provides an excellent answer to most of the outdoor recreation needs of their occupiers: small children playing in security, adults able to enjoy gardening and relaxation in privacy. However, in districts where most of the population mainly live in flats, the demand for outdoor facilities and a better environment is a primary concern, as demonstrated by numerous surveys (e.g. in Ruhr towns, Vienna, etc.).

The needs of flat dwellers, which will vary with countries and ethnic origins, are mainly related to age:

- for *very young children* with their mothers: sunny but shaded protected sites, without traffic or dogs, with lawns, traditional playgrounds, and possibly a paddling pool;
- for *children between 5 and 10:* secure areas near to their houses, protected from traffic; the school playgrounds are

often too far for children who cannot cross traffic roads by themselves; their needs are often most difficult to solve;

- for *teenagers from 12 to 16:* sports facilities and areas where they can meet in groups without disturbing the neighbourhood: parks, leisure centres or even school playgrounds;
- for *adults:* limited needs near their homes;
- for *old people:* opportunities to make short walks in a protected environment (low traffic, gentle slopes, smooth surfaces, sufficient lighting).

Sometimes incompatible, these needs are more often complementary and may build better relations between people of different ages.

Large play areas of the 'Adventure', 'Creative Play' or 'Robinson' type are attractive for the 5- to 10-year-old children but usually imply, nowadays, a supervising person and, hence, cannot be provided everywhere.

> The playgrounds in the ruins of the bombed cities in the Ruhr area, I met with in 1946 as Red Cross worker. I saw children building their towns from the rubble, laying out gardens with the flowers they could find amidst the bombed-out houses. The children were happily absorbed in creative play, despite hunger and need. It was these impressions that encouraged me to 'invent' a new kind of children's playground, the Robinson Playground, in 1953.
>
> (Lederman 1992)

Furthermore, traditional separate areas for the different ages are being abandoned for more communal open spaces, as had been done, 20 years before, for community centres.

Adapted *statutory planning procedures and building regulations* are important in order to answer these needs when new residential developments are considered. More specific regulations have been issued for new developments, which could be more beneficial if the 'playgrounds' were informal, unmanaged, not over-equipped 'play environments'. The main objectives should be to allow children and youngsters to play on their doorsteps, in front of their houses, streets and squares, with traffic controlled and streets becoming areas for games, exploration, discovery: the pre-war situation before the explosion of traffic. Different categories of 'urban squares', of 'urban inner courtyards' or 'residential streets' may bring convenient solutions, provide secure and informal playgrounds. These open areas have often been evaluated at about 20 m^2 per housing unit.

9.3.9 Planning outdoor recreation areas

Planning green areas and open air facilities at the scale of the whole city is dealt with Chapter 8.5. For individual parks, the stages are identical to those proposed for planning tourism resorts (see 6.6):

- *alternative broad concepts* proposed, taking account of the site's size, resources and capacity, of the ideas and needs of

Greenways for Geneva, Switzerland

This network of greenways (a), which has been progressively implemented since 1996, will provide pedestrian links, as far as possible distinct from the road network, taking advantage of existing parks and other green areas. The network, in particular, links schools, commercial centres and public transport poles with the residential areas. It has been based on an site-survey of all existing unbuilt areas, especially the local paths used by people living or working in the neighbourhood. The study was accompanied by proposals for 'blueways' along the lake and the river (b)

Client: Ville de Genève, Service d'Urbanisme, 1990
Planners: A&M Baud-Bovy, architects/planners, Geneva

Geneva: confluence of Rhône and Arve

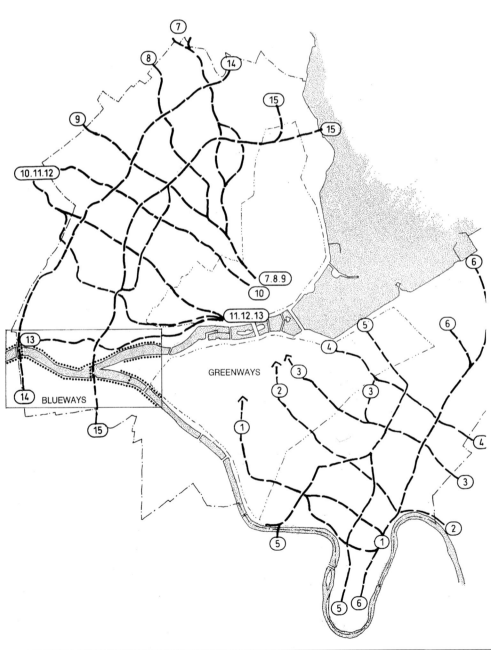

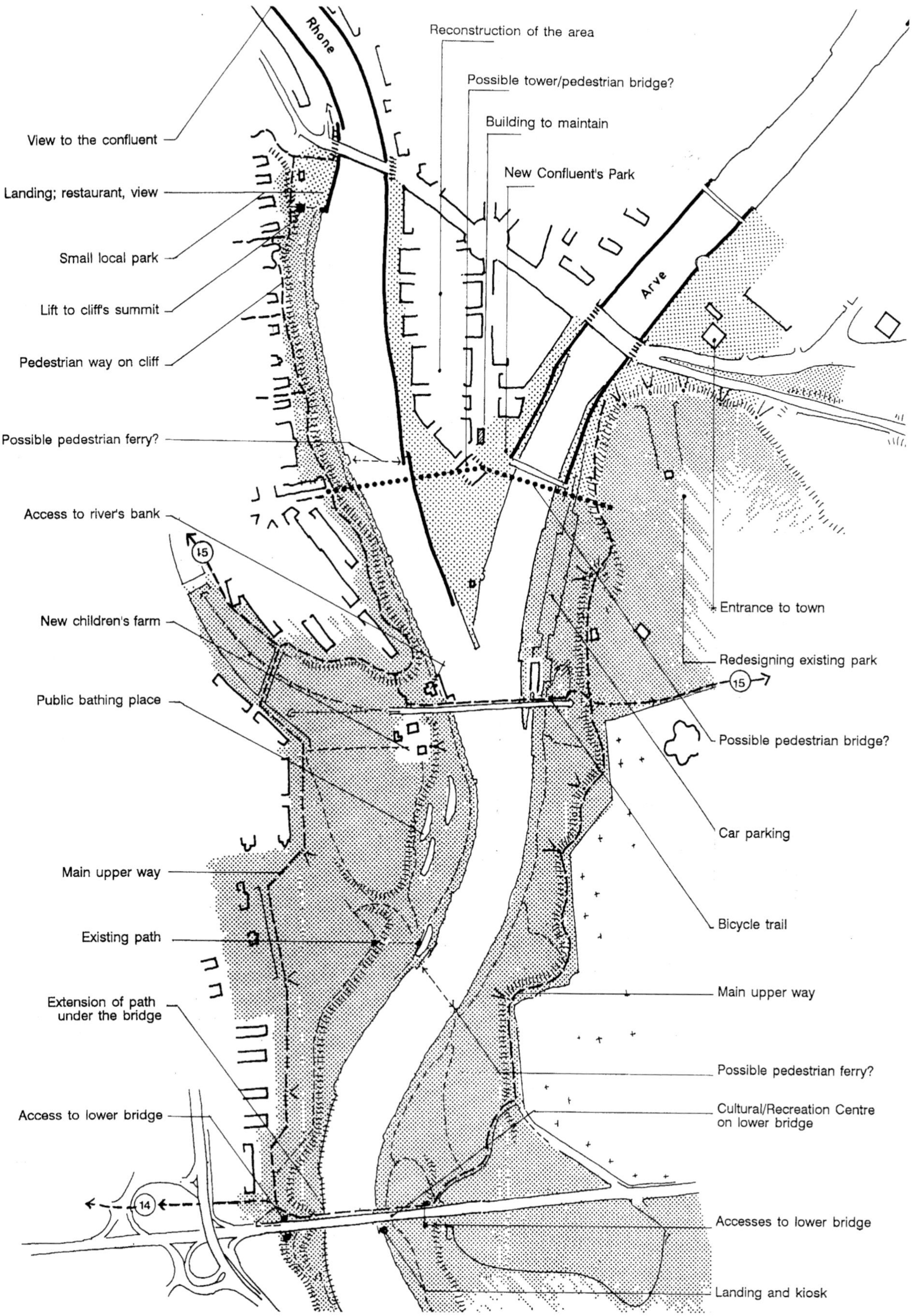
Rhone
Arve
Reconstruction of the area
Possible tower/pedestrian bridge?
Building to maintain
New Confluent's Park
View to the confluent
Landing; restaurant, view
Small local park
Lift to cliff's summit
Pedestrian way on cliff
Possible pedestrian ferry?
Access to river's bank
15
New children's farm
Public bathing place
Main upper way
Existing path
Extension of path under the bridge
Access to lower bridge
14
Entrance to town
Redesigning existing park
15
Possible pedestrian bridge?
Car parking
Bicycle trail
Main upper way
Possible pedestrian ferry?
Cultural/Recreation Centre on lower bridge
Accesses to lower bridge
Landing and kiosk
b

Viaduct Daumesnil Greenway, Paris, France

This 4-km urban greenway has been created during the 1990s on a disused railway line between the former Bastille Station (now the Bastille Opera) and the Vincennes Park, at the limit of Central Paris.

Between the Bastille and the new Reuilly neighbourhood the walkway goes along Daumesnil Avenue at the top of the viaduct (c), level with the highest floors of the apartment houses on the other side of the avenue. Workshops for craftsmen, boutiques and art galleries are being located, on lease, in the arches of the viaduct, on two levels.

The greenway enters Reuilly between high new buildings (a), crosses a bridge, to the park (with indoor swimming pool) and new apartment houses. It proceeds through older neighbourhoods, partly in cuttings, with short tunnels (b).

a

b

c

1 Bastille Square and Bastille Opera
2 New Reuilly neighbourhood
3 Nation Square
4 Bois de Vincennes Park
5 Sports Centre and Bercy Park
6 Lyon Station

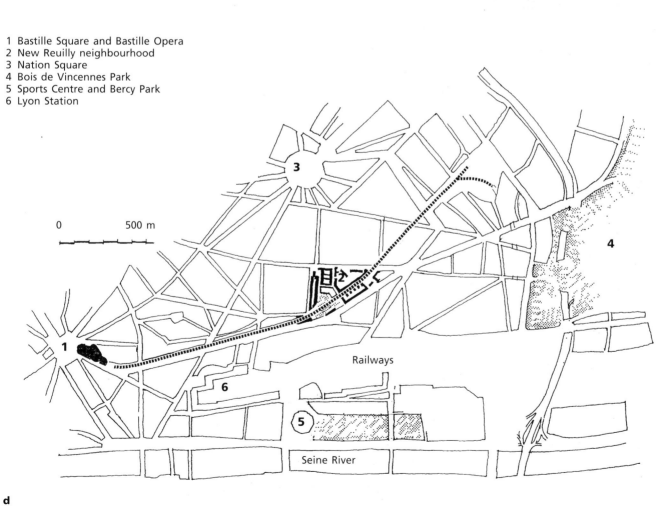

d

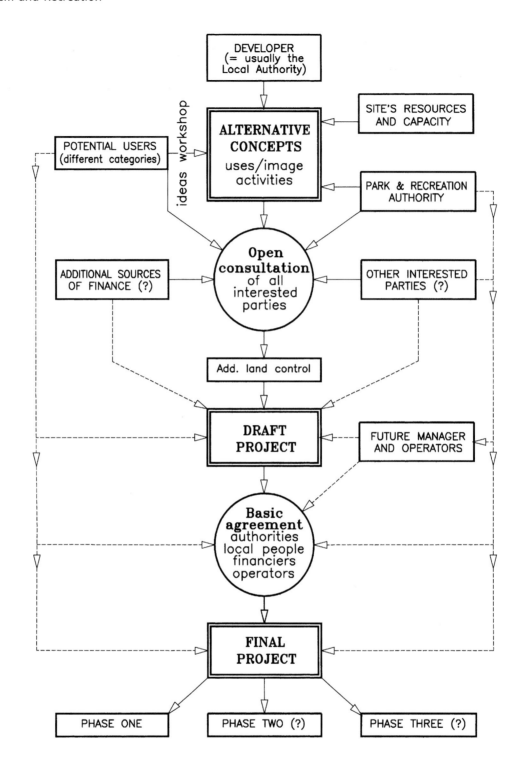

Figure 9.1

the potential users, of the objectives of the local authority (role and image of the area in the urban development, activities and facilities to be provided), and of possible conflicts with other activities;

- *permanent consultation*;
- *draft project*, evaluated by all parties;
- *final project*, schematic, followed by one or several detailed implementation projects.

The planning sequence presented in 6.6.0 should, however, be slightly adapted when planning green or mineral parks, pedestrian squares, residential streets, etc.:

- *potential users* of various categories (people living – or working – in the neighbourhood, or further away, of different origins, ages, etc.) replace the tourism notion of a more distant 'clientele'; community planning allows the potential users to take a direct part at the various stages of the planning process.

• *a park authority* (or agency, service, department, etc.) usually provides general regulations for planning and is responsible for operating the facility (although users of the park or private operators of commercial facilities could be involved).

• *additional sources of finance* (higher metropolitan authority, nearby developers, operators of commercial facilities, etc.) may participate (or not) in the project, but the main or only source of financing is usually the local community;

The planning procedure may be expressed as shown in Fig. 9.1.

Appendices: Useful data for planning development

APPENDIX A1: MARKETS FOR TOURISM AND RECREATION – INFLUENCES ON DEMAND AND TRENDS

A1.1 Measurement of recreation demand

Quantification of demands for recreation presents many difficulties. Leisure is essentially a matter of individual choice and can be readily substituted by other activities. Furthermore, the choice of recreation and range of variety considered is greatly influenced by the time available for leisure and many other personal factors such as age, marital status, income and educational background. Individual characteristics apart, recreational activities are highly dependent on the resources available within reasonable time–distance and the facilities to make proper use of them.

For purposes of planning, demand must be assessed in terms of:

Effective current demand: Statistics on the uses of leisure time are based on relatively small samples of the population subject to many qualifications and are often not directly comparable.

Latent demand: Unsatisfied demands for recreation are difficult to measure:

- many recreational pursuits are unorganized and dispersed over wide areas;
- participation is often expressed in vague terms without qualification as to frequency or time committed;
- data from specific sites or locations may not be representative of the region as a whole;
- predictions are at best based on indices which are only approximate.

Future patterns of recreational activity will not simply be the result of satisfying latent needs. As new facilities are provided, further self-generating interest will expand the demand, often at the expense of other less fashionable pursuits. **Continuous monitoring** of the influence of supply on demand is essential if a correct balance of resources and facilities is to be maintained. Equally important is the need to study the effective use of resources and limits to capacity.

A1.2 Market segmentation

The strategies for developing tourism and recreational products or services generally require two main approaches:

- *market segmentation* to identify the characteristics of likely customers enabling products to be tailored to their requirements
- *product differentiation* to distinguish particular products from the competition by emphasizing their attributes and benefits.

Market segmentation

Market segmentation involves dividing a market into meaningful sub-groups: The segments may be:

Geographic – units such as countries, regions, counties, towns and neighbourhoods indicate principal catchment areas served, population densities, time and travel distances and transportation systems involved.

Demographic – variables include age, gender, family size; stage in life cycle, occupation and income. These are usually statistically quantifiable as an indication of present and future potential market demands.

Psychographic – profiles take account of social classes, cultures, background and other influences which affect attitudes and behaviour.

Economic – divisions are based on differences in spending power. Market segmentation into socio-economic classes taking account of education and employment status is often used to provide a multi-dimensional indicator.

Behavioural characteristics are often highly influential in recreation and tourism. They set the motivations for choosing a particular interest, the aspirations of the user and the benefits sought.

Behavioural approaches are often expressed through consumer models and the steps pursued in reaching a buying decision. The benefits sought by different users of say, a leisure pool, may be fun and pleasure, learning, training for fitness, socializing, relaxing, improving general health, spectating.

These activities can be set against the local or regional organization of the participants and their demographic and socio-economic groupings. Sub-groups may also be involved such as clubs, schools and private parties seeking to hire space or facilities and the particular needs of disabled users. Similar criteria may be applied to the choice of tourism products but travel to foreign destinations is also affected by other considerations such as differences in climate and environment, comparative prices and exchange rates and extent of risk involved. Market segmentation is necessary to quantify likely demands against the facilities required to ensure that the most effective provision can be made within the constraints which are imposed (cost limits, space, resources, competition).

A1.3 Influences on demand for recreation and tourism

1 Time and opportunity

Influences	Effects: Examples
Free time	Increase with advances in technology, changes in work patterns, socio-economic changes and longevity. Generally related to GDP but affected by attitudes and roles
Holiday entitlements	Including school holidays and national and religious calendars: directly affect peak tourism and recreation demands, lengths of stay, frequency of visits
Weekend cycles	Most day recreation is concentrated into the weekends. Use levels for parks and recreation facilities are usually based on a design day
Organization, promotion	To maximize utilization of chartered transport and accommodation, inclusive travel packages set programmes for departure and return. Other packages are designed to balance hotel etc. occupancies
Geographic factors	The time–distances from main urban populations determine pressures of demand on surrounding recreational resources and the needs for user-based facilities

2 Demographic structures

Influences	Effects: Examples
Age and participation	Adult participation in vigorous games and sports reduces with age. Other pursuits are more affected by opportunity and individual interests
Gender	Women generally participate less in sport than men but more in health and body toning exercise and family-associated and socio-cultural activities
Life cycle roles	Leisure, recreation and social interests tend to progress through cycles, e.g. youth, independence, family commitments, maturity, retirement. This segmentation profiles attitudes and requirements
Population trends	Increases in older age groups in the main tourism-generating countries affects the design of products. Population escalation in developing countries increases competition for resources

3 Socio-economic characteristics

Influences	Effects: Examples
Socio-cultural attitudes	Affect the timing of holidays, propensities for travel, visitor profiles, tourism interests in sojourn, sightseeing, visiting friends and relatives; design of accommodation and facilities for recreation
Economic conditions	Economic performance has a direct bearing on government priorities, finance for recreation, relative currency values and individual disposable income, with impacts on outgoing or incoming tourism
Socio-economic segmentation	As a rule, the higher socio-economic groupings have more diverse recreational and cultural interests and experience leading to higher expenditure and more selective choice
Education and awareness	Advances in education and information have led to widening interests in culture, nature and sophisticated recreation

4 Institutional factors

Influences	Effects: Examples
Community recreation	Few recreational and cultural facilities are viable unless they are supported by high revenue-producing activities, wider subscriptions or subsidized by public authorities
Government involvement	Community recreation is usually the responsibility of municipal authorities. Specific national organizations may be set up to promote and support sport, outdoor recreation, heritage conservation, cultural interests, social tourism and tourism generally
National undertakings	State departments, national and regional parks services, and utility companies may be encouraged, even mandated, to provide opportunities for recreation compatible with their other functions
Voluntary bodies	Self-financing associations and trusts may be concerned with preserving places of historic or natural beauty for public benefit. Environmental pressure groups may exert strong influence on conservation of resources
Legislation, regulation	Government regulation of tourism and recreation is mainly concerned with environmental interests and regulation of standards
Institutions	Representative groups often set standards, codes, requirements and guidelines

5 Technological changes

Influences	Effects: Examples
Resource utilization	Improvement or replacement of existing environments to increase durability, attractiveness and recreational resources. Reclamation of extraction sites, disused industrial land and archaeology

Substitution	Construction of synthetic sports grounds, built leisure centres, fully or partly enclosed resort complexes and theme parks to enable intensive continuous use independent of outside conditions
Transport and infrastructure	Highway extensions, increases in car ownership, development of long haul and hub-distribution aircraft, high speed trains and cruise ships have brought exotic distant destinations within time and price competition for large markets
Communications and control	Rapid technical advances in communications and computer systems have led to developments in international and regional networking, information and reservation systems and control processes
Simulation	Created experiences range from animation, interaction, movement to computer simulation

A1.4 Tourism measurement

Tourism may be quantified in many ways:

Measurement	Examples
Financial	Expenditure in destinations, foreign currency transactions
Movements	Visits recorded at frontiers, traffic surveys
Consumption	Nights spent in hotels and tourist accommodation, admissions
Densities and ratios	Tourist nights/ha/annum, peak tourists/ha at locations tourists/residents, tourist expenditure/total consumer expenditure

Densities and ratios are most useful for planning purposes: they enable the volume of tourism to be seen realistically against the size, population and economic development of the destination. Tourism planning can thus be integrated into national planning frameworks. By reference to conditions experienced in other areas, the physical impacts of tourism development can be readily quantified and compared and saturation levels determined.

Statistics

Collection of tourism data involves organization and cost, the accuracy of estimates depending on the selection of samples, timing and frequency of surveys, treatment of variables and interpretation of results. Priority is usually given to the relative importance of the information such as the numbers, origins and expenditures of international arrivals which have economic and marketing implications. Domestic tourists, particularly segments involving low expenditure or/and difficult measurement, tend to be estimated from secondary data such as censuses.

A1.5 International tourism

International tourism is the largest world export industry. World Tourism Organization statistics[1] show that international tourism arrivals reached 595 million in 1996, involving 2934 million bed-nights. International tourism receipts amounted to US$425 billion accounting for more than 8.3 per cent of total world exports of merchandise and 35.4 per cent of total world exports of services. These receipts did not include expenditure on international transport which came to over US$68 billion in 1995.

Although highly sensitive to dangers and affected by economic variables, international tourism has shown resilience and overall progressive growth.

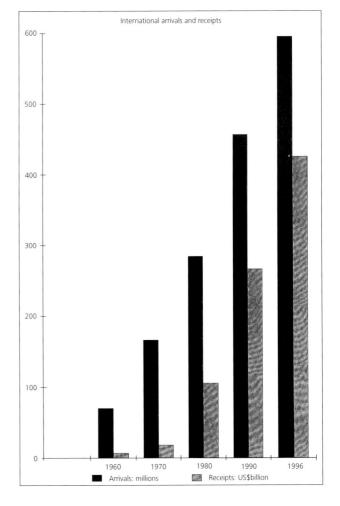

Average annual growth rates (%)	1990–1996
Tourist arrivals	4.54
Tourist nights	3.81
Tourism receipts	8.13
Tourism expenditure	7.47

Source: World Tourism Organization, 1997

[1]WTO General Assembly: Tourism Market Trends: World: 1985–1996. World Tourism Organization, Madrid, October, 1997

Whilst almost half the developed countries showed a negative balance in their international tourism accounts, the surplus balance in developing economies consistently increased from US$6 billion (1980) to US$62 billion in 1996.

Apart from cyclical seasonal fluctuations, tourism demands in a destination may change progressively or rapidly due to particular circumstances.

Changes in tourism	Examples: Factors influencing change
Progressive increases	
Improved accessibility	Regional airports, highway extensions, advances in transport.
Favourable conditions	Unique attractions, good environment, incentives, confidence.
Product enhancement	Research, investment in facilities, service and conservation.
Sustained popularity	Control over quality, extent and pace of development, continual improvements, life cycle planning.
Market development	Target marketing, reassurance of standards, image building.
Economic advances	Income growth in market countries, increased leisure time.
Rapid increases	
Staged events	World games, international expositions, special festivals.
Rapid losses	
Fear, adverse publicity	War, terrorism, epidemics, disasters, political uncertainties.
Frustration	Labour disputes, commercial failures, entry restrictions.
Progressive losses	
Perceived loss of value	Price escalation, inadequate provisions, declining standards.
Market reduction	Changes in requirements, competition from more attractive or lower cost destinations.

A1.6 Global projections to 2010

Tourism planning involves market projection over medium and long terms in order to justify the high capital investments which are invariably required for large-scale facilities and infrastructure development. Regional and national visitor statistics provide a broad indication of trends and changing patterns of tourism. They serve as a background to more specific evaluation of proposed development in selected locations.

Case Example

World Tourism Organization forecasts for International Arrivals to 2020[a]

Region	Average annual growth rates (%)			International tourist arrivals (millions)				Intraregional: long haul % split[b]	
	1995–2000	2000–2010	2010–2020	1995	2000	2010	2020	1995	2020
Europe	3.1	3.1	3.1	335	390	527	717	88:12	85:15
East Asia/Pacific	7.7	7.2	6.6	80	116	231	438	79:21	83:17
Americas	3.9	3.8	3.8	111	134	195	284	77:23	62:38
Africa	6.0	5.6	5.1	20	27	46	75	58:42	64:36
Middle East	6.9	6.7	6.5	14	19	37	69	42:58	37:63
South Asia	6.4	6.2	5.8	4	6	11	19	24:76	14:86
World[c]	4.2	4.2	4.4	564	692	1047	1602[d]	82:18	76:24

Notes (a) Figures rounded up

(b) Arrivals of residents of a country in the same region: arrivals of residents of countries outside the region as percentages of the total arrivals.

(c) These figures exclude domestic tourism (see A17)

(d) World Tourism receipts are forecast to increase from US$ 399 billion (1995) to US$ 2000 billion (2020)

Source of data: World Tourism Organization: *Tourism 2020 Vision*, 1996

Over the 25-year period, China is expected to become the leading destination for international tourists as well as a major generating country. Strong growth is also forecast for the Russian Federation, Thailand, Singapore, Indonesia and South Africa.[2]

A1.7 Domestic tourism

Domestic tourism is important as a means of extending benefits within a country as well as improving the balance of foreign tourism revenue and utilization of investments. In many countries, domestic tourism is much more significant than international tourism. Overall, the ratios between domestic tourism and international tourism are about 10:1 in terms of activity and between 3:1 and 4:1 in expenditure.

Over the period of WTO forecasts to 2020, most industrialized countries are expected to come close to their ceilings in respect of the proportions of their populations participating and the extent of participation. However, strong growth in domestic tourism is forecast for the developing countries of Asia, Latin America, the Middle East and Africa[3]

APPENDIX A2: INVESTMENT IN TOURISM AND RECREATION – METHODS AND SOURCES

Investment in tourism development is not limited to the establishment of tourist facilities: finance is also required to provide suitable infrastructure, to conserve the resources and to establish the services and supplies on which tourism products depend. In most cases this involves both public and private sector participation, although in market economies the former may be only to enable development to take place.

A2.1 Characteristics of tourism investment

The financing of hotels, tourist resorts and other related facilities usually involves a high capital investment balancing two sets of risks:

[2]World Tourism Organization, *Tourism: 2020 Vision: Influences, directional flows and key trends.* Executive Summary, WTO, Madrid, 1997
[3]World Tourism Organization, *Tourism: 2020 Vision:* Executive Summary, WTO, Madrid, 1997, p.4.

Property	Considerations
High ratio of fixed assets	Up to 90 per cent of total investment
High operating costs	60–80 per cent of revenues, limited flexibility
Long pay back period	Long term finance: 10–20 years
Fixed location	Dependency on external conditions
Marketing	
Variable demand	Seasonal cycles, long-term trends
Perishable product	Sales of room nights, seats, etc.
Price and location competition	Discretionary expenditure, choice of destination
High sensitivity to risk	Political structure, civil unrest, terrorism
Affected by economic changes	In both originating and destination countries

When privately owned accommodation predominates different sets of criteria apply

A2.2 Revenue earning potential

Development of tourism includes facilities which are capable of earning revenues, both directly from tourists to finance the costs of investment, and those which are supportive. The latter may be funded by charges on the development or more broadly out of taxation.

Revenues accruing to the development can cover a range of income streams:

- capital sales of property to individual or group owners;
- leasing of facilities to individuals, operating companies or concessionaires;
- fees, subscriptions and rentals from club and association users;
- short-term letting of rooms with or without services;
- sale of products and services.

A2.3 Accommodation

A major part of the direct investment is spent in providing accommodation. The commercial feasibility of such investment depends on a number of factors but can be considered under two main categories:

Privately owned accommodation – where property is mainly sold to individuals for second homes, or letting, development is a form of real estate business. Feasibility depends on market demand and saleable value set against the costs of development and opportunity costs of capital. Development is usually carried out in self-financing phases. Sales of property sales are sensitive to the attractiveness of the development, distance to urban catchments and economic conditions.

Specific tourist accommodation – facilities designed to accommodate short-stay visitors or a commercial business involve long-term capital and other risks. The feasibility is dependent on market and revenue projections, estimation of operating expenses and fixed costs, including the required return on investment.

Accommodation may be *fully serviced* with restaurants and other guest amenities or *self-catering*. The latter is an option increasingly offered in integrated resorts and areas in which there are alternative restaurants, etc., available.

A2.4 Other facilities

Commercial and entertainment facilities

The feasibility of restaurants, bars, shops, cinemas and other commercial investments in resorts is highly dependent on the numbers of tourists, employees and residents in the area. This often results in closures outside the tourist season, with the need to cover fixed costs in a shorter operating period, and fluctuating employment.

Created recreation

Recreation facilities can be financed in a number of ways:

* as part of the cost of accommodation;
* by wider subscription arrangements;
* through cooperative arrangements;
* by municipal funding.

Municipal funding may be financed by community charges, by the sale of other assets such as land, or by bonds with the charges levied on tourist businesses.

Supportive facilities

Infrastructural works, including the development of major roads, and transportation systems, are generally undertaken by public or private utility companies empowered to provide these services. In newly developing areas, regional state or federal funds are often allocated to subsidize or offset the initial capital investment.

The rate of development may outstrip the provision of adequate infrastructure, particularly in the communal areas outside the curtilages of properties. This may be seen in private streets, inadequate car parking, sewage and garbage pollution and frequent interruption of utility supplies.

A2.5 Public sector participation

Government participation in financing tourism and recreation development – either directly or through the agency of regional or local authorities – varies with the conditions and circumstances peculiar to each country. The main factors which have a bearing are:

* the political and constitutional system of government;
* socio-economic development of the country;
* relative importance of tourism in the economy.

Financing of revenue-earning facilities in *free enterprise market economies* is usually undertaken by the private sector whilst non-revenue-earning facilities and community recreation needs are mainly financed by state, regional or municipal authorities. However, these roles vary widely. The private sector may take responsibility for practically the whole investment, as in tourist village and condominium developments where the sale of equipped land may finance the infrastructure and community recreation facilities.

At the other extreme the state may finance all or most of the revenue-earning facilities, for example in countries having a *centrally planned economy*, or in those with a free economy where there is a need to stimulate and complement private enterprise.

Some form of state intervention is almost essential in newly developing tourist areas or where there is a need for changes.

World Tourism Organization (OMT, WTO, BTC)

The World Tourism Organization is the only intergovernmental organization that serves as a global forum for tourism and policy issues. Its members include 113 countries and territories as well as over 160 affiliated members from public and private sectors. WTO's mission is to promote and develop tourism as a significant means of fostering international peace and understanding, economic development and international trade.

In addition to statistics on world tourism, market research and economic reviews, WTO publications cover a range of topical subjects concerning tourism. Through its technical cooperation activities, the World Tourism Organization has assisted many countries in preparing planning, marketing, economic and other types of tourism studies, advising on all aspects of tourism development and training local tourism-related personnel.

Some examples of WTO projects are summarized in this book and described in WTO, National and Regional Tourism Planning: Methodologies and Case Studies, Routledge, 1994.

A2.6 Forms of financial aid

Market economies

In market economy countries, state assistance to the private sector in developing revenue-earning facilities is invariably limited to incentives which will assist investment in areas qualifying for aid.

Examples	Applications
Financial aid	
Subventions, grants	Usually up to 30 per cent maximum of cost
Long-term low-interest loans	With a specified redemption period
Participation in capital stock	Joint public and private companies
Security bonds for loans	From commercial banks and institutions
Preferential interest rates	For infrastructure development
Physical contribution	Offers of state land, infrastructure provision
Fiscal aid	
Exemption from direct taxes	For a limited period e.g. 5 years
Relief from specific indirect taxes	Duties on imports, agreements on fixed rates
Rights to transfer profits	Currency exchange concessions for set period

In each case, incentives are directed to specific types of projects, approved in advance and for limited periods of time. Criteria for assistance are based on the economic and employment benefits generated compared with costs.

Centrally planned and mixed economies

State finance in centrally planned economies usually plays a dominant role in tourism and recreation development, either directly or indirectly.

Examples	Applications
Direct capital investment through extra budgetary funds	To implement facilities: hotels, resorts, conference centres, cultural projects
Investment through allocated regional or municipal funds	For infrastructure, land acquisition, public amenities, local leisure and sports facilities
Endowment of funds	To support regional tourism enterprises, conservation projects, national parks
Grants and subsidies for conversion and improvement	For example, *pousadas*, *paradors*
Direct subsidies for social tourism development	Accommodation for young people, pilgrims, low-income families

Public sector finance is usually allocated through government departments, public institutions and joint councils set up for this purpose. Their role is to evaluate projects, determine levels of assistance, regulate expenditure and monitor results.

Governments may also be involved in operating facilities and services through state or municipal operating companies, joint stock companies or commercial contracts with hotel or facilities management companies.

A2.7 Main sources of capital finance

Public institutions financing domestic projects
These include government departments, national or regional agencies, development banks and municipal authorities distributing finance from central funds or their own resources in accordance with statutory guidelines. These institutions generally finance infrastructure works, sports and recreation development and public amenities. They may be empowered to administer incentives for private investments.

Semi-public bodies financing domestic projects
Joint public and private companies are common in countries with regional development plans. They may be involved in financing tourist projects and resorts or with both investment and operation.

Commercial undertakings for domestic projects
Loans and mortgages issued by commercial banks, building societies, insurance etc., fund managers and venture capital companies are used to fund private development. The amounts are normally limited to a percentage of the valuation, a fixed term for repayment and agreed interest charges which reflect the degree of risk.

National governmental sources funding international projects
Public or semi-public institutions entrusted by the government of a relatively rich country with the task of granting credits to governments of other, usually developing countries. Loans, often at favourable interest, are usually 'tied' to conditions.

Multinational companies
Companies concerned with tourism and large banks may set up joint stock companies to develop individual projects in which they acquire a majority interest.

Intergovernmental organizations
These include the World Bank or its affiliates including the International Finance Corporation. A wide range of regional organizations are also involved in financing individual projects.

Regional structural funds
Such funds as the European Regional Development Fund, (ERDF) and European Agriculture Guidance and Guarantee Fund (EAGGF) contribute directly to regional tourism development. For example, the ERDF may provide up to 20 per cent of costs of new or modernized accommodation and 30 per cent of infrastructure projects through quota and non-quota funds. Regional development strategies are also supported by national government funds as in the development of Casa Peril Mezzagiorno, Languedoc-Roussillon.

APPENDIX A3: IMPACTS FROM TOURISM AND RECREATION – SOCIO-ECONOMIC DATA

A distinction can be drawn between the economic impacts associated with development and those generated from tourism and recreation expenditures. The former is concerned with the impacts resulting from changes in land use, the construction and financing of tourism related facilities and the consequences of development in particular areas. Analysis of such impacts calls for project appraisal techniques as well as more broadly-based cost benefit and other methods of analysis.

Calculations of the economic benefits of on-going expenditures involve other approaches such as the multiplier concept and combined input–output models.

A3.1 Collection of economic data

Accurate determination of tourism and recreation impacts in a destination area is often difficult. This sector does not constitute an independent grouping but is linked to and dependent on other sectors of the economy. Many facilities, transport systems and services are used by local communities as well as visitors.

Surveys	Examples
International statistics	World Tourism Organization: Annual Reports
Economic reviews	Organization for Economic Cooperation and Development
Visitor expenditure	International Passenger Surveys
Household censuses	Demographic and social trends, spending travel patterns
Occupancy statistics	Hotel registrations
Visitor enquiries	Local visitor and convention bureaux
User studies	Parks, leisure centres, visitor attractions
Ad-hoc studies	Tourism economic impacts, multiplier effects
Membership surveys	Recreational and sports clubs, associations, travel agencies
Consumer markets	Commercial research of leisure purchases and trends.

A3.2 Evaluation of costs

The capital costs of purely tourist facilities is relatively easy to calculate. As an average approximation, accommodation and food services account for over half of total investment in developing tourism with proportionate capital costs as follows:

Capital costs in tourism	Average proportions %
Accommodation and food services(a)	55–60
Other tourist facilities (a)	10–15
Technical and service infrastructures (b)	10–20
Vocational training, promotion, marketing (b)	5–10
Protection and enhancement of resources (c)	5–10
	100

Notes: (a) Excluding land purchase and finance costs
(b) Depending on stage of development
(c) Landscaping and amenities

Developments centred on real estate sales often involve a higher ratio of marketing costs.

Capital investment in recreational projects depends on the extent and value of the land required and methods used for its control. Capital costs of built leisure centres have similar ratios to those for accommodation.

A3.3 National or regional income and tourism

Tourism as an export industry often plays a major role in the balance of payments and economic development of the host country and region.

Foreign tourism receipts indicate tourism dependency and may be expressed both in actual value and as percentages of the total export earnings and of the Gross Domestic Product. The *foreign tourism balance* measures the difference between foreign exchange spent in the country by foreign tourists and the money spent by nationals abroad.

The *net income in foreign exchange* is determined by deducting import leakages from the foreign tourism receipts. Leakages arise in various ways and tend to be relatively high in the initial stages of development:

- transportation by foreign carriers;
- commodity imports;
- capital goods;
- consumer goods;
- foreign investment: interest repayments;
- salaries repatriated abroad;
- publicity and promotion in market countries;
- foreign tour operators' margins.

Recreational receipts arise partly from overall tourism expenditure, partly from day visitors and partly from local users. The first two represent economic inflows to a locality whilst local usage can be measured in terms of economic gains and other benefits.

Multipliers measure the additional business output, income or employment generated as a result of the initial tourist and visitor expenditure. The magnitude of the multipliers will depend on the economy of the area, its trade patterns and leakages. In general, income multiplier values tend to be higher in a developed economy having strong inter-sectoral linkages and a lower propensity to import tourism commodities.

A3.4 Employment

Employment generated by tourists and other users may be:

Direct: in facilities and services used by the tourists: accommodation, restaurants, cafes, bars, shops, entertainment, transport, travel agencies, guides etc. These may be highly or partially dependent on tourism.

Indirect: in sectors influenced by tourism: building, maintenance, supply of consumables and durables, associated transportation, agriculture and utility services.

In most developed economies the ratio of total to direct employment in tourism is generally between 1.5:1 and 2.5:1.

The *capital:employment ratio* is particularly important in economic appraisal and may be calculated for the whole direct employment or for each type of facilities. Tourism employment has a number of serious disadvantages:

- *Seasonality:* employment fluctuation, wastage of resources, influxes of migrant workers;
- *Predominantly young workers:* leading to decline in traditional sectors of the economy;
- *Mainly operatives:* low-skill work, mainly job-trained with limited career development;
- *Tourist spending power:* distortions in values, inflation in prices and wage spirals.

Typical structures of employment in tourism and recreation	Percentage of total low-high grade
Managerial, professional	5–8%
Supervisory, technical	8–10%
Craft, skilled	17–22%
Operative, unit trained	70–60%

The *local benefits* of tourism can be increased by:

- parallel provision of education and training programmes;
- cooperative development of craft, agriculture and service industries;
- providing information and priority for local recruitment.

A3.5 State revenues and regional benefits

State benefits arise from:

- *direct taxation:* mainly on employees, tourism and transport enterprises;

- *indirect taxation:* mainly on goods consumed and customs duties
- *state ownership and participation* in tourist enterprises, leisure centres etc.;
- *invisible exports and foreign exchange:* from tourism revenues.

Participation may take the form of state financing of infrastructure, environmental improvements and municipal projects designed to generate further investment in regional plans. Loans and grants may also be provided as incentives for commercial projects

Regions with limited or poor assets for agriculture or industrial development often possess the most attractive unspoilt landscapes. Tourism can contribute to the balanced development of the country and is usually the preferred, if not the only, way of creating economic activities by transferring part of the buying power of cities and industrial areas to under-developed regions.

A3.6 Negative and unquantifiable impacts

In assessing benefits from tourism and visitor expenditures, consideration must also be given to the negative impacts and costs:

- *seasonality:* effects of fluctuating seasonal demands on employment and services
- *vulnerability* of tourism to economic or political uncertainties, either in generating or receiving countries: increased with high dependency on one market and price sensitive packaging.
- *inflationary impact* due to high demand for land, rapid rate of development of facilities and seasonal influx of high-spend population. The inflationary impact depends on the relative size of the local market compared with the tourist demand and on the economic structure of the country. It is often greatest during the initial stage of development of the economy.

Unquantifiable impacts

The intangible effects of developing or expanding tourism may be significant and even of overriding importance. They may have positive impacts, for example:

- *social welfare* for the country's inhabitants: opportunities for recreation and domestic tourism, public health improvements, the modification of behaviour patterns as a result of tourism influences;
- *amenities:* improvements in infrastructure, environment and services for tourism also benefit local populations and often attract further investment;
- national identity and pride in sport, local achievements, environment, culture and heritage. Tourism may be developed to promote awareness of, and status of a country or region.

Negative impacts mainly arise from:

- *inflationary pressures:* competition, distortions in buying power and price inflation;
- *social problems:* conflicts in attitudes; degradation of the natural and social environments of fragile populations; loss of familiar structures, leading to exploitation, begging, prostitution;
- *environmental changes*, intensified use, loss of character affecting sustainability.

Negative impacts are most evident where there are wide socio-cultural and economic gaps between the inhabitants and tourists and where development is unplanned and/or ineffectively regulated.

APPENDIX A4: TOURISM TRANSPORTATION – RECENT DEVELOPMENTS AND TRENDS

A4.1 Developments in transportation

Transport represents a major component of tourism namely:

Category	Cost relative to total cost of visit
Transportation to the destination Air, sea, road, rail or combination; scheduled, chartered or personal transport	Long haul – usually up to 50% Short haul – 10–30% depending on length of stay.
Transportation at the destination Taxis, coach trips, hired cars, local public transport, chartered craft, ski lifts.	Typically 5–8% for resort-based holidays but higher in ski areas
Transportation as a product Cruise ships, coach and rail excursions, novelty/nostalgia experiences	Cruise and train accommodation 75–90% Touring – using other hotels 15–20%

Mode of transport

The choice of transport to a destination is affected by many considerations, such as the reason for travel and practical requirements. There may also be a lack of transport infrastructures, particularly rail services or local airports.

In competitive situations such as in business trips, the modal split between transport systems tends to be determined by distances, times, convenience and costs.

A4.2 Development in air transport

Growth

Growth in international tourism reflects increases in air passenger traffic both by scheduled and chartered carriers. Passengers on international scheduled routes operated by International Air Traffic Association (IATA) members were projected to double from 256 million in 1992 to over 550 million by 2000. About 85 per cent of the international traffic was within, to or from Europe.

Investment needs

Coupled with the need to replace economically and environmentally obsolete aircraft, the increase in capacity will require 11 000 new aircraft at an estimated cost of $890 billion over the 20 years to 2010. Operating surpluses to finance previous investment have generally been inadequate, in many cases requiring governments to subsidize their national carriers.

Risk

Traffic demand is highly sensitive to changes in economic conditions, for example, on average for every 1 per cent variation in the Gross Domestic Product of European countries the demand for air travel varied by 2.8 per cent. Air transport capacity is added in units of 200 to 400 seats and $80 to $150 million of expenditure, and the difficulties of matching expensive capacity to demand has led to wide-scale losses in times of increased costs and economic recession.[2]

Inclusive travel

The rapid growth in packaged inclusive tours has been closely linked to expansion of tourism operations with mass marketing, lower pricing, inflexible advance booking giving high load factors. In 1992 chartered aircraft carried more than 60 per cent of all intra-European traffic. Emphasis on low margins with competitive low prices has made packaged products vulnerable to economic recession. The trends, as represented by the UK inclusive travel market in 1992, point to increasing demands for self-catering flight-only and long-haul traffic.[3]

Political changes

Regulation of air travel stems from the Chicago Convention 1944 with subsequent extension of the freedom of the air and bilateral and multilateral agreements. The US Airline Deregulation Act 1978 with its 'Open Skies' policy anti-trust provisions, and Directives of the European Commission illustrate current shifts towards regional deregulation.

Completion of steps towards a single aviation market in the European Union will affect tariff structures, market access, national capacity, shares and competitions. Other Directives are likely to set noise limitations and require the redesign of airports to separate international and domestic passengers.[4]

Operational systems

Technical advances include:

- computer reservation systems in Europe and America with increasing international networks;
- yield management optimization of demand, supply, load factors and fares;
- self-ticketing, automated ticket and boarding pass systems to accelerate check-in procedures.

Organizational changes

Integration: Increasing competition and technology together with the need for economies of scale are leading to the globalization of operations through airline mergers and acquisitions.

Hub and spoke operation: The economies of long-haul flights with convenient connections to intra-regional and domestic routes has led to operations being concentrated into relatively few large hub airports.

Congestion: The capacity of many air traffic control airspace areas, airports and land transport systems had become inadequate by the mid 1990s, particularly in Europe but also at a number of airports in the Asia-Pacific region and America. This congestion was projected to increase, particularly at peak times, due to inadequate investment in infrastructure and public opposition to airport developments.

A4.3 Aircraft developments

High costs of research, development and manufacture have led to rationalization into four main groupings:

Main types in use	Typical seats for passengers	Total numbers in use	Main uses
Wide bodied (16 types)	300–600	Over 2000	Long haul, high traffic routes
Narrow bodied (25 types)	120–240	Over 10000	Intra-regional, domestic and feeder routes
Turbo-prop (12 types)	Up to 70	Over 3000	Short feeder routes, developing countries
Helicopter	Generally limited to individual and emergency use		

Notes: excluding obsolescent types, including short take off and landing
Source: C. J. Blow, *Airport Terminals,* 2nd edn. Butterworth–Heinemann

Current aircraft developments are towards increasing capacity on high traffic routes with longer non-stop flights; higher fuel efficiency, sophisticated computer navigation, monitoring and control equipment and reduced noise emission to meet environmental requirements. For rapid turn around aircraft have self-contained auxiliary power, built-in air stairs and removable catering and sanitary units.

Future developments are towards further increases in aircraft capacities.

A4.4 Airport development

Development requirements

International airports require vast areas of land for the runway and terminal areas ranging from restricted sites e.g. Heathrow – 1100 ha and Schiphol – 1700 ha, to purposely-designed Charles de Gaulle – 3000 ha and Dallas/Fort Worth – 7000 ha. Extensive areas are also required for screening highway and technical infrastructures and associated developments. Regional airports with a single runway designed for the larger aircraft and terminal buildings require at least 750–1000 ha.

Public opposition and the high cost of land and infrastructure in suburban areas points to three main types of development to meet future traffic demands:

*   addition of new terminals, replacement and extension of existing airports;
*   investment in new regional airports servicing remote developing tourist regions;
*   creation of new coastal airports on reclaimed land, and artificial islands which may also be integrated with harbour developments.

Investment

The high costs of airport development and associated technical infrastructures mean that few new airports are self-financing. Investment is usually:

*   by public authorities, or
*   by the private sector with subsidized infrastructure and other development gains to offset costs, or
*   by individual airlines in terminal buildings.

Terminal capacity

Airport capacity is generally dictated by the aircraft handling system but also by the terminal facilities for processing passengers and their luggage. International terminals are usually planned to process 1500 to 3000 passengers/hr each way at peak periods, including transfers to and from hub carriers, which involves increasing difficulties in meeting peak slot demands and scheduling connecting flights.

Terminals are planned for phased expansion either by linear or pier extensions or the addition of satellites or further terminal buildings. In regional airports major congestion is liable to arise with concentrated arrivals and departures of chartered flights at weekends.

Runway capacity

International Civil Aviation classified airports must have runways of at least 3300 m to handle the Boeing 747 and other large aircraft. With advanced technical equipment a single runway can allow 30–40 aircraft movements per hour; equivalent to 25 million passengers per year.

Larger airports have twin parallel runways separated by at least 1600 m. Extensive clearance zones are required along flight paths and around taxiing areas to avoid obstacles and noise-screening by barriers, ground moulding and buildings is usually required.

Impacts

Airports create wide-ranging and irreversible impacts:

Economic

- Major generator of revenue and employment, both directly and through associated developments and induced services and supplies.
- Stimulus to tourism development in regions, with most large-scale resorts concentrated within 1 hour's transfer distance and individual hotels within 2 hours'.
- Facilitation of business travel, meetings and exhibitions through convenient access and on-site hotel development.

Environment

- Large-scale changes in land use and rapid development of terminals and associated buildings on and off site.
- Massive investment in infrastructure, plant and services.
- Increased noise climates, pollution and disturbance – ameliorated to some degree by regulating flight paths, night flights and aircraft emissions.
- Continuing pressure for progressive urbanization of surroundings and relief of traffic congestion.

A4.5 Road transport

Travel by motor car accounts for 80–90 per cent of international tourist arrivals in continental Europe and 90 per cent of domestic travel in North America. The growth in car usage reflects both the increases in car ownership and hire and the investment in road infrastructures, giving access to attractive areas. Intra-continental traffic is also influenced by the availability of ferry and rail transportation with the growth in second homes generating more frequent visits.

The benefits of travel by personal transport with the freedoms of choice in routes, stopovers and destinations, as well as the transportation of family/friends together with their luggage and sports gear, provide many advantages including the option of temporary accommodation.

Planning

Cars are likely to cause more visual impact and environmental change than the tourists themselves. The ground area taken up by car parking and access is practically the same as the unit floor space for accommodation and services and some rationalization is often required:

- separation of car parking,
- pedestrianization,
- prohibition on routes or at times,
- substitution,
- speed restriction.

Coach transport is widely used for tours, transfers and excursions as well as scheduled bus services. The trend in coach design is towards increasing sophistication, comfort and safety. Planning provisions are required for coach parking, waiting bays and luggage handling at hotels and termini.

A4.6 Rail transport

Rail travel is a relatively minor component in tourism – in the UK, for example, Intercity conveyed 7 per cent of traffic travelling over 25 miles in 1994. In most countries, railways – particularly urban commuter lines – are heavily subsidized.

Vast investments in infrastructure to increase speed and reliability, particularly in Europe and Japan, is expected to make the intercity and intra-regional trains particularly competitive with air and car travel over distances of 500 km.

Developments

- Extension of high-speed rail network in Europe linking over 30 major cities by 2005, including Eurostar services.
- Operation of 250–300 kph trains.
- High-speed rail transfers between city and airport/suburban attractions.
- Continuing novelty use.
- Nostalgia and luxury.

A4.7 Sea transport

Travel by sea may be part of the transport to a destination or a product in itself.

Ferries (vessels for short sea crossings): usually designed for car ferrying and may be based on ship, jetfoil or catamaran designs. On high density routes, modern vessels are built for speed, stability, and rapid turnaround with drive-on drive-off access through doors in the bows, stern or side. Short journey accommodation is usually based on reclining seats and sleeperettes with extensive public areas and provision for out of season cruising. *Scheduled sailings:* timetabled sailings between ports of call include:

- occasional transoceanic liners for luxury travel;
- island circuits for island hopping, exploration;
- passenger-carrying cargo boats for adventure, experience.

A4.8 Cruising

Cruising combines floating hotel facilities with transportation to a variety of destinations. Most cruises are concentrated into popular areas such as the Mediterranean, Canaries, North Africa, Caribbean, Australia–South Pacific, West Coast of North America, Rio de Janeiro, Buenos Aires as well as round-the-world voyages.

Types

- Classic cruises from the originating country – typically two weeks, 4–5 stops ashore.
- Fly–cruise – flights to and from cruise area for short cruises in warm climates.

- Cruise and stay – part cruising, part stay in hotel.
- Mini cruises – short cruises, often themed or speciality interests.
- Educational – schools, special interest groups including conducted tours, lectures.
- Sailing – in crewed yachts, sailing flotillas, adventure and training ships.
- River cruises – long and short cruises along the Nile, Rhine, Danube, Canal du Midi, Shannon.

Developments

With demographic trends towards older age groups, cruising is an expanding segment of tourism. Limitations on space necessitate small cabins – typically $15\,m^2$ with suites up to $50\,m^2$. Recreational areas such as swimming pools, also tend to be small.

To cater for all meals as well as social and entertainment needs, public areas are extensive and often ornately sophisticated. In most large luxury liners, the passenger space ratio expressed as the gross tonnage/passenger is between 30 and 40 and the ratio of passengers/crew is around 2.6 to 2.1. The trend is towards single class standards.

Modern vessels are designed to provide high stability, manoeuvrability and speed with fuel efficiency. Electronic systems constantly monitor performance, fire safety, security and navigation.

Notes

1 *World Tourism 1970–1992*, World Tourism Organization, 1992

2 Beaver, A., *Mind your own Travel Business*, Volume 1, 1993, quoting Gunter Eser, IATA Director-General, 1992.

3 McCarthy, J., *Stats M R Surveys*, Stats M R, 1992.

4 'Seven EU States abolish internal border controls', *The Times*, 25 March, 1995.

Select bibliography

ACAU (1967). *Contribution à l'étude des programmes de nouvelles stations de vacances*, Centre d'Etudes du Tourisme, Université d'Aix.

Adie, D. W. (1984). *Marinas: A Working Guide to their Development and Design*, 3rd ed., Architectural Press, London.

AFIT (1996). *Le guide de l'opérateur touristique* – Agence Française de l'Ingénierie Touristique, Paris.

Agee, J. K. and Johnson, D. R. (1988). *Ecosystem Management for Parks and Wilderness*, University of Washington Press, USA.

Anonymous (1997). *Projet de plantage à Lausanne*, in Cahiers de l'ASPAN-SO, 1996/2, pp. xvi, Lausanne.

Azeo Torr, L. (1989). *Waterfront Development*, Van Nostrand Reinhold, New York.

BACOPA (1972). *Propositions de normes théoriques d'équipement touristique*, 4 vols, Mission Interministérielle pour l'aménagement de la Côte Aquitaine, Bordeaux.

Barnett, L. A. ed. (1988). *Research About Leisure: Past, Present and Future*, Sagamore Publishing, Champaign, Il, USA.

Baud-Bovy, A.&M. (1998). Grands équipements de loisirs ouverts au public et aménagement du territoire, COSAC, Soleure.

Baud-Bovy, A.&M. (1987). *Loisirs de plein air et économie de sol*, Fond National Suisse de la Recherche Scientifique, Programme SOL, Liebefeld-Bern.

Baud-Bovy, M. (1985). *Bilan et avenir de la planification touristique*, Centre des Hautes Etudes Touristiques, Aix-en-Provence, 46pp.

Baud-Bovy, M. and Lawson, F. (1977). *Tourism and Recreation Development – A Handbook of Physical Planning*, Architectural Press, London.

Beau, B. (1992) Développement et d'aménagement touristique, Bréal ed., Paris.

Benhamou, F. (1988). *Golf: l'élu sous pression*, in Cahiers d'Espace **9**, February 1988, pp. 81–6, Paris.

Billet, T. and others (1982) *Les parcs naturels régionaux: bilans et procédures*, Fédération des parcs nationaux de France, Paris, 51 pp.

Briassoulis, H. and Van der Straaten, J., eds (1992). *Tourism and the Environment: An Overview*, Kluwer Academia Publishers, Netherlands.

Bridel, L. (1996) Manuel d'aménagement du territoire, vol. 1, Georg ed., Geneva.

Bucknall, S. (1993). 'Managing the Countryside'. In S. Glyptis ed., p. 174–82.

Büro für Strukturentwicklung (1994). *Freizeit– und Ferienzentren – Umfang und regionale Verteilung*, für Bundesforschunganstalt für Landeskunde und Raumplannung, in Materialen zur Raumentwicklung, Helf 66, Selbstverlag, Bonn.

Carlston, van Doren and others (1979). *Land Leisure: Concepts and Methods in Outdoor Recreation*, Maarouta Press, Chicago, Illinois.

Carr, S. and others (1992). *Public Spaces*, Cambridge University Press.

Cazes, G. and Poitier, F. (1996). *Le tourisme urban*, Que Sais-Je? PUF, Paris.

Cazes, G., Lanquar, R. and Raynouard, Y. (1980). *L'aménagement touristique*, Que Sais-Je? PUF, Paris.

CCRA – Comissão de Coordenação da Região do Algarve (1990). *Plano Regional de Ordenamento do Território do Algarve*, Faro, Portugal.

CHS – Committee on Human Settlements (1995). *Draft guidelines on sustainable settlements planning*, Geneva, UN Economic Commission for Europe (HBP/R.35) with Addendum 2 (HBP/R.351).

CIAG – Committee of Inquiry into Allotment Gardens (1969). *Report*, HMSO, UK.

Cocossis, H. and Parpairis, A. (1992). 'Some observations on the concept of carrying capacity'. In *Tourism and the Environment: An Overview*, Briassoulis and van der Straaten, eds. (1992).

Coleman, D. and others (1994). *North Carolina Greenways: Report to the Governor*, North Carolina Department of Environment.

Comité Régional du Tourisme d'Ile-de-France (1989). *Schéma régional de développement du tourisme et des loisirs d'Ile-de-France*, Paris.

Consulting and Audit Canada (1995). *What Tourism Managers Need to Know: A practical guide for the development and uses of indicators of sustainable tourism*, World Tourism Organization, Madrid.

Cordell, H. K. (1988). 'Outdoor Recreation: Resource Planning and Management', in Barnett, ed. 1988, pp. 143–59.

CSFSH – Comité des Stations Françaises de Sport d'Hiver (1974). *Equipement des stations*, 8, 49 rue de Pigalle, Paris.

Cumin, G. (1966). *Capacité du domaine skiable*, in Economie et Prospective de la Montagne, **7**, EPM ed., Voiron, France.

DATAR (1986). *Les parcs récréatifs*, Paris.

David, C. (1986). *Sunday gardeners*, in Cahiers de l'IAURIF **79**, pp. 57–64, Paris.

De Chiara, J. and Koppelman, L. E. (1984). *Time-saver Standards for Site Planners*, McGraw-Hill, New York.

Department of the Environment (1991). *Sport and Recreation* (Planning-Policy Guidance, Note 17), HMSO, UK.

Douglass, R. W. (1982). *Forest Recreation*, Pergamon Press, New York.

Econstat (1993). *Taking account of environment in tourism development*, Commission of the European Communities, D. G. XXIII Tourism Unit, Brussels.

Elson, M. J. (1993). 'Sport and Recreation in the Green Belt Countryside', In S. Glyptis ed. (1993), p. 131-7.

English Tourist Board (1991). *Principles for Sustainability of Tourism*, ETB, London.

Enviro, **17** (June 1994). Swedish Environmental Protection Agency, Solna, Sweden.

Erwin, S. M. (1996). Integrating GIS and CAD, in *Landscape Architecture 86/1*, pp. 26.

Evans, D. S. (1994). *National Ecotourism Strategy*, Australian Government Publishing Service.

Fahriye, H. S. (1991). 'A behavioural definition of the vernacular and implications for authenticity in regionalist architecture'. In Yenen ed. (1991), vol 2, pp. 191–204.

Fichtner, U. and Micha, R. (1987). *Freizeitparks*, Selbstverlag, Freiburg-in-Brisgau.

Fisk, D. M. and Hatry, H. P. (1979). 'Recreation Services'. In van Doren, (1979), pp. 180–99.

Flodin, C-E. *et al.* (1983). *Friytor i stadsförnyelsen*, Liber-Tryck, Stockholm.

Flournoy, W. L. (1989). *Vigilantees, the neuse, and sure salvation*, Proceedings of the Third Biennal Linear Parks Conference, Boon (NC), USA.

Flournoy, W. L. (1972). *Report to the City Council on the benefits and methodology of establishing a Greenway System in Raleigh*, Raleigh (NC), USA.

Flournoy, W. L. (1993). *Evolution of Environmental Consciousness and Emergence of an Environmentally Based Linear Parks Movement*, Proceedings of the Fifth Biennal Linear Parks Conference.

FNNPE – Federation of Nature and National Parks in Europe (1993). *Loving them to death? – sustainable tourism in Europe's Nature and National Parks*, FNNPE, D-8352 Grafenau.

Fogg, G. E. (1990). *Park Planning Guidelines*, 3rd ed., National Recreation and Park Association, Alexandria, Virgina.

Frangialli, F. (1991). *La France dans le Tourisme Mondial*, ed. Economica, Paris.

Gauthier, P. and Breel, P. (1990). *De la piscine au complexe récréatif*, Plan Urbain, contrat 449, Paris.

Glyptis, S. ed. (1993). *Leisure and the Environment – Essays in honour of Professor J. A. Patmore*, Belhaven Press, London and New York.

Gold, S. M. (1980). *Recreation Planning and Design*, McGraw-Hill Inc., New York.

Gunn, C. A. (1972). *Vacationscape: designing tourist regions*, University of Texas at Austin, USA.

Gunn, C. A. (1988). *Tourism Planning – 2nd ed.*, Taylor & Francis, New York.

Hawkins, D. E., Wood, M. E. and Bittman, S. eds (1995). *The Ecolodge Sourcebook for Planners and Developers*, The Ecotourism Society, North Bennington, Vermont.

IAURIF Institut d'Aménagement et d'Urbanisme de la Région Ile-de-France. (1995). *Plan Vert Régional d'Ile-de-France*, Paris.

IBA (1966). *The Emscher Park International Building Exhibition*, IBA Emscher Park, Gelsenkirchen.

IFLA-International Federation of Landscape Architects (1986). *IFLA Year Book 1985/86*, Versailles.

IFLA-International Federation of Landscape Architects (1992). *IFLA Year Book 1991/92*, American Society of Landscape Architects ed., Washington DC.

Inskeep, E. (1991). *Tourism Planning – An Integrated and Sustainable Development Approach*, Van Nostrand Reinhold, New York.

Jansen-Verbeke, M. (1995). Involving people: Bruges, in *Historic cities and sustainable tourism*, ICOMOS UK Conference, October 1995, Bath.

Jay-Jaton, J. C. (1983). *Pour prendre le temps d'être mieux*, Sillery, Presses de l'Université du Québec.

John, G. J. and Campbell, K., eds (1993). *Outdoor Sports: Handbook of Sports and Recreational Building Design*, Volume 1, 2nd ed., Butterworth-Heinemann/Sports Council.

KCP – Kenya Coast Planners Ltd (1975). *Development of Tourism at the Diani Resort*, Kenya Ministry of Tourism and Wildlife, Nairobi.

KVR–Kommunalverband Ruhrgebiet (1996). *Parkbericht: Emscher Landschaftspark*, Essen.

Lanquar, R. (1991). *Les parcs de bisirs,* Coll. Que Sais-Je?, no. 2577, PUF, Paris.

Laurie, M. (1983). 'A gladdened eye', in *Landscape Architecture,* **73**, p. 74.

Lawson, F. R. (1981). *Conference, Convention and Exhibition Facilities: Planning, Design and Management,* Butterworth-Heinemann, London.

Lawson, F. R. (1994). *Restaurants, Clubs and Bars: Planning, Design and Investment,* Butterworth-Heinemann, Oxford.

Lawson F. R. (1995). *Hotels and Resorts: Planning, Design and Refurbishment,* Butterworth-Heinemann, Oxford.

Lederman, A. (1992). *Twenty years of leisure policy in Europe,* ELRA Report, Zürich, Switzerland.

Lime, D. W. and Stankey, G. H. (1979). 'Carrying capacity: maintaining outdoor recreation quality'. In van Doren (1979), pp. 105–17.

Lindberg, K. and Hawkins, D. E. eds (1993). *Ecotourism: A Guide for Planners and Managers,* The Ecotourism Society, PO Box 755, North Bennington, VT 05257, USA.

Mallet, A. (1988). *Au commencement était la piscine,* in Cahiers d'Espace **9**, February 1988, pp. 98–102, Paris.

Manning, E. W. and Dogherty, T. D. (1994). *Carrying Capacity for Tourism in Sensitive Ecosystems,* Paper presented at the Conference on Sustainable Tourism, Montreal, September, 1994.

Mertes, J. D. and Hall, J. R. (1995). *Park, Recreation, Open Space and Greenway Guidelines,* National Recreation and Park Association, Arlington, VA, USA.

Monthino, L. and Curry, B. (1992). *Site selection analysis in tourism,* Cahier C/174, CHET, Fondation Vasarely, Aix-en Provence, France.

Nature Conservation Bureau (1995). *Nature Conservation in Japan,* The Environment Agency, Tokyo.

Outdoor Recreation Resources Review Commission (ORRRC) (1962). Various reports on outdoor recreation, US Government Printing Office, Washington, various reports.

Plaisance, G. (1979). *La forêt française,* Denoel Editor, Paris.

President's Commission (1987). *American Outdoors: the Legacy, the Challenge – the report of the President's Commission,* Island Press, Washington DC.

Process Architecture (1990). *Contemporary Landscape Architecture: an International Perspective,* Process Architecture, Tokyo, 256pp.

PROMOTOUR (monographic studies of numerous French winter resorts) 55, avenue de Kleber, Paris 16e.

Richter, G. (1981). *Hanbuch Stadtgrün: Landschaftsarchitektur ub Städtischen freiraum.* BLV Verlag, Munich.

Rietdorf, W. and Baeseler, H. (1979). *Freizeitanlagen,* VEB-Verlag für Bauwesen, Berlin.

Sideway, R. (1993). *Sport, Recreation and Nature Conservation.* In S. Glyptis, ed. (1993).

Simonds, J. O. (1994). *Cities 21.*

SOMEA (1968). *Studio pilota per nuevi centri turistico-residenziali,* Vol II, Associazione di Studi per le Sviluppo del Turismo in Collegamento con le Infrastrutture Autostradali, Rome.

Spirn, A. W. (1984). *The Granite Garden – Urban Nature and Human Design,* Basic Books, Harper Collins, USA.

Sports Council (1983). *Leisure Policy for the Future,* Seminar, February 1983, London.

Stankey, G. H. *et al.* (1985). *The Limits of Acceptable Charges (LAC) of Wilderness Planning,* Forest Service Technical Report, Int 176, Ogden, Utah, USA.

Tivy, J. (1972). *The concept and determination of carrying capacity of recreational land in the USE,* CCS Occasional Paper Number 3, Countryside Commission for Scotland, Perth.

Van den Borg, G. G. (1995). *Tourism and cities of art – the impact of tourism and visitor flow management,* UNESCO Regional Office for Science and Technology for Europe, Technical Report 20, Venice, Italy.

Van den Borg, G. G. (1995). *Proceedings of the International Seminar 'Alternative Tourism Routes in Cities of Art',* UNESCO Regional Office for Science and Technology for Europe, Technical Report 23, Venice, Italy.

Van Doren, C. S. *et al.* eds (1979). *Land and Leisure – Concepts and Methods in Outdoor Recreation,* Methuen & Co Ltd, London.

Walker, T. D. (1987). *Designs for Parks and Recreational Spaces,* PDA Publishers, Mesa, Arizona, 240pp.

Weixlbaumer, N. (1995). *Das Romanische Regionalparkkonzept als nachhalltige Regionalentwicklungsstrategie für Nichtsiedlungsgebiete,* in DISP 123 (October 1995), Institut für Orts-, Regional- und Landesplannung, ETH, Zürich.

Williams, S. (1995). *Recreation and the Urban Environment,* Routledge, London.

World Commission on Environment and Development (1987). *Our Common Future* (The Bruntland Report).

WTO – World Tourism Organization (1983). *Risques de saturation ou dépassement de laq capacité de charge touristique dans les destinations de séjour touristique,* WTO, Madrid.

WTO – World Tourism Organization (1985). *Rôle de l'Etat dans la sauvegarde et la promotion de la culture comme facteur de développement touristique et dans la mise en valeur du patrimoine national de sites et de monuments à des fins touristiques,* WTO, Madrid.

WTO – World Tourism Organization (1985). *Méthodologie d'établissement et d'application des plans directeurs touristiques,* WTO, Madrid.

WTO – World Tourism Organization (1991). *International Conference on Travel and Tourism Statistics – Ottawa 1991,* WTO, Madrid.

WTO – World Tourism Organization (1992). *An Integrated Approach to Resort Development: Six case studies*, WTO, Madrid.

WTO – World Tourism Organization (1992). *Sustainable Toursim Development: Guide for local planners*, WTO, Madrid.

WTO – World Tourism Organization (1994). *National and Regional Tourism Planning – Methodologies and Case Studies*, Routledge, London.

WTO – World Tourism Organization (1997). *Tourism 2020 Vision: Influences, directional flows and key trends.* Executive summary 1997. WTO, Madrid.

WTO – World Tourism Organization (1997) *Tourism Market Trends: The World.* 1997 Edition. WTO, Madrid.

Wylson, A. (1980). *Design for Leisure Entertainment*, Newnes–Butterworths, London.

Yaro, R. D. and Hiss, T. (1996). *A Region at Risk – The third regional plan for the New York–New Jersey–Connecticut metropolitan area*, Island Press, Washington DC.

Yenen, Z. ed. (1991). *International Symposium on architecture of tourism in the Mediterranean*, 3 vols, Yildis University, Istanbul.

Zoppi, M. (1988). *Progettare con il Verde*, Alinea ed., Florence.

Index

Access:
    implementation strategy, 223–4
    means of in tourism development plans,
       198–9
    recreation parks, 107
    restricting, 14
    for traffic, 39–40
Accommodation, 18–35
    balance of hotel and private, 21
    calculation in tourism development plans,
       194–8
    camping and caravanning, 19, 31–5,
       107
    hotels, see Hotels
    impact of accommodation mix on resort
       development, 21
    investment, 268–9
    main types, 18–19
    new objectives in planning, 21
    non-tourist population, 38
    private, 21, 26–30, 268
    youth hostels, 31, 32
Action programme, 169, 170
Administration, 37–9
Advertising, 225
Age, 265
Agenda 21, 8
Aid, financial, 221–2, 269–70
Air-conditioning systems, 44
Air transport, 224, 273–4
Aircraft: developments, 274
Airports, 198, 274–5
Albania: Integrated Tourism Development
    Plan, 159
Algarve, Portugal, 220
Allotment gardens, 57
Alpine resorts, 131
Alternative destinations, 14
Alternative plans, 173, 174
Alternative tourism, 11
Amelia Island, Florida, 13
Amenities: impact of tourism, 272
Amsterdam Bos, Holland, 118–19
Analytic hierarchic process, 170–3
Angling, 60
Anzère ski resort, Switzerland, 78
Apartments/flats, 26–30, 257
Aquatic parks, 50, 94, 101–3
    planning, 133–5
Asir National Park, Saudi Arabia, 122
Association for Safeguarding Recreation Areas
    around Munich, 225
Attraction parks, 96–8
    planning, 133–5
Avoriaz ski resort, France, 79

Bann Taling Ngam Resort, Thailand, 18
Back-of-house areas, 26
Bali, 130
Baltimore, USA, 239
Barcelona, Spain, 250
Bars, 26
Basic facilities, 17–18
Bastakia Conservation Study, Dubai, 233
Bathing places, natural, 57–8
Battery Park City (BPC), New York, 246–7
Beach capacities, 71–2
Beach protection, 71
Beach resorts, 18, 66–73, 82, 87, 139, 145,
    162, 195
    beach development, 71–2
    integrated resorts, 73
    public beach facilities, 72–3
Beach surveys, 71
Beds: calculation of number required, 194–8
Behavioural market segmentation, 264
Belek Hotel, Antalya, Turkey, 22
Belfast, Northern Ireland, 201
Berth capacity, 59
Bhutan, 196
Bicycle trails, 55–6, 257
Biesbosch National Park, Holland, 124
Blue Flag Campaign, 72
Boating, 59–60, 107
Boise River, Idaho, 251
Boston, USA, 209
Broad concept, 151, 152–4
Brooklyn Bridge Park, New York, 249, 256
Brooklyn/Queens Greenway, New York, 214
Bruges, Belgium, 235
Budget hotels, 19
Buffer zone, 117
Building rights: restrictions on, 225
Buildings:
    controls, 156
    distribution of, 143
    quality of construction, 143
Built areas per bed, 64
Bungalows, 26–30

Cable transporters, 83–4
Camping/caravan sites, 19, 31–5, 107
    categories, 33
    densities and sizes, 33–6
    minimum standards, 34
Canada: urban parks standards, 244
Canary Islands, 187
Canoe racing, 60
Canoe slalom, 60
Cap D'Agde, France, 68
Capital costs, 271

Capital: employment ratio, 272
Caravan sites, see Camping/caravan sites
Cariboo–Chilcotin Land-use Plan, British
    Columbia, 228, 229
Carrying capacities, 11–12
Cars, 275
Casino, 46
Casino hotels, 23
Catering, 107
    see also Food service provisions
Caudan Waterfront, Le, Mauritius, 202
Center Parks, 89, 94
Center Park, Sologne, France, 90–1
Centrally planned economies, 269, 270
Centre Equestre de Pompadour, France, 86
Cergy–Neuville recreation and sports park,
    France, 112–13
Cervinia, Italy, 132
Chailluz Forest, France, 127
Changes in requirements, 147
Changing rooms, 26
Chattanooga Greenway, USA, 218
Chester Zoo, UK, 98
Chestnut Pocket Park, Philadelphia, 249
Chicago Beach, Dubai, 24
Chicago Convention 1944, 273
Children's/games rooms, 26
Children's playgrounds, 107, 257
China, 268
CHS, 234, 257
Cinema, 46
Circuits, 203
Circulation planning, 25
Cities, see Urban centres; Urban parks
Climatic comfort charts, 185
Climatic conditions, 184
Climatic resorts, 131
Cluster groupings, 27
Coach transport, 275
Cocossis, H., 12
Coffee shops, 25, 34–5
Coleman, D., 209
Comfort charts, climatic, 185
Commercial capital, 270
Commercial facilities, 269
Commercial holiday villages, 27, 28
Communication systems, 44
Communications, 266
Community involvement in planning, 221, 245
Community recreation, 265
Community recreation centre, 48
Compatibility of activities, 60
Competing destinations, 4
Comprehensive planning, 173, 174
Computer-aided design (CAD), 178

Computerized management systems, 44
Concentric zoning, 117–21
Condominiums, 19, 26–30
Conflicts of interest, 165–7
Congestion, 274
Connecting infrastructure, 39
Conservation:
    design of isolated facilities, 203
    development vs, 7–14
Construction: quality of, 143
Consultation, 152–4
Contact with nature, 141
Control, 222, 266
Convention hotels, 23
Converted rural buildings, 88
Coordinated strategy, 220–1
Co-owners associations, 133
Cordell, H.K., 190, 242
Corsica, 200
Cost benefit analysis, 15
Costs:
    evaluation of, 271
    sports/recreational activities, 62
Countryside Commission, 220
Countryside recreation parks, 108
Countryside resorts, 85–94
    accommodation standards, 28, 29
    country resorts for rent, 19, 27, 89
    holiday parks, 89–94
    second residences, 85–8
    social holiday villages, 88–9
Courchevel, France, 132
Created safari parks, 99–101
Creativity, 164–5
Crowder's Mountain State Park, USA, 123
Cruising, 224, 275–6
    inland, 60
Cultural resources, 184
Culture, centres of, 232
Curling rinks, 84
Cycle trials, 55–6, 257
Cyclical attractions, 184
Cyprus, 161, 197

Dade County, Florida, 245
Dance halls, 46
Danish Labour Market Holiday Fund, 88
Darling Harbour, Sydney, 252–3
Day camping, 107
Demand, 2–3
    analyses, 170
    assessment of, 189–90
    influences on, 265–6
    measurement of recreation demand, 264
Demographic market segmentation, 264
Demographic structures, 265
Densities of use:
    average overall densities, 66
    average specific densities, 64–6
    recreational activities, 61
    suburban parks, 107–8
Developers, 4, 132
Development:
    vs conservation, 7–14
    evaluation of proposals, 14–16
    goals/policies, 193
    phasing, 146–51

principles of, see Principles of development
    survey of existing development plans, 192
    sustainable, 8, 9–11, 161
Diani Resort, Kenya, 38
Different experiences: providing, 135
Digital image processing, 178
Direct employment, 37, 272
Discovery, trails of, 57
Disneyland, Paris, 136–7
Distribution of buildings, 143
Distribution infrastructure, 39
District plans, 168
Domestic tourism, 4, 191, 268
Dominica: tourism sector plan, 167
Douglass, R.W., 126
Draft project, 151, 154–6
'Dry harbours', 74–7
Duisburg-North Landscape Park, Germany, 240–1

Eco-lodges, 117
'Eco parks', 251
Economic impacts from tourism/recreation, 271–3
    airports, 275
    collection of data, 271
    employment, 272
    evaluation of costs, 271
    national/regional income, 271–2
    negative and unquantifiable impacts, 272–3
    state revenues and regional benefits, 272
Economic market segmentation, 264
Economic sectors, 219–20
Ecotourism, 11
Ecotourism Society, 229–30
Eden Project, Cornwall, UK, 98–9
Effect current demand, 264
Efteling, Holland, 100
Egypt, 192
Electricity supplies, 43–4
Emergency communication systems, 44
Emergency electricity generation, 44
Employees, 37
Employment, 272
    direct, 37, 272
    indirect, 37–8, 272
    patterns, 188
Emscher Landscape Park, Germany, 217
Entertainment resources/facilities, 184, 269
Environment, 275
    guidelines for sustainable development, 10–11
    impacts from airports, 275
    impacts from recreation, 9
    impacts from tourism, 7–9
    improvement of resorts with environmental problems, 148
    master plan and environmental protection, 163–5
    quality in resources surveys, 184
    'sensitive areas' of environmental control, 226–30
Environmental auditing (EA), 14
Environmental impact assessment (EIA), 12
Environmental integration, 141
Environmental performance standards (EPS), 14

Environmental quality standards (EQS), 14
Estate agency, 133
European Agriculture Guidance and Guarantee Fund (EAGGF), 270
'European' alpine park, 21
European Regional Development Fund (ERDF), 270
European Union directives, 273
Evaux, Les, Geneva, Switzerland, 110–11
Existing development plans: survey of, 192
Extension, 146–51

Facilities:
    major, 226
    resources surveys, 187–8
    types of, 17–18
Fassbender, Eugen, 209
Feasibility analysis, 15
Feedback corrections, 175
Ferries, 275
Ferry links, 223
Final development plans, 156
Final project, 151, 156–7
Finance, 268–7
    adapating financing techniques, 221–2
    main sources of capital, 270
Financial aid, 221–2, 269–70
Financial plans:
    detailed, 156–7
    draft, 155–6
First aid centre, 26
Fiscal aid, 270
Fitness room, 26
Flaine, France, 81
Flats/apartments, 26–30, 257
Flexibility in planning, 175
Flournoy, W.L., 215
Focuses of interest, 143
Food service provisions, 34–5
Forecasting, 170
Foreign tourism balance, 271
Foreign tourism receipts, 271
Forests, 126, 127
France:
    recreational activities survey, 189
    urban parks standards, 244
Free time, 265
Fritid Stockholm, 221
Fun parks, 96–8, 133–5
Function rooms, 26

Games room, 26
Gasworth Park, Seattle, 146
Geelong Waterfront Design and Development Code (Australia), 149
Gender, 265
Geneva, Switzerland, 258–9
Geographic market segmentation, 264
Geographical Information System (GIS), 178
Geomorphology, 184
Germany: recreational activities survey, 188
Global projections to 2020, 267–8
Goals achievement matrix, 16
Gold, S.M., 4
Golf courses, 51–3
Golf hotels and resorts, 51–3

Government/state, 5
  departments, 220
  financial aid, 221–2, 269–70
  intervention in land control, 225–6
  involvement and demand, 265
  participation in finance, 269–70
  revenues, 272
  structures and policies, 160, 161
    assessment of, 191–3
Governmental agencies, 132
Grande-Motte, La, France, 76
Grassed areas, 107
Gravity productive models, 170
Great interest, resources of, 199
Greater Lyon, France, 235–8
Green Areas Agency for the Paris Region,
  225
Green belt, 209, 213
Green cities, 234
Green plans, 187, 210–211
Green tourism, 11
Greenways, 54, 209–18, 258–61
Group excursions, 224
Grouping of activities, 142
Guesthouses, 18
Gunn, C.A., 164–5
Gymnasium, 26

Hajdunanas, Hungary, 147
Harbours/havens, 72, 73–7
  basic facilities, 74
  'dry', 74–7
  planning standards, 74
Health and fitness centres, 96
Health resorts, 95–6
Heating systems, 44
Helsinki, Finland, 212
Hienghène, New Caledonia, 82
High standard hotels, 19
Hiking greenways, 215
Hiking trails, 55
Hiss, T., 234
Historic resources, 184
  protecting, 230, 232
Holiday entitlements, 265
Holiday parks, 89–94
Holiday villages, 19, 88
  commercial, 27, 28
  social, 27, 28–30, 88–9
Horse riding, 51
  trails, 56
Hostels, 19, 31, 32, 88
Hotels, 18, 23–6
  back-of-house areas, 26
  balance with private accommodation, 21
  circulation planning, 25
  effects of investment on planning, 19
  feasibility of public areas, 19
  planning of public areas, 25–6
  planning standards, 23–4
  types of, 23
  variations in room sizes, 25
Hotels garnis, 18
Hydrology, 184

Ile-De-France, Paris, 210–11, 220
Image, 141, 163–5

Implementation:
  survey of implementation framework, 192
  timescales for, 169–70
Implementation strategy, 219–26
  adapting financing techniques, 221–2
  implementing and controlling facilities, 222
  involvement of other economic sectors,
    219–20
  land control, 225–6
  need for coordinated strategy, 220–1
  organizing and promoting products, 224–5
  training tourism manpower, 222–3
  transportation, 223–4
Inclusive travel, 273
Income: national/regional, 271–2
India: Action Plan for Tourism, 175
Indirect employment, 37–8, 272
Individual facilities, 222
Individual housing units, 19
Individual properties, 27
Individual requirements: meeting, 135
Indoor facilities, 46
  standards in integrated resorts, 46
  types of, 46
Indoor sports and leisure pools, 59
Indoor sports pools, 58–9
Induced employment, 37–8
Inducement, 225
Industrial Heritage and Tourism in Scotland,
  158
Inflationary impact, 272, 273
Infrastructure, 39–45, 147, 266, 269
  access for traffic, 39–40
  communication systems, 44
  coordination of underground utilities, 44–5
  electricity supplies, 43–4
  external lighting and street furniture, 40–1
  heating and air-conditioning, 44
  parking areas, 40
  planning data for roads, 40
    see also Roads
  resources surveys, 187–8
  sanitation, 41–3
  technical, 41–5, 188, 225
Inland cruising, 60
Insect control, 184
Inskeep, E., 173
Institutional influences on demand, 265
Integrated area development plan, 226
Integrated resorts:
  beaches, 73
  planning, 132
  standards for indoor facilities, 46
Intergovernmental organizations, 270
Intermediaries, 4–5
International Labour Organization (ILO), 223
International tourism, 4, 191, 266–7, 273
  global projections to 2020, 267–8
International Union for Conservation of
  Nature, 117
Investment, 268–70
  accommodation, 268–9
  air transport, 273, 274
  attraction and theme parks, 97
  characteristics, 268
  forms of financial aid, 269–70
  hotel accommodation, 19

main sources of capital finance, 270
  other facilities, 269
  public sector participation, 269
  revenue earning potential, 268
Iran: master plan for development of tourism,
  181
Irrigation systems, 43
Isolated facilities, 203
Isolated monuments, 231

Jackson County, Michigan, 243
Jansen-Verbeke, M., 232
Japan: national parks, 120
Jay-Jaton, J.C., 189
Joint public/private development projects, 132

Kemer Tourist Village, Turkey, 20
Kentucky tourism master plan, 160
Kunfunadhoo Island, Raa Atoll, The Maldives,
  138

Laganside, Belfast, 201
Lakesides, 251
Land:
  control, 225–6
  ensuring control, 154
  reclamation, 184
  requirements for recreational activities, 61–2
  struggle for sites, 203–7
  use patterns, 178
Land-based recreational facilities, 53–7
  allotments gardens, 57
  parks, rest and playing fields, 54–5
  picnicking, 53–4
  trails, 55–7
'Land Between the Lakes', 205
Landscaping, 143
Languedoc-Rousillon, France, 162, 225
Latent demand, 189–90, 264
Launch capacity, 59
Lausanne 'Jeunotel', Switzerland, 32
Layout plans, 154
Lederman, A., 257
Lee Valley Park, England, 216
Leisure, 1, 189
Leisure centres, 48
Leisure parks, 96–128
  aquatic parks, 94, 101–3, 133–5
  attraction and theme parks, 96–8, 133–5
  natural parks, 117–28, 135, 226, 251
  planning, 133–5
  recreation parks, 104–16
  safari parks, 98–101
Leisure World, Hemel Hempstead, UK, 134
Lesotho, 150
Levels of planning, 163
Library, 46
Life cycle roles, 265
Lighting, external, 40–1
Limiting facilities, 14
Limits of acceptable charges (LAC), 12
Limni Beach Resort, Cyprus, 144–5
Limpopo Valley Game Reserve, Africa, 227
Linear parks, 215, 216–18
Linear waterways, 251, 254, 255
Loadings, electrical, 43
Lobbies, 25

Local authorities, 5, 220–1
Local planning, 163, 167–8
LOCAT model, 173
Lodges, 18
Lounges, 26
Lyon, France, 236–8

Main through routes, 203
Main tourist resorts, 199–200
Man-made dangers, 184
Manchester Tourism Development Initiative
　　(TDI), UK, 255
Manchester Velodrome, UK, 36
Manpower: training, 222–3
Marinas, see Harbours/havens
Maritime cities/ports, 251
Market assessment, 97, 188–91
　　outdoor recreation activities, 188–90
　　tourist markets, 190–1
Market economies, 269–70
Market segmentation, 264–5
Master plans, 158–263
　　aims in planning, 158
　　approaches to planning, 168–75
　　assessment of structures and policies, 191–3
　　differences in planning for tourism and
　　　　recreation, 158–60
　　fundamental planning considerations, 160–8
　　market assessment, 188–91
　　outdoor recreation in cities see Urban parks
　　preliminaries, 176
　　　　organizational framework, 176
　　　　planning objectives, 176
　　　　terms of reference, 176
　　protection of resources, 226–32
　　regional recreation plans, 203–18
　　resources surveys, 177–88
　　strategy for implementation, see
　　　　Implementation strategy
　　tourism development plans, 193–203
Mathematical models, 170–3
Mauritius: National Physical Development Plan,
　　194
Measurement of tourism, 266
Meeting rooms, 26
Metropolitan Greensward, New York, 204
Miribel–Jonage recreation and nature park,
　　Lyon, France, 114–15
Mixed developments, 23
Mixed economies, 270
Mobile homes, 33
Model boats, 60
Models, planning, 170–3
Modules for Employable Skills, 223
Monitoring system, 173–5
Monuments:
　　historic, 230
　　isolated, 231
　　monument ensembles, 231–2
　　natural, 226
'Most lovely villages of France', 232
Motels, 18
Motor cycle scrambling, 57
Mountain resorts, 77–85, 131
　　accommodation standards, 28, 29
　　average densities, 64, 65
　　cable transporters, 83–4

categories of skiers, 77
　　other facilities, 84
　　principles in planning, 84–5
　　ski trail characteristics, 81–2
Multinational companies, 270
Multipliers, 271–2
Multi-purpose hall, 46
Multivariate regression models, 170
Municipal services, 133

National identity/pride, 272
National income, 271–2
National parks, 117–22, 226
National planning, 163, 164, 165
National undertakings, 265
Natural bathing places, 57–8
Natural environment (buffer zone), 117
Natural monuments, 226
Natural resources, 184
Natural safari parks, 101
Natural sanctuaries, 117, 121, 226
Nature: contact with, 141
Nature parks, 117–28, 135, 226, 251
　　forests and recreation, 126
　　national parks, 117–22, 226
　　planning, 229–30
　　protected natural areas, 126–8
　　regional parks, 123–6, 226
　　suburban recreation and nature parks, 109,
　　　　114–16
nature reserves, 60
Naturparks (Germany), 123–4
Navigable waterways, 57
Negative features, 184
Negative impacts, 272–3
Neighbourhood recreation areas, 257
Net income in foreign exchange, 271
Netherlands:
　　structure plan for outdoor recreation, 166
　　urban parks standards, 244
New Lanark, Scotland, 234
New resort development, 132–3
　　developers, 132
　　integrated resorts, 132
　　failures/criticism, 132–3
　　operation of resorts, 133
New urban parks, 245–9
New York, 234
　　Metropolitan Greensward, 204
New Zealand Conservation Estate, 56
Niger: tourism development master plan,
　　182–3
Night clubs, 46
Non-tourist population, 7, 37
　　housing, 38
　　size, 38
Nordic skiing trails, 84
North Saskatchewan River Park, Canada, 251
Northern Ireland: tourism study of north-
　　eastern area, 178
Norway: State Council for Open-air
　　Recreation, 221
Nusa Dua, Bali, 130

Oasis Lakeland Forest Holiday Village, UK,
　　92–3
Ocean Park, Bremerhaven, Germany, 153

Olmsted, F.L., 209
Oman: implementation of development, 171
Open air pools, 58
Open air theatre, 46
Open, non-exclusive holiday parks, 94
Operational projects, 151, 157
Opportunity, 265
Orres, Les, France, 80
Out of town monuments, 231
Outdoor recreation, 188–9
　　activities, 188–9
　　in cities, see Urban parks
　　markets, 189–90
　　standards, 222
Outdoor skating rink, 84
Outfall, 43

Palace of the Lost City, Sun City, South Africa,
　　63
Parc de la Frontenac, Quebec, Canada, 116
Parc de la Vanoise, France, 121
Parco Gran Paradiso, Italy, 121
Parcs régionaux (France), 124–6
Paris:
　　Green belts, 213
　　quais, 251
Park authority, 263
Park information centre, 117
Parking areas, 40
Parks, 54–5
　　see also Leisure parks; Suburban parks; Urban
　　　　parks
Parpairis, A., 12
PASOLP approach (Products Analysis
　　Sequences for Outdoor Leisure
　　Procedure), 173–5, 207, 208
Pedestrian areas, 257
Pedestrian networks, 257
Pedestrian squares, 251–7
Pensions, 18
Peripheral zones, 117
Permanent monitoring system, 173–5
Phase 1, 151, 157
Phasing development, 146–51, 169
　　phases, 147
Philippines: tourism development, 165
Phoenix Park, Decatur, Illinois, 242
Picnicking, 53–4
Pilgrims' resthouses, Sri Lanka, 31
Planning:
　　aims in, 158
　　definition, 160
　　fundamental considerations, 160–8
　　models, 170–3
　　objectives, 176
　　processes, 160–3
　　programmes, 169–70
　　scales and levels, 163
　　with tourism products, 5–7
　　see also Master plans
Planning balance sheet, 16
Planning controls, 156
Planning procedures, 151, 152–7
　　broad concept, 151, 152–4
　　draft project, 151, 154–6
　　final project, 151, 156–7
　　framework, 152

operation, 151, 157
    phase 1, 151, 157
Playgrounds, 107, 257
Playing fields, 54–5
Pleasure harbours, 74
Policies, see Government/state
Political changes, 273
Pompadour Village, 89
Pomun Lake Resort, Korea, 67
Ponds Forge Sports Centre, Sheffield, UK, 49
Population trends, 265
Port Barcares Social Holiday Village, France, 30
Port Camargue, France, 38, 69
Port Grimaud, St Tropez, France, 67
Port Leucate–Barcarès, France, 70
Port-Ripaille, Lake Geneva, France, 87
Pousadas de Portugal, 17
Power boats, 59
Presumptive models, 170
Principles of development, 135–46
    contact with nature, 141
    distribution of buildings and focuses of interest, 143
    environmental integration, 141
    grouping of activities, 142
    landscaping, 143
    objectives, ways and means, 135–41
    quality of construction, 143
    separation of traffic, 143
    valorizing the main resource, 141–2
Priorities, 168, 169
Priority areas for development, 199
Private accommodation, 21, 26–30, 268
Private golf clubs, 51
Product analyses, 6–7
Product differentiation, 6, 264
Product positioning, 6
Products:
    planning with, 6–7
    promotion, 224–5
    recreation, 225
    tourism, 5–6, 188, 224–5
Project planning, 163
Property developers, 132
Protected natural areas, 121, 126–8
Protection of resources, 9, 13, 56, 116, 118–19, 120–5, 178, 182–3, 187, 197, 199, 200, 226–32, 233, 235
    isolated monuments, 231
    monument ensembles, 231–2
    nature parks, 226
    planning nature parks and sensitive areas, 229–30
    roads, 230
    'sensitive areas' of environmental control, 226–8
    tourists and historic monuments, 230
    towns and centres of culture, 232
Psychographic market segmentation, 264
Public address systems, 44
Public areas of hotels, 25–6
Public beach facilities, 72–3
Public facilities, 147
Public golf courses, 51
Public sector finance, 269–70
Public transport, 224

Purchase of land, 225

Qualitative analysis, 170
Quality of construction, 146
Quality control, 14
Quantitative analysis, 170

Rail transport, 275
Raleigh Greenway System, North Carolina, 214
Reading room, 46
Recreation:
    comparison with tourism, 3
    compexity of tourism/recreation system, 3–5
    definition, 1
    demand, 2–3
        measurement, 264
    differences in planning for tourism and recreation, 158–60
    environmental impacts, 9
    forests and, 126
    hierarchy of outdoor recreation spaces, 64
    interface with tourism, 1–3
    investment, 269
    master plans:
        implementation strategy, 219–22
            passim, 224
        main phases, 208
    national recreation plans, 9, 166
    regional recreation plans, 104, 105, 106, 112–13, 203–18, 228, 229, 236–8, 246–7, 248, 250, 252–3, 254, 255, 258–9
Recreation complexes/parks:
    classification, 64
    planning, 133–5
    principles of development, see Principles of development
Recreation parks, see Suburban parks
Recreation sector plans, 166, 168–9
Recreational activities 1
    cost requirements, 62
    densities, 61
    grouping, 142
    land requirements, 61–2
    market assessment for outdoor recreation, 188–90
Recreational attractions, 184–7
Recreational products, 225
Recreational receipts, 271
Redevelopment, 75, 149, 153, 201, 202, 233, 239, 240–1, 249, 250, 252–3
Refuse disposal, 43
Région Ile-de-France, 220
Regional authorities, 5, 220–1
Regional benefits of tourism, 272
Regional income, 271–2
Regional intervention, 225–6
Regional parks, 123–6, 226
Regional planning, 163
Regional recreation plans, 203–18
    extent, methodology and content, 207–8
    green belt, 209
    greenways, 209–18
    outdoor recreation areas in the city, 208
    rural areas, 209
    struggle for sites, 203–7
Regional structural funds, 270

Regulation, 225–6, 265
Rehabilitating existing resorts, 148–51
Relaxation parks, see Suburban parks
Re-planning procedures, 175
Residential developments, 51
Residents, 7, 37, 38
Resort Board, 133
Resort complexes, 19
Resorts, see Tourist resorts
Resorts Contracts, 148
Resources, 160
    hierarchy of development, 199
    increasing the value of, 141–2
    minimizing degradation, 14
    pressures on, 14
    protection of, 226–32
    utilization and technological change, 265
Resources surveys, 177–88
    existing features and potential tourist interest, 178–84
    facilities and infrastructures, 187–8
    methodology and stages, 177–8
    principles, 177
    recreational attractions, 184–7
Restaurants, 25, 34–5
Restricting access, 14
Revenue earning potential, 268
Revierpark Nienhausen, Germany, 103
Rheinaue Recreation Park, Bonn, Germany, 248
Rhone River, Geneva, Switzerland, 54
Rishiri Island National Park, Japan, 120
Risk, 273
Roads, 39–41
    access for traffic, 39–40
    lighting and street furniture, 40–1
    networks and circuits, 202–3
    parking areas, 41
    planning data, 40
    protection of, 230
    trends in road transport, 275
Robinson Playground, 257
Romania: strategic master plan for tourism development, 179
Room sizes, 25
Rowing, 60
Royal Quays, North Shields, UK, 75
Ruhr area, Germany, 104
Rule-based models, 173
Runway capacity, 274
Rural area, 209

Safari parks, 98, 100
S'Agaro, Spain, 132
Sailing, 59–60, 107
Sanitation, 41–3
    outfall and irrigation systems, 43
    refuse disposal, 43
    sewerage and sewage treatment, 41–3
    water supply, 41
Satellite imagery, 178
Scale of planning, 163
Scenic byways, 203
Scenic roads, 203, 230
Scheduled sailings, 275
Scheduling, 14
SCORP (Statewide Comprehensive Outdoor Recreation Plans), 208

Sea transport, 275
Seagaia Ocean Dome, Miyazaki, Japan, 102
Seaports, 198
Seaside resorts, 131
    accommodation standards, 28, 29
    densities, 64, 65
Seasides, 251
Seasonality, 272
Second residences, 85–8
Secondary interest, resources of, 199
Sectoral policies, 131
Sectors, economic, 219–20
Self-catering accommodation, 19, 26–30, 269
Self-sufficient, exclusive holiday parks, 94
Semi-public bodies, 270
'Sensitive areas' of environmental control,
        226–8
    planning, 229–30
Service infrastructure, 188
Sestrières, Italy, 132
Sewerage and sewage treatment, 41–3
Seychelles Tourism Master Plan, 176
Shops/shopping, 25, 35, 184
    standards, 35
Simonds, J.O., 209
Simulation, 266
    techniques for planning, 170–3
Sites:
    coordination of site works, 44–5
    planning, 27–8
    struggle for 203–7
    see also Land
Skating rink, 84
Ski resorts, see Mountain resorts
Ski rooms, 26
Ski trails, 81–2
Skiers: categories of, 77
Slalom trails, 84
Small boats, 59
Snowmobile trails, 57, 84
Social problems, 273
Social tourism villages, 27, 88–9
    standards, 28–30
Social welfare, 272
Socio-cultural resources, 184
Socio-economic influences on demand, 265
Socio-economic policies, 4
Socio-economic surveys, 192
South Antalya project, Turkey, 195
Southern Seto Nagaura, Japan, 139
Spaarnwoude recreation park, Holland, 106
Spas, 95–6, 131
    facilities, 95
    markets, 95
    planning, 96
Spatial layout, 147
Special natural reserves, 117, 121
Specific attractions, 184
Specific facilities, 17–18
Specific tourist accommodation, 269
Sports, 189
    cost requirements, 62
    densities, 61
    land requirements, 61–2
Sports associations, 133
Sports facilities, 48–53, 245
    golf courses, 51–3

grounds, 47, 48
horse riding, 51
sports halls, 48–51
standards in holiday resorts, 53
Sports-oriented recreation parks, 108–9,
        110–13, 134
Sri Lanka: tourism master plan, 164
St Lucia: tourism development strategy, 197
St Peter's Riverside, UK, 75
State, see Government/state
State of the environment (SOE) report, 14
Statistics, 266
Strategic plans, 168
Strategic town planning, 148
Stream banks, 251
Street furniture, 40–1
Structure plans, 168
Structures, government, see Government/state
Studies: extent of, 169
Substitution, 266
Suburban parks, 55, 104–16, 135, 209
    average densities, 107–8
    favourable sites, 104–7
    specific facilities, 107
Suburban recreation and leisure parks, 108
Suburban recreation and nature parks, 109,
        114–16
Suburban recreation and sports parks, 108–9,
        110–13
Sun Valley–Ketchum Resort, Idaho, 83
Support services, 37–9
Surveys:
    planning, 152, 154
    resources, 177–88
    socio-economic, 192
Sustainable development, 8, 9–11, 161
Sweden:
    protection of natural resources, 9
    urban parks standards, 244
Swimming pools, 26, 58–9
Sydney's Darling Harbour, Australia, 252–3
Synographic Mapping (SYMAP), 178
Szolnock County, Hungary, 163

Taiwan: general plan for recreation/tourism
        system, 180
Tama forest zone, Japan, 140
Team sports, 48
Technical infrastructure, 41–5, 188
    control over, 225
Technical services, 37–9, 147
Technological changes, 265–6
Telephone services, 44
Television room, 46
Television systems, 44
Tennis courts, 48
Tennessee Valley Authority, USA, 205
Tent villages, 88
Terminal capacity, 274
Thalassotherapy, 96
Thames River strategy, UK, 254
Theme parks, 96–100
    planning, 133–5
Time, 265
Timescales for implementation, 169–70
Tivy, J., 11
Tour operators, 132

Tourism:
    alternative forms, 11
    comparison with recreation, 3
    complexity of tourism/recreation system,
        3–5
    demand for, 2–3
    differences in planning for tourism and
        recreation, 158–60
    domestic, 4, 191, 268
    environmental impacts, 7–9
    forces promoting sustainable, 9–10
    impact on national/regional income, 271–2
    implementation strategy for master plan,
        219, 220
        training manpower, 222–3
        transportation, 223–4
    interface with recreation, 1–3
    international, 4, 191, 266–7, 273
        global projections to 2020, 267–8
    market assessment, 190–1
    measurement, 266
    selected indicators, 10
Tourism Concern, 11
Tourism development plans, 193–203
    additional facilities needed, 194–8
    hierarchy of development of resources, 199
    isolated facilities, 203
    local level, 13, 82, 149, 235
    main tourist resorts, 199–200
    means of access, 198–9
    national level, 9, 56, 130, 145, 159, 164,
        165, 179, 180, 181, 182–3, 186, 194,
        197
    priority areas, 199
    regional level, 162, 187, 195, 196, 200, 205
    road networks and circuits, 202–3
    towns and urban centres, 200–2
Tourism facilities, 187–8
    implementing and controlling, 222
Tourism products, 5–6, 188, 224–5
    planning with, 6–7
Toursim sector plans, 167, 168
Tourism Unit of the Commission of European
        Communities, 148
Tourist circuits, 203
Tourist and monument zones, 231
Tourist resorts, 129–33
    integrated, see Integrated resorts
    main, 199–200
    main categories, 64
    new resort development, 132–3
    operation, 133
    planning procedures, 151, 152–7
    post-war developments, 131–2
    principles of development, see Principles of
        development
    rehabilitating existing resorts, 148–51
    and tourist towns, 129–31
    traditional, 131, 133
    see also under individual types of resort
Tourist roads, 203
Tourist towns, 129–31, 232
Tourists, 1–2
    and historic monuments, 230
Towns, 200–2
    centres of culture, 232
    tourist towns, 129–31, 232

Traditional buildings, converted, 88
Traditional lifestyles, 184
Traditional resorts, 131, 133
Traditional villages, 231, 232
Traffic:
    access for, 39–40
    separation of, 143
    see also Roads
Trails, 55–7, 81–2, 107
Training, 222–3
Transfer function models, 170
Transmission voltages, 44
Transportation, 266
    developments in, 273–6
    facilities and resources surveys, 188
    implementation strategy for master plan,
        223–4
    see also under individual forms of transport
Tyne and Wear redevelopment, UK, 75
Tyresta National Park, Sweden, 125

Underwater diving, 60
United Kingdom (UK)
    recreational activities survey, 189
    urban parks standards, 244
United States (USA):
    Airline Deregulation Act 1978, 273
    National Conference on Recreation and the
        American City, 225
    National Recreation and Parks Association
        (NRPA), 172
    President's Commission, 221
    recreational activities survey, 188
    scenic byways, 203
    urban parks standards, 244
Unquantifiable impacts, 272–3
Urban centres, 200–2

Urban greenways, 209, 215
Urban isolated monuments, 231
Urban monument ensembles, 231
Urban parks, 54–5, 104, 208, 232–63
    creation of new, 245–9
    'eco parks', 251
    lakesides/seasides and stream banks, 251
    neighbourhood recreation areas, 257
    pedestrian areas and networks, 251–7
    planning outdoor recreation areas, 257–63
    planning principles, 244–5
    principles, 234–42
    standards, 242–4
Urbanization, 131–2
USSR, former, 244
Utilities, 40–1

Value: increase in, 141–2
Vanuatu: tourism development plan, 186
Vegetation cover, 184
'Venice Card', 232
Verbier, Switzerland, 38
Viaduct Daumesnil Greenway, Paris, 260–1
Vienna, Austria, 209
Village halls, 48
Villages, traditional, 231, 232
Villas, 26–30
Villes d'art, 232
Visitor centres, 46, 117
Visitor management policies, 232
Visitors, 1–2, 7
Vocational training, 222–3
Voluntary bodies, 265
Vulnerability of tourism, 272

Walking trails, 55
Walt Disney World, Florida, 100

Water-based facilities, 57–60
    natural bathing places, 57–8
    other activities, 60
    sailing and boating, 59–60
    swimming pools, 58–9
    see also Aquatic parks; Beach resorts;
        Harbours/havens
Water features, 107
Water skiing, 59
Water supply, 41
Waterways:
    linear, 251, 254, 255
    navigable, 57
Weekend residences, 85–8
Weekends, 265
Weston-super-Mare, UK, 151
Wet 'n Wild Water Park, Newcastle, UK, 50
Wienerburg suburban park, Austria, 105
Wildlife, 184
Windsurfing, 59
Winter resorts *see* Mountain resorts
World Tourism Organization (WTO) 11, 158,
    266, 269
    global projections to 2020, 267
    indicators for sustainable tourism, 10
WWF-UK, 11

Yachting, 73–7
    yachting centres, 74–7
Yaro, R.D., 234
Youth centre, 46
Youth hostels, 31, 32
Yulara Tourist Resort, Australia, 42

Zermatt, Switzerland, 38
Zoning, 14, 126
    concentric, 117–21